THE SEARCH FOR THE SELF

VOLUME 2

THE SEARCH FOR THE SELF

Selected Writings of Heinz Kohut: 1950-1978

VOLUME 2

Edited by
Paul H. Ornstein

KARNAC

First published by International Universities Press in 1978

This edition published in 2011 by

Karnac Books Ltd
118 Finchley Road
London NW3 5HT

British Library Cataloguing in Publication Data
A C.I.P. for this book is available from the British Library

ISBN: 978-1-85575-874-2

www.karnacbooks.com

Contents

VOLUME 2

VOLUME 1

35

Psychoanalysis in
a Troubled World

Psychoanalysis is under attack from various sides. As hedonistic — as puritanical. As mystical and unscientific — as hyperrational. As revolutionary — as old-fashioned and tradition-bound. As right-reactionary — as left-communistic. Such accusations may often seem justified, since psychoanalysis observes man from various sides and on different levels, uncovers many layers of human passion, explains — and while explaining removes — diverse inhibitions of human activity. Hence, one can always accuse psychoanalysis of having disregarded a dialectically opposite psychological finding or explanation with regard to each of the empirical discoveries it claims to have made, and with regard to each of the theoretical explanations it holds to be true. If analysis is put to the test in this way, the task of the would-be attacker is facilitated, while the task of the defender remains difficult indeed. The indictment is simple and concrete; the defense has to rest on the laborious study and slow integration of all the many

Based on an address given to a broad audience of students, professionals, and nonprofessionals on October 7, 1970, at the Free University in Berlin, Germany, on the occasion of the celebration of the Fiftieth Anniversary of the Berlin Psychoanalytic Institute (Karl-Abraham Institut).

This address appeared in *The Annual of Psychoanalysis* (1973), 1:3-25. New York: Quadrangle.

Although I must take responsibility for this English version of my originally German-language address, I am glad to express my indebtedness to Dr. Ernest S. Wolf, who quickly and skillfully prepared a draft of an English translation which I then took as the basis for my own efforts.

psychological insights that psychoanalysis has provided — including the acknowledged incompleteness of this science and its capacity to grow.

The analyst is on the whole not greatly upset by the aforementioned attacks, which frequently strike him as biased and pedantic; and he will tend to be philosophical about the fact that he cannot convince all the various insufficiently informed detractors of psychoanalysis of the value, the significance, the importance of this science. Still, much as the analyst may be able to discount a great number of these generally ill-intentioned and often flimsy criticisms, the problem of the worthwhileness of analysis in today's world, which is pondered by many a serious-minded and responsible observer both inside and outside the field of analysis, must not be lightly brushed aside. It is in fact fully understandable that the question should be raised whether the detailed and intensive investigation of the inner life of man can still be considered as having sufficient relevance to our deeply troubled times — and there exist indeed a number of weighty arguments that could be marshaled in support of a negative verdict.

We are living in a time of great changes. Whole populations must regroup themselves rapidly in accordance with new guidelines of communal organization. Everywhere is the individual suddenly faced with the task of aiming toward newly defined goals and meanings, of grasping new values and of making them his own, of quickly adapting to a new societal order. Such tasks arise not only in territories where a social revolution has prevailed, where a new state has been founded, or where the basic form of government has been altered, but also within those nations — the United States, for example — whose structure appears on the whole to have remained unchanged. One need call to mind only the rapid emancipation of the American Negro and his impetuous tendency to use militant means; or the rapid Americanization of new ethnic groups who, contrary to the traditions of the nation, wave the flag of amoral patriotism, who impatiently push aside all questions concerning the justice of the actions of the state, and who — contrary to historically established ideals — level their self-righteous intolerance against the man who will not disregard his moral scruples. Everywhere, new thoughts have to be thought and new plans for action devised if effective participation in the new world is to be accomplished. And everywhere are dying the Zhivagos who are incapable of adapting to the new conditions without the loss of the core of their life-sustaining traditions and ideals.

And how does depth psychology pass muster when it is evaluated against the background of the contemporary situation? Pretty badly — at least if one is satisfied with only scanning its broad outlines rather than undertaking a careful scrutiny of the actual and the potential significance of its functions.

The investigations of depth psychology must in the main be undertaken in the setting of the therapeutic situation. The patient comes to his analyst four, five, or even six times during the week, and for nearly an hour he is encouraged to talk freely about everything that goes through his head, apparently at random. The analyst, employing the skills acquired in many years of arduous professional training, listens with empathic attention to these seemingly disjointed communications; and, whenever it is appropriate, he communicates to his patient the insight he may have acquired. This process may go on for years, and if everything goes well, which luckily occurs with increasing frequency, then all this great effort will indeed lead to the deep-going improvement of a single human fate, to the new, undreamed-of psychic integration of a person who has made peace with his past, has won respect for himself, and who looks to the future with independent strength and initiative. "Well and good," it may be said, "but is all this effort worth it? All these hundreds and hundreds of hours of work, for a single individual? Is not such effort wastefulness, immoral luxury, in a time when uncounted numbers of people are struggling and suffering, and when millions perish?"

I do not wish to involve myself here in a circumstantial and petty defense of therapeutic analysis. I could stress that the assistance analysis provides is often to the benefit of very valuable individuals. Statistically it has been demonstrated — a fact of which every analyst has been aware without the aid of polls — that we do not treat the idle rich, as is often asserted, but that, in general, we help the educated and potentially creative to liberate their energies from sterile internal entanglement and thus make them available for tasks of social importance. I could also argue that each resolution of a deeply grounded psychic disturbance of an individual father or mother may benefit a whole series of generations — an analogy to (and a reversal of) the biblical punishment leveled against the children and children's children of the sinner. Of the truth of these assertions I have no doubt. But I do not believe that they, by themselves, constitute a satisfactory justification for all the time-consuming and cumbersome effort that the therapeutic endeavors of depth psychology require.

If we wish to affirm that this effort is indeed worthwhile, then we must demonstrate that its therapeutic and scientific goals carry a significance that transcends the fate of the single person and the knowledge obtained about the psychology of the individual. We must show, in other words, that psychoanalysis makes a contribution to the activation of wholesome social, cultural, and historical effects, which may influence the future of not only a handful of individuals but of large groups, whole layers of society, and — yes! — even of mankind as a whole.

W. H. Auden (1945, p. 166) may have had something similar in mind when he wrote, in 1940, one year after

Freud's death, the following beautiful lines in his poem "In Memory of Sigmund Freud":

> To us he is no more a person
> Now, but a whole climate of opinion
> Under whom we conduct our differing lives.[1]

Yes, few will doubt that Freud's work has exerted a significant influence on the conduct of life, on the *Weltanschauung* of modern man. Still, there are a number of possible objections to the assertion Auden presents to us so impressively. It could be said that it was man's outlook on the world that changed first, and that psychoanalysis and Freud's discoveries were the result, not a cause, of the new cultural attitude. (One could, of course, make the same claim with regard to Copernicus or Darwin. How is one to decide about such an issue?) Or one could take the stand that the influence of great men and of their discoveries and actions should not be overestimated. (One is reminded, in this context, of Tolstoy's opinion that even as important a figure as Napoleon was not the initiator of the events generally considered to have resulted from his actions, but that, on the contrary, he was just passively carried along by the currents of history.) True enough, terms such as "libido," "the unconscious," and "Oedipus complex" are widely used today; and people are usually ready to admit that a person's unknown thoughts and feelings may be "projected" onto others and that our parapraxes — the slips of memory, tongue, and hand — reveal our hidden intentions. And the artists, poets, dramatists — they know all this only too well. The modern psychological drama and film are frequently saturated with Freudian discoveries and insights and use them not rarely in an all too obvious, inartistically intentional manner. Is that the "whole climate

[1] Reprinted with permission of the publisher, Random House, Inc.

of opinion" of which Auden speaks? "Easy come, easy go!"
one thinks. And one calls to mind the ebb and flow of
fashions: one day they seem to dominate the world, but next
day they are gone as if they had never been around.

To be sure, the influence of psychoanalytic thought has
maintained itself for some time now in the Western world; it
appears to be more a persisting cultural style than a quickly
passing fashion. But one is inclined to remember the old
saying *"plus ça change, plus c'est la même chose."* Every
Tom, Dick, and Harry is using a few words of the psychoanalytic vocabulary, and they may have become superficially
acquainted with a few new concepts. Some people have even
learned to play analytic parlor games; that is, they permit
themselves the ill-mannered license of subjecting the actions
and the personality of their acquaintances to (generally
malicious) explanations they consider to be psychoanalytic
interpretations. In essence, however, they have remained
untouched.

The foregoing comments are only of peripheral importance, for it is by no means my intention to claim that
analysis and its insights have already exerted a deep and
genuine influence on the present generation. What I do wish
to express is the hope that the influence of analysis will
indeed be brought to bear broadly on future generations
and—what is of at least equal importance—that analysis as
an important civilizing force will become actively engaged in
man's battle for his biological and spiritual survival. The goal
of my presentation is therefore, generally speaking, a moral
one.

But first a practical and technical question: is psychoanalysis indeed able to influence society? In other words—
leaving aside for a moment the much more important uncertainty whether the broader application of the insights of
analysis would have beneficial results—do we have the means
for an effective penetration of analytic insights into society,

and is there any likelihood that analysis could ever influence the actions of large groups?

It may appear at this point that my inquiry leads into unrealistic directions. Is it necessary to demand such large effects from the professional activity of a small group of psychotherapists? Is it not enough for analysts to concentrate on their therapeutic work and to be satisfied with the appropriately circumscribed results of these therapeutic activities? Is it not a sign of insecurity when a small professional group becomes restless, begins to put on airs, and agonizes ostentatiously about the question whether it could and should influence the future of mankind?

Yes and no. I have complete sympathy for those of my colleagues who, in quiet restraint, want to focus their whole attention on the concrete problems of their therapeutic activity without spending sleepless nights over the course that mankind is taking. But I think that it also is justifiable to adopt a more comprehensive point of view. I know, of course, how tempting it is to exaggerate the importance of the small events of our workaday life and to see them in a broad historical perspective. But what I wish to affirm appears to me to be a concrete and by no means exaggerated claim, namely, that psychoanalysis — as a form of psychotherapy and as a branch of investigative science — is potentially a cultural factor of considerable importance.

Here I would point out that some of the most decisive events in history — events that ultimately came to exert a profound influence on the actions and thoughts of mankind — appeared to be small in scale and insignificant when evaluated within the framework of their original historical setting. The inconspicuous events, for example, that may have formed the historical basis of the story of the Gospels had reverberations (in the development of culture, in the shaping of morality, in the whole history of Western man) that would seem to be of incomprehensible magnitude if measured against the scale of their tiny beginnings. Clearly, it was the power of a set of ideas that prevailed here so decisively—not the weight of the bigger battalions, not, at least not in the beginning, the trumpet call of a mighty propaganda apparatus. The apparently simple and circumscribed recognition that the earth is not the center of the universe has not only revolutionized the thinking of all generations of scientists since Copernicus, it also exerted a considerable influence on cultural and historical development in areas that lie outside of the province of science (in the areas of art and literature, for example, and perhaps even in the area of political activity). Darwin's theory of the origin of species had consequences far transcending its original field of application. Out of Darwin's revolutionary approach to a sector of biology grew both a new fundamental ordering principle valid within the total biological realm and a broad new outlook on the world. Darwin's theory of the developmental transience of biological phenomena, by introducing a scientific relativism to the field that stands in sharp contrast to the preceding absolutism of man's grasp of these phenomena (exemplified by the biblical story of creation), altered man's whole outlook, from the realm of physics to that of psychology.

But why the emphasis on the banal truth that small causes may lead to large effects? Because the preceding examples can teach us the important lesson that these so-called small beginnings were small only in appearance. Their greatness remains unrecognized as long as we insist on measuring them with yardsticks and weighing them on scales that are not designed to gauge the scope of their intrinsic energy or to respond to their potential impact. One cannot determine the power of a hydrogen bomb by weighing it as if it were a stone.

There are some fields, of course, in which we are willing to treat even inconspicuous activities with respect. We do not expect a researcher who attempts to identify a new virus to be concerned only with large epidemics; we gladly allow him to spend his working days in the laboratory with his test tubes, culture media, and filters. He receives both our moral and financial support. The work of the scientist and teacher in the field of depth psychology, however, finds little public appreciation, and he will hardly be able to obtain adequate public assistance for the research he pursues in the small arena of his consulting room. The day will come, I think, when people will shake their heads in disbelief about this short-sightedness of our society.

The analyst's attention is focused on small-scale activities, and his psychological inquiry concerns apparent trifles, which seem to be far away from the events that are shaping our world. The assertion, however, that these facts speak against the importance of psychoanalytic investigation would be just as unwarranted as the conclusion that the small size of the virus or the atom negates the importance of virological or atomic research.

A short time ago a young patient reported to me that on the preceding day he had become involved in an ugly argument with a neighbor, an elderly man, who had refused him the temporary use of his driveway. Through careful psychological scrutiny of the incident, we ascertained that the apparent unfriendliness of the response of the usually friendly neighbor had not been, as the patient had thought, a reaction to his request in itself, but had been elicited by the provocative way in which he had made it. I remembered, and I reminded the patient, that a similar event had taken place once before. At that time the patient had started a serious quarrel because he had felt crowded by a man who sat next to him in a busy restaurant. I was able to demonstrate to my patient that at that time, just as now, his actions had been unnecessarily provocative and that he had left the other man no choice but to react with aggression to his own aggressivity.

I don't want to burden this presentation with a description of the details of an analysis. But I must mention briefly that both events occurred shortly before my leaving for a journey; that the patient, who had become fond of me, felt himself excluded when I told him that I would go away; that he became enraged about the inconsiderateness with which he felt treated by me; and that all these events repeated a devastating trauma of his childhood, when his beloved and admired father suddenly left the family and thus abandoned the patient.

I did not report this clinical episode in order to make propaganda for the correctness of the theories of psychoanalysis or for the usefulness of its methods; nor in order to demonstrate that in an analysis the key conflicts of a person's life are reactivated and thus become available for a new attempt to solve them. I adduced the clinical vignette in order to suggest that certain insights obtained in the analytic situation may help us understand human behavior in the broad social arena. My patient's request to use the neighbor's driveway and his wish that the other restaurant guest should move away from him were not unreasonable, and a small shift in the way he made his demands would have led in both instances to friendly compliance and would not have brought about the ugly confrontation which in fact ensued. Are such considerations without significance with regard to the understanding of the events that determine whether there will be war or peace among nations? Are we really unable to learn anything that illuminates the behavior of large groups from the careful study of the inner life of the individual? Or might we not by this road obtain insights that would allow us to cope in new ways—without having to resort to force and terror and killing—with those reality situations (social injustice, for example, or national insecurity) which up to now have been considered to be the all-important causes of the conflicts of world history?

Psychoanalysis assumes that the existence of a tendency to kill is deeply rooted in man's biological make-up and stems from his animal past. The omnipresent aggressive drive must be taken into account if we are not to yield to the lures of a shallow and misleading optimism which claims that man's pugnacity could be easily abolished if only his needs were satisfied. But analysts are also fully aware of the fact that certain external circumstances — e.g., those which bring about emotional and material deprivations — will arouse man's anger and may lead him to engage in aggressive actions. The influence of the environment on the propensity toward hostile behavior is, therefore, crucial; and the relevant external factors must be investigated thoroughly, whether we are trying to understand the aggressive reactions of the individual patient (in response to the fault-finding and belittling behavior of the marital partner, for example), or those of social groups (in response to discrimination or maltreatment), or, in the arena of world politics, those of nations and large populations (for instance, in response to territorial and mercantile injustices).

I am well aware of the danger of one-sidedness and of the loss of a balanced scientific perspective. This danger becomes especially great in areas where multiple factors are involved in the production of the phenomena we are striving to explain. Under such circumstances it is tempting to lift one set of factors from the whole intricate pattern of causes, to declare that it is primary and fundamental, and to assign a mere secondary and subsidiary role to other influences.

The depth psychologist, for example, who day in and day out observes the manifestations of the enormous power of unconscious motivations, will naturally be inclined to look upon unconscious psychic factors as the decisive, essential — i.e., as the only valid — forces in the life of individuals and of groups. The psychoanalyst must resist this temptation to espouse a naïve attitude of biased one-sidedness; he must not overrate the explanatory power of the insights of depth psychology. The analyst's insights about the role played by the unconscious forces in the depth of the personality do not, in fact, constitute a complete explanation of the behavior of either the individual or the group.

Still, there are of course many instances when psychoanalysis can make a person aware of previously unconscious motivations, thus increasing the control he is then able to exert over his behavior. Minute as the increment of understanding often appears to be, suddenly — and surprisingly! — a hitherto unbreakable deadlock may become loosened: the patient's attitude becomes more tolerant; his previously provocative behavior becomes transformed into relaxed strength and moral firmness; his aggressions begin to serve constructive aims. Can there be any doubt about the appropriateness of a judicious application of insights such as these to the understanding of the events of history? And might we not expect that an increased grasp of the causal role played by depth-psychological factors will lead us also to greater control over our historical destiny?

"Could be!" it may well be said, "but are these not just empty speculations?" The bacteriologist, the virologist, with whose small-scale research in the laboratory I compared the analytical work with individual patients, have demonstrated, after all, that their efforts lead to far-reaching benefits for mankind. Where are the analogous results of analysis? It may be true that the individual patient benefits from the research that has steadily increased the body of psychoanalytic knowledge and the technical skill of the practicing analyst. And we can perhaps also say that as a result of our persevering investigations we are now able to undertake the successful treatment of psychological illnesses that had formerly been therapeutically as unapproachable as was diabetes before the introduction of insulin. Still, analytic research has up to now given us no therapeutic techniques corresponding to the powerful therapeutic agents discovered through biological research; and, above all, it has not provided anything yet that could be made available to the population at large—nothing, for example, that comes near to equaling the brilliant successes bacteriological or virological research achieved in its fight against the great epidemic scourges of mankind.

I shall again resist the temptation of losing myself in narrow argumentation. It could, of course, be stated that the psychological knowledge slowly being accumulated as the result of work performed in the laboratory of psychoanalytic treatment is also becoming increasingly useful in the broader arena of general psychotherapy. I am thinking here, in particular, of those forms of psychotherapy which set themselves circumscribed and limited goals. The expenditure of time for patient and therapist is here significantly less than in analysis—yet, as in psychoanalysis, the therapeutic work is focused on the individual. With the possible exception of the crudest application of suggestion or of that type of psychological coercion ("conditioning") by which the patient is drilled to behave normally, there exists hardly any form of psychotherapy that does not owe a significant debt to the expanding scientific insights of psychoanalysis—whether this debt is acknowledged or repudiated.

Although claims such as these no doubt sound impressive, I must admit that the adoption and utilization of the findings of psychoanalysis by other forms of psychotherapy do not always lead to favorable results. The particular therapeutic procedure analysis employs is correlated to a specific conceptual framework and forms an integral part of the analytic situation itself. It is therefore not easy to achieve a viable transplant when the technique of psychoanalysis is employed in other therapeutic settings.

Certain forms of psychotherapeutic counseling, for example, which enjoy at present a not inconsiderable popularity, restrict their technique in the main to letting the patient say everything that occurs to him. The counselor's passive attitude seems to be similar to the analyst's attitude of expectant silence: he listens, and either says nothing or merely repeats what the patient has just said himself. But while the analyst employs his method for a specific purpose — he listens in order to understand and then explain, thus enabling the patient to enlarge his knowledge of himself — for the counselor, the method of free association appears to have become an end in itself. But when this use of free association is extolled as being superior to psychoanalysis, then the analyst cannot refrain from shaking his head in amazement. He understands, of course, how, in certain instances, temporary improvements are quickly brought about in this way. If we consider a patient, for example, who as a child had not been able to feel certain of the attention of the important adults in his environment and who never acquired a secure sense of his own worthwhileness and acceptability because he had been criticized too much and lectured at too frequently, it is evident that for such a patient simply the devoted attentiveness on the part of a therapist can be a beautiful and wholesome experience. But among the countless variations in psychological disturbances and human needs, such a constellation represents only one specific kind of problem. It is not a rarity; but it is hardly the form of psychopathology that a therapist is most frequently asked to treat.

Therapeutic benefits such as these remind me of an amusing incident that occurred during the early years of the war. I had an old alarm clock which one day refused to work and just stopped running. As a result of the conversion of industry to the production of armaments, no new clocks were obtainable. Yet nobody was willing to accept my old, cheap, nonelectric one for repair. One day I happened to pass by a small hardware store which had a sign in the window advertising the repair of alarm clocks. The owner accepted my clock without hesitation and told me to pick it up the next day. The price, he said, would be two dollars—not exorbitant, I thought, in view of the circumstances. The following day I did indeed receive my clock, which was now ticking again normally, and I happily paid my two dollars. But I was curious, of course, and I asked the shopkeeper to explain how he alone had been able to see his way clear to take on this repair and to carry it out successfully. With disarming frankness he replied that he knew next to nothing about watch repairs, let alone about the repair of alarm clocks, but that it had occurred to him one day that many of these old clocks had simply collected dust and grime in their wheels for too long and needed nothing more than some cleaning and a little oil. He decided to accept some clocks for repair, and put their movements into an oil bath overnight. If that simple process did the trick, he asked for the agreed payment. If it did not, he explained to his customer that, unfortunately, even *he* was not able to repair the clock; he then returned the clock to the owner and of course demanded no payment. There is no need to spell out the analogy between the so-called watchmaker and the practitioners of certain kinds of psychotherapy—except, I think, that my so-called watchmaker had a higher percentage of successes and knew more about what he was doing than most of the psychotherapists who borrow one or the other insight or technical rule from psychoanalysis and apply it without understanding.

But I don't want to exaggerate. Although the application of the methods and theories of psychoanalysis to many types of abbreviated psychotherapy is indeed unsatisfactory, scientifically well-founded and effective forms of short-term psychotherapy that are practiced and taught by skillful and experienced professionals do also exist. And analysts are rightfully proud of the fact that the utilization of analytic insights in brief and financially less burdensome forms of psychotherapy opens a path toward emotional health for many who might have remained bogged down in neurotic inhibitions without this assistance.

It would be tempting for the psychoanalyst who is confronted by the accusation that analysis belongs only to a socio-cultural elite to reply that the principles of analysis are indeed successfully employed in the service of briefer forms of psychotherapy which can be made available to larger numbers of those who suffer from emotional disturbances. But in the context of our present considerations, I do not believe this argument carries sufficient weight, since even the more broadly available forms of psychotherapy, which are derived from psychoanalysis, continue to deal either with the single disturbed individual or, at most — I am thinking here of forms of group and family therapy conducted along analytic lines — with only a comparatively small number of patients. Even if it should be possible in the future, therefore, to extend the availability of psychoanalytic therapy far beyond the present limits, no essential change would be achieved. For is not the problem of the relevance of psychoanalysis, as we are examining it here, to be viewed against the background of the silent assumption that mankind in its totality is in jeopardy — that it is endangered by an affliction more ominous and profound than that which is evoked by calling to mind the sum total of the misery of individual neuroses?

Yes, man is in danger. He may be on the verge of destroying himself. He cannot control his cruelty toward his fellow man. He appears to be forced to respond to differences of opinion or conflicts of interest in one mode only: through the mobilization of his readiness to fight and to destroy. The mere otherness of others frightens and disgusts him. And so powerfully impelling is the influence of these feelings on him that he would rather risk total destruction than bear the burden that an attitude of tolerance toward the demands of his fellow men and the temporary renunciation of his own demands and of his own pride would impose on him. An often-heard statement, which by now strikes us as an unimpressive truism, is that man's technological power to destroy has risen enormously, while his capacity to control his aggression has at best increased only slightly. Yet, trite as this psychosocial diagnosis appears to be, it points to the heart of the discrepancy in the development of man as an active causative force in history—a discrepancy that calls for a cure. Is it conceivable that the important insights of modern depth psychology since Freud should be irrelevant here? Clearly, we should expect them to help us as we try to control our historical fate. But do they? Does psychoanalysis, for example, make a contribution to the efforts that are being made to bring about greater harmony between ethnic and national groups? Certainly not in any clear-cut and direct way—even though we may console ourselves with the thought that some of the maxims that have been derived from the findings of analysis have filtered through to the masses and to their leaders and are thus inconspicuously and indirectly exerting their influence.

What reason can we adduce for the fact that psychoanalytic insights have not been brought to bear effectively on the great problems of our times? We will start with the simplest explanation: psychoanalysis is young. Such an assertion may well seem strange when we consider that the first psychoanalytic book—Breuer's and Freud's *Studies on Hysteria*—was published in 1895 and that the treatment of Breuer's famous case (Anna O.) had begun fifteen years earlier. We can thus say that psychoanalysis has been in existence for about eighty or ninety years—long enough, one might think, to demand from this science clear-cut achievements in the various areas of its potential application. This is indeed an opinion held by many—including numerous analysts. But it is an opinion I do not share. Analysis may of course lay claim to having provided an important new instrument which opens the path to the deeper layers of the mind; and it has clearly supplied a powerful therapeutic technique by which one can bring about the relief of certain psychic disturbances. Still, despite the accuracy of these claims, the territory staked out by them is too small. For those who thus restrict themselves to defining analysis as a circumscribed profession that employs a specific technology must concede that it is no longer young, that it can hardly expect to make further decisive advances, but has reached the final stage in its development as a limited branch of science whose almost exclusive goal has become the painstaking verification and systematic classification of the discoveries that were made in the days of the pioneers.

No, the preceding definition is too narrow. Strange as it may sound to many ears, I believe that the advent of psychoanalysis constitutes an important step in the history of science and, potentially, even a significant turning point in the development of culture. With psychoanalysis, man has succeeded in transforming introspection and empathy into the tools of an empirical science. Operations that had previously been harnessed to impressionistic, mystical, and speculative approaches have now become instruments for the systematic exploration of the inner life of man. Through the use of these methods, furthermore, a new field has been opened to science. While scientific methodology in the field of psychology formerly could be applied only to comparatively simple data concerning the behavioral surface, psychoanalysis undertakes the scientific exploration of the complex and significant dimensions of human life in depth. It has found the bridge between the two opposing approaches — understanding and explaining — to the inner life of man. It has achieved the first valid integration of, on the one hand, the observer's ability to understand the endless variety of psychological experiences through introspection and empathy with, on the other hand, the theorist's ability to conceptualize these data at higher levels of abstraction and to formulate their interrelatedness within a system of experience-distant explanations. Mystical introspection may understand, but it does not explain; and preanalytic scientific psychology explains, but it does not understand. Psychoanalysis, by contrast, explains what it has understood. This combination of empathic-introspective data-gathering with abstract formulation and theoretical explanation in the field of complex mental states constitutes a revolutionary step in the history of science. And I believe that analysis, this new and pioneering foray into the hitherto unexplored, is still in its infancy, and that our present analytic investigations do not yet penetrate very far beneath the surface.

He who has fully grasped the greatness of the step science took with the establishment of psychoanalysis will have no difficulty understanding why analytic research has up to now remained focused almost exclusively on the psychic life of the individual, why so far only one fundamental insight concerning the psychology of groups has been obtained within the framework of psychoanalytic theory: Freud's realization that the cohesion of certain groups is explained by the fact that the members of these groups hold in common the same ego ideal. It is the relative youthfulness of analysis that justifies our hesitation to transfer the knowledge obtained in the solid central sphere of our observation to the psychology of the group, i.e., to an area in which neither the new methods of observation nor the conceptual framework correlated to them can be directly applied.

Another reason why we have so far concentrated our attention on the individual is the realization that our ability to find access to the inner life of others is dependent on their willingness to reveal themselves. In general we can, therefore, undertake psychological investigations only when illness and suffering provide sufficient motivation. Without an individual's wish to seek relief or to be cured, it is usually difficult to obtain sufficient psychological data.

I am nevertheless not pessimistic. It is indeed possible to learn a great deal about the inner life of man outside the therapeutic setting. Man's wish to express himself is strong. True, the documents of self-revelation may often have the simultaneously activated tendency to hide and to disguise — perhaps just at the point where they manifestly appear to divulge some decisive secret; yet, the careful scrutiny of the available material may lead us to many insights. Freud thought, for example, that psychotic patients could not be treated by psychoanalysis because they could not come emotionally close to the analyst and lend him their trust. It was Freud's study of an available document, Schreber's *Memoirs of My Nervous Illness,* that allowed him to dispense with the investigation of the mental life of a noncooperative psychotic patient during the treatment process and yet to explain the psychopathology of paranoia (in particular its persecutory and megalomaniac delusions) more comprehensively and cogently than had ever before been done.

Are there analogous methods by which we could investigate the reactions of large groups? Are there ways by which the deep insights psychoanalysis has gained about the individual can be brought to bear on group psychology in a sensitive and creative fashion, so that we may hope to arrive at a solid understanding of the behavior of large groups and thus, in turn, may hope to make a decisive contribution to the strengthening of the self-control of these groups and of their leaders?

To be more specific, let us consider the psychic constellation called narcissism — the love for one's self — which, as we are realizing with deepening understanding, plays a decisive motivational role in group psychology. The importance of such vicissitudes in the realm of narcissism as wounded self-esteem and deflated fantasies of omnipotence cannot be overestimated—they lead to the most dangerous form of group tension: the group's readiness for aggressive action. Our broadened and deepened knowledge in these psychic areas is already assisting us to achieve respectable therapeutic successes with individual patients whose prognosis had formerly been rather poor; and the substantal insights in this area concerning the psychopathology of individual patients raise the legitimate hope that we will eventually be able to obtain analogous insights in the area of group psychology which will increase the group's ability to be the master of its own destiny.

It would not be difficult to present at this point some concrete illustrations of the important role narcissism plays in the psychic life of individuals and groups: how, for example, endless hate and lust for revenge—without regard even for one's own survival—can result from wounded self-esteem, and why these reactions come about. But I must not allow myself to be long-winded concerning a favorite topic. And instead of supplying clinical or historical illustrations, let me merely mention Kleist's *Michael Kohlhaas* (1808), a masterful German story about hurt pride and its consequences, and its English-language counterpart, Melville's great novel, *Moby Dick*, two literary masterpieces that deal with this theme— not as rigorous, scientific explorations, of course, but with the freedom an artistic medium provides.

The acquisition of psychological insights, however—be they ever so clearly formulated and validly substantiated—is only a first step. If our insights are to influence others to modify their attitudes and actions, we also must be able to count on the good will and open-mindedness of those to whom these insights are communicated. You can lead the horse to water but you can't make him drink. We will have to discover methods by which we can make the wholesome potentialities of the discoveries of modern depth psychology not only available but even attractive to the large groups. At the moment, several opportunities offer themselves to us as we strive to reach this goal. I shall discuss two of them.

The first is the mapping out of a psychological technology designed to influence the masses. I admit freely that I am not at home with such methods — indeed, I feel very uneasy about them. The skilled use of techniques to manipulate the masses smacks of demagoguery, suggests the rabble-rousing of the seducer who is able to intoxicate the listening crowds. And there is, of course, no dearth of historical examples to show how a people was led to ruin by its leader — as were the children by the Pied Piper of Hamlin. I think that we understand such events. The great seducers of mankind have retained from their childhood an unshakable conviction of being all-powerful and all-knowing. It is this pervasive sense of infallibility that shapes their attitudes and forges their actions. Such personalities are prone to formulate certain simple and clearly depicted goals — whether in the realm of religion or of politics; whether as the prophets of a salvation through physical exercise or through the eating of herbs. Although these goals may be rational in appearance, they are nevertheless the manifestations of an archaic self which, in accordance with the solipsistic conceptions of early life, is still experienced as possessing absolute power and unlimited knowledge. It is this connection with the archaic self that lends dogmatic certainty to the opinions held by such individuals, and it explains the ruthlessness with which they are able to pursue their goals. These personalities, furthermore, exert a quasi-hypnotic effect on many people. Deeply rooted in our earliest childhood there remains in us a longing to merge with an all-powerful and all-knowing ideal figure. This yearning finds an apparently irresistible fulfillment for many in their total submission to a Messianic leader and to his dogmatic beliefs.

It surely does not have to be explained why we feel instinctively repelled at the thought of advocating methods that resemble those employed by the Messianic leaders and dictators of recent history. But are we not here perhaps the victims of a prejudice? Must we not admit that there are also well-intentioned and constructive leaders who are able to employ irrational forces and to evoke irrational responses — in the service of rational and culture-building goals? What would we not have given — I am speaking here of those of my own generation who lived in Germany and Austria during the thirties — what indeed would we not have given for an inspir- ing charismatic leader who could have pitted his profoundly held humanitarian ideals effectively against that most pernicious mass seducer of our time who almost succeeded in destroying Western civilization? Under certain circumstances — we have to admit it — pure rationality, however valid its goals, must find support from the irrational depths of the archaic psyche. If not, it will remain impotent vis-à-vis the irrational forces of destruction. It was not by accident that the image of the devil was created by man's symbol-forming mind.

We must ask ourselves, in addition, whether it would indeed be possible for us to use irrational methods with conviction should we ever decide to take such a step in earnest. People who have once fully committed themselves to rationality, whether in individual psychotherapy or in the realm of social action, are in general simply not able to mobilize and exploit the charisma of archaic omnipotence. And furthermore, should we nevertheless succeed in conjur- ing up those irrational powers that are effective in the social arena in order to guide and to inspire, then we must not forget that playing the sorcerer's apprentice is not without danger. One begins by using irrational means in the service of rational ends. Yet, before one knows it, the irrational has taken over and has become our master. At first we are pre- tending omnipotence, but soon we may begin to believe in it ourselves. The kind and rational leader is now a tyrant, and the friendly mentor becomes transformed into the Messiah who brooks no contradiction. It is not hard to find examples of such inauspicious developments either in the history of nations or—I will here refrain from pointing at specific instances—in the history of psychotherapy.

The second approach to the masses and their leaders—analogous to the conditions that allow access to the psyche of the individual—is opened by the group's anxiety and need for help. We must not discount the possibility that some extreme, not yet fully foreseeable danger will in the future constitute a turning point with regard to the traditional irrationality of group behavior. Mankind may indeed be facing grave and unusual dangers, since for the first time in history the means for self-annihilation are now at its disposal. Let us assume a dawning awareness in the masses that certain convictions—such as the belief in the perfection, omnipotence, and indestructibility which each individual harbors about himself and about the group to which he belongs—prevent us from acting realistically because they make us blind to the ultimate peril. Could it not then come to pass, in a period of critical danger, that the ability to pause, to listen, to ponder may emerge—to be insightful before the irreversible deed is done? Might it not happen, under such circumstances, that the seemingly unattainable would become a reality and that the large groups, or at least their leaders, would begin to understand themselves, not only superficially but in depth? That they would grasp the significance of psychic areas which under ordinary circumstances can hardly be penetrated and mastered by the mental efforts of even the most rational and courageous individual? What I am speaking of here is the dawning recognition by the masses or their leaders of how easily the ideas of grandeur and omnipotence which are so deeply interwoven with a sense of national identity can become an unrealistic intoxicant and can thus constitute a great danger. What I have in mind, furthermore, is the recognition that neither God nor nature has bestowed on us the right to feel ourselves bigger and better than our neighbor and, what is even more important, that we do not *need* this right. That each can have pride in himself and be pleased with himself without degrading the other, without having to do away with those whose only fault is that they are different from us, and who thus remind us that we are not the only-begotten: unique and yet divinely universal.

I realize that there are objections to these thoughts. It may well be said that in moments of despair and extreme danger men tend to be less rather than more rational; that in such moments they will not turn to a rational leader, but will be swept toward the charisma of a Messiah. Yet, who can really predict how man will behave when he is face to face with ultimate disaster? At any rate: so long as there is uncertainty, it is the duty of depth psychology to be prepared for the moment when, in a situation of utmost gravity, a last chance for the ascendancy of reason might arise. We must therefore attempt to gather insights that would allow us, if the historical moment is propitious, to exert that influence on behalf of rationality in the arena of public and historical events which depth psychology has up to now exerted in psychotherapy. Beyond that we cannot see today. Yet, the mere possibility of such an intervention should be a sufficient incentive for us to devote all our resources to the broadening and deepening of our work.

But I must take a breath. From what I have said so far one might conclude that it is my intention to deflect analysts from treating their patients and to direct them instead to the investigation of groups—that I am asking them to focus their attention on social psychology instead of wasting their time with psychotherapy and the investigation of the psychology of the individual and his treatment. Nothing, however, is further from my mind. On the contrary, not only am I convinced that the abandonment of the traditional therapeutic goals and investigational tasks of the analyst and their substitution by research in the field of social psychology would lead to very meager results, but I am also certain that such a shift would bring about the drying up of the actual source from which must spring the analyst's insights concerning group psychology.

Cobbler, stick to your last! Analyst, stay in your consulting room! Don't be persuaded to relax your efforts in pursuing the work in which you have become proficient: to understand your patient, to communicate your understanding to him, and to help him through his increasing self-knowledge to become the master of his fate.

These appeals are not meant to militate against the social psychologist, or, of course, against those analysts whose predilection and talent have led them to the study of group psychology. The application of analytic insights to the investigation of this field and to related disciplines has already brought us many fine results. And nowhere is the access to the soul of man, to the peak of his love and the abyss of his hate, more open than in that singular, long-term relation between two people which is called the psychoanalytic situation. Since the fundamental discoveries of the analyst will surely continue to be made only in the central sphere of his work, he must not relinquish his therapeutic activity, for he would otherwise deprive himself of the richest source of new insights.

My conviction that the analyst must not turn away from therapeutic activity is still more broadly based. True, every successfully terminated analysis gives us the satisfaction of knowing that a human life has now been freed from the shackles of neurotic inhibitions. And we may also surely allow ourselves to feel pride when—often as the result of having been privileged to collaborate with an insightful and gifted patient—it is our good fortune to contribute a piece of new psychological insight to the enduring fund of general scientific knowledge. But each favorable therapeutic outcome, each scientific advance signifies still more. Each treatment that reaches a valid termination—yes, even each partial success that brings about the reliable modification of a hitherto deadlocked neurotic state—is an important and auspicious event with regard to the survival of what should be regarded as the essence of man. It is a victory of man's planning and thinking individuality over the impersonal anonymity of his fate-bound matrix. With every analytic success, a human being has made a step toward autonomy, toward freedom.

What I have in mind here is not the traditional conception of the victory of rationality over the irrational, the ascendancy of reason over passion. Humanness comprises not only reason and equanimity but also irrationality and passion. Still—although man as a thinking machine is no more human than man as a frenzied fanatic—a person's inner freedom and independence, the essence of his human individuality, become enhanced when he begins to discern the determinants of his goals and attitudes; when he knows why he thinks, feels, and acts as he does; and when now, because of his knowledge, it is easier for him to be in control of his feelings and his behavior and to be the master of his choices and decisions. He understands now why he always had to be cold, logical, and rational; and in consequence of this understanding, he becomes capable of passionate feelings and actions. Or he knows now why all his life he had to move from one frenzied crisis to the other, and, in consequence of this knowledge, he is now able to reflect first and not plunge into action. In the terms of Freud's well-known analogy he is no longer the horseman who claims that he wants to go where in fact his horse is taking him—he is now in truth the master of his horse.

As I get closer to the end of these reflections I realize

more and more how difficult it is to state the case of analysis without presenting the empirical evidence on which this science is built. My convictions about the broad significance of depth psychology may therefore seem fanciful to that still not inconsiderable number of skeptics who are inclined to look upon psychoanalytic therapy and research as a somewhat faddish and at any rate rather unscientific occupation.

I should nevertheless like to share with you a speculative train of thought, even though I realize that in doing so I might well run the risk of exposing myself to the justifiable reproach that I am being unscientific, and am liable to increase the very prejudices against analysis that I am trying to reduce. Let me stress, however, that I do not seek the quick acceptance of my suggestions; I have only the wish that they not be rejected out of hand and that they be given some attention. My speculation concerns the nature of the phe-nomena the psychoanalyst investigates or — to state my topic in traditional terms — the nature of the illnesses he treats.

The arguments I have been presenting up to this point are on the whole in harmony with the enlightened attitude that psychic disturbances are neither a sin nor a disgrace, but are illnesses that ought to be cured. That this view is accepted by the professional psychotherapist goes without saying. I believe that nowadays it is even held rather widely by broad, non-professional layers of the population — at least by the edu-cated. I might be too sanguine in this judgment; the old prejudices are possibly still stronger than I think. But, be that as it may, there is no doubt that the view which, according to my optimistic assessment, prevails today among the educated deserves our full support: it is the expression of a progressive and enlightened attitude.

Attractive as these humanitarian views are for us, and much as they deserve our support within the framework of present social reality, I believe that the medicotherapeutic conceptualization of psychic disequilibrium on which they are based is too confining. I believe, in other words, that we need a broader outlook. Specifically, I would like to propose that psychological disturbance should not be looked upon as a disease — or at any rate not exclusively so — but as a way station on the road of man's search for a new psychological equilibrium.

Throughout the historical period, man has had to deal increasingly with the problems posed by a world that he himself has created. The simple drives which are his natural equipment have become less and less useful to him as the social environment in which he finds himself is growing more complex. His aggressivity, in particular, was once, in his animal past, indispensable for his survival; now, on the contrary, it has become the gravest threat to his existence: he must learn to control it if human life is to continue on earth.

But to suppress human drives can also be dangerous. The capacity of our biological and psychological equipment to adapt to change is limited, and the tension imposed on us by the extensive suppression of our drives becomes intolerable before long. Freud referred to this emotional burden, in a rather understated fashion, as "discomfort" or "discontent."[2] Man feels himself imprisoned by the demands of civilized existence and strives to escape. To let himself go in orgies of lust and aggression leads to disaster. Yet, the suppression of his drives — the meek acceptance of an ascetic existence — is a feat apparently also beyond his capacity, despite the efforts of Christianity for two thousand years. Some of the gratifications from which man has obtained a modicum of relief in his

[2] The English rendition of the title of Freud's great essay *"Das Unbehagen in der Kultur"* is "Civilization and Its Discontents." Actually neither the words "discomfort" nor "discontent" do full justice to the meaning of *Unbehagen*, although "discomfort," with its milder connotation of suffering and without the implication of resentment, is the closer equivalent.

predicament are slowly becoming unavailable. There are more people and there is less space. It is getting harder to find regions in which we can satisfy our need to roam about freely. Everywhere, machines are doing the work of our muscles. And even the joys of parenthood will surely also have to be relinquished, at least by most, or else there will soon be standing room only on this earth.

Are these, then, in the bitter words of the great Austrian satirist Karl Kraus, *the last days of mankind?* I do not think so. Football and boxing, to be sure, will not be our salvation — not even the enjoyment of nature in hiking and climbing. No, what is needed to ensure the survival of the human race — and here I am revealing the perhaps overly daring hypothesis I announced earlier — is the intensification and, above all, the elaboration and expansion of man's inner life.

I know that such an assertion will be offensive to many. Western civilization traditionally extols the man of action; it demands that the individual at least be engaged in activities. To contemplate one's navel, to give oneself over to inward-looking contemplation — these are attitudes that belong in different lands, and in our culture they are supposedly confined to a minority of eccentrics who cannot successfully adapt to the ways of the world.

Well and good — but let us not judge too quickly, and first let us look about us a bit. Let us, for example, consider the widespread attempts of the young people of today to obtain pleasures and satisfactions that are largely unrelated to external activity: by giving themselves over to the intoxicating effect of drugs and rhythmical music; by immersing themselves in Eastern philosophy; or merely by maintaining long periods of a wordless physical closeness, barely touching each other in some kind of ecstasy. I am not claiming that these practices are valid solutions of the great problems of human existence. I merely want to show that the rising generation is searching and exploring — specifically, that it is attempting to find sources of fulfilling gratification that are independent of external activity.

It is safe to assume that, in the future, man's external activities will have to be restricted even further. If, under these conditions, he wishes to continue to live proudly and contentedly—without the opportunity to fasten his interest upon the absorbing challenge of the conquest of new territories, without the engagement of his energies in battles and wars, and, last but not least, without the joys of being surrounded by the exhilarating play and laughter of his children—then man's originality, indeed his genius, will truly be put to the test. Under such circumstances the goal of maintaining human life, not only as livable but indeed as worth living, this goal can be reached—and I do not discern an alternative—only through the expansion and intensification of man's inner life.

But how do these reflections bear on the topic of the significance of the psychoneuroses? I believe that these psychic conditions, which are generally conceived as diseases and which are indeed the cause of much intense suffering and unhappiness, should in certain respects be understood as man's groping toward the enlargement and intensification of his inner life. I hasten to add that we are dealing here with attempts that have come to grief. Nevertheless, I shall be bold enough to assert that these miscarried attempts should be evaluated as more courageous, and potentially more creative, than some of the forms of psychic equilibrium that make up the area of emotional normality or health.

Mental health may be defined as the psychological condition that allows a person to respond actively to his environment and to obtain satisfaction from his encounter with the world. Freud is said to have described it as man's capacity to love and to work. Such a conception of psychic normality can remain unchallenged so long as we are referring to the world of yesterday and today, to man's position as we know it from the study of history and from our own experience. Within this familiar context we will surely consider it a desirable state of psychic health when a person reflects about the physical and social environment in which he finds himself and responds to it with a full range of emotions and effective actions: rejects it in courageous rebellion where he must, and embraces it lovingly where he can.

But what will be man's psychological task in the future? Let us assume that the dread of self-annihilation will prevent humanity from engaging in wars and that the condition of enduring peace will exert a wholesome, humanizing influence on people. Let us further assume that these psychological changes (coupled with the fear of civil disorders which might lead to uncontrollable wars) will bring about a modicum of social justice. Let us finally assume that reason and self-discipline will result in world-wide agreement about the number of people that can be accommodated on this planet and will lead to the establishment of suitable safeguards that this number is not exceeded. What then?

Before responding to the challenge of this question, I will first acknowledge that I am fully aware that many readers will react with angry impatience to the foregoing considerations. It seems indeed so unlikely that the utopian conditions I have just described are realizable that I might well be told to stop worrying about the welfare of mankind in a paradise which, after all, has no chance of ever becoming established. I could match such skepticism by the rejoinder that the future is unpredictable. And, in particular, I could point out that a world-wide overpopulation and a destructive potential of the magnitude of the unchained atom are factors that combine to bring about an unprecedented psychological situation — perhaps one in which people will act more reasonably than they have so far. The essence of our problem has to be approached by a different road. If the development toward the establishment of a lasting peaceful equilibrium among people is to reach its goal, it must be maintained by the complementary cooperation of internal and external factors, i.e., by the mutually complemental interaction of certain environmental changes and man's psychological responsiveness to them. Life in a peaceful environment—although apparently the ideal state—would not be without serious psychological problems. Such an existence would, on the one hand, lead to the withdrawal of the psychic energies from the battles and problems of the external world, demanding their new employment and thus necessitating an intensification of man's inner life. But, on the other hand— and this is the crucial point of my argument—the most important precondition for mankind's approach to a state of external harmony and peace is a shift in man's psychological structure. If man could gradually withdraw from his present search for external sources of pleasure and, instead, could increasingly find contentment from the enjoyment of values that are in harmony with an intensification of his inner life, then he would *pari passu* be able to deflect his aggressive and libidinal drives from those dangerous aims which up to now have blocked the road toward the establishment of peace.

The work of the creative artist and performer and the psychological activities of those who are able to respond to art and to obtain pleasure from it should be regarded as the precursors of that ability to enjoy the pursuit of internalized interests of which I speak. Consider, for example, the powerful psychological forces which music activates in those who can enjoy it. Here, a whole universe of experiences is open to us, which is hardly related to the realities of our everyday existence—a world in which we can reap satisfactions hardly related to those external goals we traditionally strive to attain and for which we fight. It is not only art that I have in mind here but also certain aspects of science. Thinking is trial action carried out with minute quantities of energy, says Freud's (1925b) beautiful definition. Yes; but passionate reflection and mental conquest can more and more become satisfying purposes per se — and Freud himself is indeed an outstanding example of such an inward shift. Learning in order to know, reflecting in order to understand — not only to construct bridges or to organize excursions to the moon — such exercise of self-contained mental functions is a fulfilling activity for those who are adequately endowed in the intellectual and emotional sphere, allowing them to enjoy life and to consider their energies satisfyingly employed.

Stated in the most general terms, my hypothesis is the result of the application of Darwinian developmental principles to a psychoanalytic sociology. There exist countless variations within the human race. Most individuals with their specific (and, within limits, fixed) abilities and disabilities are destined for extinction when a drastically changed environment ceases to sustain them. But within the legions are a few — perhaps previously ill-adapted and weak — who will adapt to the new environment and will be able to survive, while all the countless others, the host of the formerly strong, will be destroyed.

Thus, psychic disorders may be seen as a manifestation of man's attempt to achieve the intensification of his inner life: a developmental step he must take in order to survive in his rapidly changing social environment. The neuroses as we know them have succeeded in bringing about a partial detachment of the drives from their primordial engagement with external reality; but the concomitant shift from action to thought and from the external object to the self has led here, not to creative mental activity and to the enjoyment of one's self, but to unsolved inner conflicts and psychic tension.

What is the relation between the foregoing reflections and the central subject matter of this presentation, the question whether depth psychology is still relevant in the world of today? Does the conception of the psychic disorders as man's attempt to shift his psychological energies upon his inner life throw new light on our evaluation of the importance of psychoanalysis as an investigative science and as a form of psychotherapy?

In most sciences there exists a more or less clear separation between the area of practical, empirical application and the area of concept formation and theory. In analysis, however, these two areas not only form a partnership of active, reciprocal communication and mutual stimulation which prepares the soil for many important advances in other fields of knowledge — here, they are merged into a single functional unit.

Psychoanalysis as an investigative science is inseparable from analysis as a form of psychotherapy. Not only does the therapeutic situation supply unparalleled opportunities for the systematic empirical observation of psychic processes in breadth and depth, but the aim of psychoanalytic therapy is in essence identical with the aim of science: to extend the reach of consciousness and to enlarge the ego's domain of knowledge and freedom.

A well-conducted analysis, therefore, which has been brought to a proper conclusion, provides the analysand with more than the diminution or disappearance of his painful and disturbing symptoms — existing in him now is a certain psychological openness, perhaps even a spark of that playful creativeness which turns toward new situations with joyful interest and responds to them with life-affirming initiative. Such a person may yet continue to be more easily traumatized than one who has learned to maintain a reliable yet restricting psychic equilibrium. But he will also be more perceptive and responsive than the rigidly normal.

Yes, depth psychology is still young, and its achievements are limited. But the psychoanalyst has no reason to be either ashamed of the past performance of his science or pessimistic about its future contributions. Not only can he maintain that

the venerable injunction on Apollo's temple in Delphi, "Know
thyself!" has nowhere in history found a stricter obedience
than in the sphere of his activity, but perhaps he can also
claim that he is the only scientifically systematic, yet understanding and respectful observer and helpmate in man's
attempt to achieve a new psychological equilibrium that will
be in harmony with the changed social environment of the
future.

I have now come to the end. Throughout I have tried to
refrain from offering simplistic solutions, from painting in
black and white. And I have always attempted not to obscure
the doubtful. Still, I will admit to the hope that I have not
been unsuccessful in conveying my deep conviction that the
continuing study of the inner life of man within the framework of depth-psychological treatment and investigation is an
important, a valuable, undertaking. To expand the realm of
man's consciousness and thereby that of his self-control and
creative responsiveness, during a historical juncture that
confronts him with new and difficult tasks, is a goal that calls
for both the analyst's fullest effort and devotion and the
support of his work by an understanding community.

36

Narcissism as a Resistance
and as a Driving Force
in Psychoanalysis

I hope you will not take it amiss if today I do not present you with a methodically ordered lecture. You see, I chose to devote my time to the preparation of the public address at the university.[1] I felt that as a representative of psychoanalysis vis-à-vis the public I should deliver something formally rounded there. But here I may be permitted to speak off the cuff. I am, after all, among friends who are familiar with my thoughts. The results of some of my recent investigations, however, are less well known, and it is these that I want to take up.

Narcissism as a Resistance in Psychoanalysis

The existence of narcissism as resistance — and let me say immediately that I am speaking here about narcissism as a *nonspecific resistance* against analysis — is fully acknowledged by all psychoanalysts; it is the only aspect of narcissism for

---

This lecture was given at the meeting of the German Psychoanalytic Association in Berlin on October 10, 1970. The present version was prepared from Dr. Kohut's lecture notes.

[1] [The reference is to the lecture Kohut gave three days earlier, at the Free University in Berlin. See this volume, Chapter 35.]

which all analysts make allowance in their clinical work. This, at least, is the classical attitude.

Freud, in his "A Difficulty in the Path of Psycho-Analysis" (1917b), compares his discovery of an unconscious mental life to the discoveries of Copernicus and Darwin. He says the findings of psychoanalysis are experienced as a narcissistic injury to mankind, especially the theory of unconscious mental life. Freud, then, speaks here about nonspecific resistance against the total edifice of psychoanalysis as a science.

This same attitude was gradually recognized also as nonspecific resistance of the individual patient against analytic treatment. The individual patient, in other words, believes that he wants to recognize his unconscious thoughts and wishes with the aid of analytic treatment. Yet, simultaneously, he fights against the treatment. He does not want to accept the fact that he is dominated by motivations of which he knows nothing.

This shift in emphasis of the concept of nonspecific narcissistic resistance — a shift from the general to the specific — reached a kind of climax and turning point with Wilhelm Reich. Reich formulated narcissistic resistance as character armor (1933-1934) and he maintained it was the task of the analyst to penetrate this narcissistic armor. The influence of Reich's teachings and writings on psychoanalytic theory and practice has now waned. His plastic descriptions of narcissistic resistance, however, and of the manner in which the analyst is to respond to it, have left their mark on analytic practice, even today.

The change which the idea of resistance during analysis underwent from Freud to Reich can be regarded as an example of the progressive concretization and intensification of a concept. What for Freud had been abstract and moderate — resistance motivated by fear — became for Reich something concrete, something hardened: an armor. Reich created an aggressive image implying hostility, fight, quarrel between patient and physician. The physician who wants to overcome the resistance turns into an attacker who undertakes breaking to pieces the armor of the analysand.

From Freud to Reich and beyond Reich, we see repetition-compulsion in successive generations. What has hurt the younger generation of analysts, what was suffered passively by them, was later repeated by them actively, rationalized as a moral stance. (What one has passively experienced as training analysand is then actively inflicted upon one's own patients, including one's training analysands.) After Reich's disappearance from the analytic scene, the narcissistic "armor" changed into a narcissistic "crust." This image still has not completely faded, and it still influences the technical attitude of many analysts. In spite of the moderation of the concept, from "armor" to "crust," traces of Reich's ideas are still present: the crust must be pierced.

The narcissistic resistance of which we are speaking here is nonspecific. The pathology whose revelation it opposes can be the outgrowth of unresolved conflicts in the area of object-instinctual drives: for instance,. conflicts concerning the patient's love and hate for the objects of the oedipal period. But the pathology whose reactivations in analysis the narcissistic resistance opposes can also lie in the area of narcissistic disorders.

The intensity of this nonspecific narcissistic resistance, the hardness of the analysand's narcissistic "crust," is not proportionate to the dynamic forces of the underlying pathologic conflicts or needs. The resistance is a function of the general narcissistic vulnerability of the patient. Analytic treatment as a whole offends the pride of the analysand, contradicts his fantasy of his independence, and that is why he now resists treatment — without reference to the specific details of his psychic illness.

I below submit three typical examples of nonspecific

narcissistic resistance and discuss them briefly: first two examples of narcissistic reactions to parapraxes, then an example of the narcissistic defense posture toward the analytic process (or, to express it more exactly: toward the analyst as representative of the analytic process).

First, though, some remarks about the behavior of the analyst toward parapraxes of the analysand in the early stages of analysis. In my view, it is an error if the analyst in such cases focuses on what was repressed and emerged through parapraxis. This opinion is based on many years of clinical observation; experience also taught me that nothing useful is elicited by focusing on the content of parapraxes. In the early stages of analysis — and in the analyses of some narcissistically vulnerable patients this early stage lasts a long time, often even years — the analyst should not look primarily for what was unconscious and repressed but should focus on the narcissistic injury of the analysand, i.e., he should explain to the patient that the mere fact that he has committed a parapraxis constituted a narcissistic injury. The patient feels shame, and he reacts with rage simply over the fact that a parapraxis unexpectedly got the better of him. The content of what was repressed and emerged through the parapraxis is not the most important aspect of the event. It may be mentioned, but, so to speak, only as a footnote to the interpretation proper. The proper aim of the interpretation should be the emotions caused in the patient through the feeling of relative helplessness. The temporal element — the suddenness of the loss of conscious control over one's words or actions — sometimes plays a specific (and also a specific genetic) role in this narcissistic injury through parapraxis, for instance, if a specific childhood experience concerning sudden loss of childhood self-esteem, of childhood pride, was repeated through this event.

Let us go on now to the other example of nonspecific narcissistic resistance caused through parapraxis. This example concerns not the analysand but the analyst. All of us probably have had the opportunity, for instance at a psychoanalytic meeting, to observe an analyst's public slip of the tongue. This, especially if it happens to oneself, is a very instructive event, and I advise close self-observation on the next occasion. How does the analyst behave when he makes a mistake in speaking, during a lecture perhaps, or during public scientific debate when one speaks extemporaneously? Under such circumstances one often readily admits *what* was revealed through parapraxis, often even something that was *really* hidden. But what one wants to cover up is that one lost control. "Of course I know what this means," one says; one even quickly reveals the secret. What one is ashamed of is that suddenly something broke through without one's having anything to do with this revelation. One acts as if one had almost done it intentionally; one laughs, which means that one demonstrates that one has overcome the *narcissistic* injury. (Freud explained humor [1927b] as a higher form of narcissism emerging victoriously over the inevitable injuries to one's own illusory omnipotence. My own hypothesis [1966b] is that humor represents a transformation of archaic narcissism.) It is very difficult not to react if one has publicly committed a parapraxis. In other words, making a parapraxis and then letting the others laugh without saying anything further oneself is most difficult.

And now the third example of nonspecific narcissistic resistance: the behavior in analysis of a young man, a successful journalist, who treated me and my attempts at explanations and interpretations at the beginning of the analysis with inimitable condescension. Instead of coming to terms with the content of what I interpreted (dynamically) and constructed (genetically), he criticized with disarming friendliness or superior irony the formal aspects of my endeavors: the grammar of my sentences, my choice of words, or similar matters. One simply cannot describe it, one has to have heard it to savor fully the expertise with which he tried to destroy my self-confidence, to degrade me.

When an inexperienced analyst feels exposed to such treatment on the part of a patient, he tends, of course, to react with anger, and he will be inclined to interpret the behavior of the patient as an offshoot of a "negative transference," for instance, as a reactivation of childhood hatred toward the rival of the Oedipus complex. But in the present case—and in my experience also in most similar cases— the behavior of the analysand is to be explained differently. The patient demonstrates through his behavior how *he* experiences the analysis, how my interpretations are received by *him*—how vulnerable and helpless *he* feels. One could say that he turns his passivity into activity, that he attacks *me* when *he* feels attacked. (That, however, is a comparatively unimportant explanation of his behavior. It is essentially based—at least in the case of this young man—on lessened differentiation between selfobject [analyst] and self [analysand].)

All this must be interpreted carefully and with true empathy. The analyst must not deny that the patient has indeed partially succeeded in hurting him, in inflicting real pain. And the analyst may admit—though probably only *sotto voce*—that he experienced an inclination to reactive anger. In other words: a tone of condescending kindness from the pedestal of the analyst's position must be avoided; what is needed is the analyst's expression of his sincere understanding for the position of the patient, including genetic reconstructions which explain the patient's sensitivity when he is confronted by pedagogic, didactic approaches toward him. (In connection with this patient, one might here recall Abraham's fine clinical contribution of 1919.)

In this case, and I could adduce many other clinical examples, we are dealing with a narcissistic defense. In all these cases, the analyst will try to reconstruct the specific history of the development of the patient's nonspecific narcissistic defensive posture (the analysand's nonspecific defensive narcissism). And he will try to illuminate more and more, especially in the later stages of analysis, the dynamic relationship between temporarily increased defensive narcissism and activation of specific aspects of the analysand's central pathology (e.g., especially strong shame and rage over the revelation of specific wishes and needs). Still, the narcissistic "crust" is not, by and large, specifically related to the nucleus of the neurosis; it is a general resistance against the analytic process which on the whole is not mobilized in order to obstruct the emergence of this or that specific pathogenic instinctual wish or this or that specific pathogenic infantile narcissistic need — it is directed against the analytic process as a whole.

One could talk further about the various possible reactions of analysts toward these narcissistic defense mechanisms of their patients. The central issue, however, is that it makes little difference what the analyst *does* so long as he *understands* what is going on in his patient. He can openly express his anger (as Freud did with patients who, it seemed to him, expressed their contempt for his empty waiting room by leaving the door open; he would send such patients to the door of the consulting room with the firmly expressed instruction to close it); or, as is my preference, he can suppress his anger and react with friendly understanding. Whatever we may do initially, it is ultimately our aim to help the patient understand the significance of his narcissistic reactions — the way that leads to the expansion of the patient's awareness is relatively unimportant.

A particularly instructive kind of chronic narcissistic resistance is the complex psychic formation called schizoid personality (see Kohut, 1971). This can be explained dynamically. Such individuals are vaguely aware of the fact that the cohesiveness of their self is maintained only very precariously. Because any injury of their self can lead to a catastrophic

fragmentation of the self, they protect themselves by maintaining an emotional distance between themselves and others.
(Cf. the case of Mr. H. [in Kohut, 1957e].)

Narcissism as a Driving Force in Psychoanalysis

We are speaking here about that large number of patients
whose psychopathology I have defined as narcissistic personality disorders. In the center of the illness in classical transference neuroses are structural conflicts which relate to
infantile drive demands concerning the great objects of childhood. These objects form the nucleus of the spontaneously
developing transference. In the center of the illness in narcissistic personality disorders is the disordered self. The central
content of the spontaneously developing transference is
formed not by loved or hated autonomous and independent
objects but by archaic selfobjects. These are experienced
either as a part of the self or as merged with the self
or as standing in the service of the self, i.e., as utilized
for the maintenance of the stability and cohesion of the
self.

How can one clinically differentiate a narcissistic personality disorder from a structural neurosis? On the basis of the
following empirically ascertainable fact: that, in the psychoanalytic situation, with patients with narcissistic personality
disorders a pathognomonic transference evolves spontaneously
which is directly connected with the nucleus of the psychopathology. This transference is based on a therapeutic regression to precisely that point where the normal development of
the psychic structures of the self was interrupted or where the
consolidation of those structures of the self which so far had
only been precariously established was not carried further
toward completion. The analytic situation, then, brings
about a reactivation of that developmental point in time at
which the basic disorder began. Thus, the interrupted psy-

chological growth process is given the opportunity to continue beyond the point of its arrest.

To describe this in greater detail: at the point where the psychic development is traumatically interrupted, the infantile wish or the infantile need is first intensified. In the classical transference neuroses, it is an infantile instinctual wish which, after traumatic failure, is first greatly strengthened and probably also distorted and then, in this strengthened and distorted form, is repressed. In narcissistic personality disorders, it is the need for mirroring or for merging with the idealized selfobject which, after a traumatically mortifying rejection is first greatly intensified and probably also distorted and is then, in this intensified and distorted form, either repressed or split off and disavowed. [See the remarks about "vertical splits" of the personality in 1971, pp. 183-185.] In the transference we therefore see the mobilization not of a normal but of a frustrated and therefore intensified and distorted wish or need that had been repressed or split off and disavowed. Through analysis, the connection between these wishes and needs and the central sector of the personality is re-established. But then, with the help of friendly, nontraumatic, empathic interpretations and constructions — *optimal frustration* — analysis denies direct satisfaction of the infantile wish or need and prevents retreat toward its renewed repression or splitting off. Therefore, only *one* possibility remains: further psychic development through structure building. This applies to both classical transference neuroses and to narcissistic personality disorders [cf. 1971, pp. 196-199].

In classical transference neurosis, a cohesive self cannot cope with drive demands and their frustration. The sequence of: instinctual wish, anxiety, repression of the instinctual wish, and inhibition and symptom is well known to every analyst, and therefore I need not go into this any further here. Narcissistic injuries accompany these experiences, but are here secondary. It is a cohesive self that experiences the frustrations of oedipal wishes as narcissistic trauma. It may react, to be sure, with depression and rage, but its structural cohesion is not seriously threatened. The transference leads to the activation of repressed drive demands, which now, in the working-through process of analysis, are gradually integrated into the total structure of the mature personality.

At what point in psychic development does the decisive disturbance occur that leads to narcissistic personality disorder?

As you know, I maintain that the proper appreciation of the role played by narcissism in human life demands that we posit a separate line of development for it, leading from archaic to mature forms. Specifically: we postulate two lines of development (one from archaic narcissism to mature narcissism, the other, side by side with it, from archaic to mature object love), not a single line of development (from narcissism to object love).

The symptoms of narcissistic personality disorders are the result of the defective condition of the narcissistic structures: they are manifestations of a disease of the self. The disease affects either the grandiose self or the archaic omnipotent selfobject (the idealized parent imago). Specifically, these components of the self are either fragmented or enfeebled. The development of the other parts of the personality, for instance, intelligence or drives, may have progressed comparatively undisturbed. But the narcissistic structures remained fixated in their development. In their archaic form they were either repressed or split off from the other parts of the psyche. In the latter case they can strongly dominate the patients' behavior from time to time, for example, in the form of addictionlike praise-seeking or addictionlike search for idealized selfobjects. Both these strivings can also be sexualized: we then have the different forms of sexual perversion.

Conflicts over drive aims (classical structural conflicts) are secondary in narcissistic personality disorders. In some cases the patient is involved in innumerable object relations, which can create the impression that drive-related conflicts caused his psychic illness — conflicts, in other words, which concern the patient's intense love or intense hate. However, these love or hate relationships are either defensive — attempts to ward off, through an exaggerated experience of love or hate relations, the loss of the archaic selfobject, which would lead to fragmentation of the self — or they are not expressions of object-love or object-hate at all, but of the need for self-objects in lieu of self-structure.

The spontaneously arising transference in these cases concerns the activation of the developmental stage at which the cohesive self begins to form, aided by mirroring from the side of the selfobjects of childhood and by merger with idealized aspects of these selfobjects. The structures thus formed are at first only precariously established and in constant danger of fragmentation. The formation and strengthening of the self during childhood is, in other words, the result of a long process of development. Analogously, the slowly proceeding working-through of the needs for mirroring and for idealizable selfobjects which are reactivated in the form of a narcissistic transference brings about the gradual healing of the defects in the self of the analysand.

Up to this point we discussed the narcissistic transference as a driving force toward developmental progress of the damaged self in analysis in general terms. Let us now proceed to specifics.

The genesis of the disorder can, for instance, be the insufficient mirroring of the child's self by the mother (her lack of empathy for her child's need for mirroring through the gleam in the mother's eye). The child's self can therefore not establish itself securely (the child does not build up an inner sense of self-confidence; it continues to need external affirmation). But, as was mentioned above, we do not see merely fixation on a small child's normal need for mirroring—the traumatic frustration of the normal need intensifies and distorts the need: the child becomes insatiably hungry for mirroring, affirmation, and praise. It is this intensified, distorted need which the child cannot tolerate and which it therefore either represses (and may hide behind pseudoindependence and emotional coldness) or disavows and splits off. Figure 4 is a diagram of the latter case.

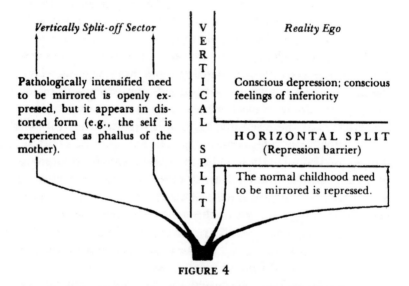

FIGURE 4

In the narcissistic transference, the infantile need for the selfobject is remobilized. (In the case shown in the diagram: the need for the mirroring selfobject.) The analyst aims at psychic reintegration of the need by reconstructing the period when, as he knows, the need was phase-appropriate and growth-promoting. Nongratification of the intensified and distorted need while yet acknowledging appropriateness of its precursor in childhood constitutes *optimal frustration* for the analysand. The analyst's acceptance of the fact that transference means reactivation of more or less normal childhood needs counteracts their renewed repression or their splitting off in distorted form. To repeat: there is only one road open to the reactivated infantile strivings for mirroring and merger with ideals: the road toward maturity. Higher forms of narcissism take shape; more precisely: the psyche acquires structures that transform the narcissistic needs.

This working-through process is kept in motion by the pressure of narcissistic needs. Again and again, in spite of strong resistance, the vulnerable, needy grandiose self offers itself to the selfobject analyst for praise, mirroring, and affirmation; or it seeks — again in spite of strong resistances — in the selfobject analyst an idealized self with which it can merge. Again and again — analogous to the conditions encountered in the classical transference neuroses where the analysand reacts to the frustration of his object-libidinal strivings — the patient reacts with regression to the frustration of his narcissistic needs as mobilized in the transference. Careful exploration of the oscillations is of great significance; knowledge of these processes contributes to their control. [See Kohut, 1971, p. 97, for a diagrammatic presentation of the usually brief but therapeutically important regressions during the working-through process of the narcissistic transferences.]

The thorough investigation of the various resistances mobilized by the analysand against the reactivation of the old narcissistic needs is, in my view, of greatest importance and will, I hope, soon be undertaken on the basis of meticulous clinical observations. In contrast to the nonspecific narcissistic resistances of which I spoke in the first part of this lecture, we are dealing here with *specific narcissistic resistances,* that is to say, in each case, with resistances against the revelation of specific narcissistic transferences in the analytic process. In the analyses of classical transference neuroses, resistances are motivated by the anxieties of a firmly cohesive self which fears either the loss of an object that is experienced as separate from the self or castration by such a separate object. By contrast, the specific resistances in the analyses of narcissistic personality disturbances are motivated by the anxieties of an insecurely established self which fears the rejection of the narcissistic needs that are reactivated in analysis, i.e., the need to be mirrored and to merge with an ideal. In other words, the specific narcissistic resistances are motivated by anxieties — I will (broadly speaking) refer to them as disintegration anxieties — which focus on the self and on an object experienced as (part of) the self. Although the analysand suffering from a narcissistic personality disorder consciously tries to express his needs openly, he nevertheless shies away from doing so because of the danger of the self's disintegration to which a possibly impending traumatic rejection of his needs exposes him. In other words, he fears the reactivation of the unempathic rejection by his childhood selfobjects, who did not respond to the need of his growing self for supportive and strengthening sustenance through mirroring and merger with the ideal.

The details of these resistances deserve, as I said, the most careful exploration. Here I can only say that they are of greatest importance during the process of psychoanalysis. They are transference resistances and, as long as they are in the ascendancy, stand in the way of the central working-through process of the analysis. They have to be dealt with time and again in the course of the treatment until they are ultimately overcome. Only then can the narcissistic transference be fully experienced and worked through. This working-through process of narcissistic personality disorders aims at integrating the repressed or split-off narcissistic structures that are mobilized in the transference into the realistic segments of the total personality. In order to achieve this end, the reactivation of these structures has to be a sustained one. With every nontraumatic frustration of the wishes of the grandiose self that are mobilized in the transference, with every nontraumatic disappointment in the omnipotent transference object, a small piece of psychic structure is laid down which increases the firmness of the self. Formerly there were gross oscillations between (1) depression and dejection on the basis of the repression of the analysand's grandiosity—to be exact: on the basis of the repression of his need for the mirroring of his grandiosity—and (2) open arrogance with self-righteous demands for an admiring audience (either on the basis of a temporary breakthrough of the archaic grandiosity across the repression barrier or, most frequently, on the basis of the displacement of the archaic narcissistic demands onto a split-off part of the personality). But gradually, as a result of the working through of the mirror transference, the analysand acquires a normal, dependable feeling of self-esteem which allows him to strive for external, self-enhancing success through realistic activities. In the area of the idealizing transference (the reactivation of the need for merger with the omnipotent selfobject), a similar development takes place. Formerly there was a quest for total merger with an omnipotent, idealized selfobject. Increasingly now, internal goal-structures are idealized instead. Previously, the patient's highly unstable self-esteem was dependent on merger with the idealized selfobject. Now the feeling of self-esteem (reacting to the vicissitudes of life with limited oscillations) can rely increasingly on the achievement of a merger between the self and its idealized goals.

I have come to the end of today's presentation. I know that I have to some extent spoken about ideas with which many of you are already familiar. Yet I hope that not only the few new details that I may have introduced today, but also, and particularly, my attempt to sketch out an over-all picture concerning the narcissistic disorders and their treatment will not have presumed on your attention in vain.

37

Peace Prize 1969: Laudation

Mr. President of the Federal Republic, Your Excellencies, Ladies and Gentlemen; dear Professor Mitscherlich!

The special edition of the journal *Psyche* in honor of Alexander Mitscherlich's sixtieth birthday contains a beautiful photograph. It shows him in the garb of the physician and medical researcher, in the white coat of the hospital or laboratory. I do not know who selected this picture — he himself, perhaps, or a colleague; but I believe that it depicts him in the role that is to him the most genuine representation of his personality: the scientific physician, the healing researcher.

The primacy of the role of medical-psychiatric researcher may indeed be the deeply imbedded knot that fastens the threads in the complex weave of his life's activities and of his personality. And it might well be true that his fellow workers see him in the same perspective. For those of his friends, however, who like myself live at some distance from him, his image is not quite so unambiguous. A number of contrasting aspects present themselves which call for separate scrutiny before one can attempt the synthesizing integration of the

Presented on October 12, 1969 in the Paulskirche in Frankfurt am Main in honor of Alexander Mitscherlich, published in the *Journal of the American Psychoanalytic Association* (1971), 19:806-818.

description of a personality and of a life's work that, difficult though it is to achieve, remains the ultimate goal of the biographer.

There is first of all the professional basis of Mitscherlich's life: the man in the white coat, the research-minded physician. Surely, for him, rooted in an academic family, with generations of great chemists as his model, this calling must be a source of life-supporting energy and professional motivation. His scientific contributions are thus, correspondingly, both impressive and wide-ranging. I will not today devote myself to a lengthy discussion of his specialized studies, even though I am aware of the fact that scientific progress depends largely on the continuous performance of circumscribed concrete scientific tasks. While his specialized studies are indeed on a high technical level, he gives of his best when he addresses himself to issues of general significance, when he provides us with panoramic overviews, for example, which lead to new insights and understanding, or when he turns to the bold organizational deed. His early study, *Freiheit und Unfreiheit in der Krankheit* (Freedom and Lack of Freedom in Disease), published in 1946, offers us a glimpse of his ability to think in breadth and depth about the nature of illness; about the interrelationship of physical and psychic disturbances; about the place of psychotherapy within the confines of medicine. And, taking due note of the importance of "the abysmal threat to which the whole of the Western World appears to be exposed" (Gebsattel, 1947, p. 44), he speaks of the incongruousness of our enormous therapeutic efforts on behalf of the single suffering individual. But, as if he were anticipating the central theme of some of his later works, he already seems to contemplate a shift in therapeutic emphasis. Observing that the effects of individual psychotherapy are tiny indeed, he adds, "Yet, we persist in applying it faithfully, *sustained by the hope,* even though we lack at present the capacity of its fulfillment, *that we will ultimately*

be able to expand the sphere of our therapeutic efficacy"
(italics added).

When Mitscherlich, just after the war, published the booklet on *Freedom and Lack of Freedom in Disease* (1946), he spoke in the preface of the isolation of the German researcher who could cast "hardly a glance at the world beyond the borders of his country." And he hoped he would contribute to setting in motion "a discussion . . . without which we have had to do for so long and for which we have such dire need." It was a full twenty years later that his treatise on psychosomatic medicine, *Krankheit als Konflikt* (*Disease as Conflict*) (1966, 1967a), was published, showing us how he had in the meantime continued to elaborate the themes with which he had formerly wrestled alone. And we can see how he, as no one else in Germany, had learned to familiarize himself fully with the work going on "beyond the borders of his country," and how he went about imparting his own knowledge to a growing number of his German colleagues. It goes without saying that Mitscherlich could never be merely the passive transmitter of the work of others, that he provided his countrymen with a synthesis which was more than a bland report of the results of research done in other lands. For occasionally, even where he seemed to be only summarizing, in the midst of the unassumingly presented material we suddenly discover thoughts of high originality. A fine example of this originality can be found in his treatise on psychosomatic medicine (1966) where he calls attention to the central position of creative fantasy at a pivotal point between the drive-laden individual and his given social environment. He speaks of the "relation . . . between, on the one hand, the pressure of fantasy which activates the individual and, on the other hand, the objectivity of the external, pre-set social patterns into which this urge can discharge its tension by expressing itself." And he states: "The degree to which . . . the given social environmental factors can interpenetrate with the

individual's creative productivity ... determines the stylistic
essence of his imagination and the extent to which it can
unfold" (p. 150). It seems to me that Mitscherlich has here
been able to bring us a step closer to the answer to an old and
puzzling question: by what means does the environment make
its often decisive contribution to the fulfilling employment of
man's creative forces? How important this contribution may
be is illustrated, for example, by the remarkable fact that five
or six of the Occident's greatest minds appeared within a
relatively short span of time in what was by modern standards
a small town — the Athens of Pericles.

Let us turn now to a second area of Mitscherlich's activity,
the sphere of social psychology, and in so doing, come nearer
to his work for peace. And here I must finally point to
something which, to be sure, could also have been stressed,
and with equal propriety, with regard to the preceding discussion of Mitscherlich's psychiatric contributions — namely,
that his psychoanalytically derived insights, his encounter
with the work of Freud, exerted an incalculable influence on
the form and content of his observations, thoughts, and
formulations. Even to speak of the influences that psychoanalysis has exerted on Mitscherlich's mode of thought is an
understatement, because this, as he says, "most precious
instrument for the psychological understanding of man that
we possess" has become fully his mental property. Whether
he is studying details concerning the psychology of the
individual or whether he is constructing comprehensive sociopsychological formulations, he always proceeds from a basis
buttressed by the empirical data of psychoanalytic observation. And it is on the strength of the fact that psychoanalytical insight is thus fully at his command that he is able, for
example, to demonstrate with convincing certainty how only
the recognition of the presence of an infantile drive can
account for the intensity of the asocial greed for possessions.
And it is similarly his psychoanalytic background that allows

him to show how the process of projection explains the formation of prejudice, the scourge of human communal life. For his most comprehensive conceptualizations, too, Mitscherlich finds support in psychoanalysis. The main lines of thought contained in his major contribution to social psychology, the book *Auf dem Weg zur vaterlosen Gesellschaft* (*Society Without the Father*), published in 1963, must to a considerable extent be regarded as applied psychoanalysis.

Society Without the Father is a difficult book. The great demands it makes on the reader are not only explainable by the fact that Mitscherlich is at home in the realms of both individual psychology and the psychology of the social group, whereas the average reader is not; there is an additional, emotional obstacle. The reader must adapt himself to a presentation in which nothing is simplified, and where much remains suspended. The contents of the treatise, in other words, cannot easily become part of the storehouse of the reader's identifiable knowledge. Yet, the basic problem Mitscherlich illuminates, without, however, offering an easy solution for it, can be lifted without undue difficulty from the intricate pattern of his book: Influences that cannot be attributed to the individual have basically altered the society in which we live. We no longer live in the security of an authoritarian state, but in a society of anonymous equals, guided by an anonymous, nonpaternalistic array of technically trained experts and professional politicians.

I shall not, in the present context, go further into the matter of how Mitscherlich presents the advantages and disadvantages of this historical development. The central question he poses — and I urge everybody to ponder this profound sociopsychological problem — is the following: how can we preserve the father-mother-oriented family structure within this broad, sibling-oriented society? The creative capacity, says Mitscherlich, which man must mobilize if he is to achieve a viable adjustment to a new social environment, will be available to him only if he has acquired in early life the nucleus of a firm yet resilient psychic structure. Such a psychological make-up, however, which is capable of spontaneous cognitive responses to new social tasks, can, as we have learned through the detailed psychoanalytic study of the growth and formation of the psychic apparatus in the individual, be developed only by those who grow up in a family in which the child can experience his father and mother as clearly demarcated, i.e., clearly differentiated figures.

Mitscherlich's contributions to medical-psychiatric research and social psychology have been substantial. None of his diverse activities, however, are as important as those relating to his role as participating citizen, as upholder of the conscience of a nation, and as social reformer.

It is not hard to perceive how Mitscherlich's deep sense of responsibility permeates every one of his activities. Even where, in scientific objectivity, he sets forth the principles of psychosomatic medicine and describes in fullest technical detail the experiments supporting the discoveries that have been made in this field, he can suddenly become the passionate champion of specific improvements in medical training, or in medical therapeutics and the care of the ill, making recommendations which are correlated with his scientific insights into the nature of psychosomatic ailments. And after he has shown us, for example, in his short but penetrating essay on Frederick II (the Great) (1969), how the Prussian Monarch's childhood experiences determined both his productive, civilizing attitudes and his inhuman, antisocial characteristics, he suddenly becomes the admonisher, who extracts from history a maxim that may be applied to the present. "If we want to distill useful ideas from history," he says, "it is no longer a question of learning from it how to expand the territory of a nation; we should rather seek for inspirations concerning the task of bringing the self completely under our control, so that we become capable, without undue loss of self-esteem, of solving international conflicts through persuasion instead of through the blind employment of power." Does not this statement constitute a fine prescription for peace?

". . . an author's words . . . are deeds," wrote Freud (June, 1935) to Thomas Mann. This sentence surely has general validity, and may thus in a broader sense also be applied to the contributions of the scientist. In Mitscherlich's case the analogy is even more specific. Time and again, true to a deep-rooted endowment of his personality, he will break the comfortable silence of prevailing indifference and speak up — either for himself alone, or as the courageous voice of the few — in order to point out needs, to suggest possible improvements or to demand that changes be made.

He is neither dreamer nor prophet. They carry the easier load. One smiles at dreamers and prophets or even admires them without fear. Their dreams, after all, are too far from reality to pose a threat. Mitscherlich has shouldered the heavier burden; he is a prophet at the dawn of change. What he demands is possible of fulfillment; and he is always aware of the resistances he will have to face. To give an unpretentious but characteristic example: when in his book *Die Unwirtlichkeit unserer Städte* (*Our Inhospitable Cities*) (1965) he calls for playgrounds for the children of the city, that is no unattainable, utopian request. And when he reinforces his demand by the assertion that a child's cramped living space may ultimately contribute to limiting the ability and scope of his intellect — who would not be swayed by the force of this argument? Yet, Mitscherlich well knows that private land will not be easily surrendered; and he compares our readiness to accept a legalized expropriation for road-building with the unwillingness to do the same for playgrounds for the children who grow up in the overcrowded and overpriced areas of the inner city. Are we here dealing with economic questions only? Or are we rather, as Mitscherlich thinks, blocked by the

immature selfishness of a generation of adults who, lacking a
sense of empathy for the needs of children, have become
unable to act with parental responsibility within the public
domain?

Permit me a digression, at this point, in order to provide
you with the outline of a principle of psychoanalytic therapy—an outline essential for understanding Mitscherlich's
mode of activity in that most significant of all of his endeavors about which I shall speak in a moment. The psychoanalytic physician opens the way toward a cure, he does not
aim at achieving a cure directly. Or, in different words: the
psychoanalyst limits his activity to the removal of obstacles
that obstruct the path to psychological health. One could
roughly liken his approach to the surgeon's attitude to a
wound. The surgeon will remove foreign bodies and perhaps
narrow the gap between the edges of the wound—the rest
must be achieved by the body's innate healing tendencies.
The psychoanalytic physician tries to liberate the misdirected
or imprisoned energies of the psyche, to make them available
to the patient. As these forces are mobilized, new solutions
for the patient's paralyzing conflicts tend to develop spontaneously: his life may unfold in hitherto untried directions.
And the originality of these new solutions and goals which
emanate from the patient's own developing personality is
often far beyond anything that the psychotherapist could
have dreamt up and suggested to his patient. I should like to
venture the assertion that Mitscherlich's most significant contribution to the cause of civilization is the experiment—
whether consciously undertaken or on the threshold of awareness—of applying this analytic principle of individual cure to
the therapeutic transformation of a whole population. Psychoanalysts are familiar with the fact that the individual
psyche will abandon rational conflict-solutions if they arouse
in him the fear of having to confront unbearable internal
tension or panic-inducing external dangers. Mitscherlich

recognizes the same psychic mechanism in the sum total of similar personalities which make up whole populations and nations. Inner and outer realities, the conscious contemplation of which would disturb the peace of our mind, are frequently dealt with by prerational psychic mechanisms, which give them short shrift. And there is, in fact, no denying that these mechanisms have their usefulness within our psychic household: it would be wasteful and inefficient to keep our most highly differentiated mental processes in operation at all times. But when we are dealing, in the developmental history of an individual, with the attempt at a total obliteration of a whole important emotional area, or, according to Mitscherlich, with the massive denial of having emotionally participated in a grandiose-gruesome chapter of national history, then the situation is indeed quite different. True, one can go on living, and sing to oneself in the tipsily blissful mood of the *Fledermaus* that "glücklich ist, wer vergisst, was doch nicht zu ändern ist" ("happy the man who will forget what cannot be changed"), but this escapist attitude costs one dear. One pays the price, says Mitscherlich, of remaining immature, and of living in emotional and cultural superficiality. Moreover — and here is the crucial point — one loses the gift of responding to the tasks posed by a new social environment with the creation of new, vigorously viable solutions for the problems of the human community.

The new task we are facing is presented to us by Mitscherlich in his *Vaterlose Gesellschaft* (*Society Without the Father*) (1963). We are confronting a new social environment, he says, which calls for the employment of our full, unencumbered powers of sociopolitical creativeness to enable us to transform our old system of values and to originate a new set of goals and ideals. And in *Die Unfähigkeit zu Trauern* (*The Inability to Mourn*) (1967), which is co-authored by his wife, Margarete Mitscherlich-Nielsen, he undertakes direct and active steps toward a national therapy, a therapy which should enable an important group within the family of mankind to play a productive role in creating the civilization of tomorrow.

The essence of this experiment in national healing has now undoubtedly become obvious. It is necessary to have dealt with the past in order to achieve emotional and intellectual mobility. The release from the past, from the co-responsibility for misdeeds that were committed years ago and from the disgrace of having then childishly and irresponsibly shared in the glamour of recklessly pursued ideas of national grandeur—this release can be achieved only through the difficult, affect-laden inner activity psychoanalysts refer to as the "work of mourning." To mourn means to revive the memories of a secretly cherished past, and then, in anguish which passes into melancholy, to relinquish that past. The hardship imposed on us by detachment from the past is as great when the emotional task concerns the giant parent figures of our individual childhood selves as it is, as Mitscherlich emphasizes, when we are confronting the idealized kings and leaders of the national past and the formerly intoxicating feeling of belonging to an all-powerful group which we had alloyed into our individual identity. If this work of mourning remains undone, then the result is psychic impoverishment. We become distant and cold—like Niobe, who turned to stone because the work of mourning demanded of her was beyond human capacity (cf. K. R. Eissler, 1963)—or else our personality becomes shallow as we espouse an attitude of empty, technology-minded optimism. Yet, in order to infuse a spirit of humanness into our civilization of gigantic industries and crowded populations, and thus to create the cultural soil in which man can survive, we must not only employ every ounce of emotional energy that can be liberated, but must be guided by the understanding for human needs and supported by the ability to be empathic with our fellow men as well as with ourselves. These are difficult tasks, indeed, and we will not be free to undertake them if we turn from the horrors of the past as if we had no emotional connection with it. "Only as we . . . become able," says Mitscherlich in a heart-rending essay (1967b) on the medical experimentation on prisoners perpetrated during the Third Reich "to achieve a modicum of mournful identification with these victims . . . will something begin to change" (p. 27).

Psychoanalytic psychologist, social psychologist, reformer —where in these manifold activities lies Mitscherlich's work for peace? The answer is: in all of them, whether they take place in the microcosm of the field of individual therapy or in the macrocosm of the social and political arena. He contributes to peace through his ministrations to the individual who, freed from paralyzing inner conflict, can now participate in the constructive work of our civilization instead of continuing to swell the ranks of the resentful seekers for revenge. And he contributes to peace on the broader stage of public life when he champions the human attitudes that must remain fused to the skills, and knowledge of the specialist— whether in medicine, or in city planning and politics—if we are to create an environment in which we can live in internal and external peace.

Mitscherlich is not an apostle of peace. He knows how easy it is to arouse enthusiasm for peace—almost as easy, perhaps, as to stir up excitement for war. But these emotional states cannot be long sustained. Just to clamor for peace is not enough. What we need are insights. Insights into the nature of man, a grasp of those specific internal and external factors that make a person more aggressive and of those that make him more ready for peace. We need the findings of depth psychology and those of a social psychology that is based on the findings of depth psychology. We need answers to such crucial questions as: What specific experiences must be provided in childhood, what specific influences must be exerted upon a person in growth and maturity, to enable him ultimately to employ his energies in the service of goals that relate to mankind's constructive best? We need the methods of science to help us solve the problem of how we can create conditions that will lead to peace. If such a science should some day come into being, a science of peace, as Mitscherlich called it in his inaugural lecture at the University of Frankfurt in 1968, it must not only illuminate the intrinsic psychological counterforces against peace, but must also identify the dangers to man's psychological health which peace may, paradoxically, bring about. If such a science of peace should ever become established in earnest, then Mitscherlich will surely be counted as one of its pioneers.

The various aspects of Mitscherlich's work and the manifold features of his personality can by no means be exhaustively treated within the framework of the present occasion. The orientation of his ethical principles, in particular the way in which he determines and purifies his values and goals on the basis of thoughtful observation, would merit special consideration. Here I will only mention a fortunate result of the specific psychic development which formed his personality: that he combines a great, discriminating intelligence with extraordinary courage, i.e., with the quality he himself defines so elegantly as that "consistency of the structure of the ego" which enables the ego to remain true to its goals, despite intimidation from without and within.

The account of Mitscherlich's achievements must now come to a close. But, Ladies and Gentlemen, there are moments in the lives of distinguished men when their lives do not belong to them; moments when they must be able to tolerate being elevated into the realm of the general and of the suprapersonal. I know that Mitscherlich dislikes both high-flown praise and empty idealization, but this is not the direction in which I am aiming. In our courageous moments we will hold fast to the realization that the achievements of the very greatest are limited, that even Goethe's proud words, uttered by the aged Faust, but surely reflecting the poet's own feelings, about the permanence of the reverberations of the work of a creative personality — *"Es wird die Spur von meinen Erdetagen nicht in Aeonen untergehn"* (*Faust II*, Act V) ("Nor can the traces of my earthly days through ages from the world depart") — must be understood as only a beautifully expressed attempt at pushing aside the thought of every man's ultimate destructibility and impermanence. No; love of truth and pride in the ability to tolerate reality without falsifying embellishment compel us to acknowledge the fact that Mitscherlich could undertake no more than a few tentative steps into a largely uncharted region. But they are a beginning to the challenging enterprise of releasing the insights of depth psychology from their moorings in individual therapy and of applying them not only to the ideas of the social and political scientist but also to the deeds of the active participant in public affairs.

What makes a man important? What makes him great? Why do we proclaim days of solemn celebration and of the awarding of prizes in which a man — and a man of science at that — may for a brief hour become the object of our applause, of the expression of our gratitude, and of our love? Is it intelligence, knowledge, energy that make a man great, that lead to the important work and to the weighty deed? Yes, all these attributes are requisite, yet something more must be added: it is a man's capacity to stimulate the creative imagination of his fellow men, especially that of the younger generation. Quite properly, Mitscherlich warns us against the tendency to glorify those who are set above us, and encourages us to develop the kind of discriminating and sober intelligence that will not childishly rely on the fancied omniscience of a father figure. But man's need for models and examples is something else again. Words and concepts must become embodied in the activity of an extraordinary person if they are to confirm our ideals and are to embolden us to act

in accordance with our highest goals. Mitscherlich's work
serves in this sense as a supporting example, and it is within
this context that we should recognize the reason for and the
significance of his selection as the Peace Prize laureate of
1969. The small forward steps of the process of the social
mutation that is required by the need to adjust to a changing society's new tasks and purposes are made possible
through the work of individuals with specific new skills and
qualities. Mitscherlich is such a new type, a man of thoughtful courage and courageous thought who tries unceasingly to
apply the best psychological insights concerning the individual to the psychological understanding of large groups and
who endeavors to make these insights available to those who
consider themselves responsible participants in our civilization
and who want to play their part in it. And it seems to me that
a dignified communal existence in which the individual is
able to live in contentment—let us call it peace—will be
reached only by taking the road Mitscherlich has pointed out
to us: the road toward courageous determination and resolute
action on behalf of goals we have set for ourselves in harmony
with the deepest scientific insights that have been obtained
about the development of man and about the forces active
in him.

38

"The Self:
A Contribution to Its Place
in Theory and Technique"
by D. C. Levin

DISCUSSION

Moderator's Opening Remarks

Dr. Levin makes a most important contribution: it is his forthright emphasis on the theoretical and technical significance of the self. Others have realized that our theoretical progress has not been matched by a corresponding improvement of our technical skills; but, dismayed by this discrepancy, they have, unlike Dr. Levin, turned away from the two essential goals of analysis as a science and as a form of psychotherapy: the formulation of explanations in the terms of psychoanalytic metapsychology, and the improvement of the patient's psychic equilibrium through the increased dominance of his ego.

There can be no objection to the study — in depth-psychological and interpersonal terms — of the wholesome effect of

First published in the *International Journal of Psycho-Analysis* (1970), 51:176-181. Dr. Levin's paper was published in the *International Journal of Psycho-Analysis* (1969), 50:41-51. Dr. Kohut moderated a discussion of this paper at the Plenary Session of the Meetings of the International Psycho-Analytic Association in Rome, 1969.

the patient's attachment to the therapist and to the current emphasis on ego change and adaptation, independent of the psychic constellation in the depth. Yet I hope that there will always also be some analysts who, like Dr. Levin, remain faithful to the maxim that if lack of therapeutic success in areas that are not yet understood metapsychologically is tolerated without the abandonment of analytic means, then the occurrence of new analytic insights is not prevented and scientific progress can be made. It is the virtue of Levin's approach that he draws attention to a new direction of potential progress in our science, with the implied admonition that we should follow through with careful investigations.

Dr. Levin then presents to us the prolegomena of a metapsychology of the self. Inevitably his formulations, first steps into a largely uncharted region, will elicit objections. Without wishing to suggest that substantial theoretical changes are advisable (see the moderator's Closing Remarks [pp. 582-588 below]), I do indeed agree with Dr. Levin that some clinical evidence exists in support of his tenet that the self may be regarded not only as a circumscribed configuration which is introspectively accessible in various psychic locations, but also as one of the "centres of identifiable function," as a "psychic entity with an experientially identifiable cohesive organization and with its own particular processes of homeostasis with the environment" (p. 43).

But now to some doubts. True, the investigator must be allowed a degree of vagueness at certain "growing points of psychoanalysis" (Gedo, 1969) until his concepts are sharpened in correlation with the clinical data. Still, I was dissatisfied with the insufficient differentiation of self and personality, as illustrated, for example, by the pivotal position assigned to Breuer's weakness vis-à-vis the consciously or preconsciously experienced threat to his existing "activities and mode of life" (p 46) or, in more theoretical terms, by Dr. Levin's attitude toward the concept of identity. He mentions — and with approval—my statement that there is "no appropriate place in psychoanalysis for the concept of identity." Yet *he* seems primarily to blame psychoanalysis for being inhospitable, while *I* thought rather that the notion of identity would not be a congenial guest. Even though the past is reverberating in a person's experience of his identity, and even though the contents of the experience of who he is or is in the process of becoming may be neither verbalizable by him nor even clear to him, identity is not a depth-psychological concept; it relates primarily to an individual's conscious and preconscious experiences of his role and personality.

The self, however, is a depth-psychological concept that can be metapsychologically defined: genetically by tracing the relationship between the present self and its archaic precursor, and structurodynamically by tracing the analogous, current transverse-sectional relationship, i.e., the interplay of the mature self, which is integrated in the adult personality, with primitive self-configurations, which are not. The study of the self in the transference allows us, for example, the reconstruction of the early developmental phase when it first becomes a cohesive unit. And we also learn to understand how during various later developmental stages—including in particular the transition from adolescence to adulthood—it oscillates, under the impact of internal and external pressures, between renewed fragmentation and regained cohesiveness. Only the uncovering of the depth-psychological dimension of the oscillations between the cohesion and fragmentation of the adolescent's preconscious and conscious self, i.e., of his so-called "identity crises," permits the explanation of these surface manifestations within the framework of a psychoanalytic metapsychology of the self. To be sure, it is instructive to examine the psychic stresses (such as the adaptational tasks of late adolescence) that trigger the fragmentation of an insecurely established nuclear self. Only the psychoanalytic investigation of the genetic determinants of the self, however — how it was built up in early childhood and what specific hindrances opposed its consolidation — and the study of the interplay of the vulnerability of the archaic self with the vulnerability of the mature self vis-à-vis an adaptational task give us access to a metapsychological explanation of the dramatic manifestations on the psychic surface and toward causal therapy.

Now a few clinical remarks. Dr. Levin shares the opinions held by most analysts that patients with disturbances of the self tend to be regressed individuals whose treatment imposes great hardships on the analyst; and/or that even in mild cases the psychopathology is widespread and has a broad effect on the experiences and behavior of the individual. By contrast, I have become convinced that psychopathology of the self may be either severe or mild, widespread or circumscribed, and that it may impose various degrees of hardship on the analyst, depending not only on the nature of the patient's disorder but even more on the analyst's familiarity with it and the therapeutic problems it poses.

The following example is adduced in support of the claim that dysfunction of the self may result not only in severe or diffuse disturbances but also in such a mild and circumscribed disorder as a parapraxis. A woman patient, trying to congratulate a former suitor on his recent engagement, had wanted to say, "I am delighted!", but said, "I am delightful!" instead. Under the impact of the attack on her self-esteem by the rejection, her conscious self-experience gave way and a specific feature of her archaic self, combined with a hitherto suppressed preconscious attitude came to view.

Dr. Levin's outlook on therapeutic technique is beyond reproach when he stresses the fallacy of structural interpretations vis-à-vis the problems of the self. "We can point," he says, "... to ... impulses and defences ... but we could only claim to have explained ... something about the symptom.... We could reformulate the problem in terms of ...

intersystemic personality structure.... Still ... much would remain unaccounted for.... We could ... guess at a specific fantasy of danger ... in terms of the chronological level of ego and superego function ... we would still not have reached ... the core of one of the most important therapeutic and scientific problems" (pp. 45-46).

I can best demonstrate my agreement with Dr. Levin's principal thesis, as well as my view that psychopathology of the self may be circumscribed and need not constitute an especially trying psychoanalytic task, by the metapsychological scrutiny of a clinical syndrome. My illustrative example is a bothersome but circumscribed and innocuous dysfunction: motion sickness.

Many cases of motion sickness are not caused by structural conflicts (for example, concerning the revival of prohibited sexual stimulation through rhythmical motion), they are manifestations of archaic insecurities concerning the stability of the self. I feel in tune with Dr. Levin's views when I say that, in nonhysterical cases of motion sickness, the self feels tossed about by an unempathic adult and cannot establish the merger into an expanded selfobject unit, the achievement of which belongs, as a prerequisite of a specific psychophysiological developmental line, to a certain early developmental phase. Disregarding subsidiary factors — such as the need for a period of adjustment (getting one's sea legs) an individual may require regardless of a developmentally acquired sensitivity to motion changes; or his innate labyrinthine sensitivity; or the nature and degree of the motion change to which he is exposed — the essence of the disorder is the patient's inability to achieve a sense of unity with the vehicle that carries him. (It is self-evident that driving a car oneself eases this achievement considerably: being in control of the car allows the driver to experience it as an extension of himself. Even people who as passengers become easily carsick, especially when they feel tossed about by an unempathic driver, will therefore hardly ever become victims of motion sickness when driving themselves.) The current situation reactivates an archaic self-fragmentation which occurred in consequence of early failures to experience a supporting adult as an expansion of the self or to merge the body-self into an idealized other. This clinical illustration demonstrates—as did the account of a narcissistic parapraxis—that psychopathology of the self need not have severe consequences, but may lead to delimited disturbances whose treatment imposes no greater hardship on the analyst than the classical transference neuroses.

In summary: it was the aim of this discussion to demonstrate my agreement with the author's principal thesis while yet expressing doubt about subsidiary points. But even with regard to the latter, I hold that some banal truths are less valuable than the unavoidable inaccuracies of work pursued by an adventurous mind on a noble scientific path. Dr. Levin's work must be evaluated within this latter context. I am grateful for having the rewarding experience of studying it.

Moderator's Closing Remarks

The discussion of the significance of the self in mental life, on which Dr. Levin had focused in his paper and which he underlined once more in his opening remarks, dealt almost exclusively with theoretical questions, in particular with the problems of clarifying and delimiting the concept of the self and of differentiating it from other related concepts, such as the ego or the personality.

Levin supported his view that the self was one of the agencies of the mind (co-equal to the ego, the id, and the superego) on clinical as well as on theoretical grounds. On clinical grounds, he felt that the self deserved to be considered one of the major psychic components of the person-

ality not only because it is, as he affirmed, the seat of the
resistances in psychoanalytic therapy and of the countertransferences (cf. his example of Breuer's reaction to Anna O.),
but also because it is the functional center of certain specific
psychic activities, i.e., of the "narcissistic transferences"
(Kohut, 1968). If the latter are unresolved, he said, they
interfere seriously with the proper termination of the analysis.
On theoretical grounds, Levin believed that the fact that
there exist separate and discrete developmental lines of
certain specific narcissistic configurations—i.e., of the "grandiose self" and of the "idealized parent imago" (Kohut,
1966b)—also supported his claim that the self is an agency of
the mind and that the analyst should therefore maintain an
equidistant neutrality toward four functional centers of the
analysand's psychic organization, i.e., toward the id, ego,
self, and superego.

The majority of the discussants, however (J. Lampl-de
Groot, A. Garma, J. Laplanche, E. Simenauer, S. Lebovici),
favored a different point of view. Lampl-de Groot and
Garma thought that the concepts of the self and of the
personality could not be sharply separated from one another;
Laplanche, Simenauer, and Lebovici maintained—in oppo-
sition not only to Levin but also to Hartmann (1953) and
Jacobson (1964)—that the concepts of the self and of the ego
should retain the confluent ambiguity that they had in
Freud's usage.

Other discussants (G. Wiedeman and T. Moser) refrained
from committing themselves to a choice concerning the issues
of conceptual definition and differentiation. They nevertheless tended to lend support to the acceptance of the self as a
delimited psychic configuration by stressing either its theoretical or its empirical (clinical) importance. Thus Wiedeman
emphasized the theoretical significance of the self by speaking, for example, of the differentiation of the self-representation and the experiencing self. Moser underlined the pivotal

nature of the empirically ascertainable position of the self by speaking about the relationship between the social role and the self, and about the psychological nutriment the self may derive from the social role filled by the individual — exemplified by the prestige (which enhances or maintains the cathexis of the self) that the role of a sought-after physician provided for Breuer.

My own reaction to these problems of concept formation, definition, and terminology is not completely settled. On the one hand, I think that at the present time the traditional theoretical framework provides adequate room for the self (as a subordinate concept), and that none of the clinical-empirical phenomena so far adduced requires the introduction of a fourth agency of the mind. On the other hand, I feel that we should not exclude the possibility that the continued investigation of the field of narcissism (e.g., of the narcissistic personality disturbances) will eventually lead to findings that could bring about a change in our theories, even in those concerning the basic constituents of the mind.

On the purely conceptual level, I would first like to stress that the notion of self, on the one hand, and that of ego, superego, and id, on the other hand, as well as that of personality, are abstractions which belong to different levels of concept formation. Ego, id, and superego are the constituents of a specific, high-level — i.e., experience-distant — abstraction in psychoanalysis: the psychic apparatus. Personality is a notion that, although often serviceable in a general sense, is (like identity) not indigenous to psychoanalytic psychology; it belongs to a different theoretical framework which is more in harmony with the observation of social behavior and the description of the (pre)conscious experience of oneself in interaction with others than to the observations of depth-psychology. The self, however, emerges in the psychoanalytic situation and is conceptualized in the mode of a comparatively low-level — i.e., comparatively experience-near

—psychoanalytic abstraction, as a content of the mental apparatus. While it is thus not an agency of the mind, it is yet a structure within the mind since it is cathected with instinctual energy and it has continuity in time, i.e., it is enduring. (Even a simple memory trace may therefore be considered a mental structure [cf. Glover, 1947].) Being a psychic structure, the self has, furthermore, a psychic location. To be more specific, various—and frequently inconsistent—self-representations are present not only in the id, the ego, and (although with a somewhat different valence) in the superego (see Hartmann, 1953; Jacobson, 1964; Sandler et al., 1963), but also within a single agency of the mind. There may, for example, exist contradictory conscious and preconscious self-representations—e.g., of grandiosity and inferiority—side by side, either occupying delimited loci within the realm of the ego or occupying sectorial positions of that realm of the psyche in which id and ego form a continuum. The self, then, quite analogous to the representations of objects, is a content of the mental apparatus, but not one of its constituents, i.e., not one of the agencies (*Instanzen*) of the mind.

As stated earlier, I do not wish to give the impression that I believe that the last word about these theoretical questions has necessarily been spoken, but I feel that the preceding conceptual considerations are not outweighed by existing opposing clinical evidence; I maintain, therefore, that we should not regard the self as one of the agencies of the mind. Being a content of the mental apparatus, however, the self should indeed be clearly distinguished from the ego and from the personality. In order to lend support to this claim and in keeping with the primacy of clinical-empirical considerations over purely theoretical ones (Freud, 1914b) at certain junctures ("growing points") in the development of psychoanalytic thought, I shall now refer to the self within the nexus of two concrete, empirically observable sets of circumstances: a developmental-genetic context, and a dynamic-structural one.

The developmental vignette refers to the birth of the self out of the fragments of autoerotic experience with the support of the "mirroring function" of the mother (Kohut, 1966b). In the terms of traditional metapsychology, this development corresponds to that from the stage of auto-erotism to the stage of narcissism (Freud, 1914b). We may assume (i.e., for example, extrapolate from the analysand's temporary regressions) that the young infant experiences his various physical and mental activities, and especially his body parts, at first separately (one by one as they are functionally cathected); but that he gradually acquires a sense of over-all unity, i.e., he acquires an awareness of the fact that the single functions and body parts belong to a greater whole, his total self, which is now also, as a unit, cathected with narcissistic libido. The mother's delighted response to the (total) child, her calling out his name, in addition to responding to the single body part or single activity or mental function that is cathected at the moment, contribute importantly to this developmental step. Disturbances in the early consolidations of the self (which predispose to a later fragmentation propensity of this structure under stress) must, of course, also be examined against the background of a maternal inability to respond acceptingly to the child, especially to him as a whole, unitary psychosomatic organization.

The second empirically accessible set of circumstances to be presented shows the self in an instructive dynamic-structural context which demonstrates the usefulness of distinguishing between the self (an abstraction derived from the introspectively observable unity and continuity of experience in time and space) and the ego (a part of the mental apparatus, a set of psychic functions). The following well-known, empirically ascertainable relationships are adduced in support of the thesis that a well-cathected, firmly cohesive self enhances the functioning of the ego, and that, in reverse, the strong cathexis of ego functions tends to enhance the cohesiveness of the self.

Concerning the former—ego functions being furthered through a cohesive self—little needs to be said, since the empirical data are directly observable and thus at the disposal of everyone. A person's secure feeling of being a well-delimited unit—i.e., his clear concept of who he is, which rests on the deep yet nameless sense of nuclear cohesiveness that is acquired early in life—is one of the preconditions for the ego's reliable ability to perform its functions. We might say that the self may serve as an *organizer of the ego activities.* If, on the other hand, the self is poorly cathected, temporarily or chronically, then ego functions may also suffer, may be performed without zest, be disconnected one from the other and be lacking in firmness of purpose and integrated cohesion. If, finally, in the course of the analysis of a pathological self, the genetic roots of the disturbance are brought into the open and if the specific working-through process leads to a firming of the structure of the self, then it can be observed that, *pari passu,* the patient's ego functions will also improve.

The reverse relationship—the enhancement of the cathexis of the self through the activation of ego functions—is also not hard to demonstrate. Here belong such everyday phenomena as the reconsolidation of a temporarily debilitated self (shaken by blows to a person's self-esteem) through physical exercise, which brings about a heightened cathexis of the body-self; or through the performance of intensive mental activities, which leads to self-confirmation. The most striking illustration of the influence exerted by the ego upon the self can occasionally be obtained at the beginning of schizophrenia. During the prepsychotic phase, the patient is aware of a disturbing decathexis of the self: he feels "different," less real, fragmented. He may then try to counteract this regression (from narcissism to autoerotism; the reverse of the normal forward move of infancy) through the frantic hypercathexis of ego functions: forced thinking, talking, writing; forced physical and mental work. The activation of ego functions may, unfortunately, be unable to consolidate the crumbling self, and the schizophrenic regression runs its course. (The overwork is then often incorrectly assessed by the patient and by his family, not as an attempt at self-healing, but as a cause or precipitant of the disease.) The success or failure of these maneuvers does not concern us here: it is the principle of the mutual relation of ego and self — and thus the heuristic value of the acceptation of the self as a delimited psychic configuration — that was to be demonstrated.

In summary: within the context of currently available psychoanalytic knowledge, it is best to confine ourselves to defining the self as an important content (a structure or configuration) within the mental apparatus, i.e., as self-representations (imagoes) of the self that are located within the ego, the id, and the superego (cf. Hartmann, 1953; Sandler et al., 1963). Although the possibility of a future acceptation of the self "as one of the centers of identifiable functions" and thus as an agency of the mind must not be ruled out, this question should not be confronted at this point. For the time being we should put aside the question of the advisability of a change in our conceptions of the basic mental constituents and should devote our efforts to the collection and the critical evaluation of relevant clinical-empirical data.

39

Scientific Activities
of the American Psychoanalytic
Association

An Inquiry

When the Executive Council of the American Psychoanalytic Association established an Ad Hoc Committee on Scientific Activities whose task it was to survey the current state of psychoanalytic scientific activities in the United States and, in particular, to assess the role played by the Association with regard to them, the extent of the field of inquiry of this body seemed on first sight to be not only broad but ill-defined. What motivated the creation of the Committee — and what motivated most of the members of the Committee — was the concern that all was not well with present-day scientific research in the field of psychoanaysis, in particular that there was a lack of original contributions, i.e., of genuine accretions to our knowledge. A drying-up of the stream of newly gained psychoanalytic insights was, moreover, considered to be an ominous sign with regard to the survival of psychoanalysis, more silently and insidiously threatening than

This paper, first published in the *Journal of the American Psychoanalytic Association* (1970), 18:462-484, is based on the records of meetings of the Ad Hoc Committee on Scientific Activities (prepared cooperatively by the Chairman and the Secretary, John E. Gedo), intracommittee correspondence, and the responses of informal consultants to these documents.

589

the noisy internal disagreements about secondary issues
among analysts, or the attacks and the ridicule still leveled
against psychoanalysis from the outside.

Principal Concerns

The Committee was, from the beginning, faced with a
number of basic questions which it debated and which it tried
to circumscribe. Need one really be concerned with the state
of health of psychoanalytic research in view of the enormous
output of papers and books in our field? And if concern is
warranted, despite the high over-all productivity, where
exactly did the fault lie? Was the quality low? Was the research done not genuinely analytic? Or were the contributions
lacking in originality?

No firm conclusions about any of these questions were
reached. The members of the Committee thought that
analysts need not be ashamed of their productivity. While
there are poor papers and books and good ones, as in other
sciences, the quality and quantity of the contributions to
scientific programs and journals in psychoanalysis are, on the
whole, quite respectable. What then is wrong, if indeed
anything is wrong? The suspicion, more hinted at than clearly
voiced by most members of the Committee, is that (a) there is
a dearth of new psychoanalytic insights in the central areas of
psychoanalytic knowledge, and (b) present-day original contributions and the research enthusiasm of analysts tend to be
devoted to the application of psychoanalytic knowledge to
peripheral areas.

Even such simple statements call up further questions. Is
there cause for dissatisfaction in view of the fact that without
doubt some good contributions to the central areas do exist,
especially some outstanding theoretical reformulations and
emendations? There are many promising applications of
analysis to peripheral fields such as to other forms of psycho-

therapy, to the understanding of the psychosomatic diseases, to child development, and to the investigation of the vicissitudes of interpersonal relations, both with regard to normal and abnormal development in early life as well as to adaptation and maladaptation in maturity. While the Committee recognized the value of a careful rethinking of our theories and of the applications of analysis to original research in more peripheral areas, it remained concerned about the insufficient involvement of present-day analysts in the most central areas of the field.

But what is this original work in the central areas of analysis which seemed to some of the members of the Committee to be of crucial importance for the survival of psychoanalysis as a science? In order to answer this question, one must attempt to define what is meant by originality and also to trace the borders that delimit the central area of analysis. These were topics to which the Committee returned repeatedly in its discussions. Only a rough summary of the deliberations in this area can be given here. The Committee concluded that the important central areas of psychoanalytic investigations concerned those new depth-psychological insights about man in health and disease that are obtained in the setting of the psychoanalytic situation itself. And the Committee felt that there existed a lessening of quality and, above all, a decline in true originality in this central area. It goes without saying that the Committee also assumed that there was at least the possibility of remedying this defect or, to say the least, that it was worthwhile investigating whether remedial actions, in particular as undertaken by the Association, could be contemplated.

In the area of our specific concern with regard to psychoanalytic creativity, i.e., the investigation of the circumstances that might be in its way and those that might further it, it soon became apparent that the Committee should not strive primarily to find answers to the many problems it encountered, and that to put forth even the most modestly phrased opinions would be less valuable than to raise and formulate questions. The Committee felt that if it could prove to its own satisfaction that the field with which it was dealing contained a sufficient number of clearly definable relevant topics, it could then offer the Association a program for the investigation of these issues. But how to bring even a preliminary order into the great number of problems which arose?

The Committee attempted, as a preliminary step, to define in metapsychological terms the position that scientific activities occupy in the psychoanalyst's psychological structure and development. It was postulated that scientific activities are to be regarded as one — and structurally the highest — step in a series of progressions toward the goal of all analysis: to encourage psychological material to become conscious and to keep it from becoming submerged again. Briefly: (1) In dreams, in some artistic productions, and in the free associations of the analysand, the essential psychological activities take place at the borders between ego and id and at the borders between the preconscious and the unconscious ego. The progress on the road toward consciousness is usually fleeting, and the gains are insecure. (2) The sharing between analyst and analysand of the knowledge gained in the first step and its expression through the explicit and precise verbalizations of the analyst's interpretations tie the psychological insights more firmly to the secondary process and make them less liable to re-repression. A second barrier — this time within the ego — has been crossed; a firmer cementing of insight to consciousness has been achieved. (3) Scientific research and its communication go yet one step further. As the Minutes of the Committee put it, "It is the aim of the psychoanalytic researcher, by raising the findings of individual psychology to more general levels, by expressing them in a carefully chosen, well-defined terminology, and by communicating them to the broad scientific community, to attach the knowledge gained to the permanent intellectual property of mankind and to protect it optimally against re-repression through forgetting or against its remaining ineffective because it is isolated from the awareness of society."

Even in the Committee's first attempt at creating a theoretical framework for its deliberations it went a good deal further than the preceding formulation and, for example, examined the various different, yet specific resistances that oppose the process of becoming conscious encountered at these various levels of the psychic apparatus — particularly at the level of scientific formulation and scientific communication. Only one detail should be added here, namely, that the Committee did not indulge in a wish-fulfilling idealism, i.e., it realized that, under the pressure of extensive untoward circumstances, the most securely fastened scientific gains (psychological or other) might again disappear from the awareness of man. The members of the Committee were familiar with the fact that a gulf filled with mysticism and superstition[1] separated for over a thousand years the investigative genius of the man of classical antiquity from that of the man of the Renaissance. Twentieth-century totalitarianism, with its antipsychological attitudes and its emphasis on the reform of social conditions, might similarly wipe out the gains that modern depth psychology has achieved since Freud. Although the Committee was aware that even the

---

[1] The fact that mysticism is here juxtaposed to superstition, and that both are contrasted to "investigative genius" is not meant to carry a pejorative implication. Still, however the contribution to human culture of the profound mystic thinkers of the Middle Ages is to be evaluated, their attitude toward man's inner experience was further from that of empirical science (detailed observation leading to theory) and closer to that of art and religion (direct search for ultimate truths through the total response of the observer). The present report is not, however, the place to attempt the definition of the dividing line between mystical introspectionism and introspective-empathic, empirical depth psychology.

greatest efforts to support and invigorate psychoanalytic research had limitations and could be swept away by the
currents of history, it envisioned no alternative but to work
toward the goals it considered right.

It is unprofitable within the present context to continue
these sociohistorical speculations or to pursue a broad approach to the examination of man's struggle to increase the
realm of his consciousness. But the general considerations,
and especially the metapsychological schema, should be kept
in mind as a background during the ensuing examination of
some of the factors that might shape the development of the
psychoanalytic researcher. The Committee discussed various
influences on creativity which are exerted on the potential
contributor to our science during four crucial points in his
career: (1) his selection as an applicant for psychoanalytic
training; (2) his training analysis; (3) his training at the
psychoanalytic institute; and (4) his environment after
graduation.

The Process of Selection

The question of whether the current selection process
might deprive us of potential contributors to our field was
raised repeatedly in the Committee's discussions and in many
replies of its consultants (see introductory footnote). Especially frequently referred to was the conflict between (1)
choosing candidates for their promise of clinical competence
and responsibility toward their patients, and (2) choosing
candidates whose fluid psychological make-up would raise the
hope of creative contribution, but might entail the risk of
lack of discipline and unpredictability in the clinical situation.

The composition of selection committees was discussed
from the point of view of the possibility that some solid
clinicians and administrators—and even some conscientious
investigators—might not be in tune with the truly creative

whose minds often appear confused on superficial scrutiny, but that they might be impressed by the solidly reliable or the intellectually brilliant, by-passing those whose potentially creative pathology seems too close to the untreatable or to the morally unstable. Much, of course, can be said in defense of conservative admission procedures, and much was indeed said in defense of the stable, the predictable, and of those whose high intellectual endowment is not embedded in an all-too-pathological personality.

A number of possibilities were suggested for the harnessing of creative pathology in the service of progress in our field, such as the organization of collaborative research enterprises between those who do solid clinical work and those whose unusual modes of thinking and psychological perception might permit them empathic access into areas that cannot be penetrated by the ordinary mind.

Inevitably, the question of medical education was brought up, together with the old problem of whether medical preselection constituted a narrowing influence, weeding out *ab initio* some restless personalities who might provide new insights to our field if given the appropriate psychoanalytic training, but who cannot tolerate the discipline imposed by the necessity of mastering the enormous bulk of nonpsychological subjects medical education demands of its students. Or, stating the problem in reverse, it was questioned whether the present policy of restricting admission for full training to graduates from medical schools (plus a few carefully selected others, mainly psychologists, for "training in research") deprives analysis of people (with different personality make-ups, and cultural and educational backgrounds) whose outlook on the human psyche differs from the outlook of those whose scientific predilections (including the predominant research interests) have been shaped by prior training in medicine (or psychology). The Committee wondered whether selection of analysts with nonmedical backgrounds — teachers, educators, ministers, artists, philosophers, philologists, jurists, historians,

art historians—might not bring to psychoanalytic research
the vigorous impulse to expand in new directions that it seems
to lack.

The age factor, too, was considered, with emphasis on the
question whether the empirically ascertained fact of the
youthfulness of the original contributor in physics and math-
ematics was totally irrelevant with regard to psychoanalysis.
Although most of the members of the Committee assumed
that a certain ebbing of instinctual pressures is necessary for
the objective assessment of the instinctual life of man, which
our science demands, they also felt that such judgments
should not be made *ex cathedra,* but that some experimentation was indicated.[2]

At no time during all these considerations did the Committee forget that the future creativeness it wanted the
selection process to retain for our field occurred in different
types; that originality could be found within a spectrum that
reaches from the creative clinician, on the one hand, to the
creative theoretical synthesizer, on the other; and that the
selectors must therefore take into account that the presence of
highly specific potentialities in a candidate might have to be
weighed against the fact that he will not be able to become a
well-rounded general psychoanalytic practitioner.

The Training Analysis

The Committee did not attempt to come to definitive
conclusions with regard to the influence of the training

[2] In context of the concern with the applicant's age, Dr. John Frosch
directed my attention to the relevant fact that some medical schools have
now "established track paths of study so that if someone wants to become a
psychiatrist he follows this track almost from the beginning." Dr. Frosch
suggests that, under these conditions, medical students might be encouraged to turn toward analytic training early and "if possible, to start
their courses [at the analytic institute] when they enter their elective
period." He believes that analysis might in this way acquire candidates who
are likely to devote themselves to research.

analysis on creativity. Again, the emphasis was placed on the formulation of questions to be studied and on problems that could be investigated by future workers with specific interest in this area. None of the members of the Committee, it must be emphasized, thought simplistically that the training analysis should have the direct task of producing, or even of freeing, creativity. But at least some of the members of the Committee thought that specific investigations of various types of creative personalities in psychoanalysis might benefit some gifted candidates indirectly, and the science of psychoanalysis secondarily. What are the specific hindrances to empathic data-collection, which is a necessary precondition to certain types of creative pursuits? What are the endopsychic factors that might paralyze the ability for theoretical formulations at levels transcending the twosome of the analytic situation and supervision? Are classroom inhibitions and inhibitions against the preparation of written reports grist for the mill of the training analysis, as are the student's conflicts with regard to his clinical work with supervised cases? And what are the obstacles that stifle the ability to indulge in fantasies and to contemplate the formulation of plans concerned with the communication of insights to a broadened audience through the publication of papers or through verbal presentation at professional gatherings? For the training analyst to be aware of the specific vulnerabilities and inhibitions of the potentially creative can hardly be anything but beneficial if his attitude remains compatible with basic analytic neutrality. Enforced productivity is no more desirable than any other surface adjustment in the realm of mental health and, if brought about, will overburden the psyche of the analysand and lead to ephemeral adjustment rather than to the exercise of a freely chosen enjoyable activity which can be maintained for a lifetime. That these considerations regarding the influence of the training analysis on creativity are not empty speculations can be seen from the reply of one of our respondents, a training analyst with long years of experience, who wrote as follows: "A great deal depends upon the analyst and the kind of analysis a student receives. I reanalyzed five analysts who developed a generally recognized analytic creativity only in the course of the reanalysis. I believe that I know the reason: I was particularly concerned about the analysis of their difficulties in this area."

Despite its emphasis on the formulation of questions and on the delineation of problem areas worthy of further study, the Committee did not restrain itself from pursuing specific inquiries when a hypothesis introduced into the discussions seemed to be especially promising. For example, the suggestion was made that creative research in the field of psychoanalysis is frequently stimulated by the researcher's unresolved psychopathology in areas where neither the training analysis nor later attempts at self-analysis were able to provide solutions. It was hypothesized that the lack of resolution of these creativity-stimulating areas of psychopathology is due neither to the intensity of the endopsychic resistances that opposed the training analysis nor to failings of the training analyst (i.e., countertransference manifestations), but to the fact that the limitation of current psychoanalytic knowledge does not allow the analytic resolution of the training analysand's psychopathology in a particular area. In addition, the potentially fertilizing power on creative psychological research that is exerted by endopsychic tension states may be blocked if the incompleteness of the training analysis is not faced up to. For instance, the areas of remaining psychopathology may be concealed by the exertion of the analysand's ego to conform with the training analyst's wish. Thus, due to faulty perception or narcissistically motivated distortion, the training analyst may communicate his erroneous belief to the analysand that the latter has achieved psychoanalytically valid ego mastery when in fact he has not.

The foregoing hypothesis concerning the relation between the training analysis and the future creativeness of the analysand, and many other cognate topics are, in the opinion of the Committee, a worthy subject for systematic investigation in a framework independent of the narrowing focus of educational considerations in the strict (i.e., the administrative-organizational) sense of the term.

Training at the Psychoanalytic Institute

Several members of the Committee affirmed the desirability of stimulating the students' research interest through courses that focus on research methodology. Some also felt that talented students should be encouraged either to engage in research projects of their own or to participate in the research activities of their instructors. The pros and cons of such undertakings must be weighed carefully. Routinization, even of activities intended to stir up interest in research, might stifle spontaneous creativity rather than further it. Concentration on research goals at a time when the student is struggling with conflicts aroused by the therapeutic encounter with his supervised cases may interfere with his working-through processes in this more basic area by offering him research as an intellectualizing escape from the appropriate emotional reactions to the personalities of his patients and of their transference demands. In other words, the investigation of the *how* and the *when* of such measures appeared to the Committee as often more important than the examination of the content of specific research courses or of the administrative details relating to students' research activities. The atmosphere that prevails at the psychoanalytic institute is probably more important than the concrete measures taken by the institute in this area. Is the institute primarily a professional school that teaches specific technical, therapeutic skills, with theory and research offered only as secondary topics? Does the faculty believe that psychoanalysis is a closed system, that the transmission of a basic storehouse of knowledge to the students is the primary goal of the curriculum, that the student is expected to read a prescribed list of titles — and sometimes, *horribile dictu,* that he should ingest parts of articles or even selected paragraphs in them! — and pass examinations in order to become an analyst? Or is the prevailing atmosphere one in which it is the essential educational goal to teach the student a mode of observing and of thinking? Are the faculty members themselves engaged in research activities, and do they transmit by example to the potentially creative students a model of their struggles with the conceptualization of empirical material?

A number of the Committee's consultant-respondents expressed their specific predilections with regard to the kind of atmosphere they felt would enhance the research potential of gifted students. One, for example, an outstanding contributor to psychoanalysis, emphasized that technique courses were especially stultifying devices in this respect, and that the model of the team approach to research problems that was presented to students at some training institutions was not an appropriate basic model for psychoanalytic research (which this researcher felt was essentially a lonely pursuit). The same respondent also felt that an applicant's or student's expression of his hope that psychoanalytic research should (and ultimately would) achieve the methodological exactness of physics or biology was a clear sign of lack of talent for our field and that it should be evaluated negatively in the selection process and during training. (Although the members of the Committee tended to concur with this consultant, it must be added that such rules of thumb are at times misleading and that an expressed desire for precision has to be evaluated carefully by the selectors before broadly negative conclusions can be drawn.)

Anna Freud has stated that the most important contribution the institutes can make to the maintenance of genuine psychoanalytic research is through the enhancement of the students' capacity to think metapsychologically. This view was interpreted by the Committee as meaning that the basic metapsychological viewpoints constitute a theoretical framework that cannot be curtailed or discarded without severe narrowing of our capacity to understand and communicate observational data. The gravest danger to which analysis is exposed is the undisciplined approach of investigators — a danger that can be averted only by the preservation, in practice and in research, of the rational and orderly framework of our theory. As Anna Freud put it in a communication to the Committee: "What is getting lost gradually in present-day analysis is the ability to think 'metapsychologically,' which does not mean 'theoretically, divorced from clinical material,' but means to look at clinical data from all four or five metapsychological aspects simultaneously and to relate them to each other, especially with regard to their relevance for the dynamic function of the ego in therapy." Clearly, Anna Freud, by her emphasis on the crucial importance of metapsychology, underlined not only that specific theoretical courses should transmit the knowledge of basic metapsychology to our students, but, even more, that metapsychological thinking should naturally pervade the thinking habits of all teachers — whether they teach theoretical or clinical subjects. Anna Freud implied that the secure possession of this basic mode of thinking was a crucial precondition for the preservation of psychoanalytic research as such.

*The Postgraduate Atmosphere and the
Psychoanalytic Investigator*

The Committee considered what particular factors in the psychoanalytic community in general and in psychoanalytic organizations, national and local, enhance the production of original research in psychoanalysis. It was the opinion of the majority of the members that the hierarchy of values currently prevailing in the psychoanalytic community and its organizations does not provide optimal encouragement for those who want to devote themselves to the gathering of new insights about the human psyche derived from the clinical situation and formulated in the precise conceptualizations of psychoanalytic metapsychology—for those, in other words, who wish to work in the central areas of psychoanalytic research. The major prestige values for most of those analysts who are not primarily attracted by a financially lucrative practice lies in the area of psychoanalytic education (especially with regard to their attaining the status of training analyst and teacher at the institute) or in attaining administrative-organizational positions rather than in the area of psychoanalytic research. And even within the area of psychoanalytic research, most analysts are inclined to look upon research in the central areas as either unpromising or old-fashioned. Most support—financial and moral—tends to go to the applied field: to the investigation of therapeutic technique, to psychosomatic research, to research about psychoanalytic education, to the psychologically and sociologically sophisticated investigation of interpersonal relations.

If these opinions of the majority of the members of the Committee are correct, the next step would be to ponder the ways and means by which a more favorable balance could be restored, i.e., how to encourage and support research efforts in the central areas. Would the institution of specific prizes or other honors for relevant meritorious research be of help? Could the Association collect and distribute money in support of research, even to the point of allowing some especially gifted people to dispense wholly or partly with private practice as the sole source of their income? Could the Association set up advisory boards of experienced research analysts to counsel younger researchers in the planning of their research?

Should established members of the profession try to encourage research by younger colleagues, or would it be best to advise against this until maturity and increasing clinical experience make valid research possible? The question of nonmedical researchers was again brought into focus, and the bestowal of a distinctive membership title in recognition of research achievement, either in addition to regular membership or alone, was contemplated by the Committee.

Many other points concerning postgraduate arrangements that might stimulate research were touched upon. The daring suggestion was made that the talent of some highly creative people — independent of their medical status — whose psychopathology might prevent them from being directly responsible as therapists, and who are thus excluded from the direct gathering of clinical data in the analytic situation, could yet be harnessed in the service of research through the intimate cooperation with a gifted clinician who supplies the raw data for discussion and further investigation. It is difficult to know whether such arrangements would indeed be workable. Yet, relevant experiments could be undertaken and organizational support could be enlisted for a pilot study of this type. A related though less adventurous possibility might also be worth considering, namely, the undertaking of research through the cooperation of predominantly clinical and predominantly theoretical minds. Again, the support of such organized ventures and the arrangements for them — including the assignments of topics to be investigated — might well come from the Association.

A good deal of debate focused on the question whether the major scientific forums of the Association — the meetings and the *Journal* — could be improved in the service of increasing the quality of scientific production in the central areas of psychoanalytic research. For example, should there be more vigorous, honest, and frequent confrontations of people who hold divergent scientific views by prolonged

mutual supervision of clinical cases, as was suggested by one
of our informal consultants? If so, the organization and cost
of such a stimulating undertaking might well be carried by
the Association. But surely not every researcher — and this
probably holds true for many who pursue genuinely original
research goals — would thrive in an atmosphere of confrontation and debate. Many creative minds in psychoanalysis
tend to flourish in solitude, since their very sensitivity to and
perceptivity of psychological material is bound up with a low
stimulus threshold and, hence, with some degree of intolerance for the public battleground of opposing scientific opinions. Would there thus — in addition to setting up new and
expanded opportunities for scientific exchange and debate —
also be an advantage in the creation of scientific media in
which debate and discussion are eliminated, e.g., a forum in
which papers containing novel and daring ideas could be
presented without immediate public discussion? Would it be
worthwhile to experiment with programs in which certain
sections consisted only of the presentation of papers without
the opportunity for critical public reply? It is at least possible
that some creative people shy away from having their papers
publicly discussed and from being exposed to having to think
on their feet in order to justify a daring new thought to a
clever discussant who appears to make mincemeat of it. In
the same vein, another informal consultant suggested that
psychoanalytic journals have an "idea section" in which new
insights would be printed with a minimum of scientific
responsibility — as a stimulus for further thought in areas that
are only dimly understood at the present time.

Other Factors Influencing Research Activities

During the discussion of the career of the researcher from
the time of his selection to the period when he is engaged in
his final work as a full-fledged member of the scientific com-

munity of analysts, the Committee had to face a variety of other questions which were related to the major problem area. Of these more general topics only two groups will be taken up here: those that relate to scientific methodology, and those that relate to the personality structure of potentially creative workers in analysis.

The Committee members addressed themselves to the question of whether psychoanalytic creativity in the central areas of psychoanalysis was hampered by insufficient familiarity with (or training in) general scientific methodology or whether specific features of psychoanalytic methodology in particular required more intensive systematic investigation. The details of even the comparatively brief discussion this problem area elicited cannot be given here, except to say that it centered around the comparative importance of the empathic data-collection step in our science that precedes the subsequent (or near-simultaneous) step of the formulation of explanations on theoretical levels. Surely, the attainment of explicit conceptualizations in this area would lead to directly and indirectly wholesome results. Not only might direct clarification be achieved in this puzzling field (which, in itself, could be considered a valuable scientific contribution) but, indirectly, certain obstacles to creativity that are related to difficulties within the field of methodology could be better understood and thus perhaps more easily overcome. What, for example, are the specific disturbances of empathy that oppose the gathering and discernment of significant new psychological configurations? And what are the specific difficulties that might oppose the undertaking of those steps that lead away from direct experience in order to arrive at the abstractions of our theoretical language, i.e., to metapsychological formulations? A host of relevant topics were identified in this context; for instance, on the one hand, the trend to cling to an experience-nearness of theory by those who stay close to the data of introspection — the introspectionists and

phenomenologists among us—and, on the other hand, the
trend of the behaviorists and social psychologists within our
ranks to stay close to the observed data of direct behavior.
The Committee, of course, did not advocate a simplistic,
wholesale rejection of either viewpoint, but it maintained that
a clear delimitation of the theories derived from these different viewpoints would clarify the special position of psychoanalytic metapsychology. Metapsychological formulations are
not to be regarded as being in opposition to those of other
levels of observation and theory, but as expressive of a mode
of thinking that is appropriate to the specific grasp of endopsychic and interpersonal phenomena provided by the
psychoanalytic method. Metapsychological formulations are
thus high-level scientific abstractions, expressed with the aid
of a specific set of symbols; they are not only serviceable in
psychoanalysis, but should ultimately become the instrument
of interdisciplinary communications.

Loosely related to the preceding considerations is another
topic on which the Committee touched on many occasions:
the various fields open to psychoanalytic investigation and
what specific talents might impel analysts to investigate them.
Some of the relevant questions were already taken up in the
discussion of selection procedures. It should be emphasized
again, in this context, that potential creativity must sometimes be assessed as weighing heavily in the balance if an
applicant's psychological adjustment is judged to be precarious. Further, in our assessment of the processes of selection and of training, and in our scrutiny of scientific activities
after graduation, we must always remember that there are
various kinds of workers who bring different talents to our
field. We should measure neither excellence nor average
qualifications by the simple criterion of the desirability of the
balanced performance of a general practitioner of psychoanalysis. The physician-psychiatrist-analyst's controlled wish
to cure, the achievement of optimal objectivity in the realm

of therapeutics, are the favorable outcome of developments toward secondary autonomy of functions in personalities whose early sensitivities might have been fostered by crucial experiences around sadistic impulses and reactively mobilized pity and desire to save lives and to relieve suffering.[3] The investigative urge may originate in the sphere of merging and detaching, on the one hand, and of infantile sexual curiosity, on the other. Again, the usefulness of the outcome depends not so much on the origin of the preoccupation as on the degree of secondary autonomy it attains. Nevertheless — and disregarding other factors — the end result will be different with different central motivations. Even in the field of research, there will be those who will remain closer to the quasi-medical process of cure, while others will be drawn more to psychological investigation, even though the setting in which their material is obtained is the clinical situation. Freud's maxim was that the analyst's principal aim should be not to cure but to understand and explain — the cure will follow automatically. One might thus assume that it was the voyeuristic element that played the predominant role in the primordial steps to Freud's investigative genius. At any rate, the problems of therapeutic management, and even those of a theory of technique, did not stand high on his list of interests.

Be that as it may, the existence of a variety of investigative tasks and kinds of research minds deserves our interest. The appropriate enhancement of psychoanalytic research talent will be furthered greatly on all levels of the analyst's career if we distinguish between general theorists and clinical investigators, for example, and original thinkers and synthe-

---

[3] These considerations are not meant to account fully for a person's wish to become a physician. The search for prestige and the influence of culturally transmitted hierarchies of values may well play a greater role nowadays than the motivating power exerted by repressed personality structures acquired on the basis of childhood conflicts.

sizers. The question whether there are general depth-psychological factors that might account for the development of research talent remains unanswered.

Lack of mastery over reaction formations that enter into the wish to relieve suffering and to cure is undoubtedly a grave hindrance to scientific progress, inasmuch as the use of libidinal supplies for the *direct* relief of suffering and for facilitating gross identifications with the analyst impedes the objective assessment of the psychological field necessary for gradual ego expansion. On a more superficial level, concern for the analysand might sometimes stand in the way of publishing important scientific findings. In order to protect the patient against the remote possibility of being upset should he find out that his analyst had used some data from his analysis, significant material is either withheld or distorted and expurgated to the point of irrelevance. Thus, the science of analysis is deprived of important data, and a host of future patients are harmed indirectly.

Having alluded to some obstacles encountered by those whose motivations to become analysts stemmed from conflicts in the sadism-pity area, we now turn to those whose motivation relates to a libidinal hypercathexis in the visual-cognitive area. Here we are not only dealing with the comparatively small obstacle posed by circumscribed blind spots that interfere with clinical proficiency, but also with the more subtly disturbing influences that prevent the perception of the total psychological field. A researcher's capacity for clear and even outstanding perceptivity within the confines of a limited, dazzlingly illuminated field of interest may frequently be accompanied by a stubborn inability to see and evaluate other areas, leading to an imbalanced assessment of the psychological field, to playing up certain factors to the detriment of others—all as a consequence of the incomplete mastery and integration of infantile precursors of his research interest that led to a damaging segmentation of his talent.

Organizational Implementation

The Committee offered specific suggestions concerning organizational activities which relate to the area surveyed. In the following, these are presented in the form of three alternatives: the minimum proposal, the intermediate proposal, and the maximum proposal.

The Minimum Proposal[4]

The minimum proposal suggests no more than the adoption of appropriate measures to ensure a carefully planned distribution of the reports of the meetings of the Committee and its correspondence, including a digest of the replies from those of its consultants who agree to have them made available. The material contained in all these documents should serve to illuminate problems surrounding the continuing scientific advancement of psychoanalysis, an area which is at present the responsibility of the societies and institutes, of the major branches of the Association (Council and Board) and its committees, and of certain already functioning specialized bodies (such as some of the study groups of the Committee on Psychoanalytic Education [COPE], e.g., those on Selection and on Training Analysis).

The Committee hopes, in particular, that the example of its work will lead to the creation of committees on scientific activities by the societies and institutes throughout the country, which will continue to debate and to investigate the relevant problems on the local level and will implement its recommendations through appropriate local improvements.

---

[4] The suggestions made here are, of course, to be included among the intermediate and the maximum proposals, just as those of the intermediate proposal are to be included in the maximum proposal. [Ed. fn. The "Intermediate Proposal" was accepted, and a Standing Committee on Scientific Activities has been active since its creation by the Executive Committee of the American Psychoanalytic Association, in December 1971.]

The Intermediate Proposal

The essence of this set of suggestions is to establish, within the framework of the Executive Council, a (standing) committee on scientific activities under whose aegis a series of study committees would function. The organization of this committee would be similar to that of the Committee on Psychoanalytic Education. Its major activity would be the systematic study of topics relevant to questions of analytic research creativity. A Committee on Scientific Activities would in essence have no executive functions, but it may submit practical suggestions to the Council, which might then create action committees—either as subcommittees of the Committee on Scientific Activities or independent of it. Such an action committee may conclude, for instance, that a wholesome influence on the prestige of independent research would be exerted by granting a yearly award for the best essay on a clinical or theoretical topic by a student at an accredited institute. The Executive Council might then create a body to implement the suggestion to make further concrete proposals (e.g., whether a monetary award should be given, whether the paper should be printed in the *Journal,* whether the student should read his paper at a meeting of the Association, etc.) and would select a panel of judges.

The foregoing example was intended only to illustrate a secondary issue: the relation between the deliberations of a committee on scientific activities—in the main, a federation of study committees—and an action that might be contemplated as the outgrowth of the studies made.

What are some of the areas for study by the subcommittees of a committee on scientific activities? It is not difficult to enumerate a variety of fascinating and important topics, yet a mere listing cannot evoke the depth and subtlety of the problem areas in each case. Judgment should be withheld until the distribution of the reports of the meetings of the Ad Hoc Committee on Scientific Activities (see the relevant suggestions about the distribution of documents in the preceding minimum proposal) will allow greater familiarity with the details of the discussions held by the Committee. In this way glimpses can be obtained of the spontaneous interest elicited by a great number of topics and of the potential value of investigating them as thoroughly as possible. Despite the shortcomings of a headline-type presentation, the following random enumeration of relevant topics may transmit the sense of the potential fruitfulness of their investigation that was felt by the Committee members.

1. Personality types and their relation to productivity and creativity in the clinical and theoretical areas. The implication of increased knowledge in this sphere for the selection of applicants and the training of students.

2. What is psychoanalytic research as differentiated from research *about* psychoanalysis, and from nonanalytic research?

3. In what areas and by what methods can and should analytic researchers cooperate with those in other fields or with researchers who work with different methods?

4. The relation between psychoanalytic education and psychoanalytic research. What type of research, if any, should be taught and/or encouraged in psychoanalytic institutes?

5. The training analysis examined from the point of view of the student's research potential. The topic of research inhibition.

6. Practical problems. How to provide time and money for the psychoanalytic researcher. The pros and cons of financial grants. Support through the Association. The organization of national research teams — a potentially important activity of the Association in view of the fact that there are only a few analytic researchers in many locations, and that national teams with Association support would enable

them to work together with peers who have the same research interest.

7. The influence of the over-all climate on research. How to increase the prestige of the researcher. Prizes, awards, scholarships, lectureships. An examination of the comparative prestige enjoyed by the researcher, the training analyst, the widely sought-out prosperous clinician. Research organizations and special classes of membership for researchers.

This list could easily be continued, as a glance at the reports of the meetings of the Committee would show. It would, of course, be one of the first tasks of a standing committee on scientific activities, as the roof organization of the study committees, to select a few especially promising topics and to suggest for appointment those analysts who seem best suited to study a particular topic.

The Maximum Proposal

This involves reorganization of the American Psychoanalytic Association as the embodiment of the tenet that the three major areas with which organized psychoanalysis is concerned — the professional, the educational, and the scientific — should have equal representation. The Executive Council would thus be *primus inter pares* of three separate organizational branches rather than of two as heretofore. It would retain its dominant administrative position in the total organization, but in combination with special responsibility for professional affairs. The Board on Professional Standards with its special responsibilities for educational affairs would be retained, and a board on scientific activities with special responsibilities for the scientific pursuits of analysts would be added. The innovation would thus be the institution of a scientific branch to correspond in stature and relative autonomy to the educational branch. Existing scientific committees, such as the Program Committee, the Com-

mittee on Liaison with the A.A.A.S., the Committee on
Indexing, and the Editorial Board of the *Journal,* would form
part of this third branch of the Association. In addition, the
board on scientific activities would be able to pay greater
attention to the study and support of scientific activities than
is possible within the present organizational framework, and
a number of new activities could be undertaken under its
aegis. To mention only a few examples: a committee to facilitate research cooperation between members in distant locations, a committee to provide financial support for meritorious research or to aid with grant applications, a committee to
give methodological advice to younger researchers, and, as
discussed in the preceding section, a group of committees,
organized in analogy to the subcommittees of the Committee
on Psychoanalytic Education, to study the various problem
areas concerning psychoanalytic research and creativity and
to report their results to the Association from time to time.

The advantages of such reorganization are obvious:
Setting up a scientific branch would put scientific activities
on a level of importance equal with the professional responsibilities of the Association and with its concern for educational
matters. The new branch would grant scientific activities a
degree of independence from professional concerns. Thus, for
example, the opposition to the participation of nonmedical
research talent in psychoanalytic research—motivated largely
by professional concerns—might become less serious if the
Association's support of scientific activities was handled
independently from the administration of the therapeutic-
professional activities. The fellows of the scientific branch of
the Association would be analysts who are competent in the
area of the scientific matters with which the Association must
deal. For example, they would be chosen by the societies and
institutes because of special talent for and interest in scientific
matters. Thus, they would not be analysts with predominantly professional-therapeutic or educational concerns, but

those to whom — for whatever reasons of talent or personality make-up — the scientific progress to be achieved by analysis occupies the highest position in their scale of psychoanalytic values.

What are the disadvantages? They are considerable, but not as easily formulated as the advantages. The major disadvantage is that the change requires undertaking something new and untried — and it is a social fact that major new and untried steps are generally shunned by organizations, when there is no obvious dire need for reform. Things are, after all, going well. The scientific programs of the meetings of the Association are filled, the productivity of the membership is high, and the quality of the contributions, though uneven, is, on the average, acceptable. Thus, in the absence of severe intraorganizational tensions such as those that motivated the setting up of the educational branch, there would seem to be insufficient reason to undertake a major reorganization which would demand a great deal of work, tolerance for the uncertainty of new developments, and pose a threat to the present distribution of prestige.

To some at least, the advantages of setting up a scientific branch of the Association would be worth the price. There is good reason to believe that among the obstacles that stand in our way as we attempt to add new insights to the existing depth-psychological understanding of man is our tendency to drift toward a predominantly therapy-oriented attitude, and to acquiesce, as an outgrowth of this attitude, to the increasing professionalization of our training institutions. If these conditions do indeed prevail, then the creation of a scientific branch of the Association, with the prestige that its position would command, might well be considered a wholesome, strategic undertaking in an area that is of deepest concern to all who wish to maintain the vitality of psychoanalysis.

40

Thoughts on Narcissism
and Narcissistic Rage

One of the gems of German literature is an essay called
"On the Puppet Theater" by the dramatist Heinrich von
Kleist (1777-1811), written in 1811, not long before he
ended his short life by suicide. Kleist and his work are almost
unknown outside the circle of those familiar with the German
language, but my fascination with his short essay—and with
one of his stories—has had, as I can see in retrospect, a particular significance in my own intellectual development: it
marks the first time that I felt drawn to the topic that has
now absorbed my scientific interest for several years.

Ever since reading Kleist's essay during my school days I
had puzzled about the mysterious impact the plain account
has on the reader. A male ballet dancer, we are told, asserts
in a fictitious conversation with the author that, by comparison with human dancing, the dance of puppets is nearly
perfect. The puppet's center of gravity is its soul; the
puppeteer need only to think himself into this point as he is
moving the puppet and the movement of its limbs will attain
a degree of perfection that cannot be reached by the human
dancer. Since puppets are not bound down by gravity, and
since their physical center and soul are one, they are

This essay was presented in an abbreviated version as the A. A. Brill
Lecture of the New York Psychoanalytic Society on November 30, 1971. It
was first published in *The Psychoanalytic Study of the Child* (1972), 27:
360-400. New York: Quadrangle Books.

never artificial or pretentious. The human dancer, by
comparison, is self-conscious, pretentious, artificial. The
author responds to the dancer by recalling how, some years
ago, he had admired the grace with which his nude male
companion had set his foot upon a stool. Mischievously he
had asked him to repeat the motion. He blushed and
tried — but became self-conscious and clumsy. ". . . beginning
at this moment," Kleist writes, "a puzzling change took hold
of the young man. He began to stand in front of the mirror
for days; . . . [An] incomprehensible force appeared to
encage . . . the play of the motility that formerly had so freely
expressed his emotions" (my translation).

It is not my intention to bring our psychoanalytic knowledge to bear on this story. But the psychoanalytic reader will
have no difficulty identifying the problems with which the
writer of the story was preoccupied: apprehensions about the
aliveness of self and body, and the repudiation of these fears
by the assertion that the inanimate can be graceful, even
perfect. The topics of homosexuality (see Sadger, 1909), of
poise and of exhibitionism, of blushing and self-consciousness
are alluded to; and so is the theme of grandiosity in the
fantasy of flying — the notion of "antigravity" — and that of
merger with an omnipotent environment by which one is controlled — the puppeteer. Finally, there is the description of a
profound change in a young man, ushered in by the ominous
symptom of gazing at himself for days in the mirror.

Of all the facets of narcissism, only one is missing in
Kleist's essay: aggression as it arises from the matrix of narcissistic imbalance. It is a striking manifestation of the unity of
the creative forces in the depth of the personality of a great
writer that Kleist had indeed dealt with this theme a year or
two earlier, in the story of *Michael Kohlhaas* (1808), a grip-
ping description of the insatiable search for revenge after a
narcissistic injury — in its field, I believe, surpassed by only
one work, Melville's great *Moby Dick*. Kleist's story tells of the

fate of a man who, like Captain Ahab, is in the grip of interminable narcissistic rage. It is the greatest rendition of the revenge motif in German literature, a theme that plays an important role in the national destiny of the German nation, whose thirst for revenge after the defeat of 1918 came close to destroying all of Western civilization.

In recent years I have investigated some phenomena related to the self, its cohesion and its fragmentation (Kohut, 1966b, 1968, 1970a, 1971). The present essay gives me the opportunity to turn from the former topic to the relationship between narcissism and aggression. I shall first deal once more with the work that lies behind, draw attention to topics that are in need of emphasis and point up areas that will provide a basis for subsequent formulations.

The Self and Its Libidinal Investment

The Influence of Parental Attitudes on the Formation of the Self

If I were asked what I consider to be the most important point to be stressed about narcissism I would answer: its independent line of development, from the primitive to the most mature, adaptive, and culturally valuable. This development has important innate determinants, but the specific interplay of the child with his environment, which furthers, or hinders, the cohesion of the self and the formation of idealized psychic structures, is well worth further detailed examination, especially with the aid of the study of the varieties of the narcissistic transferences. In this essay I shall add only one small point to the results I have previously reported, namely, that the side-by-side existence of separate developmental lines in the narcissistic and in the object-instinctual realms in the child is intertwined with the parents' attitude toward the child, i.e., that the parents sometimes relate to the child in empathic narcissistic merger and look upon the child's psychic organization as part of their own, while at other times they respond to the child as to an independent center of his own initiative, i.e., they invest him with object libido.

On the Acceptance of an Affirmative Attitude Toward Narcissism in Theory and Practice

My second retrospective point refers to a broad question. In assuming an independent line of development in the narcissistic sector of the personality, a development that leads to the acquisition of mature, adaptive, and culturally valuable attributes in the narcissistic realm, I have, of course, taken an essentially affirmative attitude toward narcissism. But while I have become convinced of the appropriateness of this affirmative outlook on narcissism, I am also aware of the fact that it may be questioned, that indeed there exist a number of arguments that can be marshaled in opposition to a consideration of narcissism as an integral, self-contained set of psychic functions rather than as a regression product; that there exist a number of obstacles that stand in the way of its acceptance as potentially adaptive and valuable rather than as necessarily ill or evil.

One aspect of classical theory (see, especially, Freud, 1914b, 1915a, 1917c)—and the, in general, appropriate conservatism of analysts concerning changes in theory—may adventitiously play a role in this regard. We are used to thinking of the relation between narcissism and object love in a way corresponding to the image of the fluid levels in a U-shaped tube. If the level of fluid in one end rises, it sinks in the other. There is no love where there is toothache; there is no pain where there is passionate love. Such thought models, however, should be replaced when they cannot accommodate the data of observation. The sense of heightened self-esteem, for example, that accompanies object love demonstrates a relationship between the two forms of libidinal cathexis that does not correspond to that of the oscillations in a U-tube system. And while the behavior of the fluid levels in the U-tube, and Freud's amoeba simile (1914b, p. 75), are models that adequately illustrate the total preoccupation of the sufferer with his aching tooth and the waiting lover's obliviousness to rain and cold, these phenomena can be readily explained in terms of the distribution of attention cathexes and do not *require* the U-tube theory.

Be that as it may, more formidable than the scientific context, in which the term narcissism may have acquired a slightly pejorative connotation as a product of regression or defense, is a specific emotional climate that is unfavorable to the acceptance of narcissism as a healthy and approvable psychological constellation. The deeply ingrained value system of the Occident (pervading the religion, the philosophy, the social utopias of Western man) extols altruism and concern for others and disparages egotism and concern for one's self. Yet, just as is true with man's sexual desires, so also with his narcissistic needs: neither a contemptuous attitude toward the powerful psychological forces that assert themselves in these two dimensions of human life nor the attempt at their total eradication will lead to genuine progress in man's self-control or social adaptation. Christianity, while leaving open narcissistic fulfillment in the realm of the merger with the omnipotent selfobject, the divine figure of Christ, attempts to curb the manifestations of the grandiose self. The current materialistic rationalism in Western culture, on the other hand, while giving greater freedom to the enhancement of the self, tends to belittle or (e.g., in the sphere where a militant atheism holds sway) to forbid, the traditional forms of institutionalized relatedness to the idealized object.

In response to ostracism and suppression, the aspirations of the grandiose self may indeed seem to subside, and the yearning for a merger with the idealized selfobject will be denied. The suppressed but unmodified narcissistic structures, however, become intensified as their expression is blocked; they will break through the brittle controls and will suddenly bring about, not only in individuals, but also in whole groups, the unrestrained pursuit of grandiose aims and the resistanceless merger with omnipotent selfobjects. I need only refer to the ruthlessly pursued ambitions of Nazi Germany and of the German population's total surrender to the will of the Führer to exemplify my meaning.

During quiescent historical periods the attitude in certain layers of society toward narcissism resembles Victorian hypocrisy toward sex. Officially, the existence of the social manifestations emanating from the grandiose self and the omnipotent selfobject are denied, yet their split-off dominance everywhere is obvious. I think that the overcoming of a hypocritical attitude toward narcissism is as much required today as was the overcoming of sexual hypocrisy a hundred years ago. We should not deny our ambitions, our wish to dominate, our wish to shine, and our yearning to merge into omnipotent figures, but should instead learn to acknowledge the legitimacy of these narcissistic forces as we have learned to acknowledge the legitimacy of our object-instinctual strivings. We shall then be able, as can be observed in the systematic therapeutic analysis of narcissistic personality disturbances, to transform our archaic grandiosity and exhibitionism into realistic self-esteem and into pleasure with ourselves, and our yearning to be at one with the omnipotent selfobject into the socially useful, adaptive, and joyful capacity to be enthusiastic and to admire the great after whose lives, deeds, and personalities we can permit ourselves to model our own.

Ego Autonomy and Ego Dominance

It is in the context of assessing the value of the transformation (rather than of the suppression) of the archaic narcissistic structures for man as an active participant in human affairs — *l'homme engagé* — that I would like to mention a conceptual distinction I have found useful, namely, the demarcation of *ego dominance* from *ego autonomy* (see Kohut, 1971, p. 187). There is a place for ego autonomy: the rider *off* the horse; man as he reflects coolly and dispassionately, particularly as he scrutinizes the data of his observations. But there is also a place for ego dominance: the rider *on* the horse; man as he responds to the forces within himself, as he shapes his goals and forms his major reactions to the environment; man as an effective participant on the stage of history. In the narcissistic realm, in particular, ego dominance increases our ability to react with the full spectrum of our emotions: with disappointment and rage or with feelings of triumph, controlledly, but not necessarily restrainedly.

A Comparison of the Genetic and Dynamic Importance of Narcissistic and Object-Instinctual Factors

In my retrospective survey I shall now take up the question whether by focusing our attention on narcissism we may not run the risk of disregarding the object-instinctual forces in the psychic life of man. We must ask ourselves whether our emphasis on the genetic and dynamic importance of the vicissitudes of the formation and cohesion of the self may not lead to a de-emphasis of the crucial genetic and dynamic role played in normal and abnormal development by the object-instinctual investments of the Oedipus complex.

A short while ago, a younger colleague who has followed my work on narcissism with interest reviewed the relations between the generations in our field and, speaking for the rising generation of analysts, suggested that the anxiety of the older group was not so much "that we become grownup, but that

we become different" (Terman, 1972). I thought that the
clear implication of this incisive statement was that the older
generation was concerned less about being endangered by the
oedipal killing wish than about being deprived in the narcissistic realm — and I felt strongly inclined to agree with this
opinion. But then I began to worry. Am I the Pied Piper who
leads the young away from the solid ground of the object-
libidinal aspects of the Oedipus complex? Are preoedipal and
narcissistic factors perhaps no more than precursors and trim-
ming? And will the preoccupation with them become a focus
for the old resistances against the full acceptance of the emotional reality of the passions of the oedipal drama? Does not,
behind the preconscious fear that the younger generation will
be "different," lie the deeper and more powerful fear of
their wish to kill, for which the narcissistic concern is only
cover and disguise?

I shall not attempt to pursue this question directly. I
assume that it is not going to be answered in the form in
which we see it now, but that it will some day be superseded
by a reformulation of the nexus of causal factors in early life.
(The work of Gedo and Goldberg [1973], for example,
constitutes, I believe, a significant step in this direction.) In
the meantime we must, without prejudice, study all analytic
data — oedipal and preoedipal, object-instinctual and narcissistic — and determine their developmental and genetic significance.

We shall therefore do well to refrain from setting up a
choice between theoretical opposites concerning the question
of the genetic importance of the young child's experiences in
the narcissistic and in the object-instinctual realm. An
examination of two topics will, however, illuminate the
relative influence that these two sets of early experiences exert
in later childhood and in adult life. The first topic concerns
the significance of the pivotal developmental phase in which
the nucleus of a cohesive self crystallizes; the second concerns

the interplay of pathology of the self (narcissistic pathology) and pathology of structural conflict (oedipal pathology).

The Prototypical Significance of the Period of the Formation of the Self. Concerning the first of these two topics it must be stressed that, like the persisting influence of the vicissitudes of the Oedipus complex, the vicissitudes of the early formation of the self determine the form and the course of later psychological events that are analogous to the crucial early phase. Just as the period of pubertal drive increase, for example, or the time when a marriage partner is chosen constitute emotional situations in which a dormant Oedipus complex is prone to be reactivated, so do certain periods of transition which demand from us a reshuffling of the self, its change, and its rebuilding, constitute emotional situations that reactivate the period of the formation of the self. The replacement of one long-term self-representation by another endangers a self whose earlier, nuclear establishment was faulty; and the vicissitudes of early pathology are experienced as repeated by the new situation. Extensive changes of the self must, for example, be achieved in the transition from early childhood to latency, from latency to puberty, and from adolescence to young adulthood. But these sociobiologically prescheduled developmental processes are not the only ones that impose on us a drastic change of our self; we must also consider external shifts, such as moves from one culture to another; from private life into the army; from the small town to the big city; and the modification in the self that is necessitated when a person's social role is taking a turn—whether for better or worse, e.g., sudden financial success or sudden loss of fortune.

The psychopathological events of late adolescence described by Erikson (1956)—I would call them the vicissitudes of self-cohesion in the transitional period between adolescence and adulthood—should therefore neither be considered as occupying a uniquely significant developmental position, nor should they be explained primarily as due to the demands of this particular period. (These stresses constitute only the precipitating external circumstances.) But an adolescent's crumbling self experience should in each individual instance be investigated in depth — no less than in those equally frequent and important cases of self fragmentation that occur during other periods of transition which have overtaxed the solidity and resilience of the nucleus of the self. Why did the self break down in this specific adolescent? What is the mode of its fragmentation? In what form is the task of the construction of a new self — the self of young adulthood — experienced? How does the present situation repeat the early one? What traumatic interplay of parent and child (when the child began to construct a grandiose-exhibitionistic self and an omnipotent selfobject) is now being repeated for the patient, and — most importantly — how is it revived in one of the specific forms of the narcissistic transference?

To repeat: just as the object-instinctual experiences of the oedipal period become the prototype of our later object-instinctual involvements and form the basis for our specific weaknesses and strengths in this area, so do the experiences during the period of the formation of the self[1] become the prototype of the specific forms of our later vulnerability and security in the narcissistic realm: of the ups and downs in our self-esteem; of our lesser or greater need for praise, for merger into idealized figures, and for other forms of narcissistic sustenance; and of the greater or lesser cohesion of our self during periods of transition, whether in the transition to latency, in early or late adolescence, in maturity, or in old age.

Pseudonarcissistic Disorders and Pseudotransference Neuroses. The relationship between the focus of the development

---

[1] To be exact, one would have to call this point in development the *period of the formation of the nuclear self and selfobject.* The archaic selfobject is, of course, still (experienced as) part of the self.

of the object-instinctual strivings, the Oedipus complex, and the focus of the development in the narcissistic realm, the phase of the formation of the self, will be further illuminated by comparing two paradigmatic forms of psychopathology: nuclear oedipal psychopathology that is hidden by a broad cover of narcissistic disturbance; and narcissistic disorders that are hidden by seemingly oedipal symptomatology.

Concerning the first, a brief remark will suffice. Every analyst has seen the gradual emergence of the oedipal passions and anxieties from behind a broad cover of narcissistic vulnerabilities and complaints, and he knows that the careful observation of the oedipal transference will also reveal how the narcissistic manifestations are related to the central oedipal experiences. How, for example, a sense of low self-esteem relates to phallic comparisons and a feeling of castration, how cycles of triumphant self-confidence and depression relate to fantasies of oedipal success and the discovery of being in fact excluded from the primal scene, and the like. Surely, I need not elaborate further.

Now to the second form of paradigmatic psychopathology. I have chosen to focus on a specific, somewhat complex type of narcissistic disorder, despite its comparative infrequency, because its examination is very instructive. (Cases, it may be added, in which the narcissistic blows suffered by the child in the oedipal phase lead to the first straightforward breakdown of the self are much more common.) I believe that, among the, in principle, analyzable disorders, it confronts the analyst with one of his most trying and difficult therapeutic tasks. These patients initially create the impression of a classical neurosis. When their apparent psychopathology is approached by interpretations, however, the immediate result is nearly catastrophic: they act out wildly, overwhelm the analyst with oedipal love demands, threaten suicide — in short, although content (of symptoms, fantasies, and manifest transference) is all triangular oedipal, the very openness of their infantile wishes, the lack of resistances to their being uncovered, are not in tune with the initial impression.

That the oedipal symptomatology in such cases (e.g., of "pseudohysteria") is not genuine is generally accepted. However, in contrast to what I believe to be the prevailing view that we are dealing with hidden psychosis or with personalities whose psychic equilibrium is threatened by severe ego weakness, I have become convinced that many of these patients suffer from a narcissistic personality disturbance, will establish one of the forms of narcissistic transference, and are thus treatable by psychoanalysis.[2]

The nuclear psychopathology of these individuals concerns the self. Being threatened in the maintenance of a cohesive self because in early life they were lacking in adequate confirming responses ("mirroring") from the environment, they turned to self-stimulation in order to retain the precarious cohesion of their experiencing and acting self. The oedipal phase, including its conflicts and anxieties, became, paradoxically, a remedial stimulant, its very intensity being used by the psyche to counteract the tendency toward the breakup of the self—just as a small child may attempt to use

[2] See in this context the differentiation of *psychosis*, i.e., permanent or protracted fragmentation of the nuclear grandiose self and the nuclear omnipotent selfobject, and *narcissistic personality disturbance*, i.e., insecure cohesion of the nuclear self and selfobject, with only fleeting fragmentation of these configurations. See, furthermore, the classification of the disorders whose essential psychopathology consists in permanent or protracted fragmentation of the self or selfobject, i.e., the psychoses. They fall into three groups, namely: the frank *psychoses* where the symptomatology openly reflects the breakup of the nuclear narcissistic structures; the *latent psychoses* or *borderline cases* where the symptomatology hides to a greater or lesser extent the fact that a breakup of the nuclear narcissistic structures has taken place; and the *schizoid personalities* where a breakup of the nuclear narcissistic structures (the development of an overt or latent psychosis) is the ever-present pathognomonic potentiality, which is, however, prevented by the patient's careful avoidance (through emotional distancing) of regression-provoking narcissistic injuries (Kohut, 1971, Ch. 1).

self-inflicted pain (head banging, for example) in order to retain a sense of aliveness and cohesion. Patients whose manifest psychopathology serves this defensive function will react to the analyst's interpretations concerning the object-instinctual aspects of their behavior with the fear of losing the stimulation that prevents their fragmentation; and they will respond with an intensification of oedipal dramatizing so long as the analyst does not address himself to the defect of the self. Only when a shift in the focus of the analyst's interpretations indicates that he is now in empathic closeness to the patient's fragmenting self does the stimulation of the self through forced oedipal experiences (dramatizing in the analytic situation, acting out) begin to diminish.

It might bear repeating at this point what I have, of course, already said in earlier contributions: that the only reliable way by which the differential diagnosis between a narcissistic personality disturbance and a classical transference neurosis can be established clinically is by the observation of the transference which emerges spontaneously in the analytic situation. In the classical transference neurosis, the vicissitudes of the triangular oedpial situation will gradually unfold. If we are dealing with a narcissistic personality disturbance, however, then we will witness the emergence of one of the forms of narcissistic transference, i.e., of a transference in which the vicissitudes of the cohesion and (fleeting and reversible) fragmentation of the self are correlated to the vicissitudes of the patient's relation to the analyst.

If we wish to state the difference between classical transference neurosis and narcissistic personality disturbance in metapsychological terms, then we must focus on the structure of the psychopathology. Concerning the two aforementioned contrasting paradigmatic disorders, for example, we can say the following. In the pseudohysterias we are dealing with patients who are attempting to maintain the cohesion of an endangered self through the stimulation that they derive from

the hypercathected oedipal strivings. An overt oedipal symptomatology is used to keep hidden self pathology within
bounds. In the pseudonarcissistic disorders, on the other
hand, we are dealing with patients who are attempting to
come to terms, not only with the object-instinctual conflicts,
wishes, and emotions of the oedipal period, but also — a point
deserving emphasis — with the narcissistic injuries to which
their securely established self had been exposed within the
context of the oedipal experience. The presence, in other
words, of narcissistic features — and even their initial predominance within the total picture — does not alter the fact that
the essential psychopathology is a classical psychoneurosis.

Organ Inferiority and Shame

My comments so far may be regarded as an attempt to
tidy up the house before going on a trip. The work on the
libidinal aspects of narcissism, in other words, is more or less
done, but I wish to straighten out odds and ends before
leaving it behind. The trip should lead into the rugged ter-
rain of narcissistic rage, and, later, into the far-off region of
group psychology. A glance, however, at a topic that lies in
the main within the familiar area of the libidinal cathexis of
the self, yet extends into the unfamiliar territory of narcissism
and aggression, should serve as a bridge to the new undertaking. Let me refer to this topic by what is nowadays a
somewhat discredited name:[3] "organ inferiority" (Adler,
1907).

In his "New Introductory Lectures" (1933, p. 66) Freud
took the writer Emil Ludwig to task — without naming him,
however. Ludwig had, in one of the biographical novels
(1926) that were his specialty, interpreted the personality of

[3] Freud (1914a), however, spoke of "the valuable work he [Adler] had
done on 'organ-inferiority' " (p. 51).

Emperor Wilhelm II in accordance with the theories of Alfred Adler. He had explained the Hohenzollern's readiness to take offense and to turn toward war as reactions to a sense of organ inferiority. The Emperor had been born with a withered arm. The defective limb became the sore that remained sensitive throughout his life and brought about the character formation that, according to Ludwig, was one of the important factors leading to the outbreak of the First World War.

Not so! said Freud. It was not the birth injury in itself that resulted in Emperor Wilhelm's sensitivity to narcissistic slights, but the rejection by his proud mother, who could not tolerate an imperfect child.

It takes little effort to add the appropriate psychodynamic refinements to Freud's genetic formulation. A mother's lack of confirming and approving "mirroring" responses to her child prevents the transformation of the archaic narcissistic cathexis of the child's body-self, which normally is achieved with the aid of the increasing selectivity of the mother's admiration and approval. The crude and intense narcissistic cathexis of the grandiose body-self (in Emperor Wilhelm's case: the withered arm) thus remains unaltered, and its archaic grandiosity and exhibitionism cannot be integrated with the remainder of the psychic organization, which gradually reaches maturity. The archaic grandiosity and exhibitionism thus become split off from the reality ego ("vertical split" in the psyche) or separated from it through repression ("horizontal split"). Deprived of the mediating function of the reality ego, they are therefore no longer modifiable by later external influences, be these ever so accepting or approving, i.e., there is no possibility for a "corrective emotional experience" (Alexander et al., 1946). On the other hand, the archaic grandiose-exhibitionistic (body-) self will from time to time assert its archaic claims, either by bypassing the repression barrier via the vertically split-off sector of the psyche or by breaking through the brittle defenses of the central sector. It will suddenly flood the reality ego with unneutralized exhibitionistic cathexis and overwhelm the neutralizing powers of the ego, which becomes paralyzed and experiences intense shame and rage.

I do not know enough about the personality of Emperor Wilhelm to judge whether the foregoing formulation does indeed apply to him. I believe, however, that I am on more solid ground when I suspect that Emil Ludwig did not take kindly to Freud's criticism. At any rate he later wrote a biography of Freud (Ludwig, 1947) which was the undisguised expression of narcissistic rage — so coarse, in fact,[4] that even those inimical to psychoanalysis and Freud considered the crudity of Ludwig's attack an embarrassment, and disassociated themselves from it.

Be this as it may with regard to Emperor Wilhelm and his biographer, I have no doubt that the ubiquitous sensitivity about bodily defects and shortcomings can be effortlessly explained within the metapsychological framework of the vicissitudes of the libidinal cathexes of the grandiose self and, in particular, of the grandiose-exhibitionistic body-self.

The topic of the sense of inferiority of children about the small size of their genitals (in the boy, in comparison with the penis of the adult man; in the girl, in comparison with the boy's organ) may warrant a few special remarks. Children's sensitivity about their genitals is at its peak during the pivotal phallic phase of psychosexual development — later sensitivities concerning the genitals must be understood as residuals (e.g., during latency) or as revivals (e.g., during puberty) of the exhibitionism of the phallic phase. The significance of the

---

[4] Lionel Trilling (1947), who reviewed Emil Ludwig's book *Dr. Freud*, closed his remarks about this biography with the following trenchant sentence: "We are not an age notable for fineness and precision of thought, but it is seldom indeed that we get a book as intellectually discreditable, as disingenuous and as vulgar as this."

genitals during the phallic phase is determined by the fact that at this period they temporarily constitute the *leading zone of the child's* (bodily) *narcissism*—they are not only the instruments of intense (fantasied) *object-libidinal* interactions, they also carry enormous *narcissistic* cathexes. (The narcissistic cathexis of feces during the anal phase of development and the narcissistic cathexis of certain autonomous ego functions during latency are examples of earlier and later leading zones of the child's narcissism during preceding and subsequent stages of his development.) The genitals are thus the focal point of the child's narcissistic aspirations and sensitivities during the phallic phase. If we keep these facts in mind and emphasize in addition that the exhibitionistic component of infantile narcissism is largely unneutralized, then we will also understand the much-disputed significance of infantile penis envy. This topic has aroused a great deal of unscientific and acrimonious discussion, even leading to the ludicrous spectacle of opposing scientific line-ups of men who assign the phenomenon exclusively to women, and of women who deny either its existence or its importance.

Some of the difficulties may resolve themselves if the intensity of the exhibitionistic cathexes is taken into account and particularly if we do not underestimate the importance of the *visible* genital in this context: in other words, if we keep in mind that the narcissistic demands of the phallic period are no more—but also no less!—than an important instance in the developmental series of demands for immediate mirroring responses to concretely exhibited aspects of the child's body or of his physical or mental functions. That his penis will grow is small consolation for the little boy; and that a complex but invisible apparatus will be maturing that will enable her to bear children is small consolation for the little girl within the framework of the psychology of childhood exhibitionism—notwithstanding the simultaneous existence of other sources of direct narcissistic gratification and of acceptable substitutive mirroring which enhances the acquisition of sublimations in children of both sexes.

The shame of the adult, too, when a defective body part is looked at by others—indeed, his conviction that others are staring at it![5]—is due to the pressure of the unmodified, archaic, exhibitionistic libido with which the defective organ has remained cathected. And the self-consciousness concerning the defective organ and the tendency to blush when it is being scrutinized by others are the psychological and psychophysiological correlates of the breakthrough of the unmodified exhibitionistic cathexes. (I shall return to this topic in the context of the metapsychology of narcissistic rage.)

The Motivational Role of Disturbed Narcissism in Certain Types of Self-Mutilation and Suicide

Related to the preceding formulations about "organ inferiority" are those concerning the self-mutilation of the psychotic, and certain types of suicide. With regard to both self-mutilations and suicide, one must differentiate the motive for these acts from the ability to perform them.

The motivation for the self-mutilations of psychotics emanates, I believe, in many instances not from specific conflicts—such as incest guilt leading to the self-punitive removal of an organ which symbolizes the evil penis. It is rather due to the fact that a break-up of the body-self has occurred and that the fragments of the body-self that cannot be retained within the total organization of the body-self become an unbearably painful burden and are therefore removed. The schizophrenic who (like the young man in Kleist's essay on the

---

[5] This quasi-delusion is, I believe, a manifestation of the archaic exhibitionistic urge which is isolated from the rest of the psychic organization and projected (with reversed aim) upon the person who is the supposedly gloating onlooker. The relation between this phenomenon and the paranoiac's delusion of being watched is obvious.

puppet theater) looks into the mirror for hours and days attempts to unite his fragmenting body-self with the aid of his gaze. If these and similar endeavors (e.g., stimulation of the total body-self through forced physical activity) to replace the cohesion-producing narcissitic cathexes fail, then the organ is removed.

The understanding of the motivation for self-mutilation is not, by itself, sufficient to explain the actual performance of such acts. A person may sense in himself the analogue of the Biblical command, "If thine eye offend thee, pluck it out" (Matthew 18:9), but he would still be unable to obey this order. The ability to perform an act of gross self-mutilation depends, in some instances at least, on the fact that the organ the psychotic removes has lost its narcissistic libidinal cathexis; i.e., it is no longer part of the self and can therefore be discarded as if it were a foreign body. This explanation applies to those instances in which the act of self-mutilation is performed calmly by the psychotic patient. Self-mutilations performed during stages of emotional frenzy may have different motivations, and the ability to carry them out rests on the almost total concentration of the psychotic's attention on some delusional aim. The ability to carry out the act, then, does not rest on the fragmentation of the body-self, but is based on a scotoma of the psychotic's perception—similar to those instances when soldiers during a frenzied attack on enemy lines may temporarily not be aware of the fact that they have suffered a severe physical injury.

Analogous considerations also apply to certain kinds of suicide with regard to both the motivation that leads to the act and the ability to carry it out. Such suicides are in the main based on the loss of the libidinal cathexis of the self. Analogous to certain self-mutilations, such suicide does not emanate from specific structural conflicts — it does not constitute, for example, a step taken in order to expiate oedipal guilt. Characteristically, these suicides are preceded, not by

THE SEARCH FOR THE SELF

guilt feelings, but by feelings of unbearable emptiness and deadness or by intense shame, i.e., by the signs of profound disturbance in the realm of the libidinal cathexis of the self.

Narcissism and Aggression

The hypothesis that a tendency to kill is deeply rooted in man's psychobiological makeup and stems from his animal past — the assumption, in other words, of man's inherent propensity toward aggression (and the correlated conceptualization of aggression as a drive) protects us against the lure of the comforting illusion that human pugnacity could be easily abolished if only our material needs were satisfied. But these broad formulations contribute little to the understanding of aggression as a psychological phenomenon. It is obviously not enough to say that such phenomena as warfare, intolerance, and persecution are due to man's regression toward the undisguised expression of a drive. And the often-heard complaint that it is the thinness of the civilized layer of the human personality that is responsible for the evils wrought by human aggression is appealing in its simplicity, but misses the mark.

True, the protagonists of the most dreadful manifestation of aggression in the history of modern Western civilization proclaimed loudly that their destructive acts were performed in the service of a law of nature. The Nazis justified their warfare and the extermination of those they considered weak and inferior by seeing their misdeeds within the framework of a vulgarized Darwinism: the inherent right of the stronger, and the survival of the fittest race for the good of mankind. But I do not believe that, despite their own theories, we can come closer to understanding the Nazi phenomenon by conceiving of it as a regression toward the biologically simple, toward animal behavior — whether such a regression be extolled, as it was by the Nazis themselves, or condemned and despised, as it was ultimately by the rest of the world.

It would, on the whole, be pleasant if we could do so; if we could state—in a simplistic application of a Civilization-and-Its-Discontents principle—that Hitler exploited the readiness of a civilized nation to shed the thin layer of its uncomfortably carried restraints, leading to the unspeakable events of the decade 1935 to 1945. But the truth is—it must be admitted with sadness—that such events are not bestial, in the primary sense of the word, but are decidedly human. They are an intrinsic part of the human condition, a strand in the web of the complex pattern that makes up the human situation. So long as we turn away from these phenomena in terror and disgust and indignantly declare them to be a reversal to barbarism, a regression to the primitive and animal-like, so long do we deprive ourselves of the chance of increasing our understanding of human aggressivity and of our mastery over it. The psychoanalyst must therefore not shrink from the task of applying his knowledge about the individual to the field of history, particularly to the crucial role of human aggression as it has shaped the history of man. It is my conviction that we will reach tangible results by focusing our attention on human aggression as it arises out of the matrix of archaic narcissism, i.e., on the phenomenon of narcissistic rage.

Human aggression is most dangerous when it is attached to the two great absolutarian psychological constellations: the grandiose self and the archaic omnipotent object. And the most gruesome human destructiveness is encountered, not in the form of wild, regressive, and primitive behavior, but in the form of orderly and organized activities in which the perpetrators' destructiveness is alloyed with absolute conviction about their greatness and with their devotion to archaic omnipotent figures. I could support this thesis by quoting Himmler's self-pityingly boastful and idolatrous speeches to those cadres of the S.S. who were the executors of the extermination policies of the Nazis (see Bracher, 1969, p. 422-423;

see also Loewenberg, 1971, p. 639) — but I know that I shall be forgiven for not displaying this evidence here.

On Narcissistic Rage

In its undisguised form, narcissistic rage is a familiar experience which is in general easily identified by the empathic observer of human behavior. But what is its dynamic essence? How should it be classified? How should we outline the concept and define the meaning of the term?

I shall first respond to the last of these interrelated questions. Strictly speaking, the term narcissistic rage refers to only one specific band in the wide spectrum of experiences that reaches from such trivial occurrences as a fleeting annoyance when someone fails to reciprocate our greeting or does not respond to our joke to such ominous derangements as the furor of the catatonic and the grudges of the paranoiac. Following Freud's example (1921, p. 91), however, I shall use the term *a potiori* and refer to all points in the spectrum as narcissistic rage, since with this designation we are referring to the most characteristic or best known of a series of experiences that not only form a continuum, but, with all their differences, are essentially related to each other.

And what is it that all these different experiences, which we designate by the same term, have in common? In what psychological category do they all belong? What are their common determinants? And what is their common metapsychological substance?

It is self-evident that narcissistic rage belongs to the large psychological field of aggression, anger, and destructiveness and that it constitutes a specific circumscribed phenomenon within this great area. From the point of view of social psychology, furthermore, it is clearly analogous to the fight component of the fight-flight reaction with which biological organisms respond to attack. Stated more specifically, it is easily observed that the narcissistically vulnerable individual responds to actual (or anticipated) narcissistic injury either with shamefaced withdrawal (flight) or with narcissistic rage (fight).

Since narcissistic rage is clearly a manifestation of the human propensity for aggressive responses, some analysts believe that it requires no further explanation, once the preconscious motivational context in which it is likely to occur has been established. Alexander, for example, dealt with this important psychological phenomenon by identifying its position in a typical sequence of preconscious and conscious attitudes. He attempted to clarify the psychological significance and the metapsychological position of shame and rage, these two principal experiential and behavioral manifestations of disturbed narcissistic equilibrium, in a paper (1938) that has influenced the relevant work of a number of authors (e.g., Saul, 1947; Piers and Singer, 1953; and, with wider individual elaborations, Eidelberg, 1959, and Jacobson, 1964). In this contribution he presented the schema of a self-perpetuating cycle of psychological phenomena—an explanatory device which is appealing in its pedagogical clarity and in its similarity to formulations cogently employed in other branches of science, e.g., in physics. He described the dynamic cycle of hostility→guilt→submission→reactive aggression→guilt, etc. He thus restricted himself to explaining narcissistic rage (in his terms: reactive aggression that follows upon a shameful submission) in the context of the motivational dynamics of (pre)conscious experiences and overt behavior without investigating this phenomenon in depth, i.e., without attempting to uncover its unconscious dimensions and its developmental roots.

Narcissistic rage occurs in many forms; they all share, however, a specific psychological flavor which gives them a distinct position within the wide realm of human aggressions. The need for revenge, for righting a wrong, for undoing a hurt by whatever means, and a deeply anchored, unrelenting compulsion in the pursuit of all these aims, which gives no rest to those who have suffered a narcissistic injury—these are the characteristic features of narcissistic rage in all its forms and which set it apart from other kinds of aggression.

And what is the specific significance of the psychological injuries (such as ridicule, contempt, and conspicuous defeat) that tend to provoke narcissistic rage; and how do these external provocations interact with the sensitized aspects of the rage- and revenge-prone personality?

The propensity for narcissistic rage in the Japanese, for example, is attributed by Ruth Benedict (1946) to their methods of child rearing through ridicule and the threat of ostracism, and to the sociocultural importance the Japanese attach to maintaining decorum. Small wonder, therefore, says Benedict, that "sometimes people explode in the most aggressive acts. They are roused to these aggressions not when their principles or their freedom is challenged . . . but when they detect an insult or a detraction" (p. 293).

The desire to turn a passive experience into an active one (Freud, 1920, p. 16), the mechanism of identification with the aggressor (A. Freud, 1936), the sadistic tensions retained by those who as children had been treated sadistically by their parents—all these factors help explain the readiness of the shame-prone individual to respond to a potentially shame-provoking situation by the employment of a simple remedy: the active (often anticipatory) inflicting on others of those narcissistic injuries which he is most afraid of suffering himself.

Mr. P., for example, who was exceedingly shame-prone and narcissistically vulnerable, was a master of a specific form of social sadism. Although he came from a conservative family, he had become very liberal in his political and social outlook. He was always eager to inform himself about the national and religious background of acquaintances and, avowedly in the spirit of rationality and lack of prejudice, embarrassed them at social gatherings by introducing the topic of their minority status into the conversation. Although he defended himself against the recognition of the significance of his malicious maneuvers by well-thought-out rationalizations, he became in time aware of the fact that he experienced an erotically tinged excitement at these moments. There was, according to his description, a brief moment of silence in the conversation in which the victim struggled for composure after public attention had been directed to his social handicap, and, although all acted as if they had not noticed the victim's embarrassment, the emotional significance of the situation was clear to everyone. Mr. P.'s increasing realization of the true nature of his sadistic attacks through the public exposure of a social defect, and his gradually deepening awareness of his own fear of exposure and ridicule, led to his recall of violent emotions of shame and rage in childhood. His mother, the daughter of a Fundamentalist minister, not only had embarrassed and shamed the boy in public, but had insisted on exposing and inspecting his genitals—as she claimed, to find out whether he had masturbated. As a child he had formed vengeful fantasies—the precursors of his current sadistic enactments—in which he would cruelly expose his mother to his own and to other people's gaze.

The heightened sadism, the adoption of a policy of preventive attack, the need for revenge, and the desire to turn a passive experience into an active one,[6] do not, however, fully account for some of the most characteristic features of narcissistic rage. In its typical forms there is utter disregard for

---

[6] Many psychotherapists, including psychoanalysts, traumatize their patients unnecessarily by sarcastic attacks on their archaic narcissism. Despite the analyst's increasing understanding of the significance of the reactivation of the patient's archaic narcissistic demands, such tendencies are hard to overcome and the analyst's inappropriate sarcasm intrudes again

reasonable limitations and a boundless wish to redress an injury and to obtain revenge. The irrationality of the vengeful attitude becomes even more frightening in view of the fact that — in narcissistic personalities as in the paranoiac — the reasoning capacity, while totally under the domination and in the service of the overriding emotion, is often not only intact but even sharpened. (This dangerous feature of individual psychopathology is the parallel of an equally malignant social phenomenon: the subordination of the rational class of technicians to a paranoid leader and the efficiency — and even brilliance — of their amoral cooperation in carrying out his purposes.[7])

Two Phenomena Related to Narcissistic Rage

I shall now examine two forms of anger which are related to narcissistic rage: the anger of a person who because of cerebral defect or brain injury is unable to solve certain simple problems, and the anger of a child who has suffered a minor painful injury.

The "Catastrophic Reaction" and Similar Occurrences. If a person with a brain defect strives unsuccessfully to perform some task that should be easily accomplished — naming a

---

and again. The difficulty is, in some instances at least, due to the fact that the psychotherapist (or analyst) had himself been treated in similar fashion (by his parents and teachers, for example, and, specifically, by his training analyst). The fact that an analyst will persist, despite insight and effort, in his nontherapeutic sarcasm toward his narcissistic patients is evidence for the power of the need to turn a passive experience into an active one. In addition, we must not disregard the fact that the motivator of the deleterious attitude (i.e., the urge, which is deeply rooted in the unconscious, to inflict a narcissistic injury on others) can easily be rationalized: The therapist's attacks can be justified as being undertaken for the good of the patient and in the service of realism — or a maturity-morality.

[7] For a discussion of these events in National-Socialist Germany see Rauschning (1938). The relation of Speer, Minister for Armaments and War Production — an organizational genius — to Hitler is especially revealing in this context (see Speer, 1969).

familiar object, for example, or putting a round or square peg into the fitting hole—he may respond to his incapacity with the intense and frenzied anger that is known as "catastrophic reaction" (Goldstein, 1948).[8] His rage is due to the fact that he is suddenly not in control of his own thought processes, of a function people consider to be most intimately their own—i.e., as a part of the self. "It must not be! It cannot be!" the aphasic feels when he is unable to name a familiar object such as a pencil: and his furious refusal to accept the unpleasant truth that his incapacity is a reality is heightened by the fact that his spontaneous speech may be comparatively undisturbed and that his sensorium is clear.

We take our thought processes as belonging to the core of our self, and we refuse to admit that we may not be in control of them. To be deprived of the capacity to name a familiar object or to solve a simple problem is experienced as even more incredible than the loss of a limb. We can see our own body and, since perception is primarily directed toward the outside world, it is easier to think of our body in objective terms. The unseeable thought processes, however, we consider inseparable from, or coinciding with, our very self. The loss of a limb can therefore be mourned, like the loss of a love object;[9] a defect in the realm of our mental functions, however, is experienced as loss of self.

An attenuated variant of the catastrophic reaction is familiar to all: the annoyance when we cannot recall a word or name. And our patients, especially early in analysis, ex-

---

[8] The organic defect itself undoubtedly contributes to the diminution of the capacity to control emotions and impulses. Yet, many patients who respond with the catastrophic reaction under comparatively bland conditions (e.g., in the harmless test situation) will not react with equal intensity under different circumstances which might arouse anger (e.g., when they are being teased or otherwise annoyed).

[9] Tolstoy's description of Anatole Kurágin's farewell to his amputated leg is a deeply moving illustration of this process (1866, Book 10, Ch. 7, pp. 907-908).

perience slips of the tongue and other manifestations of the
unconcious as narcissistic blows. They are enraged about the
sudden exposure of their lack of omnipotence in the area of
their own mind — not about having disclosed a specific unconscious wish or fantasy. ". . . the trace of affect which follows the revelation of the slip," Freud says, "is clearly in the
nature of shame" (1901, p. 83).

It is instructive to observe our own behavior after we have
made a slip of the tongue, especially under circumstances
such as a lecture in which our exhibitionism is mobilized. The
victim's reaction to the amusement of the audience is very
specific: he either pretends that the revelation had been intentional or he claims that he understands the meaning of the
slip and can interpret it himself. Our immediate tendency is
thus to deny our loss of control rather than to obliterate the
unconscious content. Or, expressed differently: our defensive
activity is motivated primarily by our shame concerning a defect in the realm of the omnipotent and omniscient grandiose
self, not by guilt over the unconscious forbidden sexual or
aggressive impulse that was revealed.

The excessive preoccupation with a situation in which one
has suffered a shameful narcissistic injury (e.g., a social *faux
pas*) must similarly be understood as an enraged attempt to
eradicate the reality of the incident by magical means, even
to the point of wishing to do away with oneself in order to
wipe out the tormenting memory.

The Child's Reaction to Painful Injuries. The other phenomenon that illuminates the significance of narcissistic rage
is the emotional reaction of children to slight injuries. When
a child has stubbed his toe or pinched his finger, his response
expresses a number of feelings. We might say with Freud
(1926) that in the child's feelings "certain things seem to be
joined together . . . which will later on be separated out" (p.
169). The child gives voice not only to his physical pain and
fear, but also to his wounded narcissism. "How can it be?

How can it happen?" his outraged cries seem to ask. And it is instructive to observe how he may veer back and forth between enraged protests at the imperfection of his grandiose self and angry reproaches against the omnipotent selfobject for having permitted the insult.[10]

The Experiential Content of Narcissistic Rage

The various forms of narcissistic rage, the catastrophic reaction of the brain-damaged, and the child's outrage at being suddenly exposed to a painful injury are experiences that are far apart in their psychological impact and social consequences. Yet, underlying all these emotional states is the uncompromising insistence on the perfection of the idealized selfobject and on the limitlessness of the power and knowledge of a grandiose self which must remain the equivalent of "purified pleasure" (Freud, 1915a, p. 136). The fanaticism of the need for revenge and the unending compulsion of having to square the account after an offense are therefore not the attributes of an aggressivity that is integrated with the mature purposes of the ego—on the contrary, such bedevilment indicates that the aggression was mobilized in the service of an archaic grandiose self and that it is deployed within the framework of an archaic perception of reality. The shame-prone individual who is ready to experience setbacks as narcissistic injuries and to respond to them with insatiable rage does not recognize his opponent as a center of independent initiative with whom he happens to be at cross-purposes. Aggressions employed in the pursuit of maturely experienced causes are not limitless. However vigorously mobilized, their

[10] When the archaic selfobject does not provide the needed narcissistic sustenance or does not prevent or dispel the child's discomfort, it is held to be sadistic by the child because it is experienced as all-powerful and all-knowing, and thus the consequences of its actions and omissions are always viewed by the child as having been brought about intentionally.

aim is definite: the defeat of the enemy who blocks the way to
a cherished goal. The narcissistically injured, on the other
hand, cannot rest until he has blotted out a vaguely
experienced offender who dared to oppose him, to disagree
with him, or to outshine him. "Mirror, mirror, on the wall,
who is the fairest of them all?" the grandiose-exhibitionistic
self is asking. And when it is told that there is someone fairer,
cleverer, or stronger, then, like the evil stepmother in "Snow
White," it can never find rest because it can never wipe out
the evidence that has contradicted its conviction that it is
unique and perfect.

The opponent who is the target of our mature aggressions
is experienced as separate from ourselves, whether we attack
him because he blocks us in reaching our object-libidinal
goals or hate him because he interferes with the fulfillment of
our reality-integrated narcissistic wishes. The enemy who calls
forth the archaic rage of the narcissistically vulnerable, however, is seen by him not as an autonomous source of impul-
sions, but as a *flaw in a narcissistically perceived reality*. The
enemy is a recalcitrant part of an expanded self over which
the narcissistically vulnerable person had expected to exercise
full control. The mere fact, in other words, that the other
person is independent or different is experienced as offensive
by those with intense narcissistic needs.

It has now become clear that narcissistic rage arises when
self or object fail to live up to the expectations directed at
their function — whether by the child who more or less phase-
appropriately insists on the grandiosity and omnipotence of
the self and the selfobject or by the narcissistically fixated
adult whose archaic narcissistic structures have remained unmodified because they became isolated from the rest of the
growing psyche after the phase-appropriate narcissistic
demands of childhood had been traumatically frustrated. Or,
describing the psychodynamic pattern in different words, we
can say: although everybody tends to react to narcissistic in-

juries with embarrassment and anger, the most intense experiences of shame and the most violent forms of narcissistic rage arise in those individuals for whom a sense of absolute control over an archaic environment is indispensable because the maintenance of self-esteem—and indeed of the self—depends on the unconditional availability of the approving-mirroring selfobject or of the merger-permitting idealized one.

However different their manifestations, all instances of narcissistic rage have certain features in common because they all arise from the matrix of a narcissistic or prenarcissistic view of the world. The archaic mode of experience explains why those who are in the grip of narcissistic rage show total lack of empathy toward the offender. It explains the unmodifiable wish to blot out the offense that was perpetrated against the grandiose self and the unforgiving fury that arises when the control over the mirroring selfobject is lost or when the omnipotent selfobject is unavailable. And the empathic observer will understand the deeper significance of the often seemingly minor irritant that has provoked an attack of narcissistic rage and will not be taken aback by the seemingly disproportionate severity of the reaction.

These considerations are, of course, also valid within the context of the psychoanalytic situation. Everybody tends to react to psychoanalysis as a narcissistic injury because it gives the lie to our conviction that we are in full control of our mind (Freud, 1917b). The most severe narcissistic resistances against analysis, however, will arise in those patients whose archaic need to claim omniscience and total control had remained comparatively unaltered because they had been too rapidly, or phase-inappropriately deprived of an omniscient selfobject or had received inadequate confirmation of the phase-appropriate conviction of the perfection of the self.

Can Ego Dominance Over Narcissistic Rage
Be Achieved Through Psychoanalysis?

Can narcissistic rage be tamed, i.e., can it come under
the dominance of the ego? The answer to this question is affirmative — but the "yes" must be qualified and defined.

When, during the analysis of a narcissistic personality
disturbance, a defensive wall of apparent tranquility that had
been maintained with the aid of social isolation, detachment,
and fantasied superiority begins to give way, then one has the
right to regard the emergence of narcissistic rage, of sudden
attacks of fury at narcissistic injuries, as a sign of the
loosening of a rigid personality structure and thus of analytic
progress. These developments must therefore neither be
censured by the analyst, nor hastily identified as a part of an
archaic psychological world, but must for some time be
accepted with implicit approval. Yet, whether present from
the beginning of the analysis in the narcissistic analysand, or
arising after a therapeutic loosening of his personality, such
rage must not be confused with mature aggression. Narcissistic rage enslaves the ego and allows it to function only as its
tool and rationalizer. Mature aggression is under the control
of the ego, and the degree of its neutralization is regulated by
the ego in conformance with the purposes for which it is employed. The mobilization of narcissistic rage is therefore not
an end point in analysis, but the beginning of a new phase — a
phase of working through which is concluded when ego
dominance in this sector of the personality has been
established. The transformation of narcissistic rage is not
achieved directly — e.g., via appeals to the ego to increase its
control over the angry impulses — but is brought about indirectly, secondary to the gradual transformation of the
matrix of narcissism from which the rage arose. The analysand's archaic exhibitionism and grandiosity must be gradually transformed into aim-inhibited self-esteem and realistic

ambitions; and his desire to merge into an archaic omnipotent selfobject has to be replaced by attitudes that are under the control of the ego, e.g., by his enthusiasm for meaningful ideals and by his devotion to them. Concomitantly with these changes the narcissistic rage will gradually subside and the analysand's maturely modulated aggressions will be employed in the service of a securely established self and in the service of cherished values.

The relinquishment of narcissistic claims—the precondition for the subsidence of narcissistic rage—is, however, not absolute. (See in this context Tausk, 1913.) In accepting the existence of an unconscious psychic life, for example, we analysts are not unconditionally renouncing a narcissistic position that has sustained the cohesion of the self, but we are shifting the focus of our narcissism to different ideational contents and are modulating the neutralization of the narcissistic cathexes. Instead of sustaining our sense of self-assurance through the belief in the all-encompassing scope of our consciousness, we now gain a new self-respect from such derivatives of the relationship with the omniscient and omnipotent selfobject as the joy in the superego's approval of our stamina in tolerating unpleasant aspects of reality or the joy of having lived up to the example of an admired teacher-figure, Freud.

My emphasis on the fact that narcissism need not be destroyed, but that it can be transformed is in tune with my support of a nonhypocritical attitude toward narcissism as a psychological force *sui generis*, which has its own line of development and which neither should—nor indeed could—be relinquished. In the psychoanalytic situation, too, the analyst's nonhypocritical attitude toward narcissism, his familiarity with the forms and transformations of this psychic constellation, and his uncensorious recognition of its biological and sociocultural value will diminish the analysand's narcissistic resistance and rage against the analytic procedure. The analyst's accepting objectivity toward the patient's narcissism cannot, of course, do away with all narcissistic resistance and rage, but it will reduce the nonspecific initial resistance against a procedure in which another person may know something about one's thoughts and wishes before one knows them oneself. Through the diminution of the *nonspecific* narcissistic resistances, moreover, recognition of the significance of *specific* narcissistic resistances as repetition and transference is facilitated.

The analyst must therefore at first not ally himself unqualifiedly with the patient's reality ego when it rejects the claims of the unmodified grandiose self or when it tries to deny the persisting infantile need for full control over the narcissistically invested selfobject.[11] On the contrary, he must even be understandingly tolerant of the rage that emerges in the patient when his narcissistic needs are not totally and immediately fulfilled. If the analyst maintains his empathic attitude toward the patient's needs and toward his anger, and if, in response to the analyst's attitude, the patient's reality ego, too, learns to be understandingly accepting of the demands of the grandiose self and of its propensity for rage, then there will be a diminution of those nonspecific resistances in which the patient who feels treated like a naughty child begins indeed to act like a misunderstood naughty child. Only then will the specific resistances against the uncovering of specific repressed needs, wishes, and attitudes be brought into play. The nonspecific narcissistic resistances are in general accompanied by a great deal of rage; the specific resistances, however, are usually characterized by the presence of hypochondria and of other vague fears. The

[11] This advice is valid not only when the grandiosity is on the whole in repression (horizontal split in the psyche), but also where archaic narcissistic claims are by-passing the reality ego (vertical split), i.e., where the ego is disavowing the presence or significance of the narcissistic claims and enactments (see Kohut, 1971, pp. 183-186).

transference reactivation of the original need for approval through mirroring, and for the merger with an idealized archaic object, increases narcissistic tension and leads to hypochondria; and it creates the vague dread of having again to suffer the old traumatic rejection from the side of an environment that will not respond empathically to the rekindled narcissistic needs of childhood.

The Transformation of Narcissistic Rage into Mature Aggression. It is often more revealing to examine transitional phenomena than the extremes of a spectrum of contrasting manifestations; and it is often more instructive to study intermediate points in a developmental sequence than to compare its beginning with its end. This maxim holds true for the study of the transformation of narcissistic rage into mature aggression: the way stations of this development and the remaining imperfections deserve our attention.

Patient A.'s insufficiently idealized superego could not provide him with an adequate internal supply of narcissistic sustenance (see the discussion of this case in Kohut, 1971, pp. 57-73), and he needed external approbation in order to maintain his narcissistic balance. He therefore became inordinately dependent on idealized figures in his environment whose praise he craved. Every time they remained unresponsive because they failed to sense his need, he became enraged and criticized them with bitterness and sarcasm during the analytic sessions. When, however, as a result of the extensive working through of his idealizing transference, his structural defect became ameliorated, his rage changed. He continued to complain about the current stand-ins for the archaic idealized figure (his father who had disappointed him in his early life), but his attacks became less bitter and sarcastic, acquired an admixture of humor, and were more in tune with the real shortcomings of those whom he criticized. And there was another remarkable change: while he had formerly nourished his grudges in isolation (even in the analytic sessions his complaints were predominantly soliloquy, not message), he now banded together with his fellow workers and was able to savor, in enjoyable comradeship with them, the pleasure, of prolonged bull sessions in which the bosses were taken apart. In still later stages of his analysis when the patient had already mastered a large part of his psychological difficulties, and especially when certain homosexual fantasies of which he was very ashamed had disappeared, some anger at idealized figures for withholding their approval continued to be in evidence — but now there was not only benign humor instead of sarcasm, and companionship instead of isolation, but also the ability to see some positive features in those he criticized, side by side with their defects.

Another clinical example: patient P., whose attitude toward his eight-year-old son was very revealing.[12] He was in general on excellent terms with the boy and spent a good deal of time with him in enjoyably shared activities. He could, however, become suddenly outraged about minor transgressions, and would then punish the child severely. Slowly, as the analysis proceeded, he became aware of his narcissistic vulnerability and realized that he tended to respond with violent anger when he felt frustrated by narcissistically cathected ob-

---

[12] I examined another, though not unrelated, aspect of this patient's behavior earlier in this presentation. (He is also referred to, but in a clearly different context, in Kohut, 1971, pp. 321-324.) At a meeting of the Chicago Psychoanalytic Society (September 25, 1962), in discussing a presentation on psychosomatic disturbances, I described a transient speech disorder of the then three-and-a-half-year-old son of Mr. P. I interpreted the child's stammer as a reaction to his father's narcissistic involvement with him and to his father's insistence on absolute control over him.

[Kohut refers here to Augusta Bonnard's "Impediments of Speech: A Special Psychosomatic Instance," published in *The International Journal of Psycho-Analysis* (1963), 44:151-162. The following is Kohut's discussion as summarized by J. Kavka in the *Bulletin of the Philadelphia Association for Psychoanalysis* (1962), 12:176.

Heinz Kohut indirectly observed the temporary occurrence of stammering in the three-and-a-half-year-old son of a male analysand whose

jects. Yet, he was at first unable to recognize the often seemingly unmistakable fact that he reacted to the trauma of a narcissistic injury by becoming unduly harsh toward his son. He remained convinced that his severity was objectively justified, was adamant in the defense of his behavior, and claimed that consistency and unbending justice were better for his son than ill-placed kindness and unprincipled tolerance. His rationalizations seemed foolproof for a long time, and no headway was made in the analysis. His moralistic punitiveness finally began to subside and was replaced by his growing empathy for his son after the memory of certain childhood scenes was recovered in the analysis and after their dynamic significance was understood. His mother had always reacted with severe, morally buttressed punishments when he attempted to extricate himself from her narcissistic universe. He now did likewise when he felt that an alter ego tried to withdraw from him—either the analyst through activities (such as a temporary interruption of the treatment) that upset the balance of the narcissistic transference, or the son through activities that demonstrated his growing independence from him. It had usually been one of the latter moves—such as the son's stepping over to the neighbor's garden without having asked the father's permission; or his

---

pathology lay between perversion and (paranoid) psychosis. The borders of the patient's personality were blurred, and he often reacted to his own perverse transgressions by becoming harshly critical toward his son. Kohut speculated that such criticism (which is not related to a child's impulses, but is due to the child's inclusion into the narcissistic system of the educator) cannot become part of the child's superego; instead, there is a fixation on a more primitive phase of drive control through a narcissistically experienced "object." No object-directed rebellion against the father (or against the superego) is possible. The tongue becomes the battleground of preverbal rage in the service of a rebellion that has no differentiated object and is thus estranged from the child's ego. The success of Dr. Bonnard's therapeutic work may be partly due to the fact that her attention to the child's tongue movements helps him to establish ownership and mastery of this organ.]

returning home late even by one or two minutes—that the patient had considered a serious misdeed and had punished severely.

In both of the preceding examples I restricted myself to presenting a sequence of clinical events demonstrating how narcissistic rage subsides (and is gradually replaced by aggressions that are under the control of the ego) in consequence of the analytically achieved transformation of the narcissistic matrix from which it arises. The first example (Mr. A.) illustrates how the patient's sarcastic rage gradually became tamed and how his empathy for the targets of his rage increased as his neediness vis-à-vis the idealized object diminished. The second example (Mr. P.) illustrates how the patient's moralistic punitiveness gradually became tamed and how his empathy with the victim of his rage increased as he began to master his narcissistic involvement with alter-ego figures and grasped the fact that he was repeating a crucial situation from his own childhood.

Therapeutic Implications. I have now reached a point at which the convergence of clinical experience and theoretical reflection permits me to summarize and to restate certain conclusions. Our therapeutic aim with regard to narcissistic rage is neither the direct transformation of the rage into constructive aggression nor the direct establishment of controls over the rage by the autonomous ego. Our principal goal is the gradual transformation of the narcissistic matrix from which the rage arises. If this objective is reached, the aggressions in the narcissistic sector of the personality will be employed in the service of the realistic ambitions and purposes of a securely established self and in the service of the cherished ideals and goals of a superego that has taken over the function of the archaic omnipotent object and has become independent from it.

It must be admitted that in practice, e.g., at the end of a generally successful analysis of a narcissistic personality disturbance, it is not always easy to assess to what extent the propensity for narcissistic rage has been overcome, not always easy to know whether the aggressions are now the activities of a mature self and are under the dominance of the ego. But, as is true in general with regard to the completion of the analytic task in other sectors of the personality, so also here: we must make no excessive demands on our patients or on ourselves. On the contrary, the patient should openly face the fact that there exists in him a residual propensity to be temporarily under the sway of narcissistic rage when his archaic narcissistic expectations are frustrated and that he must be alert to the possibility that he might be overtaken by a tantrum. Such squarely faced awareness of the existence of residual psychopathology will stand the patient in good stead when after the termination of the analysis he has to tend his psychological household without the aid of the analyst.[13]

The persistence of some subtle and seemingly peripheral manifestations of psychic malfunctioning is sometimes more dependable evidence of the incompleteness of the analytic work than the occasional recurrence of gross behavioral disturbance under stress. In the area of our scrutiny, in particular, we can say that the subtle manifestations of the persistence of a patient's inability to mobilize even a modicum of empathy and compassion for the person who is the target of his anger, and his arrogant and rigid refusal even to try to consider the other's position or motivations, are a more reliable indication that the analytic work in the narcissistic sec-

[13] I am here advocating the taking of an attitude of tolerance vis-à-vis a relationship between ego and id that is neither one of ego autonomy nor of ego dominance—i.e., that is less than optimal. The comparative evaluation implied in this context warrants a metapsychological elucidation. Ego autonomy is achieved when the ego can function without being disturbed by pressures from the depth. Ego dominance is achieved when the archaic forces have become integrated with the ego and when their power can be employed in accordance with the ego's purposes. When I speak acceptingly of a former patient's postanalytic attitude of alertness with regard to the

tor is unfinished than the conspicuous manifestations of his propensity to react occasionally — and under unusual stress — with the flare-up of the kind of rage which, before the analysis, had occurred frequently and in response to minor provocations. Patient P.'s unfeeling moralism toward his son, and the immovable dogmatism of his conviction that he was acting appropriately when meting out the punishments, demonstrated more clearly that his behavior was in essence motivated by narcissistic rage than did the severity of the penalties he imposed on the child. True enough, the penalties were disproportionate. (Unsurprisingly, they consisted mainly in the vindictive re-establishment of his narcissistic control in the form of the prolonged withdrawal from his son of such privileges as leaving the house, or in the boy's being banished to his room.) They were never inflicted, however, in an uncontrolled or in a sadistic manner.

A Metapsychological Formulation of Narcissistic Rage

The scrutiny of aggression as it is interrelated with the area of narcissism has, up to this point, been focused on the phenomenology of narcissistic rage and on the explanation of

---

possibility that he might be overtaken by an attack of narcissistic rage, I am endorsing a condition that is, according to strict definition of these terms, neither ego autonomy nor ego dominance (although it is closer to the former than to the latter state). I am here referring to the ego's surveillance of untamed archaic forces: of the ego's handling or manipulating them. Such a relationship between ego and id may be considered a tolerable imperfection if it concerns a narrow sector of the psyche, i.e., if, on the whole, a broad transformation in the area of the relevant psychopathology has taken place.

An analogy from another field may illustrate my meaning concerning the type of imperfection I have in mind. I once knew a man who had so many muscular tics and spasms (probably on an organic basis) that his volitional motility was severely interfered with. He had, however, learned to wait for an appropriate tic movement that he could exploit for the action he wanted to perform.

the matrix of archaic narcissism from which it arises. As my final task I shall now attempt to explain narcissistic rage in metapsychological terms — even though I know that metapsychology has fallen into disrepute and is considered by some to be hardly more than a sterile thought exercise.

In previous contributions (Kohut, 1966b, 1968, 1971) I provided a metapsychological formulation of the emotion of shame. I said that it develops under the following conditions. Exhibitionistic libido is mobilized and deployed for discharge in expectation of mirroring and approving responses either from the environment or — I spoke in this context of "shame *signals*" — from the idealized superego, i.e., from the internal structure that took over the approving functions from the archaic environment. If the expected response is not forthcoming, then the flow of the exhibitionistic libido becomes disturbed. Instead of a smooth suffusion of self and body-self with a warm glow of approved and echoed exhibitionistic libido, the discharge and deployment processes disintegrate. The unexpected noncooperation of the mirroring object creates a psychoeconomic imbalance which disrupts the ego's capacity to regulate the outpouring of the exhibitionistic cathexes. In consequence of its temporary paralysis, the ego, on the one hand, yields to the pressure of the exhibitionistic urge, while, on the other hand, it strives desperately to stop the flow. The exhibitionistic surface of the body-self, the skin, therefore shows, not the pleasant warmth of successful exhibitionism, but heat and blushing side by side with pallor.[14] It is this disorganized mixture of massive discharge (tension decrease) and blockage (tension increase) in the area of exhibitionistic libido that is experienced as shame.

---

[14] I am grateful to Dr. Milton Malev for bringing my attention to the following passage from the Babylonian Talmud (Epstein, 1962, p. 58B): "He who makes *pale* the face of his companion in public [i.e., embarrasses his companion], it is as if he had *spilled his blood*" (my italics). This statement not only predicates the intense painfulness of narcissistic injuries, it

Similar considerations apply to the experience of narcis-sistic rage. But while the essential disturbance underlying the experience of shame concerns the boundless *exhibitionism* of the grandiose self, the essential disturbance underlying rage relates to the *omnipotence* of this narcissistic structure. The grandiose self expects absolute control over a narcissistically experienced archaic environment. The appropriate mechan-isms — they belong to the aggression-control-power sector of the personality — are set in motion, in expectation of total dominance over the selfobject. When the environment fails to comply — be it the unempathic mother who does not respond to the child's wishes or the table leg that noncompliantly is in the way of the child's toe or an analogous unempathic archaic object in the world of a narcissistically fixated adult — then the formerly smoothly deployed forces become deranged. Paralleling the processes described with regard to shame, we see discharge and inhibition side by side or in rapid succession, except that here, as stated before, the un-derlying force is not the grandiose self's boundless exhibition-ism, i.e., its insistence on being admired, but its omnipo-tence, i.e., its insistence on the exercise of total control. It is the disorganized mixture of massive discharge (tension de-crease) and blockage (tension increase) in the area of unneu-tralized aggression, arising after the noncompliance of the ar-chaic selfobject, that is the metapsychological substratum of the manifestations and the experience of narcissistic rage.

Chronic Narcissistic Rage

If the rage does not subside, it may be added here, then the secondary processes tend to be pulled increasingly into the

---

also appears to take for granted that the physiological correlate of the painful experience is a derangement of the distribution of blood (pallor and blushing: "makes pale the face" and "spilled his blood") in the exhibi-tionistic surface of the body, especially in the skin of the face.

domain of the archaic aggressions seeking to re-establish control over a narcissistically experienced world. Conscious and preconscious ideation, particularly as it concerns the aims and goals of the personality, becomes more and more subservient to the pervasive rage. The ego, furthermore, increasingly surrenders its reasoning capacity to the task of rationalizing the persisting insistence on the limitlessness of the power of the grandiose self: it does not acknowledge the inherent limitations of the power of the self, but attributes its failures and weaknesses to the malevolence and corruption of the uncooperative archaic object. We are thus witnessing the gradual establishment of *chronic narcissistic rage*, one of the most pernicious afflictions of the human psyche—either in its still endogenous and preliminary form as grudge and spite, or, externalized and acted out in disconnected vengeful acts or in a cunningly plotted vendetta.[15]

Concluding Remarks

A number of the topics discussed in this essay, especially those taken up in the retrospective survey of my earlier work (i.e., on the libidinal investment of the self), were of necessity only sketchily formulated and need elaboration. But what I regret even more than the shortcomings of this condensed

---

[15] The relation between acute and chronic narcissistic rage in the area of the omnipotence of the grandiose self is paralleled by the relation between acute shame and chronic feelings of inferiority in the area of the exhibitionism of this narcissistic structure.

For completeness' sake it should also be mentioned here that narcissistic rage, especially in its chronic form, when it is blocked from being directed toward the selfobject (which is experienced as being outside the self or body-self), may shift its focus and aim at the self or at the body-self. The result in the first instance is self-destructive depression; the consequence in the second instance may be psychosomatic illness. It should be noted in this context that patient P. suffered not only from the manifestations of acute and chronic narcissistic rage, but also from a severe degree of hypertension.

presentation is that I was unable to demonstrate the application of my older formulations about narcissism and of the preceding considerations about narcissistic rage to group psychology, to the behavior of man in history.

I hope very much that further efforts in this area will prove to be fruitful. But this is for the future, and I would like to mention only this much. I have begun work proceeding in two directions. First, regarding the contribution which the understanding of narcissism can make to the understanding of the formation and cohesion of groups: particularly the fact that group cohesion is brought about and maintained not only by an ego ideal held in common by the members of the group (Freud, 1921) but also by their shared subject-bound grandiosity, i.e., by a shared grandiose self. Indeed, there are groups that are characterized by the fact that they are held together by this latter bond — crudely stated, by their shared ambitions rather than by their shared ideals. Secondly, the psychic life of groups, like that of individuals, shows regressive transformations in the narcissistic realm. When the deployment of higher forms of narcissism is interfered with (such as in the area of the grandiose self, through the blocking of acceptable outlets for national prestige; and in the area of the idealized parent imago, through the destruction of group values, e.g., religious values), then the narcissism of groups regresses, with deleterious consequences in the realm of group behavior. Such regressions become manifest particularly with regard to group aggression, which then takes on, overtly and covertly, the flavor of narcissistic rage in either its acute or, even more ominously, in its chronic form.

But this is work that still needs to be completed, even in its preliminary form, and I must resist the temptation of saying more about it at this point.

41

"On the Adolescent Process as a Transformation of the Self" by Ernest S. Wolf, John E. Gedo, and David M. Terman

DISCUSSION

The thesis developed by Drs. Wolf, Gedo, and Terman strikes me as correct, even though I am missing the psychoanalytic material that would corroborate the theories advanced.

What is the self, this continuum in time, this cohesive configuration in depth, the "I" of our perceptions, thoughts, and actions? We have two choices as we wish to define the self. We can make it a basic axiom of psychoanalytic theory: see it as the center of our being from which all initiative springs and where all experiences end. Some theorists — existentialists, certain psychoanalysts (e.g., Schafer, 1973) — do indeed make this choice. I do not, however, for two reasons. First, the postulate of a single, central self leads toward an elegant and simple theory of the mind — but also toward an abrogation of the importance of the unconscious. Second, this definition of the self is not derived from psychoanalytic material but from conscious experience; and it is introduced,

Presented at a meeting of the Chicago Psychoanalytic Society, May, 1972.

from the outside as it were, in order to create a rounded-out, cohesive theory of thought, perception, and action.

Even though the second choice—my choice—does not give us an equally elegant theory, I prefer to define the self as an abstraction derived from psychoanalytic experience, i.e., I see it as a content of the mind. As a result of this approach, we recognize the simultaneous existence of contradictory selves: of different selves of various degrees of stability and of various degrees of importance. There are conscious, preconscious, and unconscious selves; there are selves in the ego, the id, and the superego; and we may discover in some of our patients contradictory selves, side by side, in the same psychic agency. Among these selves, there is one that is most centrally located in the psyche; one that is experienced as basic, and is most resistant to change. I like to call this self the "nuclear self." It is composed of the derivatives of the "grandiose self" (i.e., the central self-assertive goals and purposes of the individual) and of the derivatives of the "idealized parent imago" (i.e., the central idealized values of the individual in the superego).

Now, what strikes me as correct about the thesis presented to us by Wolf, Gedo, and Terman is the claim that this nuclear self (in its self-assertive and in its idealistic dimensions) undergoes a significant test and, under favorable circumstances, a significant firming during adolescence. In other words, I think it is appropriate to stress that the impact of drive maturation in combination with changing social expectations (the task of functioning in accordance with the maturing drives; the task of accepting oneself as male or female; and the task of forming long-term goals and purposes and guiding ideals that are in harmony with the goal-directed aspirations of the self) puts the assertive aspects and the ideals of the self of the early adolescent in jeopardy. I also think it appropriate to stress that the transformation of the self—of its ambitions and ideals—reactivates old fears of self-disintegration. It is the pressure of these fears that prompts the adolescent to seek a variety of supports. The authors underline, rightly, I think, the importance certain peer relationships may have for the adolescent in this context. These peers may serve as alter egos and as confirming reflections and extensions of the endangered self; they may provide increased security through contact with sameness; may increase the feeling of cohesion through the maintenance of empathic contact with identical others and, in particular, through sharing the same ideals.

I was in my own adolescence a member of a secret society, and I know that certain features of my adult personality are derived from these experiences. I am thinking here of a characteristic idealism I have: on the one hand (on the negative side), I am at times prone to become a bit of a pollyanna; on the other hand (on the positive side) I have not only the capacity to be enthusiastic myself, but also the ability to inspire enthusiasm in others for the causes in which I believe. Here, then, are features that belong to my nuclear self as it became shaped and firmed during adolescence. But I know that I also harbor other selves, which are in contradiction not only to the one I alluded to, but also with each other, and, furthermore, that the conscious and preconscious aspects of this "idealistic" self of which I spoke are only the surface of a psychic sector that dips deeply into the unconscious—in other words, I know that my adolescent idealism has precursors in my childhood and infancy. I also know that this adolescent self—which was firmed in specific turmoils of my adolescence with the aid of a secret society of alter egos—that this self is now gradually changing. The influence of aging (and with it the inescapable necessity of facing the reality of the final dissolution of individual existence) is producing a shift. There is less enthusiasm in me now (and less Pollyanna) and more concern for the continuity (i.e., for the survival) of the values for which I have lived.

Be that as it may, the point I wish to make is that even the *nuclear* self changes and that, under the impact of new internal and external factors, the task of reforming the self is repeatedly imposed on us, and may evoke in us, temporarily, old fragmentation fears until a new self is again firmly established.

But to return to adolescence. Are we seeing sexual drives and defenses against them during this period of transition, or the vicissitudes of the self? I don't think that we should expect to see either the one or the other, but both. To be more exact: I think it is fruitful to examine adolescence from both points of view. We will then find that in certain adolescents the conflict about sex (the resurgence of incestuous sexuality) is paramount, while in others the danger of the dissolution of the self (the reactivation of earlier fragmentation fears) is the main problem. I have tried to outline, in earlier contributions (Kohut, 1971) how one goes about this differentiation. Here I would only like to say, on the side of the authors, that not everything that looks like sex is sex. That beautiful movie, *The Last Picture Show*, for example, is indeed filled with the sexual activities of adolescents. But there is little joy or significance in their sex. Intercourse for them, I felt, was not an exhilarating goal, sought by them despite anxiety and conflict, but an escape from dreariness and depression. There are only two positive, nondepressive features in the life of the adolescents of this town—the friendship between two adolescents and the concern for young people by one older man. What lies behind the emptiness, the depletion of all these adolescent selves? The oedipal rejection? The victory of the father over the son? Or is the implication, as I think likely, that there is parental disinterest in the younger generation, and that the whole dying town, the dying society of the town, is a symbol for the unresponsiveness, the unempathic self-absorption of the parents.

42

The Future of Psychoanalysis

I have spoken on many festive occasions but never on one that focused on me. It is a strange experience. I feel that I cannot do wrong, since you are willing today to forgive me my shortcomings; nor can I do right, since, measured by what I can achieve in reality, your expectations are undoubtedly too high. But I shall not worry and shall let my thoughts flow — not unchecked, of course, but also, as befits the mood of the occasion, without the rigor and caution I would usually be inclined to apply.

I shall begin with two personal stories. The first is no more than an anecdote with easily graspable meaning. The second, however, although the account of a real event, has taken on the coloring of a private myth. It has become interwoven with those elements in me that transcend the personal: the goals and ideals — *our* goals and ideals — to which I have increasingly devoted my life.

Here is the anecdote, and you will have no trouble understanding how it relates to the present moment. Sixteen years ago I returned for the first time to Vienna, the city where I was born and raised, and which I had left nearly two decades before. I was with my wife and my then seven-year-old son. Among the people there whom I had not seen for all those

Presented at a banquet honoring Kohut on his sixtieth birthday, May, 1973. A Symposium on Psychoanalysis and History preceded the banquet. This essay was first published in *The Annual of Psychoanalysis* (1973), 3:325-340. New York: International Universities Press.

years was an old uncle who was a man of considerable influence. On the day before we were to leave, this uncle suddenly
expressed the wish, probably in anticipation of his
death — which indeed occurred not long after our departure
— to make a gift to my son. That evening we joined him for
dinner, after which he took us to the largest toy store in town,
Muehlhauser's — the F.A.O. Schwarz of Vienna — a large establishment with several floors of toys. It was nine o'clock in
the evening: the store — as do all stores in Vienna — had closed
at six, but because of my uncle's political influence, I suppose, a phone call had summoned the management.
Somebody was waiting, let us in, locked the doors behind us,
and turned on the lights; and we were there all by ourselves.
My uncle looked at my son, who was gazing at his surroundings with big eyes, and said: "You may have anything here
you like." At first my son was speechless and paralyzed. But
some prompting from the attending manager of the store
loosened him up, and we found ourselves upstairs in the section where the electric trains were soon circling around their
various complex tracks. And then the balance began to shift.
"Can I really have everything?" my son asked. "Yes, everything!" So, hesitatingly at first, but in ever quickening succession, he began to point at various items in the display. This?
he asked. Yes, of course! And this? and this? Of course. Then
give me this! he ordered. Yes. And this! he commanded. The
clerk who accompanied the manager took his orders and, one
by one, put things away into boxes — engines, cars, stop signs;
bridges, houses, mountains — just as fast as my son's demands
were expressed. I saw my son's face becoming flushed with
excitement; a dream was coming true, the world of limitations and reality was giving way. The old uncle, the manager,
the clerk, all watched — for different reasons — the spectacle
with glee. But I became more and more uncomfortable, and
finally I said, softly but firmly, "I think that we have now
enough."

This evening, here, on the occasion of the meeting, conceived by Dr. Ernest Wolf, with which you are honoring me,
receiving a beautiful gift from the candidates at the Institute,
learning that a great university is bestowing an honorary
degree on me, hearing John Gedo's review and generous
evaluation of my work, seeing and enjoying the presence of
this gathering, which includes some of the finest minds of
modern psychoanalysis, I feel that it is *I* who need a father to
tap me on the shoulder and tell me: Wake up! Enough!

I do not have such a father any more and for a lifetime
have had to be, as all of us must be, my own father when I
am in danger of overstimulation; I have to set my own limits
and curb the onrush of painful excitement by my own
devices. The father that I have set up in myself, that internal
ally who helps me maintain the integrity of myself under psychologically trying circumstances, has taught me, from way
back in my life, to turn to reflection, to the search for meanings and explanations. And I have learned that the enjoyment
of these mental activities must often take the place of the direct gratifications that are hard to keep in bounds. And, increasingly, and with changing emphasis in the course of my
life, these thoughts and reflections have become attempts to
understand myself, to understand other individuals, and also,
most recently though tentatively and with great caution, to
understand man as he feels, reacts, behaves in the arena of
history.

And here comes the second memory, to which I referred
earlier as a personal myth. It is the memory of the only time I
saw Freud—that symbol of the father, that embodiment of
the curbing and explaining efforts of which I spoke. It was a
moment that was the low point of my life, yet also, in its propelling power, a high point—the wellspring of the most important commitments of my future. It was in 1938 when, on a
sunny day in Vienna, I went to the railroad station because I
had learned that Freud was going to leave our city. I cannot

tell you the story, because there is no story to be told. I was a young man; the world that I had known, the culture in which I had grown up, had crumbled — there was nothing to hold on to. Yet, here was the symbolic event: an old man was leaving the city of my parents, and I, a young man, was tipping my hat as the train took him away.

I shall not dwell any longer on the personal. Just as that moment at the railroad station became the germinal point for my professional and scientific future, just as it turned me, over the years, from efforts concerning myself to the attempt to help others and to make contributions to science, so shall I now, having touched on this pivotal moment in my life, turn toward general reflections, in particular concerning that great content of my life, of the lives of so many of us here: the science of psychoanalysis, the psychology of the depths of the human soul. The question to which I shall address myself this evening concerns not the value or the validity of the contributions made so far by individual psychoanalysts, not even the significance of the immense oeuvre of Freud, but the *vitality* of psychoanalysis — in other words, I shall address myself to the question of its future.

Festive occasions frequently engender a cheap optimism: impermanence and insignificance are denied, and a prosperous future is cheerily predicted. Or such occasions may provide a forum for cheap pessimism, for the Jeremian outcry of the aged who proclaim the inevitable decline and fall of everything — a forum for those, in other words, who predict that the younger generation, and all who will follow them, will fail. I hope to avoid both of these positions as I evaluate the future of psychoanalysis.

Let me begin by stating a conclusion first. Contrary to the opinion of a number of thoughtful colleagues, I have become convinced that, judging by *intrinsic* factors, analysis has great potentialities, that this science, this new and pioneering foray into the hitherto unexplored, not only has a future but also is still quite young, that our present analytic investigations do not yet penetrate very far beneath the surface. Yet, I must add to this seemingly overoptimistic credo that I believe that psychoanalysis will, before long, be exposed to the potentially most significant moment of its early internal development: the moment when there will be no more analysts who have come under the direct influence of Freud and his charisma — even in a brief glance at a railroad station.

What I am speaking about is the moment when Freud who, as an archaic image is still living on concretely in those who serve as substitutes for him, will die a second time, i.e., will finally die. I am speaking of the moment when the community of analysts will realize that they have not inherited an identification, goal-setting as well as curbing, but have been given the legacy of an opened door, allowing entry into the vast unexplored area into which the first explorers could make only a few halting steps.

The realization of the death of the father, of the disappearance of an idealized figure, can have two results. It can bring about rebellious destruction: after discarding the father's values and goals, the new generation then turns away from the labors that were imposed by the idealized figure's goal-setting demands. Or it can bring about a surge of independent initiative: after the integration of the father's values and goals has been accomplished, the youthful minds of the new generation penetrate further into the regions that the ancestral efforts had made accessible.

It is my prediction, then, that psychoanalysis is not far from an important point in its development. At that point, it will be decided whether a critical developmental task will be avoided or whether it will be engaged. In the first case, analysis will enter a period in which it will restrict itself to continuing its careful codification and systematization of the already explored, and will then die. In the second case, it will enter a more or less prolonged period of questioning its past, of struggling against the temptation of rebelliously discarding its inheritance, followed by the examination of daring new paths into new territories. This will be a period of great danger, of excited battles and debates — but analysis will have a chance to emerge from it, to go on to live and to thrive.

The future generation of psychoanalysts will have to accomplish two specific tasks before it can mobilize the creative initiative and, secondarily, the resources of talent that will enable it to move more deeply into the territory of man's psychological experiences. I have already mentioned the first of these two tasks. It is the full integration of the inherited value system that now guides us. This task includes not only those comparatively minor though by no means insignificant modifications achieved through separating the wheat from the chaff, the essential from the unessential, but also the correlated undoing of certain regressive changes in the ideals that have brought about compliance that is not based on the comprehension of the meaning of the inner demand — ritualistic obedience to the letter rather than to the spirit of the inner command. The second task is the re-evaluation of the inherited value system itself and even, if necessary, its substantial transformation, in order to bring it into harmony with the character of the new generation and to make it relevant to the problems and tasks with which the new generation will be confronted by the surroundings in which it will live. About the first task I can speak with assurance; about the second, however, only tentatively, because the validity of my statements here depends on the validity of certain predictions about the nature of the future environment, specifically, about the nature of the psychological environment in which the man of tomorrow will live.

What is the essence of the present value system of the psychoanalyst? Does it require further integration? Has it undergone regressive changes that need to be reversed?

The highest ideal of the psychoanalyst is his commitment

to truth. Specifically, he strives to see psychological reality clearly and realistically, to unmask and discard the illusions and falsifications that arise in consequence of wish-fulfilling tendencies in himself and in those he wants to help. These tasks are the essence. The rest are instrumentalities in the service of the search for unembellished and unmitigated psychological truth. The uncovering of the repressed with the aid of free associations and dream analysis; the use of the couch, of daily interviews, on the one hand; the tolerance, for tactical reasons, for the temporary maintenance of illusions, on the other hand—all are, despite their importance, tools in the service of the principal ideal: to expand the realm of awareness, to establish what is fact and what is fancy with regard to man's psychological life.

What are the obstacles in the path that leads to this ideal? I shall not take up here those extensively studied dynamics of psychic life—the defenses and resistances—that stand in the way of living up to the ideal, but shall address myself to the problem of the integration of the ideal itself.

For a number of reasons, I have on this occasion avoided technicalities, particularly the use of technical terms. But it is clear to those who are familiar with my work that I am speaking here of the process that in the treatment situation I call transmuting internalization. Certain patients who as children were deprived of the opportunity to merge themselves psychologically into a powerful figure in their environment, who were deprived of the security of feeling themselves a part of such a person, will during analysis attempt to accomplish a psychological task that was not completed in childhood. Although such a patient will begin by identifying himself with the gross and manifest features of the admired therapist, he will go on, if the process is not interfered with, to discover, little by little, the therapist's realistic shortcomings. In so doing, as he is discarding his relationship to an illusionary idealized person, he is strengthening certain structures in his own

personality that had been laid down insufficiently, particularly in the area of his guiding values and ideals. The ultimate
result of this process is not the incorporation of the *analyst's*
values and ideals, but the idealization of standards that are in
harmony with the *analysand's* personality and relevant to the
tasks with which *he* is confronted in his *own* life.

The coming generation of psychoanalysts will similarly
have the opportunity to divest its image of Freud of certain
specific features that have remained concrete, and thus to
achieve a genuine integration and strengthening of its ideals.
The replacement of a concretely experienced archaic object
by a strong set of ideals and values, furthermore, is likely to
be followed by a surge of independent initiative, which in the
case of the scientist may lead to renewed scientific advances.

What are the features that are likely to prove genuine in
the analyst's ideals, and what will be discarded as bound to
Freud's personality (his idiosyncrasies, as it were); to the atmosphere that surrounds a period of pioneering discoveries;
and to the historicocultural environment in which Freud and
his collaborators lived and worked?

Although I am here predicting that a future generation of
analysts will not retain a number of their presently held ideals
derived from Freud when they have ultimately formed
ideals that have become truly their own, the consideration of
this possibility does not mean that my admiration for Freud's
personality and genius has lessened.

Let us, for example, examine Freud's (1912b) advice that
analysts should "model themselves during psycho-analytic
treatment on the surgeon, who puts aside all his feelings, even
his human sympathy" (p. 115). Let me say first that, while I
know that Freud's actual behavior toward his patients could
indeed be full of human warmth, I have little doubt that the
emotional reserve expressed in the quoted statement was in
harmony with an integral part of his particular personality. I
am convinced, furthermore, that Freud's injunction was quite

appropriate at the time it was given—a time when the effect
on the analysts' psyche of the prolonged exposure to the
childhood passions of their analysands had not yet been tested
and when the danger of overinvolvement and irrational response must have required emotional detachment as a pro-
tective shield. Still, even though I am thus of the opinion that
Freud's advice was more determined by his personal needs
and by time-bound factors than he was able to recognize, and
that the analyst of today or tomorrow need not continue to
idealize an attitude that may not be in harmony with *his*
personality—an attitude, furthermore, that is no longer required in our day when the growing familiarity with our
subject matter enables us to be indeed much more relaxed
than was possible for the analysts of the early days—this
opinion does not diminish my admiration for Freud.

Or, to give another example, let us assume that—perhaps
in reaction to having been duped in childhood, or in reaction
to being exposed to humiliations from the very society that
claimed to be guided by the ideal of love for the fellow
man—let us assume that such experiences prompted Freud to
demonstrate that man's religion-building capacity was deleterious and that its creations had to be rejected as nursemaids' tales (1927a). Or consider the following statement,
which is in a similar vein: "If I had another life of work
ahead of me," he wrote in 1936 (concerning what he called
"such distinguished guests as religion, art, and others"), "I
would dare to offer even those high-born people a home in
my lonely hut" (E. L. Freud, 1960, p. 431). If it could be established that there was a genetic connection between, on the
one hand, Freud's capacity to dissect the great values of man
and to determine their derivation from the primitive and
archaic in the human soul and, on the other hand, his
growing up as a member of a minority group surrounded by
the values of a majority which, despite professing high beliefs
of kindness and love, humiliated and persecuted him and

those with whom he identified, such a discovery would neither diminish Freud's human or scientific stature nor could it be used as an argument against the validity of his conclusions. Yet, if the analyst of the future, or if this or that analyst now, does not share Freud's emphasis on the unmasking of, let us say, religious values, I see no reason why he should feel either disloyal to Freud or unfaithful to the scientific tenets of psychoanalysis.

Or, as a final example, take Freud's touching admission concerning his attitude toward the insane ". . . that I do not care for these patients, that they annoy me, and that I find them alien to me and to everything human" (Schur, 1966, p. 21). What exemplary openness he showed here about this trait in his personality, especially when it is viewed against the background of the profound explanations of serious mental disorders that he had given to the world, in spite — or perhaps even because? — of his need to keep an emotional distance from the psychotic mind (cf. Eissler, 1971, pp. 318-320). And yet, I have no hesitations in adding that this specific attitude does not belong to the intrinsic value system of the analyst, and that even its current remote derivatives — such as the occasionally encountered insistence that therapeutic techniques involving empathic responsiveness toward archaic mental states must not be called psychoanalysis — may well be discarded by the analyst of the future, who will not be afraid that every move into new territory exposes him to the danger of the irretrievable loss of his professional identity.

As I mentioned earlier, the task of integrating an ideal and our attitude toward it not only requires the discarding of the concrete features of the ideal that belong to its precursor, the idealized person, and to our relation with him, it also involves the undoing of certain regressive changes — the reversal of the regressive development from idealized value to archaic command, from living according to the spirit of the ideal to the ritualistic and often fanatically pursued observation of accessory formalities.

The regression of values is a historicopsychological fact that can be easily observed. And I believe, by the way, that here is one of the many areas to which only the historian trained in depth psychology and the depth psychologist trained in history, if they have achieved a synthesis of the points of view and of the operations of the two disciplines, can address themselves with the hope of achieving a thorough grasp of the phenomenon. Values, like people, are subject to developmental changes. They are most attractive in their early prime — not perhaps when they have just been created, but not long thereafter. They are youthful then, carried with enthusiasm, and, while already purified of the excited intolerance that, at the beginning, accompanied the overcoming of the former oppressors in the heated battles of the revolutionaries, they are imbued with the glow of a meaning that is still in contact with the pressing task of reform to which they are related. The liberators of yesterday, however, may become the oppressors of tomorrow. And their values, too, may undergo a change. The content of the values remains the same, but instead of being beacons of progress they now become the code of the narrow-minded and, finally, the rationalizations of a new tyranny.

These considerations apply, not only to the historical development from national, social, and political liberation to a renewed tyranny, but also to the development of a science. Indeed, I believe that the exhaustion of the vitality of some sciences is related more to such psychological factors, manifested in a curve from excited discovery over status-preserving professionalism to extinction, than to such abstract cognitive issues as the obsolescence of a paradigm (Kuhn, 1962) and the like. Or, in still different terms, one might say that a science grows older in proportion to the shift of its emphasis from the *field* it investigates to the specific *tools* it employs in investigating it.

Why is it, for example, that so few members of the faculties of the history departments of our great universities are here today? Why have they not come to find out what the psychology of the depths of the human soul may have to offer to them? I believe I can discern at least one strand in the complex weave of their reasons for staying away. It is related to the pride of the historian in a specific brand of vision and, in the obverse, to the contempt for the different tools employed by the psychoanalyst's perception. Professor Schorske, who understands me well, when I posed this question to him, responded in a fine formulation. "I am sure you must know," he said, "that the problem of a confining idealization applies in any intellectual discipline, surely in the field of history." Yes, I do know. And I am grateful to be able to quote him, rather than be required to talk about my own field, where I would have no trouble in demonstrating the presence of similar trends.

But having spoken of the need for the next generation to integrate its ideals and free them from impurities, let me now focus attention on the examination of a specific creative endeavor that the next generation will be able to undertake once the consolidation and purification of its value system has been accomplished: the re-evaluation of the basic values themselves, not just their integration and modification.

To change one's values is a staggering psychological task. And to advocate such a change, perhaps even to predict that such a change might come about, is likely to expose the advocate, perhaps even the cautious predictor, to the anger of those whose values seem to be under attack.

Why should it be so hard to change one's values? Although I cannot speak at length about my own views on the psychology of values and ideals this evening, a few general remarks are indispensable before I can turn to my specific prediction.

Our values and ideals occupy the position in our psyche that in the beginning of our lives was held by the idealized omnipotent adult who, on the one hand, towered above us but into whom we, on the other hand, merged ourselves and whose power we then experienced as our own. Our values and ideals have retained the qualities of absoluteness, unmodifiability, and supremacy that characterized the idealized selfobject; and questioning them, suggesting that they can be changed, appears to deprive us of this all-powerful part of ourselves — a threat to which we react with indignation and with the tendency to fight. Still, values do change, and the ability to change them is surely compatible with mental health. On the other hand, it is one of the characteristic features of average mental health that *some* values exist at any given point in time that we *experience* as being absolute and unchangeable.

I should like to emphasize another rule concerning the general psychology of values. What we identify as our values and ideals relates to psychological patterns that are not yet established with complete firmness — despite the paradoxical fact that we experience the content of these values and ideals as absolute and unchangeable. Values and ideals, in other words, are psychological structures that guide us toward certain goals even though we still harbor some reluctance to do their bidding. Values can therefore have two fates. Their content can change, i.e., they can be replaced by new values; or they can disappear. They disappear if our reluctance to live in accordance with them ceases. They have then become ego functions, a content of the ego. It is in this sense that we should understand one of Freud's favorite quotations, F. T. Vischer's saying, *"Das Moralische versteht sich von selbst"*: what is moral goes without saying, requires no effort, or, with Jones (1955, p. 416), "is self-evident."

And now a final general remark. It is instructive to observe the emotions that accompany the change and the disappearance of our values and ideals. A change in values and ideals, especially when they begin to give way under the pressure of a different set of values of greater vitality, is first reacted to with rage, with the furious resolve to preserve the prized internalized selfobject at all costs. But, once the old ideal has been replaced by the new one, the new one is now held to be as perfect and absolute as had been its predecessor. (In the historical arena, analogous phenomena can be observed in wars of religion and other ideological clashes.) In the second case, however, i.e., when values disappear and become ego functions, there is no rage, but rather a subtle sadness— a melancholy at the loss of a long-term protector and leader.

But now I must leave generalities behind and reveal the specific change in the hierarchy of values that will, I believe, occur in psychoanalysis. The full integration of his ideals may allow the analyst of the coming generation to become the pacesetter for a change in the hierarchy of values of all the branches of science concerned with man, through a shift of emphasis from a truth-and-reality morality toward the idealization of empathy, from pride in clear vision and uncompromising rationality to pride in the scientifically controlled expansion of the self.

I admit to feeling almost defenseless when I now imagine the reactions that my prediction will evoke from two sides. Defenseless vis-à-vis those who will immediately reject it on the grounds that I am advocating or welcoming a regressive development from science to kindly sentimentality, and even more defenseless vis-à-vis those who will immediately tend to accept it with enthusiasm on the basis of the mistaken notion that the pious injunction "love thy neighbor as thyself" will again come in the ascendancy, although now in a scientific guise.

In addition, since I can foresee that my hypothesis will quickly be drawn into the ingrained emotional dialectic of maleness versus femaleness, of paternal versus maternal attitudes, I hasten to stress my conviction that empathy is not a sex-linked capacity. It is a broad, autonomous mental function, present in all human beings, present at every level of development — from the baby's first instinctive enmeshment with his human surroundings to those rigorously controlled mental processes that supply the primary data of observation to any science of complex psychological states.

My prediction, as I shall try to demonstrate, is based on careful observation and sober reflection. The facts on which my conclusion rests were not only obtained during decades of clinical work with adults, but were also derived from observing the young, specifically the questioning attitude taken by many of the young people of today toward our value system, toward that seemingly absolute and unchangeable value system that was implanted in us as the quintessence of the scientific ideal of the nineteenth and twentieth centuries — in our case transmitted to us via beliefs held by Freud. And lastly, I also took into account my impression that the psychological tasks the coming generations will have to face will be different from ours because the sociocultural milieu in which they will live will be different.

I have already mentioned the deleterious *intra*professional effect of tool-and-method pride: it de-emphasizes discovery, it emphasizes formal refinement and conservatism. And I have also spoken of the deleterious *inter*professional effect of tool-and-method snobbishness: the wasteful isolation from one another of the various branches of science. These two losses, however, seem to me to be of lesser importance and more easily opposed or remedied than yet another one. Modern scientists, by their pride in the perfection of their operations and in the exactness of their conceptual and technological framework, have not only become isolated from the community at large, but — an especially regrettable, an ominous development — their activities are increasingly experienced as irrelevant by some of the most committed and searching minds of the younger generation. And indeed, if we survey the grave, the ominous events that have been shaping man's historical destiny during this century, the scientist can hardly see himself as having been more than a dehumanized technician, *internally* helpless, with his ingrained tool-and-method pride, to relate in depth to the crucial issues of our times. Will it be the psychoanalyst who will here lead the way? Will it be the example of psychoanalysis that will demonstrate to the other branches of science that the use of tools and methods involves no more than the employment of ego functions? The analyst, as does every man of science, has, of course, the right to enjoy the exercise of his abilities and skills to the fullest, but there is no need for the idealization of these functions. I believe that once we relinquish the idealization of our tools and methods, the exhilarating expansion of the self, a new kind of humanitarianism in the form of a scientific empathy, will gain ascendancy.

Empathy is, I am convinced, not just a poor relation of those other forms of cognition that we hold in high esteem because we consider them functions of our prized intellect. Empathic modes of perceiving ourselves and our surroundings exist from the beginning of our lives side by side with other, nonempathic, modes of perception. And empathy, as holds true for nonempathic cognition, has its own line of development, can be trained, refined, and employed with scientific rigor. Psychoanalysis is par excellence the science of empathy, of that "mechanism," as Freud (1921) said, "by means of which we are enabled to take up any attitude at all towards another mental life" (p. 110n). As a newcomer to nineteenth-century science, psychoanalysis has always felt methodologically insecure in comparison with the established sciences. And we have underplayed or hidden our reliance on empathy, have been ashamed of it as not scientific. I believe that the psychoanalyst of the future, if he can become unashamedly proud of his stance of scientific empathy, will be able to provide all the sciences of man with that common ideal—an organizing principle of their various specialized activities — for which they will have an increasing need in the world of tomorrow.

What was the world of yesterday in which psychoanalysis was born? What will be the world of tomorrow to which psychoanalysis may yet make its weightiest contributions?

The world of yesterday (which seems to those of us who are of middle age and beyond to be the world of today) was still the world of the individual — a world descended from the Renaissance. It was the world of the independent mind — of the proud scientist: standing tall, clear-sighted. And it was also the world of intense interrelationships between clearly defined people. It was a world that exposed the child to over-stimulation by involving him in the emotions and conflicts of the adults who surrounded him, exposing him to a degree of participating excitation and temptation that his psyche was not yet ready to handle. This was the time when psychoanalysis was born. It gathered its data through the activities of the nineteenth-century scientist, proud of his intellectual clarity, eager to distance himself from a demimonde of sentimental fuzziness, of tenderhearted perception. And it set about investigating the personalities and lives — whether in terms of psychopathology or in terms of normal variation — that had been formed in consequence of the exposure to the clashes of clearly delimited individuals and of families and groups made up of clearly delimited, of strongly — perhaps too strongly — interrelated people. This is the matrix of analysis as we know it from our literature and as we still tend to view it today.

The world of tomorrow, however, is not likely to be the same. Changes are not abrupt, of course, and just as the older generation sees only the yesterday in the today, so may the younger generation see only the tomorrow as significant and overlook the potent remnant of a past whose influence is still felt everywhere. What will be the sociopsychological essence of the world of tomorrow? Will it remain a world of individuals as was the world of yesterday? Will the children and grownups of tomorrow's world continue to confront the problems of overinvolvement and overstimulation—of traumatic interpersonal conflicts that have become endopsychic? For the answer to these questions, I turn to the prophets of all psychocultural tomorrows, the great artists, poets, and writers. They are no longer dealing with the problems of psychological man as we have known him; indeed, they seem strangely unpsychological to us so long as we remain walled off from the problems of tomorrow's world. I will not call as my witnesses the most profound prophets of this tomorrow— the musicians of atonal sound, the sculptors of disjointed form, the painters of disintegrated line and color, the poets of decomposed language—who in their work are demonstrating the breakup of the unresponded self and its artistic reassemblage. I will instead turn to a writer whose message, perhaps because his genius was not quite of the order of the greatest in those other fields, may therefore speak more clearly to our average minds. I ask you to think of the writings of Franz Kafka, in particular of *Metamorphosis, The Trial,* and *The Castle.*

Mr. K. is Everyman, the Everyman of a tomorrow that, I believe, is already discernible today. He is the Everyman who had been exposed to the unempathic indifference of his family and who has therefore remained grotesquely grandiose and thus estranged from the world. And he is the Everyman who feels that society, too, that latter-day extension of the family, is indifferent to him and who therefore wanders through the world, empty, flat, yearning for something he can no longer understand because the part of himself that once was eager to demand welcoming empathy and empathic response has long been buried and has ceased to be available to him. The cold voices of the family speak of him as the cockroach, in the impersonal third pronoun, and to the unreachable judges of the trial and to the unreachable rulers high up in the castle he has become a number, rejected without even an attempt to justify his rejection in individual terms.

Is this truly the world of tomorrow? Yes and no. "No" if we understand this question in a literal sense, but "yes" if we attempt to focus with predictive empathy on the leading psychological problems the man of tomorrow will have to face — indeed is already today increasingly facing.

Most analysts will, I believe, agree with me that the forms of the psychic illnesses we are treating are changing, that, even though they might still be in the majority, we are seeing fewer people whose disorder is the result of unsolvable inner conflicts, and increasingly more who suffer from having been deprived of the give and take with a close and interested environment that would have enabled them to shed the asocial grandiosity of infancy and thus become self-confident and secure participants in a meaningful world of adults. But I do not have to evoke the specialized professional experiences of the analyst to make my point. Who has not felt a whiff of the cold anonymity of the Trial when he was caught as a patient in the wheels of a big impersonal hospital? Who has not stood anxiously in line somewhere, while somebody behind a desk was delaying his response to him, and was thus — for one terrible fraction of a second — demonstrating his power over him? I believe these indignities — although they have undoubtedly always existed — have now taken on an ominous symbolic flavor. They point to a future to which only a few of the greatest artists have begun to respond in depth.

What I am saying is that, in a world of stablized populations, of increasing uniformity, of lessened space to roam in, of mass movements and efficient totalitarianism, the individual will be confronted by new problems of psychological survival. A shift from the joys of action to the enriching potentialities of his inner life may well be one of his avenues of escape, as I have suggested in another context (Kohut, 1973).

The expansion of the self, its increasing capacity to embrace a greater number and a greater variety of others through a consciously renewed and cultivated deepened empathy may be a second one. And psychoanalysis appears to have emerged just at this crucial time to be man's scientific leader in both of these directions.

From the beginning of life, it is empathy, the psychological extension of an understanding human environment, that protects the infant from the encroachment of the inorganic world. And it is human empathy, as we mirror and confirm the other and as the other confirms and mirrors us, that buttresses an enclave of human meaning — of hate, love, triumph, and defeat — within a universe of senseless spaces and crazily racing stars. And, finally, it is with our last glance that we can yet retain, in the reflected melancholy of our parting, a sense of continuing life, of the survival of essential human sameness, and thus protection against the fallacy of pairing finiteness and death with meaninglessness and despair. This is an axiomatic belief, no more provable than the Hitlerian dogma that only eternal war and destruction are reality. And if I say that in the hierarchy of the values of science in general and of psychoanalysis in particular the primacy of empathy will be established, I cannot prove the validity of this future pre-eminence any more than one could prove that tool-and-method pride, the pride in clear vision and in the undistorted perception of reality deserve the crown.

I will stress once more that our unashamed commitment to the survival of human life, the commitment to contribute our share to the preservation of the vitality of a fulfilling human life, is not only compatible with scientific rigor, but that scientific rigor is indeed indispensable. True, a patient who had been overstimulated as a child will, despite his noisy love-demands, experience a calm, objective therapeutic atmosphere as basically wholesome and in the long run as a support during the task of raising his conflicts into awareness and solving them. And the emotionally undernourished patient will, despite his overt self-centered coldness, experience a positively toned atmosphere of nonrejecting empathy as being in the long run the appropriate medium for the performance of *his* therapeutic work. But these considerations concern only the emotional climate in which the therapeutic interactions take place, not the details of analytic technique and the dynamics of the cure. Analysts do not hold the simplistic view, for example, that people who suffer from early deprivations must now have them made up for by a belated therapeutic compensation. The image of the aging Ferenczi allowing his patients to sit on his knees, trying to provide them with the love of which they had been deprived in their childhood (Jones, 1957), does not represent our ideal. We are aware of the complexity of the results of early deprivation; but we do not encourage the therapeutic reemergence of childhood demands in order to give now what had been missing in the past so that their curbing and transformation can finally be achieved. The position of primacy in our hierarchy of values that will be attained by the ideal of achieving an ever broadening and deepening scientific empathy for the varieties and nuances of human experience relates, in other words, to a broad motivational context, not to a set of rules concerning methods and operations. Or, to express the same thought in still another way, our leading ideal will not be passionate truth-finding softened by humanitarian considerations but the empathic expansion of the self with the aid of scientifically trained cognition.

But I must come to a close. Despite the apparent complexity of my presentation, my argument was simple. I believe that psychoanalysis will in the not too distant future examine itself afresh, will reorganize its basic stance, will transmute its inheritance into new, creative initiative. And, because it is the science that reaches farthest into the breadth and depth of the human soul, I suggest that it will be the leader in the revolutionary undertaking of shifting the hierarchy of the values of the scientist of the future. Pride in clear vision and realism will turn into the nonconflictual enjoyment of *ego functions*. But scientific empathy, the broadening and strengthening of this bridge toward the other human being, will be the highest *ideal*. If the analyst will lead the sciences of tomorrow into this direction, he will most significantly have entered the decisive battle of the future: the struggle between the human world, a world in which the varieties of psychological experience are cherished, and a nonhuman world, the world foreseen by Kafka, whose regimentations and regularities resemble the inexorable laws that establish the organization of inorganic matter. We cannot predict how this battle will end or where the victory will ultimately lie. But we do know on which side the psychoanalyst must fight, upon which side psychoanalysis, this new sun among the sciences of man, will shed its understanding warmth and its explaining light.

43

The Psychoanalyst in the
Community of Scholars

As a psychoanalyst, I am accustomed to seeing the world
and its events as they are reflected in the experiences of the
individual. I am thus tempted to react to the honor bestowed
upon my work and myself by speaking in personal terms of
what the support of a great institution such as this University
has meant to the thinking, working, and creating self. The
moral support that institutions can provide for the lonesome
worker is indeed important. I feel, however, that the
significance of the occasion is not definable within the framework of individual psychology, and I have accordingly
decided on a subject for my talk more in keeping with the
deeper meaning of this day. The title of my essay, "The Psychoanalyst in the Community of Scholars," is therefore meant
to indicate that I have set my sights on a broad topic: I shall
examine the relationship of psychoanalysis to the university;
or, stated in more general terms, I will discuss some
problems of the integration of a new system of thought,
psychoanalysis, into the established body of the intellectual
life of our time as it is represented by our universities.

As all of us know, and as we seem to have accepted with
some resignation and without too many questions — although

First published in *The Annual of Psychoanalysis* (1973), 3:341-370.
New York: International Universities Press. This address was given at the
University of Cincinnati, November, 1973, in response to Kohut's receiving
the honorary degree of Doctor of Science.

we should be deeply disturbed and puzzled by the fact—psychoanalysis and the universities have on the whole not been on good terms. It remains illustrative of the lack of integration of analysis within the university that when Freud finally, after many delays, received his professor's title from the University of Vienna, it was given to him not for having taken some of the most daring steps in the intellectual history of modern times,[1] but for his solid, yet by no means world-shaking contributions to neurology and neuropathology.

It would be a worthy challenge for a skilled and unbiased historian to investigate the relationship between psychoanalysis and the universities, to identify the factors responsible for the attitudes of mutual suspiciousness and mutual contempt that are undoubtedly still prevalent and—how could he resist the temptation?—to evaluate which one of the two sides is to be blamed more for this unwholesome situation.

I am not a historian—unfortunately. If I had another life to live, I think I would try to become one because I am convinced that a new and revolutionary science of history is the logical next step, the natural development that ought to follow the revolutionary step Freud took with regard to the psychology of the individual. Being neither a trained historian of the traditional type nor, of course, that revolutionary historian of whom I like to dream, I must restrict myself here to a few comments. What is the explanation for the lack of integration of psychoanalysis within the mainstream of modern science?

---

[1] As I have stated in earlier communications, and as will become apparent again in the course of the present one, I believe that the crucial significance of Freud's contribution lies neither in his invention of the enormously fruitful methodology of psychoanalysis nor even in the vast number of psychological discoveries he was able to make with the aid of his new methods, but rather in his having created a science that allowed empirical conceptual access to a field which heretofore had been open only to the nonscientific responses of artists and writers, i.e., a science of the human soul in all its complexity.

It is frequently thought that common prejudice has played a role in blocking the way to the acceptance of Freud's work. "Rest assured," Freud wrote to a friend in 1908, "that, if my name were Oberhuber, . . . my innovations would have met with far less resistance" (Abraham and Freud, 1965, p. 46). Perhaps so — but I do not think that this sociological explanation is satisfactory. Prejudice may well have contributed to the delay in Freud's obtaining his professorship at the University of Vienna. But even had Freud been a member of the ethnic and religious majority in Austria, I believe that psychoanalysis as a body of science would still not have been accepted by his great alma mater. No, the narcissistic tensions aroused by differences in ancestry were not the essential difficulty. The contributions to the traditional branches of science made by numerous other scholars and scientists of Freud's religious extraction, whatever personal rejections they may have had to suffer, were after all accepted by the University of Vienna and became fully integrated into the body of knowledge that was recognized as valid science by its faculty. And if anyone still doubts the essential correctness of this view, I recommend that he read (in Rosenbaum, 1954) the touching correspondence between Freud and Hebrew University, that young representative of traditional scientific thought. Freud begins the correspondence hopefully — he speaks of "our university" in his first letter of October 16, 1933 — but in his final letter of December 5, 1933, he is referring coldly to "the University of Jerusalem" — with the same disappointment concerning the acceptance of psychoanalysis to which he had felt exposed throughout his life by almost all institutions of higher learning.

Another well-known explanation for the nonacceptance of psychoanalysis is derived from the analyst's experiences in individual psychotherapy; it is the claim that the rejection of analysis is due to "resistance." As you know, the term "resistance" refers to the fact that the confrontation with unconscious mental contents increases the repressive forces. Analysis confronts man—layman and scientist alike—with all those strivings within himself which he has painfully learned not to know; no wonder, then, that people in general and scientists in particular will reject a science that threatens the maintenance of the established repressions.

This is simple and persuasive reasoning; but I think it is no more adequate than the explanations based on social considerations. It would require a paper of its own to defend this assertion against the objections that could be raised at this point. Suffice it to say that the mechanism in question is undoubtedly frequently in evidence when people are for the first time confronted with specific psychoanalytic findings. And it would also not be difficult to point out certain individuals in whose case the loudly voiced and angry rejection of psychoanalysis does clearly rest on personal psychological dynamisms that are indeed akin to resistance. But I do not believe that the lack of integration of the body of knowledge accumulated by psychoanalysis into the scientific sectors of our civilization can be explained in this way. Psychoanalysis was, after all, created by man and is deeply understood by many people. Various aspects of analysis, furthermore—albeit highly selective ones—have found increasing acceptance inside and outside of science. Why, then, does the gap between analysis and the sciences still persist? Why is the bestowal of an honorary doctor-of-science degree upon an analyst *for his psychoanalytic work* still an event of some significance in 1973, more than seventy years after the publication of "The Interpretation of Dreams," more than ninety years after the first analytic observations (the case of Anna O.) were recorded (Breuer and Freud, 1893-1895, pp. 21-47)? No! Scientists with their (on the whole) greater than average ability to accept facts, whatever their emotional connotations, should be expected to have learned by now to make the necessary psychological adjustments and, within their strongly walled-off autonomous egos, to have furthered the work of the integration between psychoanalysis and the established scientific disciplines.

One of the profoundest explanations of the psychological forces that oppose the acceptance of analysis was given by Freud nearly sixty years ago. Put briefly, Freud (1917b) said that analysis—in particular its central claim of the existence of unconscious mental processes—tended to be rejected because it had made a discovery that offended man's delusional but tenaciously held conviction that he was master in his own psychological household. To paraphrase Freud's reasoning succinctly: his findings—like those of Copernicus and Darwin before him—constituted a narcissistic blow to people and they reacted with narcissistic anger in the form of attacks on psychoanalysis.

I have always had the greatest admiration for this deceptively simple essay by Freud, and I continue to hold his formulation in high regard. It is my conviction, however, that it refers to a factor that is in the long run no more decisive than the social and psychological forces of which I spoke earlier. All these explanations—and yet another one to which I will turn shortly—neglect the presence of counterforces, the creation of countercurrents if you will, that enable man through the use of a variety of psychological means to accept the seemingly unacceptable. It may be an unpleasant blow to our pride to realize that we don't live in the center of the world, that our earth is a negligible speck of dust in the universe—still, we all have managed to accept this fact without suffering from lowered self-esteem. It may be unpleasant to realize that we were not separately and uniquely created by God as the ultimate product of his creative ability, that mankind is at best a small link in the developmental chain of living matter. Still—disregarding the Monkey Trial—we all have managed to accept this aspect of reality as well and don't seem to be unduly depressed about it. Indeed, I believe that most people experience a distinct pride after having acknowledged the explanatory power of these theories: an enhanced feeling of well-being, a narcissistic increment, which is based on their having been able to rise above themselves through the action of their mind, to participate in a surpassing reality through the acceptance of a truth that has validity beyond the limits of their individual existence.

I must turn to yet another psychological impediment, which, in my opinion, accounts at least as much for the isolation of psychoanalysis among the sciences as do social bias, resistance against the repressed, and the rejection of the notion of an unconscious mind. It is a psychological constellation that is not only responsible for the gap separating psychoanalysis from the other sciences, but also tends to divide other branches of science from one another. I have called this divisive force tool-and-method pride, or tool-and-method snobbishness (Kohut, 1975a, p. 335).

I deliberately chose this descriptive term in the hope that it would be easily understood. It refers to the increasing esteem in which the specific methods developed by each branch of science in the pursuit of its goals tend to be held, to the awe, even, with which the devoted specialist ultimately looks up to the idealized methodology of his field. The characteristic mixture of pride in his technical and conceptual methodology and contempt toward the uninitiated, which the specialist tends to develop, leads not only to the isolation of the various branches of science from one another, but also to the internal rigidification of each branch of science and thus to its lessened vitality as it shifts its emphasis from the field being investigated to the specific means it has developed in order to explore it.

Although my remarks about this point must be brief, I do not want them to be simplistic. I know that sometimes means and ends cannot be neatly separated, that—as was certainly true for depth psychology—the discovery of a pioneering method can be the decisive step which opens a new field. I am not speaking against the importance of method, nor am I belittling methodology and specialized skills; I am only saying that they should not be idealized, that, in psychoanalytic terms, they should remain ego functions. The ability to master them to perfection should be enjoyed by the practitioner. If the attainment of technological mastery becomes the supreme ideal of any branch of science, however, then its creative spirit will be stifled and its survival will be in doubt.

This is a broad topic and one that I cannot pursue very far today. Let me call to mind, however, the moving and beautiful portrayal in Wagner's *Die Meistersinger* of the problems posed in this conflict and of the balanced human attitude their solution requires. The guild of the Meistersingers stifled the free expression of art by more and more rigidly applied rules. Yet, the greatest among them, Hans Sachs, not only retained his receptivity for a beautiful song even though it transcended the narrow rules, but also could simultaneously maintain the realization of the value of a conservative methodology. *"Verachtet mir die Meister nicht, und ehrt mir ihre Kunst!"* ("Do not hold the masters in contempt, but do revere their art!") he tells the creative rebel who feels that the tool-and-method pride of the established profession has left no room for his originality.

To return to my main line of thought, let me again express my conviction that there is little question that one of the barriers which has isolated psychoanalysis from the established branches of science has been tool-and-method pride; and that there is little question, furthermore, that the responsibility for the existence of this barrier is shared by both sides. I would also suggest that the increasing rapprochement between psychoanalysis and the established sciences is due to the fact that this particular wall is gradually being lowered through mutual adjustments. It is being lowered through the efforts made by some workers in the established sciences; by

experimental psychologists, for example, who are beginning
to treat the data collected by psychoanalysis with respect and
who are enriching their own research by focusing their attention on topics that have been made accessible to them by
analysis. And the barrier is also being lowered through the
effort of some psychoanalysts; by those, for example, who are
attempting to prove the correctness of some of the empirical
findings of psychoanalysis with the aid of the traditional
methods of science, specifically, through the methods of
statistical evidence.

I have now reached a turning point in my reflections.
Having examined a number of factors that might explain the
lack of a full integration of psychoanalysis with the established sciences, and having come to the conclusion that none
of them, alone or in combination with the others, can account for the relative exclusion of the psychoanalyst from the
community of scholars, I now turn to features of psychoanalysis that are indeed responsible for its continuing isolation.
Instead of addressing this crucial issue directly, let me first
consider an important question that might be raised at this
point.

Is it really true that analysis is not accepted by our
modern Western culture? Has it not, on the contrary, become
one of the pillars on which the modern world rests — like
dialectic materialism, relativity and quantum physics, and
the visual world of Picasso? And is it really true that analysis
is not accepted by our universities? Has it not, on the contrary, exerted a strong influence upon certain activities carried out within the universities? We need think only of many
departments of psychiatry and schools of social service, of
some departments of psychology, of social and political
science, history, theology, anthropology, and even jurisprudence, to realize that psychoanalysis has achieved a solid
foothold in the universities. And in other important areas of
modern Western civilization — consider, for example, the psy-

chological novel, the psychological play and movie—the influence of analysis is often so great that it appears at times to interfere with the unfolding of the genuine virtues of the creations in these fields by bringing in psychological understanding from the outside, as it were, instead of letting it emerge from the depth of the creative writer's soul. Yet, despite the scholarly eclecticism at universities, which extends its tolerance toward analysis, and despite the enthusiasm with which some of the insights of psychoanalysis are employed by certain groups of artists, I remain unconvinced of the acceptance of analysis by our culture.

Let me give you a concrete illustration of the puzzling nature of the serious difficulties faced by the attempt to bring about a valid integration of psychoanalysis with other scientific disciplines. An increasing number of professional people from various fields—from psychology, anthropology, jurisprudence, for example—are nowadays undertaking psychoanalytic training. I do not deny the desirability of this enterprise—indeed, I have been its staunch supporter for many years. But I have also been disconcerted about one paradoxical result of such training. Having undergone the training, the trainee will not infrequently move into one of two directions: he may, after a while, emotionally and intellectually return to his original discipline with little obvious enrichment from the psychoanalytic experience—or he may become a psychoanalyst, more or less dropping the knowledge and skills of his primary profession. And even where an unusually gifted person is indeed able to achieve an apparent integration—such as a skilled historian's now greater ability to write pathographies of historical personages—it strikes me that he is now (in essence) using two separate skills side by side, that the two branches of science have not achieved a new synthesis through the emotional and intellectual work of an individual who was trained in both of them. One is reminded of the mode of perception in the figure-ground experiments: one sees either one configuration or the other; but it is impossible to see both of them at the same time.

We are thus still left with a puzzling question concerning the relationship between psychoanalysis and the other sciences, i.e., we must still define the nature of the obstacle that stands in the way of the true acceptance of the central area of the methods and findings of psychoanalysis by the other sciences.

There is, indeed, no lack of evidence for my assertion that the solid integration of psychoanalysis with the other sciences has not yet taken place. Not only does the acceptance of psychoanalysis always seem to be only temporary and to remain precarious—witness the repeated assertions that analysis has become old-fashioned, that it has been superseded by more modern developments—and not only is it usually accompanied by loudly voiced expressions of uneasiness and caution, but also, and most importantly, I believe that the acceptance of analysis always concerns only its peripheral areas. Indeed, I cannot shake off the uncanny impression that analysis is losing its essence in the process of being accepted, that, in particular, it is in danger of drifting toward the repudiation of its proudest achievements when it tries to become acceptable to the other branches of science. The feeling of uneasiness I experience under these circumstances is not due to any particular professional snobbishness on my part, is not related to any feeling of superiority about the analyst's proficiency in the use of the psychoanalytic situation; it is akin to my dismay when I see how the profoundest insights obtained by analysis about the tragic condition of man are being put to use in cleverly concocted movies, plays, and novels. In either case, when analysis presents itself through the medium of art or when analysis becomes, as it were, all science, when it is no more than subtle phenomenology or when it tries to become all dry, quantifying formulation—in either case do I recognize incompleteness, in either case do I know that an integral part of this great new edifice of human thought is now missing.

It may seem that the object of all these complicated reflections is simply to observe — as is often said with reference to the profession of medicine — that psychoanalysis is partly art and partly science, and that I do not like it when it becomes completely one or the other. One could put it that way; but I don't think that one would have done justice to the problems involved. True, it is my wish to demonstrate that psychoanalysis in its very essence consists of two seemingly antithetical constituents, of which one may be especially attractive to the artistic temperament while the other will be more in tune with the sober intellect of the scientist's personality. It is , however, not my primary aim here to describe the emotional responses of different people to the different facets of analysis: I wish to define, if ever so briefly, that two-layered substance of analysis which I believe accounts for its revolutionary nature, which in fact sets it apart from the established sciences, which explains its singular position in modern culture, and which is, in particular, the most important cause of the fact that it is not fully integrated with the other branches of science and thus with the universities.

The aim of science is to provide explanations of the phenomena observed by man, in order to ultimately increase his mastery over nature. As far as the interests of science itself are concerned, this mastery is confined to the realm of cognition, although intellectual progress may lead secondarily to increased technological control. In order to achieve cognitive mastery over the world he observed, scientific man had to rid his thought processes of certain archaic or infantile qualities: he had to give up subjectivity (i.e., he had to learn to observe external phenomena and to explain them in their interactions as, in essence, unrelated to himself); he had to relinquish the animistic conception of nature (i.e., he had to realize that natural phenomena are not to be explained in analogy to self-experience: as volition or emotion, for example); and he had to learn to move in his explanations increasingly away from his sensory impressions. To give a simple illustration: a flash of lightning is not to be understood as a god's angry attack on man; it is to be formulated in mathematical and physical terms as a discharge process between different levels of electrical tension.

I believe it is the incompleteness of man's cognitive development—his unacknowledged, still persisting temptation to return to animistic thought and to anthropomorphic concepts—that has created a defensive hypersensitivity to psychoanalysis, a science that seems to be unscientifically animistic and anthropomorphic because it deals with the inner life of man. Psychoanalysis is the science of complex mental states, the science of man's experiences. It thus poses the ultimate challenge to scientific thought: to be objective and (in its explanations) phenomenon-distant in the area of the subject, the human soul, the human experience itself. It is the emotional hardship of meeting this challenge, not the complexity of the intellectual work, that accounts for the fact that psychoanalysis was of necessity a very late development in science. And the full integration of analysis with the established sciences will, therefore, be the manifestation of a decisive progress in man's acceptance of scientific thinking.

The difficulty of taking this step toward the integration of analysis with the body of the established sciences is great, and more than good will and the overcoming of the usual tool-and-method pride is required to achieve it. The emotional attitude needed if this task is to be truly faced is not a tolerant welcome to a feeble straggler, but open confrontation with a trailblazing pioneer. The completion of the task is, as I see it, in jeopardy from both sides: from the side of the traditional scientist who walls himself off against analysis out of fear that the acceptance of its methodology will undermine the constructed edifice of scientific thought; and, even more importantly, from the side of the analyst who, in his wish not to appear unscientific, tries to adopt not only the formal style of the theories of the established sciences but even their methods of observation.

This uneasiness among analysts is not new. Freud expressed it as early as 1895, in the "Studies on Hysteria," when he acknowledged that his case histories sounded "like short stories and . . . lack the serious stamp of science"; this appearance, he added apologetically, was due to the nature of the subject matter and not, he said, to "any preference of my own" (Breuer and Freud, 1893-1895, p. 160).

Is the suspicion of the other sciences justified that psychoanalysis is unscientific? Is the analyst's uneasiness that his activities may "lack the serious stamp of science" warranted? I do not believe the answers to these questions are difficult to find.

Each empirical science begins with observations, with single items, or with sets and combinations of them; these are then brought into an explanatory (causal) relation with other single items in the field of observation, or with sets of them, in order to explain their behavior. We have the mass of a stone, the mass of the earth, and the speed of the stone's fall; and by correlating these three observable items we are led to an explanatory assumption, to the hypothesis, let us say, of a gravitational pull of masses. Or we observe the fact that a person's ideation is leading him to a certain wish, see then that he reacts with anxiety to this wish, and, finally, we witness the disappearance from consciousness of the ideation concerning the wish; and by correlating these three observable items we are again led to an explanatory assumption, let us say in this case to the hypothesis of a mechanism of repression. It is thus not any unusual quality of its explanations that makes psychoanalysis different from the other sciences but rather the great complexity of the elements of its primary observations. Psychoanalysis does not deal with psychological phenomena of the order of simplicity that would, for example, be given if we measured the time that elapses between the occurrence of a sudden loud noise and the startle reaction. Should an analyst who observes a person's response to an experience in his current life resembling that of a specific traumatic experience in his childhood attempt to break up these two experiences — that of yesterday and that of his childhood — into minutiae, he could not go very far in this direction without losing the grasp of the essence of the events, without dealing with irrelevancies.

In this context it is of interest to ponder Goethe's famous refusal to accept Newton's theory of color, particularly Newton's claim that the summation of all the colors of the spectrum would give white or, in the reverse, that white light could be dissolved into the colors of the spectrum (by being refracted via a prism). There is no doubt that, although Goethe was wrong as far as the physics of light is concerned, his position was valid within the context of a psychological theory of colors. (Cf. Heisenberg, 1952, pp. 60-76, esp. p. 64, where he says: "It is clear to all who have worked . . . on Goethe's and Newton's theories, that nothing can be gained from an investigation of their separate rights and wrongs. . . . basically the two theories simply deal with different things.") From the point of view of the observer's experience, white is a phenomenon that cannot be meaningfully understood as the summation of the colors of the spectrum.

It is not easy for the mind of modern man, steeped from childhood in the outlook of the physical and biological sciences, to accept the fact that a scientific attitude toward a world of subjective experiences is no less valid (and in certain contexts vastly more relevant) than the scientific attitude toward a world of objective sensory data. The following reflections, however, will demonstrate that each of the two approaches is valid within its own (operationally defined) sphere. For the physicist, the essential nature of the phenomena perceived by man's senses as heat and color is identical. He conceives of them in the analogizing imagery of waves and differentiates them only by the different frequency of these waves along the time axis. The energic constellations experienced by man as the sensation of heat and as the perception of redness thus form an unbroken continuum for the physicist, notwithstanding the fact that one kind of receptor in man's biological equipment (certain sensory end organs in the skin) is attuned to heat, while another one (certain sensory end organs in the retina of the eye) is attuned to the color red. From the point of view of the psychologist who deals with man's experiences, however, warmth and redness may have vastly different connotations—as evaluated by the psychologist, warmth and redness may be clearly disparate experiences that do not form a continuum.

It may be objected here that it is the very hallmark of science that it is able to go beyond the perception of the senses, and that it is therefore a characteristic achievement of science to discern unity (a continuum) behind phenomena that to mere sensory perception appear to be diverse (discontinuous). Such an objection, however, is based on an antipsychological bias and thus on circular reasoning. True enough, the investigations of science will at times lead to results that may appear bizarrely at variance with the impressions of everyday life. Science will indeed sometimes discover alikeness, relatedness, continuity, when the common-sense approach can only see dissimilarity, lack of relatedness, and discontinuity. And, by contrast, science will also sometimes discover diversity, essential unrelatedness, or lack of continuity, where the unscientific observer obtains the impression of unity, relatedness, or continuity. But such discoveries, which are at variance with common-sense perception and judgment, are not restricted to observations within the sphere of the physical and biological sciences; they occur also in scientific psychology and, par excellence, in depth psychology, i.e., within the sphere of the psychology of complex mental states. The claim, for example, of the essential psychological unity of the triad of orderliness, penuriousness, and obstinacy (Freud, 1908a) may strike the common-sense observer as preposterous — yet, to the depth-psychological scientist the genetic-dynamic interrelatedness of these psychological features is as obvious as is the fact for the physicist that heat and redness occupy neighboring positions in the spectrum of energic constellations. Or, to end these reflections on a less technical note, the physicist conceptualizes temperatures of various ranges as only quantitatively different, whereas for the psychologist it is obvious that coldness, warmth, and heat may be qualitatively divergent experiences, symbolizing (e.g., in dreams) cold emotional indifference, warmly empathic (maternal) care, and scaldingly destructive criticism.

But if the psychoanalyst will not abandon the position that his subject matter is man's inner experience, how can he prove that he is able to discern with any degree of certainty the experiential configurations with which he deals? Just as the observer in the other empirical sciences must ultimately rely on his sensory impressions, however refined they might have become through instrumentation, so must the psychoanalytic observer ultimately rely on introspection and, especially, on vicarious introspection, i.e., on empathy, for the gathering of the meaningful and relevant data in the field of his observations (see Kohut, 1959b). He uses his sensory impressions, of course, as he hears the analysand's words and observes his gestures and movements, but these sensory data would remain meaningless were it not for his ability to recognize complex psychological configurations that only empathy, the human echo to a human experience, can provide. An unreliable instrument! some might say. Yes and no. The answer is yes, if the instrument is handled without care and training, if intuition is relied upon instead of persevering, waiting, checking, and comparison. The answer is no, however, if we recognize the need for the continuous study of safeguards against error, for watchful alertness to the possibility that our bias might lead us to erroneous perception, and for arduous practice in the use of the instrument. It may well be, furthermore, that training in empathy requires the overcoming of specific obstacles. In some individuals, at any rate, the access to the empathic capacity seems to have been blocked by the development of the nonempathic mode of cognition — perhaps analogous to the relation between the phylogenetic stunting of man's olfactory sense and the evolutionary ascendancy of his vision. But, unlike smell, empathy — i.e., cognition via the narcissistic investment of the other — is still a powerful, potentially reliable, and at any rate irreplaceable instrument of observation. And training in its use imposes tasks upon the analyst that are in essence the same as those that are confronted by all the other empirical sciences, i.e., by those empirical sciences where the observed is essentially dissimilar to the observer — by the biologist, for example, who examines stained tissue sections through the microscope — by those sciences, in other words, where empathy must not be employed.

I trust that I have now made clear why I must object when psychoanalysis is welcomed among the fashions of the day on the basis of the erroneous notion that it is no more than a specific, sophisticated art — an art of understanding people via the resonance of empathy. And I trust I have also succeeded in demonstrating why I must reject the acceptance of psychoanalysis among the sciences of our times when this acceptance rests on the restrictive approval of its explanatory formulations and on the rejection of the empathic mode of its data-gathering processes, which is looked upon as an undesirable shortcoming, to be superseded, the sooner the better, by traditional methods of scientific observation. Both of these positions disregard the very nature of psychoanalysis — of this important advance along man's road toward the increasing ascendancy of his intellect. Both of these positions disregard the fact that the decisive step analysis has taken in the development of scientific thought is that it has combined empathy and traditional scientific method, that it has introduced scientific truth-finding with regard to processes that can become accessible only through the scrutiny of the inner experiences of man.

Let me pause here for a moment and clarify the purpose of the preceding reflections. As I have already intimated: I think that the present occasion transcends the personal, that it represents a step toward the integration of analysis into the community of scholars. My effort to define those qualities of analysis that I believe contain its essence were therefore intended to deepen the channel of communication between psychoanalysis and the other sciences, which, I feel, has been opened today. But I do not wish to leave it at that. Feeling accepted, I will not only acknowledge a gift, but will offer something in return.

What can analysis, this newcomer to modern science, contribute to the more established fields? What can analysis give to the other sciences, from whom it has received — or with whom it shares — the striving for scientific objectivity and for experience-distant explanations? The answer is: the introduction of empathy into the field of science.

I know that while you may be taken aback by this statement you will, after all I have said, not be afraid that I am calling here for a return to sentimentalizing anthropomorphism, to an animistic perception of the world. No, what I have in mind is something else. I am thinking of the introduction of empathy into the university in two specific, interconnected ways: first, its employment as a tool of observation, a move that will increase the depth and breadth of the investigations conducted by a number of traditional scientific disciplines; and, second, its employment as the matrix into which all scientific activities must be embedded if they are not to become increasingly isolated from human life, if they are not to be our inhuman masters instead of our servants and tools.

You may well wonder at this point whether I am not exaggerating the importance of the role of empathy—in human life in general and as a potential ingredient of science. Was it not enough that I argued its case as a legitimate and valuable instrument of scientific observation in the service of the science of complex mental states? Am I not going too far when I now also claim that with its aid the formulation of new research aims of other sciences can be facilitated, that—to state it concretely—the psychoanalyst, because of his training in empathy, may be able to help other researchers gain access to new areas of investigation, outline problems that the workers in the established fields have failed to recognize, and pose questions that they have not yet raised? Are these assertions not extravagant? you will ask. Yet, I am crowning it all by proclaiming that empathy should become the guiding ideal of all the sciences, that the scientist's commitment to it should take the place of the pride in his methodological and technological expertness which he has felt up to now.

I must admit that these statements may well seem fanciful and idiosyncratic—or worse: that they may seem to constitute simply another instance of the idealization of a specific tool, and of the conceited conviction that a position of superiority is bestowed upon those who have become experts in its use.

But this is not my view. Skill in the use of empathy as a tool of observation no more bestows a position of superiority on the depth-psychologist than skill in the use of the telescope on the astronomer, or skill with the electron microscope on the virologist. I do not even claim that the psychoanalyst's knowledge of the deeper reaches of man, his familiarity with man's most profound strivings and conflicts, gives him the right to assume a position of leadership with regard to the evaluation of the hierarchy of human activities and thus of the significance of the goals and aspirations of the scientist and scholar within the social fabric of the university. No, while in certain respects the psychoanalyst may explore the human soul more deeply and broadly and in greater detail than do other observers of man, his vision of man tends to be restricted by the fact that he observes people in a specific therapeutic context and in a specific setting—the psychoanalytic situation. The analyst is indeed able to learn a great deal that is applicable to the grasp of man's general behavior; I would nevertheless consider it to be the expression of the conceit of the specialist were the analyst to claim that he necessarily knows more about man than, let us say, the anthropologist, the historian, the sociologist, or the political scientist. What is needed in this realm is the cooperation of specialists, and thus their mutual enrichment, but not the ascendancy of one branch of the sciences of man over the others.

The situation is different, however, with regard to the full appreciation of the significance of the important role empathy plays in all human life, a significance that vastly transcends that of its usefulness as a tool of scientific observation. Here, at least at this point in the history of human thought, it is indeed the psychoanalyst who has the broadest access to the relevant data. He knows that, despite its essentially narcissistic nature, empathy is a fundamental mode of human relatedness; that it is not only a powerful basic psychological bond between individuals, but that indeed it constitutes the very matrix of man's psychological survival. And since today's occasion has assigned to me the role of addressing the community of scholars as the representative of psychoanalysis, I feel justified in pursuing the task of demonstrating to you the enrichment that the appropriately tempered acceptance of the empathic outlook would provide for the sciences.

First, however, let me summarize my opinions of the importance of empathy in human life in general by compressing my views into three propositions: (1) Empathy, the recognition of the self in the other, is an indispensable tool of observation, without which vast areas of human life, including man's behavior in the social field, remain unintelligible. (2) Empathy, the expansion of the self to include the other, constitutes a powerful psychological bond between individuals which — more perhaps even than love, the expression and sublimation of the sexual drive — counteracts man's destructiveness against his fellows. And (3), empathy, the accepting, confirming, and understanding human echo evoked by the self, is a psychological nutriment without which human life as we know and cherish it could not be sustained.

As viewed in the context of the present-day problems of science, no further explanation of the foregoing definitions should be necessary here.[2] The fact, however, that an entire older generation of scientific psychotherapeutic depth-psychologists had to fight the primary battle of their lives against unscientific "cure through love" (Freud, 1907, p. 90), had to take up militant positions as defenders of a scientific "explaining" psychology against a merely "understanding," i.e., unscientific, psychology (cf. Hartmann, 1927), makes an expansion of my previous statements advisable at this juncture. Specifically, I shall now discuss briefly the relation between the first of my propositions (that empathy, correctly employed, is an indispensable tool of scientific observation) and the other two (that empathy constitutes a psychological bond between individuals and groups which diminishes their aggression; and that empathy is an important source of psychological nutriment without which psychological life as we know it could not be sustained).

Those who feel that our primary battle must still be

[2] For extensive discussions of scientific empathy, see Kohut, 1959b; 1971, pp. 300-307; and 1973, pp. 528-529. [See also 1977, pp. 302-310.]

against mysticism, occultism, and sentimentalizing obfusca-
tion will not only continue to stress the purely cognitive
aspects of empathy as a data-gathering instrument, operating
via "vicarious introspection" (as I did in my essay of 1959),
but will also shy away from emphasizing the importance of
the valuable effects of empathy in the social field (as I am
now doing in propositions [2] and [3]). I have no doubt that
the battle against mysticism has not yet been won and that
the fight against unscientific sentimental psychology must be
continued. I am convinced, however, that, taking a broader
view, this issue should now be seen as a subsidiary one, and
that the task of integrating tool-and-method science into a
larger matrix of human values is now becoming paramount.

Looked upon solely as a tool of observation, as a specific
cognitive process — one might indeed call this aspect of empathy "the empathic process" as Dr. Warren Bennis (1974)
has suggested — empathy is value-neutral. It can only be
correct or incorrect in its perception of the actualities of the
inner life of another individual. And it may also be rightly asserted, in opposition to my propositions (2) and (3), that empathy (even correct empathy) can serve inimical ends, is often
used for destructive and asocial purposes.[3]

There can be no doubt, however, that under normal circumstances empathic modes of perception are, from the beginning of life, amalgamated to feeling states that are characterized by an intermingling of two experiences (see Kohut,
1971): (a) the child is able to understand the selfobject via
empathy, and (b) simultaneously, he feels empathically
understood by it. And it is this set of experiences which par

---

[3] In this context we need only think of the psychological means, empathically attuned to the psychological state of an opponent, employed in
war propaganda to make an enemy lose courage and give up the fight; or
of the skills of the salesman who, empathically assessing the victim's readiness to be persuaded, will use these empathic data in order to sell inferior
merchandise.

excellence reassures the child that he is not losing control over the selfobject and thus assuages his destructive narcissistic rage (see Kohut, 1972b). There can also be no doubt that the beginnings of empathic cognition occur within a specific matrix which sustains the healthy narcissism of the individual by providing psychological nutriment to the self (for example, through "mirroring" [see Kohut, 1971]). As with the maturing of the individual, furthermore, the cognitive aspect of empathy will be employed with increasingly appropriate discretion by science, generally, when it investigates man but not when it investigates man's nonhuman environment, so also with the aggression-reducing and with the self-esteem-nourishing and humanness-sustaining aspects of empathy. The empathic bridge to the inner life of the other, to his experiences, and the empathic bridge of others to us, to our experiences, continue to assuage our rage and destructiveness and continue to sustain our humanness. But we are now also able to maintain control over the noncognitive dimensions of empathy: restrain them where they interfere with our objectivity, but give them free rein where they serve our larger goals. Within the area of the present inquiry, our ideal as scientists can be condensed into a single evocative phrase: we must strive not only for scientific empathy but also for an empathic science.

I am eager to turn to the task of providing concrete illustrations of the interaction between the empathic process as a mode of cognition, on the one hand, and the wholesome social effects of empathy, on the other hand, in order to illuminate the potential role empathy can play for science. Before doing so, however, I will again present my reasoning — but now in the form of a brief summarizing statement. Yesterday's depth psychology had the obligation of defining its borders as clearly as it could — it had to emphasize that it did not employ the nonscientific methods of a cure through love which characterize so many therapeutic cults. This obligation has not ceased, of course; but our priorities have changed. I believe that present-day depth psychology—employing scientific empathy—no longer needs to see the struggle to establish itself as a science as its major task. On the contrary, it is my conviction that, having secured its own position as a science, it is now able, indeed it is now obligated, to assist the other sciences, particularly as organized in the universities, in their task of determining a matrix of meaning—empathic science—for their activities. It must offer its help, as the community of scholars attempts to re-examine the hierarchy of its values, in order to chart its course in today's—and tomorrow's—world.

But enough of generalities and abstractions! I know that they do not convince and I shall therefore turn again to the specific and concrete. I shall begin by giving you two examples which will illustrate my claim that empathy, as an instrument of observation, has important, and in certain fields irreplaceable, perceptive powers—that, with its aid, certain aspects of human life can be understood and therefore recognized, which without it would not be understood and would therefore remain unseen. Specifically, I shall describe two instructive instances which indicate the existence of as yet largely untapped potentialities of this psychological function, demonstrating that people with unusual gifts for empathy, or people whose empathic function has had the benefit of special training, will remain open-minded, and thus able to see reality in a new light, where others, with lesser gifts or lesser training, can react only with stereotyped indignation or with hate. Allow me, then, to describe two such instances in which empathy transcended the boundaries usually imposed on it. The first is an example of untrained, naïve empathy; the second is more mundane: it occurred in the course of my professional work.

My first illustration concerns an episode in the life of the folk singer Bob Dylan (Hentoff, 1964) which took place years ago, shortly after the assassination of President Kennedy, at a time when our grief and horror about this event were still fresh and intense. Dylan was to receive an award from a civil-liberties group. Aware of the profound difference between himself and the conventional, middle-class gathering at which the honor was being bestowed on him, he wanted to demonstrate something of his own essence, which he felt in danger of deserting by accepting the award. Thus, instead of giving voice to his appreciation and pledging support for the causes of the civil-rights movement as was expected of him, he shocked his audience by talking about Lee Oswald. This is what he said: "I told them I'd read a lot of his [Oswald's] feelings in the papers, and I knew he was up-tight. [I] said I'd been up-tight too, so I'd got a lot of his feelings. I saw a lot of myself in Oswald, I said, and I saw in him a lot of the times we're all living in. And, you know," Dylan continued, "they started booing. They looked at me like I was an animal."

Dylan's responsiveness to human isolation, to the despair that motivates the perpetrator of a crazy deed, has a touch of the genius that allowed Dostoyevsky to grasp the humanness of the sinner, to extend his ability to recognize essential human alikeness to the farthest reaches of depravity — it was a feat of empathy. Whatever the admixture of nose-thumbing rebellion in Dylan's provocative act, he yet demonstrated that a self may expand its borders to comprehend another human experience even when this empathic resonance leads to social ostracism, to rejection, even when the temptation to join in the prevailing mood and thus to reap the rewards for not up-setting an established psychological equilibrium seems irresistible.

The second example, too, concerns the recognition of human suffering in human depravity. But it is not naïve; it does not have the flavor of that mixture of rebellion and saintliness that characterizes Dylan's stance; it illustrates the sober scientific or professional use of empathy by a trained observer. It occurred in my function as a supervisor of an analyst in training whose patient was a lonely man who suffered from the feeling that he was different from the rest of humanity and that he was thus unacceptable. We had made some progress in understanding his experiences, present and past, and the analyst had begun to transmit to the patient our understanding of how the rejection of his maleness, of the boyish core of his personality, by his bizarre and unpredictable yet powerful mother had affected him, and how deprived he had felt by the withdrawal of his more humanly predictable but weak and retiring father. In response to feeling understood by the analyst, the patient had become less suspicious and thus less cautious in his communications. It was at this point that he began to give accounts of his unspeakable cruelty to animals, which strained our empathic capacity, our tolerance, to the utmost. In his childhood he had had pets to whom he was kind much of the time, but whom he would occasionally beat unmercifully, often without any provocation, to the point of injury or even death. Hard as it was to maintain our empathic intention in the light of these stories from his childhood, our task became even harder with regard to the accounts of his present activities, particularly his behavior to his cats, whom he usually pampered but whom he would suddenly pick up and smash against the wall, again often to the point of injury or death.

I do not wish to burden you with the most appalling details of the patient's actions; even without hearing about them you will surely understand that we were upset and indignant. Indeed, we felt close to abandoning the analyst's tolerant attitude of readiness for empathic comprehension. We felt close, in other words, to following the example of those therapists who have reported wholesome consequences when, in analogous circumstances, they openly expressed their indignation and, as they saw it, reacted honestly and appropriately to a patient's wrongdoings. We did not take this road, but gritted our teeth and continued to attempt to understand the meaning of the patient's activities. Was he trying to frighten the therapist? Was he trying to make himself unacceptable out of fear of the increasing affection he might have felt for the therapist? Was he expressing hatred for somebody in a symbolic way, or was he giving beatings in order to revenge himself for beatings he had received? None of these interpretations and attempted reconstructions[4] hit the mark — although the last was indeed not far off target. The empathic insight leading us to the correct understanding of the patient's behavior to animals came not from the student analyst but from me. It came from me — or it came from me first — not because I possess any extraordinary powers in the area of scientific empathy, but mainly, I believe, because — unlike my student — I was not directly exposed to the impact of the patient's upsetting accounts.[5] I understood that this patient's behavior to animals was a

[4] I am presenting the various psychological configurations obtained through trial empathy in order to demonstrate one aspect of *scientific* empathy. The use of empathy in depth psychology is not based on the not-further-to-be-defined intuition of the observer — it is a specific, disciplined cognitive process. The trained analyst learns to resist being convinced by the Aha! experience of empathic pseudoclosures. He patiently defines the greatest variety of possible configurations and then evaluates the emerging material — including the patient's reaction to trial interpretations — as evidence for or against the correctness, the exactness, and the relevance of the meaning he had attempted to define.

[5] The relatively shielded position enjoyed by the supervisor (or consultant) deserves serious attention as a methodological factor in psychoanalytic research. The benefits resulting from the protection of the consultant's cognitive processes (including the greater relaxation with which he can extend his empathy toward the data) have to be weighed against the detrimental effect resulting from the possible distortion of the material through its passage via the analyst and through the artifacts introduced by the supervisory situation. On balance, I believe that the advantages may often be greater than the disadvantages — especially where the investigation concerns emotionally trying, regressive forms of psychopathology. And I believe, therefore, that the situation we have traditionally used as a teaching device is also a promising instrument of research.

wordless description of how he had felt when he was a child. At that time he had felt cruelly tossed about and smashed — just as the animals felt now when he tossed them about and smashed them, i.e., when he repeated the bizarre behavior of his mother, who seemed to understand him and thus led him to expect sensible empathic responses to his needs and aspirations, but who then, unpredictably, ridiculed and rejected him, and bitingly and sarcastically belittled the very attributes he had just proudly exhibited to her. Indeed, at such moments he was exposed to tortures and injuries equivalent to those he inflicted on his pets. No saying, in my view, is more erroneous than the one about the sticks and stones that break your bones and the words that never hurt you.

I will forego, here, the attempt to marshal the evidence to support the reconstruction I presented and restrict myself to expressing the hope that it will be taken on trust that the analytic interpretations based on that reconstruction had a wholesome effect on the patient and on his subsequent behavior. I cite this case as an example of humanizing, of healing empathy, of empathy as a bridge between human beings — as a demonstration of the type of empathy that is capable, not only of safeguarding humanness within our increasingly inhuman world, but also of reclaiming psychological territory that seems to have become irretrievably dehumanized and of returning it to the domain of living, feeling man.

With the preceding examples, I have attempted to demonstrate the power of empathy both as an instrument of cognition and as a civilizing force. In these two broad realms, empathy seems to me to be irreplaceable. The importance of the empathic mode of man's relation to his human environment, the importance of that "mechanism by means of which we are enabled to take up any attitude at all towards another mental life," as Freud put it (1921, p. 110n), can, I believe, hardly be overestimated. If I had sufficient time at my disposal, I would be able to demonstrate that empathy, the res-onance of essential human alikeness, is indeed — from birth to death — the power that counteracts man's tendency toward seeing meaninglessness and feeling despair; that the wide-spread existential malaise of our times rests not so much on a philosophical but rather on a concrete experiential basis; that our propensity for it is due to the insufficient or faulty em-pathic responsiveness we encountered during the crucial period when the nucleus of our self was formed. And I could show how the intense needs of those whose self has thus been undernourished make them the easy prey of any seducer who promises to relieve their sense of emptiness, of any make-believe that will, even if only temporarily, give them that feeling of being empathically valued and accepted which they should have internalized as children and which they should now possess as their unquestioned psychological property. If this feeling is lacking, then any relief is welcome — whether it is provided by drugs and wordless touching in encounter groups or by nationalistic ecstasy and merger into mystical experience.

But do I then suggest that science, that the universities, should supply the emotional substance that fulfills these needs? Am I suggesting that the universities should embrace a quasi-religious mystique of empathy, a religion of empathy which is to take the place of the religion of love? Of course not ! Neither do I expect — or even want — our professors to be saints, nor do I believe that any of the current sainthood fads — think of the Jesus freaks and of the pseudo-Buddhists among the young — will carry us toward a solution of our problems.

But there exists among the best, perhaps, of our young people a new attitude that deserves our attention. It is an attitude of naïve unworldliness coupled with a disinterest in and often contempt for the traditional values of our culture. On first sight, it might seem to be nothing more than the attitude we have learned to expect from adolescents. But it is part of the stable outlook of these young people, often persisting long into adulthood, and, while it is unworldly, it is by no means unrelated to the world. These young people show us that the ideals we are offering them — specifically, the ideals of scholarship and of truth-finding research which reached the peak of their power at the end of the nineteenth century — that these ideals no longer sustain and lead them. Clear-vision and tool-and-method pride, the ideal of the search for truth, sustained our learned communities well into the beginning of our century. But we have also seen the isolating effects of scientific pride; we have seen how easily the tool-and-method-oriented scientist submitted, with undiminished pridefulness, to the totalitarian regimes of this century and hence to some of the most inhuman goals the world has ever known.

Science cannot prove, of course, that man should be guided by humanitarian ideals, just as it cannot prove — as it tried to do on the basis of a vulgarized Darwinism when it allied itself to the fascist regimes of the early part of the century — that *in*human ideals, the gospel of the survival of the fittest, are justified. Still, while our scientific insights concerning the importance of the empathic bond between people do not lead us to a proof of the validity of humanitarian ideals, they go a long way toward increasing our awareness of how much of the human essence we abandon when our overriding pride imbues the specific ego functions involved in truth-finding, rather than the expansion of our selves that we undertake in order to sustain the fellow human being.

What I support, then, is the infusion of our specialized activities with a new kind of humanitarianism — not with the humanitarianism of the Age of Reason which accompanied the formation of our universities as we now know them and which has grown old, uninspiring, and ineffectual, but with the new and scientifically buttressed recognition that man cannot fulfill his essential self in any better way than by giving emotionally nourishing support to man, i.e., to himself and to his like.

No governmental system of regulations, no social apparatus providing for reasonable economic equality, no international union of nations maintaining world peace, however noble their aims and however efficient their technology, can, on the basis of their technological perfection alone, give the fundamental emotional sustenance to man that he needs for his psychological survival. Even if the aims of these institutions are chosen in harmony with the results of the best scientific studies undertaken by experts trained at our universities in the traditional fields of knowledge, even if their methods have been refined on the basis of experiments carried out by our most advanced academic researchers, institutions alone cannot sustain man any better than sufficient calories, optimal temperature, and bacteria-free cleanliness can sustain the psychological and biological survival of our babies. Food, warmth, and cleanliness are of course indispensable; and so are the great social institutions of man. But unless the food, warmth, and cleanliness are provided with empathic human responsiveness, and unless the child's growing body and forming personality are responded to with empathic acceptance, the baby's growth and survival will not be sustained.

We must not, of course, caricature a principle by its exaggerated application to details. I believe the physicist should continue to probe the secrets of the atom, the surgeon to refine his skills, and the historian to devote himself to the objective discovery of facts and documents. But if the university is nothing more than an organization that provides laboratories for its researchers, libraries for its scholars, and salaries for its employees, if it is no more than an aggregate of specialized technicians, each trying to explain a sector of reality with his own tools, then it will continue to lose its rele-

vance for a younger generation that is already deeply disen-
chanted. The preaching of the old values of scholarship and
of Nobel Prize-seeking research will not do, nor will the
expansion of divinity schools and of departments of
philosophy where, all too often, lines of thought are being
pursued uneasily, whose irrelevance the best of the faculty
have themselves long recognized within the silence of their
souls. And, much as I love the subject matter of the
humanities, I do not believe that the emphasis on this branch
of learning to the detriment of the hard sciences will give to
our great centers of scholarship the vitality they need.

How, then, can the universities, how can the sciences
amalgamate their knowledge to life-sustaining goals and thus
become once more the intellectual leaders, the pioneers of
our society, become once more the embodiment of ideals that
are acceptable to our young?

Freud (1925b) once defined thought in the following
beautiful way. Thought, he said, is "an experimental action"
carried out with "small expenditure" of psychic energy (p.
238). I believe that an analogous definition can be applied to
the activities of the university. Just as it is the function of
thought to rehearse various courses of possible action before
the whole personality decides to which particular one it will
commit its energies, so it is the function of our universities to
undertake experiments that should determine the direction of
man's commitments in the larger arena of civilization. Our
universities should be the proving ground where scholars test
alternative means of support for the survival of human life in
its physical, biological, and psychological dimensions.

Will the university again be a community of scholars
rather than just a place where separate, technique-defined
specialties are held together by administrative convenience?
Can universities, can one university, undertake the daring
step of becoming a microsociety, an enclave within the
framework of society at large, which in trial actions under-

takes the self-examination of social processes that cannot be performed outside its walls?

This is not the place to spell out the details of specific "experimental actions," of—I am using the hallowed term with some reluctance—specific research projects that a university might undertake in order to make a contribution to the definition and solution of some of the crucial problems of our age. Still, I have to present at least some concrete, illustrative examples of questions scholàrs might ask who have recognized that the employment of empathy can indeed enrich their work.

Take, for instance, even the maxim of the life-sustaining, civilizing, curative power of empathy itself. It is obvious that as soon as we turn from the assessment of the role it plays in the relationship of two individuals—be it mother and child, or psychotherapist and patient—and begin to examine its potentialities in the social arena, the psychoanalyst's knowledge alone will not carry much weight. Clearly, it would be suicidal to apply the two-step procedure of empathic understanding and scientific explanation directly to some of the sources of evil in our world. It is one thing to grasp the human suffering hidden behind a patient's cruelty to animals, it is another thing to be tolerant and understanding toward the antihumanitarian activities of a dangerous fascist politician and the appeal he exerts upon the multitudes. Even if we acquire increasing understanding of the psychology of the charismatic or messianic leader, even if we grasp the psychological needs of those who follow him, our tolerant communication will not set up the move toward health in the political arena that we are able to achieve in the therapeutic situation. It is here, however, where the university, through the cooperation of scholars from a variety of fields, can devise a framework of experimental actions within its own microcosm, can formulate answerable questions and thus throw light on the limitations as well as on the possible extension of the effectiveness of empathy in the social field.

Although outside the scope of conventional research, the goals to be reached through investigations that require the employment of empathy (in addition to the use of the traditional tools of scientific cognition) are not chimerical. Neither would it be impractical to pursue them. True enough, courage would be required if a university were to make a serious attempt to implement the kind of program I have in mind. But we should take it for granted that every decisive step in the history of science, every pioneering move forward in man's grasp of his world, requires the overcoming of prejudice, requires courage, requires the ability to survive despite ostracism and ridicule. The move, furthermore, toward a redefinition of the guiding philosophy of the university does not have to occur with revolutionary speed; it may proceed by way of small testing steps, let us say in the form of a limited number of investigations, which in their aim and methodology are influenced by the analyst's knowledge of man's problems and man's personality.

I suggested some time ago, for example, that a university hospital would be a splendid testing ground for the investigation of the dehumanizing effect of the large institution, of the specific fear of losing his self to which the individual is exposed when he finds himself caught within the machinery of an impersonal process—even when the goal of the process is beneficial to him. Would not such an investigation provide a fine opportunity for the cooperation of scientists of various disciplines? The literary scholar could study the meaning of Kafka's insights concerning the man who finds himself in nonresponsive surroundings, from *Metamorphosis* to *The Trial* and *The Castle*; and he could cull the essential lessons to be learned from the keen observations provided by Solzhenitsyn in his *Cancer Ward*. The psychoanalyst could examine the reactions of those of his analysands who were exposed to the process of diagnosis and treatment in a big medical institution. Observers trained in empathy could interview individual patients at various stages of processing and could attempt to determine how one could best relieve their loneliness and fright; or how one could tap the emotional resources of those who face the last step of human existence.

The application of the results of such a research project would be of great value in transforming the hospital — the place where at one time or another most of us have to live through hours of gravest concern; the place where most of us will die — from a factory that houses diagnostic and therapeutic machines into a dwelling place for human beings. My proposal to study the hospital was made primarily not in order to bring about humanitarian improvements in a specific setting, great as the need for these specific improvements might be, but with a much broader aim in mind. This study and others like it would, I believe, increase our understanding of some of the central psychological problems of modern man: the understanding of man's problems in a world — the world of tomorrow — where the individual will be increasingly pitted against surroundings that reduce him to painful anonymity, that deprive him of his most precious possession, his self.

Let me give you one final example of an area in which the insights of the psychoanalyst might stimulate and enrich scholarly investigations within the broader social field. The observation of certain specifically vulnerable individuals has taught us that they may react to the loss of empathic responses from others by experiencing themselves as dead, inanimate, nonhuman — in particular, as machines (cf. Tausk, 1919). And I have reached the additional conclusion that the not-infrequent delusion harbored by certain mentally ill patients that they are being watched, that they are being penetrated electrically by someone who reads the secrets of their thoughts, expresses their perception of a world that to them has become devoid of empathy. Such patients demonstrate via their delusions that they experience their surroundings, not as warmly empathic, not as reflecting their presence with pleasure and as responding to their needs, but as cold, indifferent, mechanical, nonhuman, machinelike, and thus as hostile to their survival. These are manifestations of individual personal deprivation, the revival of a person's tragic early childhood—a childhood, for example, in which he had been confronted by bizarrely unempathic parents.[6] And

[6] The significance of certain psychopathological phenomena can often be grasped more readily when they are the manifestations of a minor deviation from normal mental functioning (i.e., when they occur fleetingly and have not overwhelmed the patient's personality) rather than the symptoms of a major disturbance (i.e., when they have established themselves for protracted periods and have overwhelmed the healthy sectors of the patient's personality). These considerations apply also with regard to the recognition that the delusion of being observed by rays and other electrical devices is the expression of the patient's experience that a deterioration of empathy from the side of his environment has taken place. My own first lead to this insight came as I was listening to the report (Palombo, 1972) of the treatment of a seven-year-old boy who was in general in good touch with reality and, although beset by fears and inclined to be suspicious and provocative, clearly not psychotic. At a time when the therapist had aroused hope in the boy that he would be empathically responsive to his needs (and thus be different from his parents), the therapist responded to a communication of the child in a way that the child experienced as unempathic. The child, who had been looking forward eagerly to the more intensive schedule of psychotherapy the therapist was now introducing, had discovered a dispenser of orange juice in one of the clinic offices and had asked the therapist to give him some of the juice. Instead of reacting on the basis of understanding that the child's wish expressed his eager and hopeful attitude toward what he trusted he would now obtain in the therapeutic relationship, the therapist thought he had to curb the child's wish for direct oral gratification. The child responded by developing the conviction that the pens the therapist carried in his shirt pocket were microphones that transmitted his confidences to a tape recorder and thence ultimately to the child's parents. I think the child's temporary paranoid delusion is to be understood as a message to the therapist: "You are just as coldly unempathic as my parents!" Although this clinical vignette can be no more than an illustration, since I neither treated the child nor followed the ongoing

social analogies to these experiences also exist. Think of the ill-defined anxiety that reports about the use of electronic bugging and wiretapping by governmental agencies arouse in most of us. I do not believe it is mainly guilt — realistic and conscious or even unrealistic and unconscious — that is responsible for the discomfort we feel. I think, rather, that the ominous quality of the use of these devices stems from the fact that they constitute a replica in the social field of the dehumanized corruption of empathy that plagues the psychotic patient who suffers from the delusion of being observed. The delusion portrays the transformation of empathy into a force that coldly and inimically intrudes into the patient's self instead of modulating its responses to his needs. Similarly, through the use of bugging and wiretapping, the social environment seems to have undergone a pernicious change: instead of being benevolently responsive to the individual, it has become a hostile force trying to penetrate into his most private communications and thus into his thoughts.

Would not insights such as these, obtained with the aid of the trained empathic perception of the depth psychologist, be of great value to the historian, the political scientist, the sociologist, the anthropologist? Would not the synthesis of these insights with those obtained by means of traditional non-empathic methods of investigation lead the way to the definition of new problem areas and to the formulation of significant new testable hypotheses? Would we not via this route illuminate the workings of certain important forces that are active in the society in which we live? And would we not, perhaps, with the aid of our increased understanding, also be enabled to increase our control over these forces?

---

process of therapy as a consultant, I have since observed similar instances in my analytic practice in which an analysand's association temporarily took on a paranoid flavor after I had been unempathic and was thus experienced by the patient as the traumatically unempathic parent of his childhood.

But enough! I am in danger of burying my message, my assertion, under the mass of evidence adduced in its support. Let me, instead, repeat my claim. It is the claim that psychoanalysis, as a system of thought, can make a contribution to our universities which no other science is able to make at this time: not only by adding its specific tools and methods and its specific findings to the armamentarium of methods employed by the sciences and to the fund of knowledge gathered by them, but also by helping the university to redefine its goals, by helping the individual scholar to reassess the hierarchy of his ideals.

Psychoanalysis is neither starry-eyed and sentimental about the human personality nor out of touch with the basic psychological needs of man. It neither preaches the inhuman gospel of the conception of man as a Darwinian animal who, uninfluenced by altruistic values, submits to the law of the jungle, nor dispenses armchair ideals of boundless humanitarianism, nor proclaims a gospel of suprahuman love. Yet, when in the search for meanings and ideals we arrive at the axiomatic conclusion that it is man's ultimate purpose to support the survival of man, then psychoanalysis should be able to supply those empirical data of observation that allow us to define realizable goals for our society by taking into account the deepest insights science has so far achieved about the nature of the human soul.

There are critical periods of transition in the developmental history of the group as well as of the individual — periods when an established equilibrium has to be abandoned, when a new self has to be formed. The outcome of the struggle during such periods decides whether man will move toward health or illness, toward forward-moving new solutions, or whether he will decline. Our civilization appears to be faced with the challenge of finding new ways for human survival in a mass society. The university as we have known it — as it grew from its humanistic beginnings in the Renaissance to its modern culmination: its imposing achievements in biology and physics—expressed the aspirations of the thinking, searching individual who had emerged from medieval anonymity. But as social surroundings have changed and have themselves become the greatest danger to man's survival, the universities have not sufficiently responded. They have carried on business as usual in pursuit of their old purposes and, simultaneously, have tended to adapt to the new surroundings without attempting to redefine their role and to reassess the structure of their goals. And in particular —and here lies, I believe, the gravest consequence of their inertia—they have not mobilized their resources in the service of the shift of aims from the conquest of nature toward the control of human destiny that the changing pattern of civilization demands.

A significant number of scientists have already begun to realize these facts. They have not yet acknowledged that they, and thus the universities, have become increasingly less relevant to modern man, but they have clearly grasped that they are often used by forces with whose aims they do not agree. The example of the technological exploitation in war of basic scientific findings—from physics to psychology—is the most obvious one; but there are many others. The reaction of science, of the universities, to these evils has been more or less makeshift and on the whole ineffective. I do not wish to belittle personal courage in this respect, and I do not deny that instances of individual resistance to the exploitation of scientific thought have made their historically significant mark. But individual courage is not enough. What is needed is a transformation of the guiding system of ideals within the scientific community.

Man used to take for granted that he was helpless vis-à-vis the powers of nature, the helpless victim of storm and plague; that he could do no more about these forces than resign himself and pray. Science has changed this sense of resignation.

Physics and biology have provided us with explanations that have become the basis for a technology that has given man mastery over forces which—so he had believed—would remain forever beyond his control.

But having gone some distance toward the conquest of nature, man still considers himself to be helplessly carried along by the currents of history and by the tidal waves of cultural change. Although there is less prayer now, there is resignation and, at times, even a snobbishly aristocratic pessimism that rejects the supposedly hollow optimism of the attempt to influence the course of history and to control the speed and direction of cultural change. Taking the long view, however, we may well be less helpless than we think. With the advent of depth psychology, man is beginning to have instruments and concepts that give him greater access than ever before to the forces that motivate him. The attainment of a broader understanding of his own aims and purposes can bring him, in turn, closer to an effective control over his own actions.

It is here that the courageous scholar and scientist must again become the intellectual leader of man, must supply man with the reasoned blueprints for mastery in hitherto unconquered realms.

To put the matter in a nutshell, the university's failure has been to carry on its traditional labors in the pursuit of specialized endeavors while closing its eyes to the tragedy of man, who suffocates in an increasingly inhuman environment that he himself continues to create. The present isolation of psychoanalysis from the universities should thus be taken as a sign that an unhealthy cultural stalemate has not been fully broken; its beginning integration is not only a step toward the full mobilization of a creative struggle for new meanings and ideals and new scientific goals, but also indicates the presence of a movement toward renewed cultural health.

44

Letter to the Author: *Preface to* Lehrjahre auf der Couch *by Tilmann Moser*

I see that you want me to write a foreword for your book. Well, I cannot deny that about a year ago when I read your manuscript for the first time, I was sufficiently impressed by it to volunteer a preface. I must admit that I feel less ready now and approach the task with some hesitation. Still, I will not evade the assignment. There may even be some advantage in the fact that nearly a year has elapsed since I first read your psychoanalytic memoirs and that I have gained some emotional distance with regard to them. I can now see more clearly much that speaks against your work, or at least much that *seems* to speak against it. And since the questions I have about your book will probably also come to the minds of some of your readers, I can probably be most helpful by taking them up and by responding to them.

Very well: what are the objections that can be raised against your confessions? Let me begin in my professional capacity. The fact that I have many years of professional experience behind me is important in the present context because you, by contrast, are a young analyst and must feel insecure

---

This was written in 1973. Moser's book appeared in Germany in 1974. The English edition, *Years of Apprenticeship on the Couch*, was published by Urizen Books (New York) in 1977.

when older colleagues tell you that by describing your own
analysis — what is more, your training analysis — you did something analytically suspect — especially in view of the fact that
you devoted yourself to the writing of your book at the time
of the termination of your analysis and shortly after it had
ended.

I have over the years given some thought to the termination of analyses, and have also written on this subject. And if
you had asked me, say, ten years ago, what I thought of an
analysis that ends with the analysand writing the story of his
treatment and wanting to publish it, I would certainly, without much reflection, have expressed the opinion that something had gone wrong. A good analysis, I would probably
have said, ends with the analysand in a state of mourning
over the final relinquishment of his childhood objects as they
had been reactivated in the transference. The valid termination of an analysis, I would have said, imposes a task of such
magnitude upon the analysand, namely, that of separating
himself from the analyst and from the great figures of his
childhood, that little emotional energy could possibly remain
for other tasks. The *inner* work of the analysis, I would have
thought, must certainly be expected to continue for a while
after termination, but writing down an account of what had
transpired during the treatment, especially an account that
aims at publication, I would surely have considered a form of
acting out, as constituting merely a repetition of infantile experiences, indicating that a sufficient mastery of these experiences had not been achieved. The good analysis, by contrast,
I would have concluded, leads to remembering the wishes
and conflicts from childhood and to accepting that these
wishes and conflicts do not belong in adult life.

But, as you know, I have come to change my mind concerning these matters. The opinions I formerly held are quite
correct insofar as they relate to the analysand's persisting love
and hate for the great figures of his childhood. If at termina-

tion the analysand has not come to recognize these old attachments, if he has not come to realize that they do not belong in his adult life, then his analysis will end with his acting out his old wishes and conflicts. And his frantic activities will alert his analyst to the fact that further analytic work is yet to be done. I will not go into technical details here; there are certain activities from the side of the analysand even at the end of the analysis of the usual psychoneuroses that do not indicate an incompleteness of the analytic work. But by and large, it is correct to say that unusual activity from the side of an analysand at the termination of the analysis of a classical transference neurosis is an indication that the analysis was not completed.

The judgment, however, that the analysand must be engaged in quiet mourning at the end of his analysis is not correct, not even in principle, when the analytic work had had to deal mainly with problems of disturbed self-esteem. The painful relinquishment of former grandiose conceptions of the self that analysands who suffer from disturbances of the self have to achieve may still be regarded as analogous to the painful relinquishment of the attachment to the parents and to the brothers and sisters that must be achieved by analysands who suffer from unresolved emotional conflicts concerning the important figures of their childhood. And a kind of sadness is indeed also experienced at the end of those analyses that dealt with the disturbed self of the analysand: sadness over the loss of the analysand's former grandiose conception of himself, sadness over the loss of the old idealized images of power and perfection into which he once felt himself merged. But something else happens here, something for which there is hardly a parallel in the analyses that deal with the classical neuroses: the gradual transformation of the archaic grandiose self, and of the archaic omnipotent imagoes of childhood into which the self was merged, lead to the gradual increase of creative initiative, to the emergence of the urge to create and to the liberation of creative energy, i.e., to the activation of talents which before the analysis existed only in a rudimentary form (usually having emerged only fleetingly during adolescence). These creative action patterns are now being nourished by the strong, newly transformed powers that had previously been bound to infantile forms of self-aggrandizement. I am tempted to speak further about these fascinating matters, but must restrain myself; after all, I am not composing a book, I am writing a preface.

A further objection that will surely be raised about your memoirs concerns the question whether the description of an analysis for the public—your description of your own analysis—does not offend against the canons of good taste.—Something tells me that this second question has greater weight than the first. We are here dealing with distinctions that are not easily made. The problem of drawing the line between the offensiveness of the obscene and the attractiveness of a nonhypocritical affirmation of the enjoyment of sexuality is not far removed from the subject I am here considering. One's attitude in this area is influenced by a variety of factors, and it is likely to remain relative. The writer's intention is certainly of considerable importance here—whether he aims at a sensational effect, or whether he has other, higher, motives for his revelations. But his intention is not everything. What an author may write with good intention may yet call forth experiences in the reader that belong to a much lower sphere of emotions than that in which the author wanted to place his work. In a certain respect, the emotional climate of analysis resembles that of sexual love. In both situations intensive feelings toward another person arise, and in both situations the presence of a third person destroys the essence of the experience. The presence of a third person—not to speak of the addition of several others—leads either to a flattening of the emotions or to their primitivization. The love relationship turns into a sexual orgy, the

analytical twosome into a tense social group where the wishes
that have been activated tend not to be absorbed by their
expression in words but by their expression through action.
The psychoanalytic situation is in its essence a private one. It
represents the attempt of a human being to be honest with
himself, to understand with growing clarity what it is that he
had formerly repudiated in himself—he learns to look at the
unaccepted part of himself as a first step on the road to
changing it. One's own shame is often so great that one can
persist with this work only with the benevolent help of another. The notion that the patient should be able to trust
many benevolent helpers in this task—that the patient should
presume that a whole group will want to assist him, that he
will find a benevolent public that will help him overcome his
shame—this notion does not appear to me to be among the
expectations of modern man.

But, my dear colleague, I feel certain that the fact that
you are revealing some of your most private experiences to a
broad audience in the account of your analysis does not trans-
gress the limits set by the rules of good taste. I have little
doubt, of course, that some individuals will turn to your book
with the expectation of satisfying their unsublimated
curiosity, that some will buy it motivated by the openly
admitted or disavowed wish for sexual stimulation. But I do
not believe your book will provide these satisfactions for the
reader; you simply did not write that kind of book. It is the
form that separates art from smut. Whatever motivation
might have driven you to reveal your experiences to a broad
audience, it was not crude exhibitionism. You sensed that you
had received something from your analysis, something great
and broadening that you wanted to share with many others in
the world. The message of your book—I admit that the form
in which it is presented strikes me at times as all too personal
and intense—concerns the healing power of analysis, it concerns the wholesome, health-giving power the expansion of

self-knowledge can provide, the salutary quality of a process — the analytic process — that is able to liberate a person's creative energy. I agree with the content of your message, but want to extend it by spelling out directly what you surely wished to imply: namely, that in order to provide all the aforementioned benefits an analysis must tune in on the patient's specific personality and psychological needs; that it must not be a procrustean bed of preconceived notions concerning the nature of the patient's psychological disturbance.

If this is indeed what you wanted to say, if I have understood you correctly, then we have found a further reason why you should not let yourself be troubled by misgivings about the question whether your memoirs might be too open and too revealing. Your book is, after all, primarily an enthusiastic testimonial; or, stated in different terms, to reveal yourself was not an end in itself: you revealed yourself in the service of your grateful message concerning the healing power of psychoanalysis. Still, as I said, I wondered about the intensity of your need to persuade others by sharing your experiences with them. Here lies, I believe, some not fully mastered emotionality, perhaps an outgrowth of the fact that an important unconscious position had not been dealt with sufficiently in your analysis. It may be a manifestation of the irony of the workings of unconscious processes that, believing you had overcome your disappointment about the deidealized father, you have now returned after all to a position of father-idealization; believing you had learned to shrug away the soul-saving sermons preached by your grandfather, you are now preaching your own soul-saving sermon in the area of psychology. Perhaps your message to the multitudes about salvation in the field of psychotherapy carries the traces of the old belief in the message of salvation of which you thought you had rid yourself.

I do not want to dwell on these uncertain explanations. Whatever the sources of your enthusiasm may be — enthusi-

asm for your analyst; for the analytic investigators, beginning
with Freud, who contributed to the process of the analytic
science; and for the whole edifice of psychoanalysis — I am
grateful that you have preserved — or regained — the ability to
be enthusiastic. I am especially grateful for your enthusiasm
because I have regretted for a long time that a whole younger
generation — the generation that followed the one to which I
belong — including the very best of its representatives, seems
to have lost the capacity for enthusiasm. The incapacity of
these young people to experience enthusiasm can perhaps be
understood as a reaction to the gullibility of their fathers who
allowed themselves to be led astray by the Führer. Still, however understandable the excessive need for objectivity among
your generation may be, I believe that it is misdirected.
Enthusiasm, in and of itself, is not reprehensible. Only the
enthusiasm for what is evil must be fought. Without the
capacity to be enthusiastic one is soon lost in the world of
action. One has to be able to react from the depths of one's
soul if one wants to maintain oneself in the social and
political arena, if, in the field of social and political action,
one wants to be a staunch fighter in support of what is good.

But these thoughts lead too far afield. I must leave them
to turn to the consideration of another of the possible objections to your book. This objection, the third and last, is, like
the first one, related to a technical problem in analysis. But
unlike the first, it concerns your position as analyst, not
your position as analysand. The objection, in other words, is
raised in view of the fact that your analysis was not only a
therapeutic analysis, undertaken in order to cure your personal psychological disturbances, but also a training analysis,
that is to say that it constituted a step in your education toward becoming an analyst. I know, of course, that one can
hold the opinion, and in a sense rightly so, that there is no
difference between a training analysis and a therapeutic
analysis; that every training analysis is in fact therapeutic.

But while such an opinion is correct, it is too narrow. It is too narrow because the training analysand's wish to become an analyst, in addition to his wish to attain psychic health, plays a considerable role in the psychic transformations that are taking place during his analysis and, in particular, it influences the training analysand's outlook on the termination of his analysis. The analysand who is not becoming an analyst has nothing else to do with his newly won insights but to use them for his own subsequent life, for the maintenance of his own psychic equilibrium. Once his analysis is over, he will to a large measure apply his psychological discoveries only to himself. The situation of the future analyst, however, is different. Upon termination of his analysis he is called upon to take one further step, sometimes even two. He must detach from himself the insights he has obtained in his analysis and amalgamate them to the broadly applicable tenets of psychoanalysis — and he must perform this cognitive transformation without the loss of the personal gains he has made.[1] The insights an analyst gains during his training analysis must have produced in him the conviction that the teachings of analysis are not dry dogma unrelated to life, but that they are derived from experience. And although he cannot have encountered in his own analysis everything that the science of analysis has come to know, he will at least have learned from his experiences how other insights are derived from the analytic investigation of those whose personalities are different from his own. This last-named benefit is especially important with regard to still another step, a third step, the psychoanalyst can take. This step leads him from the therapeutic experience with his analysands in the analytic situation toward scientific investigation; it is a step from the specific to the general. There is a good deal more that could be said

---

[1] To some extent this maxim also applies to the postanalytic task of those who enter other professions that deal with the inner life of man.

about many aspects of this important move that many analysts do indeed make in the course of their professional career; but here I want to focus only on one question concerning both of the steps that lead beyond the therapeutic gains that result from the training analysis, namely, the question whether the publication of the account of your own analysis will not prove to be a hindrance in your professional future.

This is a serious question and deserves serious thought. I will begin by dividing it into two parts. (1) Will the loss of anonymity that will result from the publication of the autobiographical account of your analysis make the analysis of your future analysands more difficult? (2) Will the mental image of you that the still undecided potential patients will form on the basis of your memories selectively attract some who will then hurry to your office and repel others who will then shun your consulting room?

The first danger is, in my estimation, not a very serious one. The maxim that the analyst has to be anonymous is correct in principle; its concrete interpretation, however, that the analyst should be no more than a mirror reflecting back to the patient the impressions that proceeded from him, is psychologically erroneous. The principle is quite correct; but the terms neutrality and anonymity should not carry the implied injunction that the analyst must not respond with a full range of human reactions or that the patient must be prevented from knowing anything about his life and personality. In every analysis a baseline composed of the patient's realistic impressions about the analyst is soon drawn, a stable background to the analytic work composed of certain recognizable human features of the analyst establishes itself within the patient's mind. It is against these realistic givens of the analytic situation that the analysand's personality and the figures of his childhood are set off. The analyst must concentrate on directing his full empathic attention on the patient and on the patient's personality, he must not use the analytic situation as a stage for the expression of his own individuality, which is allowed to manifest itself only in a subordinate way in his responses to the analysand. If these conditions are fulfilled, then the analytic work will unfold freely—whether the analyst had been unknown to the analysand before the analysis or whether the analysand knows many intimate details of the analyst's life and personality. In either case, the analyst soon learns to recognize the deviations from reality that are revealed by the analysand's communications—be they distorted perceptions of the analyst's appearance or personality or inappropriate reactions to his interpretations. And every analyst must learn, of course, neither to deny the analysand's correct perceptions nor to overlook the distortions that emanate from the transference. I do not believe, therefore, that the actual knowledge about you that your patients will obtain from your published revelations will be an interference. On the contrary, your courage, your capacity to look into psychic depths in spite of your fear, may well assist your analysands to deal with their fear and shame, may help them to resist the temptation of turning away from the painful confrontation with unpleasant psychic reality that the analytic process imposes on them.

The second part of the last question, however, raises a problem that I find it more difficult to be reassuring about—especially in view of the fact that you stand at the beginning of your professional career as an analyst. I do indeed fear that the publication of your book will lead to a regrettable narrowing of your experience. I believe, in other words, that the publication of your book will have the result that certain personality types will feel attracted by your personality as it is revealed in your memoirs and that others will stay away who, had they not read your book (or heard about it), would have become your patients. That is a pity, because the young analyst who initially is still caught up in his

personal problems and who tends to see the psychological
world too narrowly as patterned like his own must gradually
become acquainted with the full range of man's psychological
experiences—many of them quite different from those he
became acquainted with in his own analysis. To be sure, no
analyst feels equally at home with all personality types. We
all have limits, often probably set by early childhood experience, and there are some limits beyond which we cannot step
without exposing ourselves to great difficulties. Every analyst
learns to avoid certain groups of analysands, either because
they depress him or make him fearful, or because it is difficult for him to understand them in depth. What a shame,
therefore, to see a situation that, at the very beginning of
your career, lessens your chance to become acquainted with
the broad spectrum of psychological experience, in sickness
and health, with which the psychoanalyst deals in his professional life. This is a risk that you will have to weigh for yourself. I assume that you have already given thought to this
problem, that you have decided that the limitation of which I
spoke will not be too great. I hope so, for the sake of your
future as an analyst.

But now I must close. Having discussed a number of details with as much cautious objectivity as I could bring to the
task, I will give up my reserve and tell you that your book has
given me much pleasure. I am an enthusiastic analyst who
believes that analysis is a science with a great potential for
further development, despite the fact that it will before long
be able to celebrate its hundredth anniversary. Indeed, I
think that in certain essential ways analysis as a science is not
only still young, but that it is still in its infancy. One of the
dangers that threatened analysis during its early years was
lack of scientific discipline; and Freud rightly warned his colleagues to be on the alert concerning what he called "wild
analysis." But while it must be admitted that the dangers of
unscientific wildness have not yet passed, I think that the

greater threat to which analysis is exposed today is that of premature senility. The greatest present danger to analysis, as I see it, is the loss of the spirit of adventure, of exploration, of the courage to undertake new forays into the still unknown regions of the psychological universe. And how are we to deal with this danger? The answer to this question is not hard to give. If analysis is to fulfill its inherent potential, it needs courageous workers; it needs young and creative workers who have grasped the essential nature of the scientific inheritance bestowed on them by the great pioneers, it needs young and creative workers who are not paralyzed by the fear of the injunctions of empty traditionalism. It is my awareness of these needs that made me read your book with pleasure. I saw it as the manifestation of a youthful and creative spirit—a spirit I find fully compatible with the essentials of the analytic tradition. I can thus think of no better way of ending this preface than by expressing the hope that the readers of your book will be able to step beyond their preoccupation with this or that detail that they might wish to question; that they will accept it, as I came to do, as a testimony to the vitality—the present vitality—of our great and growing science.

45

Remarks About the Formation of the Self

LETTER TO A STUDENT REGARDING
SOME PRINCIPLES OF PSYCHOANALYTIC RESEARCH

Thank you, dear Dr. L., for giving me a copy of your essay on narcissistic and oedipal fixations. You did an excellent job of condensing the aspects of my work relevant to your topic, and, although there are some questions here and there that I could raise and attempt to answer, I can say that your over-all understanding is good and you have stated the major points clearly and correctly. I shall not bore you with praising the results of your considerable labor, however, much as they deserve to be praised, but shall express my gratitude for your efforts on behalf of my work, in the best way I know, by sharing with you some reflections your essay stimulated in me.

Before confronting some of the most crucial theoretical problems raised by your essay, I would like to clarify an issue that to my mind, while of the greatest clinical importance, is not of overriding theoretical significance. When discussing self-pathology we have in the past, for simplicity's sake, usually spoken only of one type of self-disturbance, namely, fragmentation. I would like to stress here, however, that an

---

In its original form (as "Letter to Dr. L.), this essay, written in May, 1974, was presented in two parts at two consecutive sessions of the Wednesday Research Seminar of the Chicago Institute for Psychoanalysis in January, 1975.

insecurely established self reacts to the selfobject's failure to supply it with (sufficient or appropriate) narcissistic sustenance in a variety of ways and that temporary fragmentation is only one of them, albeit an important and characteristic one. Apart from fragmentation, there are the various regressions of the self and its two major constituents (the grandiose self and the idealized parent imago) to more archaic yet still cohesive forms; and there is, above all, the simple enfeeblement of the still coherent self in the form of a drop in self-esteem (experienced as empty depression).

Fragmentation, however, as I said before, does frequently occur. Although, as you know, it is incomplete and fleeting in the narcissistic personality disorders, yet it has come about, its presence is unmistakable. Its most frequently observed manifestations are (1) the patient's temporary hypochondria, i.e., the experience of (preoccupation with and worry about) single body parts and single mental and physical functions which are beginning to replace the experience of a total mind-body self, (2) the patient's disorganized appearance, particularly the lack of harmony in the way he dresses, and (3) certain behavioral changes, such as the use of stilted language and affected gestures, which are the result of the fact that his mental and physical functions are beginning to be deprived of the organizing influence provided by the inclusion into a total self.

After the preceding clarification concerning the fact that fragmentation is only one of the forms of self-pathology, albeit a leading one, I will now turn to the central problem areas that I would like to examine in response to your work. In reading your essay I noticed that you seemed just a little impatient with me for being overly tentative — for "implying" rather than "stating," as you put it — and I know you are not the only one who has felt that way about a certain cautiousness in some of my conclusions and formulations. Let me take, as an illustration, a sector of my work on narcissism which I myself would regard as containing one of my most significant findings: the discovery that in the narcissistic personality disorders the cohesion of the self is insecure, that it depends on a relation to selfobjects, that the self reacts to the faulty empathy of the selfobjects (or to analogous disturbances) by breaking up and that these events repeat, in reverse, a progressive movement of early childhood: a stage in which the child experiences only single body parts and single bodily and mental functions is superseded by a stage in which the child experiences himself as a cohesive body-mind self—a development that is aided by the wholesome, i.e., development-enhancing influence of the selfobjects of childhood.

But wait! I made a mistake here which is of crucial importance. The words "findings" and "discovery," which I used, can properly be employed for the swings in the clinical situation, which indeed I have observed hundreds of times and which, I am convinced, can be checked by any practiced, open-minded, empathic clinical observer. These words should not have been used with regard to the hypothetical progressive movement of which the clinical phenomenon is supposedly the regressive reversal. You know, of course, the difference: the one is a directly observable finding, describable through the presentation of concrete data which can be gathered by the empathic observer; the other is more distant from empirical reality: it is a reconstruction of the past based on what is clinically observed in the present.

It is here that I believe it behooves us to be more cautious and tentative, it is here that the analytic researcher as an empirical scientist must evaluate the reliability of the means of verification at his disposal, must estimate the strength of the support he can muster for his hypothesis.

And what are the possibilities for the support of this reconstruction about early development, which occupies such a basic position in my work? I shall give you three, and I shall give them to you in the order of the increasing solidity of the evidence they are adducing. The first is the documentation of the consistency of the reconstruction with previous conceptualizations, in particular with a statement Freud made concerning a step of libidinal development; the second is the demonstration that the hypothetical mental phenomena of early childhood are analogous to directly observed mental phenomena during certain states of adult life—particularly the transference states of patients with narcissistic personality disorders—when the psychic organization is similar to that of the still feebly constructed psyche of the child; the third is the collection of supportive data obtained via a more or less direct empathic penetration into the mental life of childhood itself.

(1) *Consistency with previous conceptualizations.* When, in consequence of my observations during the analysis of patients with narcissistic personality disorders, I began to suspect that the temporary regressions from the cohesive self to a state of self-fragmentation constituted the (albeit distorted) activation in reverse of certain archaic normal stages of earliest mental development, I was pleased to discover that Freud had already briefly alluded to such a development in 1914 when he made the statement, not further elaborated, that "there must be something added to auto-erotism . . . in order to bring about narcissism" (1914b, pp. 76-77). And since with the term autoerotism Freud referred to single drive elements and the cathexis of single "erotogenic zones" (as I see it, to the child's experience of single, unconnected body zones), while with the term narcissism he referred to the cathexis of the totality of the body and mind (as I see it, to the child's experience of the total bodily and mental self), I considered Freud's distinction the drive-psychological analogue of my own distinction between two stages in the development of the self, namely, the distinction between a stage of "unstable, prepsychological fragments of the mind-body-self and its functions" and a stage of "psychologically elaborated, cohe-

sive configurations" (Kohut, 1968). And I thought I had been able to extract a more explicit meaning from Freud's rather cryptic remark that "there must be something *added* [italics mine] to auto-erotism — a new psychical action — in order to bring about narcissism." The new "action" of which Freud speaks is, I believe, nothing else but the birth of the nuclear self.

Should someone question my use of Freud's brief remark in buttressing my claim, I would not find it easy to show convincingly that the analogy between my formulation and Freud's tersely expressed suggestion could indeed be seen as a support for my hypothesis. I would probably try to demonstrate that Freud's hint was derived from a host of preconsciously synthesized empirical impressions and that the whole body of psychoanalytic theory as built at that time, particularly the theory of hypochondria, was consistent with both Freud's terse statement and my own more broadly based and elaborated theory. But since, as I said initially, the consistency of my assumptions with certain tenets of classical psychoanalytic theory carries the least weight in the present context, I shall not pursue this line of argument any further but, turn to the area in which the most extensive support for my theory can be found.

(2) *Extrapolations from clinical behavior.* Here, the area supporting my basic theoretical assertion is so broad that it is impossible to do it justice in any concise summary, since almost my whole work on narcissism, on the self, and on the narcissistic personality disorders could be referred to in this context. A look, however, at the diagram illustrating the typical regressive swings that occur during the analysis of narcissistic personality disorders (Kohut, 1971, p. 97) will demonstrate the nature of the clinical evidence I used to support the hypothesis of a developmental sequence "from a stage of the fragmented self . . . to a stage of the cohesive self — i.e., the growth of the self experience as a physical and mental unit

which has cohesiveness in space and continuity in time" (Kohut, 1971, p. 118).

It is my impression that most analysts will consider the clinical evidence from which I extrapolated my developmental thesis the most important support for it — its form and content correspond most intimately to the form and content of the analyst's professional thinking; the single observations that provide clinical evidence lie in the very center of his experience, and he can repeat them on his own in his daily work. It is my own feeling, however, that — despite its obvious value — extrapolated evidence without the further support of directly recalled memories from childhood and of empathically undertaken observations of the relevant behavior of children is insufficient. It is for this last line of support that I now turn to my next and final point.

(3) *Childhood memories and first-hand empathy with the experiences of children.* In view of the fact that the hypothesis in question concerns a specific sequence of the psychic development of childhood, it is clear that confirmatory evidence relating directly to the child's experiences will *prima facie* weigh heavier in the balance than the supportive weight of the arguments just given, especially when the data derived from directly recalled childhood experiences and the data obtained via the direct empathic observation of children relate to an age not too distant from the age at which the developmental sequence in question is supposed to be taking place. Let me give you four examples of the kind of evidence that relates more or less directly to childhood which I was able to marshal in support of my hypothesis.

(a) The first example concerns the blissful interplay of a proud mother and her happy child (see Kohut, 1966b). Here, the empathic observer should be able to obtain direct evidence for the oscillations between the child's reaction to the mother's attention to single body parts and single mental and physical functions and his reaction to her attention to his total presence—evidence, in other words, for alternating experiences in the child, the manifestations of which, in pathological distortion, we are able to see in the analysis of adults with narcissistic personality disorders. And he should also be able to witness the gradually increasing predominance of the second attitude, i.e., how the mother's shift of attention toward the whole child is responded to by the firming of his experience of a total body-mind-self—a total body-mind-self which he exhibits with delight to the delighted mother, even in the preverbal stage. (b) The second example concerns the effect on the child of the mother's calling him by name. Simple as this step might be, it is, I believe, a very important one; and the various ways in which the child's name is called out by the mother as she shifts her attention from specific parts of his body and from his specific physical and mental functions "to the total child," to the totality of "his presence and activities" (Kohut, 1971, p. 18), will decisively influence the feeling tone of the child's initial experiences of his cohesive self, i.e., of his self "as a physical and mental unit which has cohesiveness in space and continuity in time." Does the child hear his name as the expression of the mother's approving enjoyment as she shifts her attention to his total presence? Or does he hear his name only when he has displeased the mother? Or, finally, does she fail to call him by name as an outward manifestation of her lack of emotionally valid interest in him?[1] Clearly, the claim that the mother's various responses in this area will either promote or hamper the establishment of the cohesive self is open to investigation: it is a

---

[1] The cold voices heard by the paranoiac become understandable when seen in this genetic context—they are the expression of the lack of the self-objects' capacity to mirror the child's total self and a reflection of the lack of cohesion of the patient's self-experience which is correlated to the self-objects' failure. Kafka described this situation poignantly in *Metamorphosis:* Gregory Samsa experiences himself as nonhuman while his parents in the next room speak about him in the third person singular.

subsidiary hypothesis which can be either proved or disproved by direct observation. (c) The third example from my collection of empirical data in support of the hypothesis that a stage of self-cohesion follows upon a stage of isolated body parts and functions is a negative one, namely, the fact that mothers who are afraid of losing the child as an appendage of their own self (a self they experience as being incomplete) turn the child's attention to single body parts and functions at the very moment when he tries, in the hope of obtaining the confirming approval for an as yet insecurely completed developmental step, to offer his total self for her enjoyment and confirming approval. (In this context, see the childhood memory from Patient B.'s latency period [Kohut, 1971, p. 121], undoubtedly a telescoped memory which is the carrier of many earlier similar experiences. "Don't move your hands while you are talking!" the mother said, just as he was proudly and excitedly telling her of a great self-esteem-enhancing success.) (d) The fourth, my final and in many ways favorite example of empirical proof for the hypothesis of a developmental sequence from a stage of single parts and functions to one of self-cohesion, is the little-piggy game played by mothers and children. The psychological precondition for the success of this game is given by the fact that a cohesive self has already been established, but that its cohesion is new and therefore still insecure. (The game, in other words, contributes to the mastery of traumatic states — analogous traumatic states occur in all transitional stages of development — that occur in the transition toward the experience of a total body-self. It would not be enjoyable if it were played before the establishment of a cohesive self or if it were played after the self has become securely entrenched.) One secret of the success of the game is the mother's empathic grasp of the degree of the child's ability to tolerate this threat to his newly formed cohesion. In focusing on each of his toes, one by one, she takes the small toddler's barely established cohesive body-self apart — yet, watching his tense face (which, however, after many repetitions simultaneously expresses glee at the anticipated joyful resolution), she does not allow the threat to become too great, and just at the right moment she will embrace the whole child and the fragmentation is again undone (Kohut, 1971, p. 119).

The purpose of my preceding discussion was, as you may remember, to explain to you the cautiousness of my hypothetical reconstructions. Yes, many of my hypotheses are presented cautiously and even, perhaps, tentatively, despite the evidence I may have been able to amass. But analysis is an empirical science, and we must therefore differentiate clearly the utility of its axiomatic tenets, such as the heuristic value of its "ordering principles," which can be firmly asserted, from the truth value of those of its formulations and hypotheses (e.g., of its genetic reconstructions) which must initially be regarded as being in doubt. They may be either correct or wholly or partially in error, and they are therefore in need of support through empirically obtained data.

Since you are familiar with my contributions to analytic theory, I know that you will not suspect me of harboring an antitheoretical bias. Nothing, indeed, could be further from the truth. But I do believe that analysis has, particularly in recent times, turned too far away from what I consider to be its essential activity: the use of empathy — persistently employed, carefully checked — as a research instrument in the investigation of the complex mental states of man. Here, correctness of the results of our efforts can never be established with certainty; we can only strive to increase the probability that our claims are valid by supporting them through empirical data and by examining them — in analogy with the use of the experiments of let us say the classical physicist — with the aid of conscientiously pursued thought-experimentation.

It may well be that the researcher trained in physiology or experimental psychology will be taken aback by my claim that "thought-experimentation" can, in the realm of depth psychology, take the place that the (physically carried-out) experiment has in the established empirical sciences. It would lead me too far afield within the present context if I were to discuss this issue at length, but let me give you one concrete illustration.

I shall take as my example one aspect of my hypothesis concerning the development of the narcissistic sector of the personality. I had for a long time taken for granted that the self, in inverse order to its fragmentation under untoward circumstances, was formed through the coalescence of its parts — that the child's experience of himself as a body-mind unit (which has cohesion in space and continuity in time and which is a center of independent initiative) established itself gradually through the coalescence of the experiences of single, unconnected body parts and of isolated bodily and mental functions. And it was on the basis of this assumption (one, I believe, shared by most of those familiar with my work, including you) that I began to adopt the term stage of self nuclei for the stage that precedes the formation of the "cohesive self," the stage I had formerly referred to as the stage of "unstable, prepsychological fragments of the body-mind self and its functions," and which I later simply called "the stage of the fragmented self."

Two reasons made me look favorably on this designation and prompted me to use it (first, next to and later, in replacement of my earlier terms). It seemed to me to constitute an improvement over the term fragmented self because I thought this latter term might be taken as implying regression and pathology rather than the "inherent progressive developmental potential toward unification and cohesion" (Kohut, 1971, p. 29, n. 15) I had in mind. The second reason is that the meaning it evoked appeared to me to be in tune with my previously mentioned belief (held largely preconsciously, however) that the experience of a total self was formed through the coalescence of the experiences of parts. The experiences of isolated body-mind fragments that preceded the formation of the self could, in other words, be seen as nuclei[2] which would gradually coalesce to form the child's experience of a total self.

On further reflection, however, I have become doubtful about the correctness of a theory claiming that the formation of the self comes about via the coalescence of the experiences of "fragments" or "parts." And since, as I said before, the term self nuclei appeared to me to carry such a meaning, I have become rather disinclined to continue to employ it, despite its attractive evocativeness of an "inherent progressive potential." A development via coalescence seems indeed to take place with regard to the complex web of cooperating interrelated ego functions, and thus Glover's term ego nuclei appears to me to be an acceptable one, even though I would not want to affirm my final commitment to this opinion without further research. With regard to the implied hypothesis, however, that the cohesive self comes into being through the coalescence of self nuclei, I believe not only that there is no proof for the existence of such a specific process, but, on the contrary, that there is some evidence on which to base the rejection of such a claim.[3]

[2] The term self nuclei is an adaptation of Glover's term ego nuclei (1932b). My attention was drawn to it by Gedo and Goldberg (1973) who used it in a related context. They, however, (personal communication) did not intend to convey the meaning of "coalescence of parts" by the use of this term, which I had intended to convey through its use when I began to adopt it.

[3] I should like to stress here that my present inclination to reject the theory that the formation of the self-experience takes place via the gradual coalescence of the experiences of body-mind parts does not imply, of course, that I am abandoning the developmental theory that the stage of parts (fragments) is followed by the stage of the (whole) self. On the contrary, I believe that the existence of this developmental sequence is now firmly established. But, as I shall try to demonstrate, the later stage begins at the point when the (separately developing) self has become strong

What specific data would one have to adduce in order to support the hypothesis that the "cohesive self" develops out of "self nuclei"? I can think of several approaches by which one could proceed. (1) One could carefully observe adult patients during the time when a regressive self-fragmentation is undone (e.g., during analysis after a correct interpretation of the transference trigger that brought about the fragmentation). If one could show, for example, that "nuclei" of the body-self, i.e., body parts experienced in isolation, begin to coalesce with surrounding "nuclei" to form larger units of body-experience during the period preceding the restitution of the cohesive self, then one could conclude that a similar mode of coalescence might also have occurred in normal development. And (2) one could apply the above-mentioned principle in the empathic scrutiny of the experiences of small children as they move from the hypothetical "stage of self nuclei" to that of the "cohesive self."

It is not my intention to undertake here the detailed examination of the already available evidence in order to answer the question whether the establishment of the cohesive self does indeed take place in a way that is analogous to that posited by Glover for the building up of the apparatus of the ego. What evidence I have at my disposal inclines me to assume that the development of the child's experience of his "self" does not take place in a way that could be formulated as a coalescence of "nuclei," but that the developmental path of the experience of his self is separate from that followed by his experience of the single body parts and single bodily and mental functions. I think that the child's experience of his body parts and of their functions and of his various mental activities has its own line of development; that this development leads toward the increasing neutralization of

---

enough to gain ascendancy over the experiential world of the body-mind parts.

these experiences, toward the increasing recognition of the spatial interrelatedness of various body parts and of the cooperation of their various functions, and toward the increasing recognition of the relationship of individual body parts and their individual functions to reality (to objects). The child's self experience arises separately, increasing in importance as it develops next to and, more and more, above his experience of body parts and single functions. And finally, the child reaches a stage in which the progressively tamed experience of single parts and functions has become related to the total experience of a cohesive self — the parts, in other words, do not build up the self, they become built into it.

I hope that you will still remember the wider context in which I have been presenting these thoughts. I am explaining the reason for the tentativeness, the cautiousness with which I tend to present new theoretical conclusions and formulations. On the general level dealing with the methodological preferences of psychoanalytic research, I am trying to demonstrate anew the validity of Freud's view that psychoanalysis is, first and last, an empirical science — a view he illustrated in a great image, comparing its observations with the immutable foundations of a building, and its conceptualizations as a discardable superstructure. (See — or I should rather say, "read and read again!": Freud, 1914b, p. 77.)[4]

[4] My endorsement of Freud's affirmation of the primacy of observation in psychoanalysis may warrant a qualifying statement.

(1) The emphasis on observation as the most competent judge and ultimate arbiter in matters of scientific truth, and the acknowledgment that observation is the irreplaceable instigator of that specific mental stance of the scientific observer which I should like to call his *readiness to see new configurations*, do not, of course, at all negate that investigative processes exist in psychoanalysis that do not arise from the clinical field, but grow preconsciously from the matrix of introspective observation and thought-experimentation.

(2) It is clear, furthermore, that scientific observation, even when it is not mingled with consciously undertaken reflection and thought-experimen-

I have now come to the end of the first part of the present considerations. In spelling out the empirical basis of my work in some detail I am pursuing two purposes—one I hope has already become clear, the other I have yet to explain.

My first purpose in demonstrating the observational data from which my theories concerning the self were derived, and in outlining some of the operations that led to the formation of these theories, was that I wanted to express and lend support to views I hold with regard to the hierarchy of the goals of the scientific depth psychologist at the present point of the development of psychoanalysis. I believe—I repeat: at this juncture!—that it is of crucial importance for us to assert the primacy of the task of empirical observation (mainly in the clinical situation), followed by the formulation of tentative theories that are derived from these observations. To the task of perfecting our theories, however, through working over, correcting, and rearranging older theories formulated by preceding generations of analysts on the basis of (clinical) observations made long ago, I would assign—once more: at this stage!—second place. I hold, in other words, that it is an error to believe that analytic research has reached a final stage of development in which we can do no more than emend, refine, and clarify our theories—a stage in which we cannot discover anything new. I hold the very opposite to be true. As I expressed it in a previous context, "analysis, this

tation (which some might consider hidden sources of theory-admixture), can never be pure. Every researcher holds some theoretical concepts that serve as a framework for his observations. They make it possible for him to fit the data of his perception into a known context (or to recognize that they do not fit into it). There is, however, a decisive difference between the tentative and ad hoc use of preformed, vaguely outlined configurations during the act of observation which makes possible the collection of data and the development of sharply defined mental configurations, i.e., of theories to which the researcher has a long-term, conscious commitment, which is followed by a systematic series of observations designed to prove or disprove these theories.

new and pioneering foray into the hitherto unexplored, is still in its infancy, and our present analytic investigations do not yet penetrate very far beneath the surface" (1973, p. 529). The first of the two purposes, therefore, was to demonstrate the fact that the depth-psychological field is still largely unexplored and that we must, therefore, unhesitatingly extend our investigations by moving into new directions and into greater depths.

In addition, I pursued a second purpose which I shall now define, even though you will not be able to appreciate its full significance before you have become acquainted with some of the specific views concerning the depth-psychological field I have yet to outline. To anticipate briefly: I shall deal, within the framework of empirical depth psychology, with a dimension of human psychological life, with a set of functions of the self, undisturbed and disturbed, or, if you wish, in health and in disease, which up to now has not been in the focus of scientific investigations, but has been approached through the work of artists, theologians (such as Tillich), and, especially in recent times, philosophers (particularly existential philosophers such as Sartre and Camus—in the latter's *Sisyphus*, for example). I shall, in other words, speak scientifically, i.e., psychologically, about an area to which certain philosophers and theologians refer as existential malaise or existential anxiety—of our time and, in extension, of all times—within the framework of existential philosophy or theology, i.e., nonscientifically, and, at times pointedly so, nonpsychologically. Still, however great his loyalty to empirical science might be and however loudly affirmed by him, the psychologist who approaches topics that have traditionally been the focus of nonempirical speculation will soon be suspected by his colleagues of having lost his scientific bearings. In order to be able to accept the fact that these topics can be fruitfully investigated by scientific methods, we must first rid ourselves of the prejudice that only those processes that are regulated by the laws of the pleasure principle can be considered to be legitimate targets for our investigative efforts. The area of which I am speaking lies "beyond the pleasure principle." I hasten to point out, however, that I am using this term in a sense different from the one Freud had in mind when he introduced his theory of the death instinct. (Freud's theory, it might be added, is, I believe, regarded by most modern analysts as not necessarily erroneous, but as lying outside the borders of an empirical science.)

What are the phenomena that lie within the area "beyond the pleasure principle" in the sense in which I would like this term to be understood? What, in other words, are the data that we can here examine, in harmony with our basic stance as empirical scientists and our rejection of the speculative approach of the philosopher?[5] The answer to these questions

[5] It is important to stress that the psychology of the self, while directing the focus of its observations to experiences dealt with by mystics, vitalists, and theologians, deals with these phenomena from the point of view of the empirical scientist. The recognition, for example, that the self arises in a matrix of empathy, and that it strives to live within a modicum of empathic responses in order to maintain itself, explains certain needs of man and illuminates the function of certain aspects of institutionalized religion, thus allowing us to appreciate certain dimensions of the culture-supportive aspects of religion and making it less necessary for us to see religion only as an illusion. And while the insights of the psychology of the self enable us to shed our intolerant attitude toward religion, the science of the self will not therefore become a religion, but will remain science. And the same holds with regard to therapy. The analyst's acceptance of the fact that the psychoanalytic process must encompass the recognition of the needs of the self enables him to become tolerant vis-à-vis the analysand's hope that he will obtain empathic responses concerning his ambitions and his idealizing needs. But the analytic procedure will not therefore become a quasi-religious cure through love and kindness, will not rest on corrective emotional experiences in the sense of Alexander's brief psychotherapy (i.e., will not rest on the acquisition of gross identifications with a messianically accepting and forgiving kindly therapist), but will continue to be brought about, with the aid of newly gained insights by processes that lead to the rearrangement of faultily laid down psychic structures and to the acquisition of transmuted and firmly internalized new ones. And while, furthermore, the insights provided by the psychology of the self lead us to the abandonment of our

is simple: it is the area of the self and its vicissitudes. Indeed, it was the study of this area, and certain basic conclusions that I could draw on the basis of this study, that enabled me to turn from the hypothesis that the self develops through the coalescence of fragments or nuclei to the one to which I am now committed, namely, that it comes into being separately, that from the beginning, however rudimentary it might then still be, it is a psychological whole that is superordinated to the psychological parts.

In the following I will explain to you the basis for my interrelated conclusions that the fate of the self is experienced by us as being beyond the pleasure principle and that it has, from its beginning to its end, a developmental line of its own. In view of the fact, however, that I intend to present my findings in this field in a different context, I shall be brief with regard to it. Examining such diverse areas as (1) the course of specific clinical analyses which led to the analysands' increased ability to live their life in accordance with the pattern of their nuclear self, (2) the personality of solitary resisters against totalitarian political power, and (3) the psychology of the tragic hero in drama and religion, I came to the conclusion that our task of understanding the psychological problems of the human condition would be decisively facili-

---

former pejorative attitude toward narcissism and to a shift in our therapeutic aims from the attempt to rid the analysand of his narcissism to the liberations of the demands of his self, these shifts in our stance will bring about neither an espousal of a mystique of creativity and a rejection of man's more mundane pursuits nor the unshackling of dangerous vanity, grandiosity, and selfishness, on the one hand, and of ecstatic devotion to messianic leaders, on the other. On the contrary, the therapeutic mobilization of these forces leads to the analysand's increasing mastery over them and to his ability to employ them for the benefit not only of himself but also of society. In facing all these apprehensions, with regard to our now shedding our former intolerance and contempt toward narcissism, we will do well to remember the fears of those who long ago attacked Freud and his early followers for endangering man and society by unleashing man's sexual drives.

tated if we approached it via two roads. The first approach is the traditional psychoanalytic one: it is determined by the conceptualization of man as in conflict over his pleasure-seeking drives—*Guilty Man*; the second approach, however, has not been spelled out by traditional psychoanalysis: it is determined by the additional conceptualization of man as blocked in his attempt to achieve self-realization—*Tragic Man*. As I said before, these two conceptualizations are by no means unrelated to the hypothesis of separate lines of development for the child's experience of his single body parts and single physical and mental functions, on the one hand, and for his experience of himself as a cohesive continuum, a self, on the other hand. Indeed, the assumption that the child's experiences of single parts and functions follow one line of development while his experience of the self follows another is not only compatible with the aforementioned assumption concerning the double nature of man (Guilty Man; Tragic Man), but the two assumptions are interwoven and mutually supportive.

Let me present my argument in the briefest form by drawing the outlines of a separate development of single drives and functions, on the one hand, and of the self, on the other hand. We begin, then, by examining—via thought-experimentation—the psychological conditions prevailing during a hypothetical stage of intense primitive experiences of the type to which Freud referred as autoerotic. There is no superordinated psychological structure (i.e., no self) present at this stage (or, at any rate, only a very rudimentary one), and the child senses with intense pleasure each properly stimulated body part, each properly stimulated area of his skin and mucous membranes, each properly modulated sensory impression, as well as each individual motion of each of his limbs and organs, especially when it evokes the selfobject's adequate response. All these experiences, as I said, are intense and pleasurable ("infantile sexuality"). But if the selfobject's responses to those psychophysiological needs of the child which are correlated to the functions of these body zones (erotogenic zones) are inadequate or inappropriate (because the selfobject is unempathic), then the child experiences intense frustration, painful overstimulation, primitive anxiety, and primitive rage. There is no need to pursue the details of the further development of the child's experiences of body parts and functions, for this is the familiar territory of Freud's great discovery (Freud, 1905b) of the epigenetic sequence of leading organ zones, from oral to phallic predominance. What I want to emphasize in the present context is that this pleasure-seeking aspect of the experiential world of our body-mind organization persists throughout life: it becomes, on the one hand, the world of aim-inhibited gratifications and pleasures and, on the other hand, the world of (structural) conflicts, of tension, anxiety, and of guilt. The fact that, at about the age of five when the child's pleasure-strivings are organized in relation to intense phallic experiences, a decisive shift toward ego-superego ascendancy takes place—i.e., the ascendancy of adaptation to reality and of conscience over the drives—determines, of course, the nature of his central conflicts in this realm (the Oedipus complex) and thus the nature of man's leading guilt (about incestuous libido and aggression) and of his leading anxiety (castration fear).

    If we now turn to the area of the self, we can only admit that its hypothetical beginnings are as much shrouded in mystery as are the beginnings of the experiential world of single body parts and their functions (from which Freud extracted the generalizations of his libido theory). It is my impression (see Kohut, 1972b) that, from early on, the child's empathic environment reacts to him with two sets of responses: one is attuned to his experience of single parts of his body and of single bodily and mental functions, and another is attuned to his beginning experience of himself as a larger, coherent and enduring organization, i.e., to him as a self.[6] If careful observation of parental (especially of maternal) attitudes toward the baby should confirm this impression, one could take this finding as a support for the theory of the existence of a primitive self at very early stages of life. The fact, furthermore, that the baby reacts with rage to unempathic responses from the side of the early environment may also be interpreted as supporting the theory of a rudimentary self at the beginning of life—narcissistic rage, it may be argued, presupposes an active and reactive self which insists on control over a dimly sensed selfobject.[7] But, however uncertain we may be about the beginnings of the self, we stand on firmer empirical ground with regard to its further early development. Insofar as I have extensively discussed these later (yet still early) stages in my writings on narcissism, there is no need to give you here a résumé of the early experiences of the self that are concerned with the child's grandiosity and exhibitionism (the grandiose self), on the one hand, and with the child's including himself into the powerfulness of the omnipotent selfobject (the idealized parent imago), on the other. Suffice it to say that a reliably cohesive and enduring self-experience seems to be acquired by gradual steps. When the self is finally well established, it takes its position, as a superordinated structure, above the experiential world of

---

[6] Concerning the hypothesis that, in addition to these two sets of responses toward the child, there may exist still another basic parental attitude, see the remarks on pp. 768-770.

[7] Freud's statement (1915a, p. 137) that ". . . the attitudes of love and hate cannot be made use of for the relations of *instincts* to their objects, but are reserved for the relations of the *total ego* to objects" might be thought of here. On first sight it seems to support my speculation. In reality, however, it belongs in a different context. When Freud states that "love" and "hate" are related to "the total ego," he gives expression to the view that complex psychological attitudes require the involvement of the total personality; he does not consider a rudimentary self which reacts to its loss of control over a dimly recognized selfobject.

single parts and functions. This latter world of experiences, however, continues to exist.

Although these two realms of psychological experience are present side by side — or rather: one above the other — the psychological direction into which the realm of the self propels the life of the individual is decisively different from that which is favored by the realm of the parts and single functions — in Freud's terms, the realm of the pleasure-giving erotogenic zones and of the (first autoerotic, but ultimately object-instinctual) drives correlated to them. The self, whether in the sector of its ambitions or in the sector of its ideals, does not seek pleasure through stimulation and tension-discharge; it strives for fulfillment through the realization of its nuclear ambitions and ideals.[8] Its fulfillment does not bring *pleasure*, as does the satisfaction of a drive, but triumph and the glow of *joy*. And its blocking does not evoke the signal of *anxiety* (e.g., of castration anxiety — anxiety concerning the loss of the penis as the supreme source of pleasure), but the anticipation of *despair* (e.g., of shame and empty depression — anticipatory despair about the crushing of the self and of the ultimate defeat of its aspirations). Tragic Man does not fear death as a symbolic punishment (castration) for forbidden pleasure aims (as does Guilty Man); he fears premature death, a death which prevents the realization of the aims of his nuclear self. And, unlike Guilty Man, he accepts death as part of the curve of his fulfilled and fulfilling life.

I am worried about the possibility that these considerations might appear to you as all too speculative, philosophical, and unscientific. While I do know that I am able to show the relevance of the preceding thoughts, with regard to not only psychoanalytic psychology in general but even many

[8] Once these basic ambitions and ideals have been laid down permanently, I like to refer to this most central narcissistic sector of the personality as the *nuclear self*.

details of clinical work, I will not in this letter try to demonstrate, as I shall do elsewhere, the results, in theory and
practice, that the systematic application of these ideas can
bring about. But I do hope that I have been successful in explaining to you why I have become increasingly inclined to
hold the view that we should not conceptualize the birth of
the self experience as coming about through the coalescence
of self nuclei, i.e., through the joining together of disconnected experiences, but that we should think of the experience of
the self, on the one hand, and of the experience of single
body zones and of single mental and physical functions, on
the other hand, as two aspects of man's psyche, both with
their own genesis, their own development, and their own relationship to the environment.

We must, of course, also undertake a systematic study of
the mutual influence these two realms exert on each other. I
have already a number of times pointed out the organizing
effect which the presence of a firm self has on the pleasure-
seeking aspects of man's psyche, or, more broadly speaking,
the role played by the cohesive self in man's life within the
confines of the pleasure principle. But the various ways by
which a person can achieve an equilibrium between these two
realms, or the various personality structures characterizing
different individuals in whom the one or the other of these
two realms has ultimately achieved a position of predominance, these are matters still awaiting detailed — and unpreju-
diced — scientific scrutiny.

I can mention only a few features of the interrelationship
of these two areas, for it would take a paper of its own to do
more. To begin with, we must acknowledge the fact that
observation in the psychological realm is facilitated when
there is conflict and disharmony, and that therefore our
descriptions tend, unfortunately, to focus on pathology rather
than on normal development. Even the nomenclature I am
suggesting (the terms Guilty Man and Tragic Man) relates to

the area of frustration and conflict instead of focusing on the area of positive goals, i.e., on the pleasures of the senses (however "sublimated" these pleasures might be) and on the joy of self-realization (however primitive and crude this joy might be). My decision to classify the duality of man's major goals in accordance with his failures rather than his successes is, however, not only justified by the fact that pathology is more open to analytic observation than is health, it also reflects the actual predominance of conflict, and of frustration and unfulfillment in human experience over inner peace and satisfaction and accomplishment. But, to introduce my brief outline of the different ways in which these two dimensions of man's psychic life can relate to each other, let me first state the obvious, namely, that man's two major tendencies (his searching for pleasure and his striving to realize the pattern of his self) can either work together harmoniously or they can be in conflict with each other.

I shall first schematically sketch out the psychological conditions prevailing in those individuals in whom there appears to be no major conflict between the pleasure-seeking and the self-expression-seeking sectors of the personality. One might be inclined to assume that the absence of conflict is due to the fact that these two major strivings are of equal strength, that an equilibrium of forces exists. While such a condition might occasionally be found, I do not believe it can in general account for the absence of disturbing conflicts in this area. It is the evaluation of the nature of the relation between the two sectors of the personality rather than quantitative considerations that will explain to us why some individuals achieve a more or less harmonious and happy life while others are either deeply unhappy or bemoan the sterility of their existence. The predominance of one sector of the personality does not lead, in other words, to pathological results if the other, the weaker, sector can accept the subsidiary role. The predominance, on the one hand, of the self-realizing ten-

dencies over the pleasure-seeking drives does not lead to conflict if the pleasure-seeking sector (the sector of single functions) subordinates itself smoothly to the supraordinated goals
of the self; no conflict, in other words, arises under these conditions if the individual is able to enjoy the exercise of his
special talents and of his workaday skills in the service of the
nuclear ambitions and ideals of the self. The predominance,
on the other hand, of the pleasure-seeking tendencies does
not lead to conflict if the self can subordinate itself, i.e., if
the self is able to relinquish its insistence on the expression of
its basic design and is satisfied with the limited supraordinated function of lending a sense of wholeness and
continuity to the area of pleasures and skills, of lending a
sense of purposive unity to man of love and work.[9]

Having briefly examined instances where there is no serious tension between the sector of pleasure-seeking Guilty
Man and the sector of self-expression-seeking Tragic Man, I
turn now to those where there *is* conflict and disharmony. Instead of addressing myself to presenting the different variants
of imbalance in this area, I shall condense my task by making
one specific assertion which I will support by adducing the illustrative example of one specific life. My assertion is simply
that the presence of disharmony and conflict between the two
realms of the personality may not stifle a gifted individual's
productivity; that it may perhaps serve as a stimulus for
creative responses—even if the contest between the two

---

[9] It might well be asked here whether such a personality organization
does exist in reality, i.e., whether an individual can indeed resign himself
to the abandonment of the goal of expressing the basic design of his
nuclear self without becoming depressed. The answer is not clear-cut, but I
believe that an individual who has walled himself off from his nuclear ambitions and ideals can yet attain a joyful existence if he is able to see himself
as a functioning particle in a large social organization. This kind of psychological balance might well be of great importance in the totalitarian
societies of our time and could become the healthy norm in the mass
societies of the future.

realms for the dominance of one over the other remains un-resolved throughout a whole (unhappy) lifetime.

Tolstoy's life was an endless struggle between pleasure-seeking, working Guilty Man and self-expression-seeking, creative Tragic Man. Luckily, Tragic Man predominated for sufficiently long periods to allow him to create novels which, like all great works of literature, revitalize those who are open to being affected by them. The deep reverberation of our nuclear selves as we participate in the works of great novelists or dramatists intensifies our reactions to the world and thus heightens our self-awareness; the work of the great novelists and dramatists enables us to experience our existence more fully, to participate more profoundly in the eternal cycle of life and death. Millions of readers — both simple and sophis-ticated — have lived their lives more intensely than they could ever have done via the unaided contact with their own drably experienced surroundings while seeing the world through the eyes of Tolstoy, the story-telling genius. But there was also another Tolstoy, clearly discernible both in the data of his biography and in some of his (lesser) writings. This is not only Tolstoy the gambler, drinker, and philanderer, but also, in the obverse, Tolstoy the man filled with disgust for woman, guilt-laden with the need to expiate, to mortify the flesh. When Tolstoy the creator was dominant, the writer's enor-mous talents were harnessed to the task of projecting the broad design that had been formed by his volcanic creative self. The bulk of the nonmoralizing panorama of the world contained in *War and Peace* is surely the greatest manifesta-tion of tragic Tolstoy, deeply in tune with the drama of human existence, despite the fact that even this masterpiece contains some sermonizing passages and chapters — emana-tions of Guilty Man. But whenever Tolstoy the pleasure-hunter or the guilt-laden moralist predominated, his creative self became subdued — temporarily, as happened repeatedly throughout his life, or protractedly, as happened ultimately during his last years. At such times the creative core of Tolstoy's self lost contact with the executory powers of his personality because his energies were absorbed by the pursuit of untamed drive aims; and then his self, instead of being the initiator of creative activity, became the servile organizer of expiatory religious attitudes. If during such periods his productivity did not dry up altogether, his writings became moralizing, religious, philosophizing. And the work he produced at such times — e.g., certain philosophical chapters toward the end of *Anna Karenina*, or the late novels such as *Resurrection* — lost the power of his amoral realism and must, as I am inclined to believe — in comparison with his greatest creations — be judged as inferior.

In the foregoing, I focused on the realm of the mature levels of the experiential world of body parts and of single physical and mental functions, on the one hand, and on the realm of early levels of the experiential world that are connected with the nuclear self, on the other hand. And the examination of the relation between these two realms has, I trust, illuminated a number of features of human psychology. I shall round out my sketch of the relation between the world of parts and the world of the self by turning to the experiences of the child. Here, too, it must be emphasized that our subdivision of the child's experiential world (and of the empathic responses of the selfobject that are correlated to it) into two parallel sectors is only a first schematic conceptual step. Important though this step is, it would lead us to a distorted perception of psychological reality if we did not acknowledge that, although these two realms aim into two divergent psychological directions (within the pleasure principle; beyond the pleasure principle[10]), there also exists from

---

[10] I cannot elaborate here on my assertion that the realm of parts lies within the pleasure-reality principle while the nuclear self pursues its aims "beyond the pleasure principle." I intend, however, in the future

early on the possibility of smooth cooperation between them. Body parts and single physical and mental functions are not only the foci of intense pleasure-strivings — whether "auto-erotic," "narcissistic," or "object-libidinal" — they are also simultaneously the representatives of the self, i.e., they are the leading narcissistic zones of the body-mind self (see Kohut, 1971, pp. 215-218). They are not only involved in the child's guilt conflicts over pleasure aims but are also carriers of the child's narcissism. In this latter context they constitute the experiential content of those actions and fantasies through which the child expresses his exhibitionism and the sense of his greatness, and they also become the foci of his despair and shame. In normal development, it must be emphasized, the child's enjoyment of body parts and of physical and mental functions is no more antagonistic to his joyful experience of the total self than are the experiences of narcissism to those of object love (see Kohut, 1972b). On the contrary, a person's ability to experience the pleasures of body parts and single functions is enhanced by the security provided by the organizing schema of his total body-mind self. And I must only add here that the cohesion of the body-mind self is in turn decisively strengthened by the presence of a strong nuclear self, i.e., by the direction-setting influence of a person's basic ambitions and ideals which had been laid down in early childhood via the empathic responses of the selfobjects. In the reverse direction, finally, the experience of a well-functioning psychological system of single parts and functions (embedded in a firm body-mind self) which is serving our pleasure-aims and our self-preservative aims (i.e., our aim to preserve body and mind as a source of pleasure) enhances our ability to realize in work and deed the basic pattern of our personality,

---

to buttress this claim by presenting material concerning an analogy between this dualistic concept of man and the dualistic concept of the world that is implied in the formulations of modern physics.

i.e., to reach the goals set by our nuclear ambitions and ideals.

I have now come to the end of my reflections about certain aspects of your review of my work. I should like to round out my response by referring to another point of your survey, namely, the diagrammatic rendition of the development from autoerotism to narcissism to object love, on the one hand, and to higher forms (i.e., transformations) of narcissism, on the other. Here again we are confronted with a subtle divergence of opinions, namely, whether your teacher's diagrammatic rendition (see Figure 5) of the contrast be-

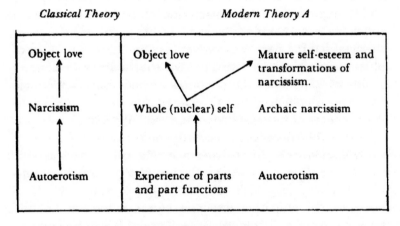

FIGURE 5

tween classical theory—the single-line development from autoerotism via narcissism to object love—and my earlier views referred to as "Modern Theory A" in Figure 5—the "Y"-shaped development in which the step from autoerotism to archaic narcissism forms the stem of the "Y" and the further movements from archaic narcissism to object love, on the one hand, and to mature narcissism, on the other hand,

form its two branches—is preferable to a verbal presentation.

I can, of course, raise no objections if a teacher introduces
his students to the complexities of our science through the use
of simple diagrams—on the contrary, I admire his ability to
do so.[11] But I would stress that it should be clearly understood that such diagrams in depth psychology are merely
teaching devices. They are useful for the acquisition of
knowledge; they become a hindrance, however, when
teacher and students begin to forget that it is the totality of
the empathically observed psychological data and their inter-
relation and not the condensations of the diagram that constitute the decisive reality. Viewed from this perspective, I
think that verbal presentations, even if offered tentatively and
cautiously—implying, rather than stating with conviction and
certainty—have the advantage of leaving the researcher
greater freedom to change his mind on the basis of newly perceived facts and of newly perceived relationships between
them. The change of the single-stemmed "Y" of Figure 5 into
the visual representation (in Figure 6) of two streams of devel-

Modern Theory B

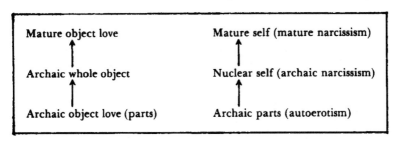

FIGURE 6

[11] You may know that in my own past teaching at the Institute, I
frequently resorted to diagramlike sketches on the blackboard. And in my
writings, too, I use diagrams—though much more sparingly—to ease the
reader's way toward the grasp of complex relationships.

opment, side by side, is, I believe, not as easily brought about — and the "Y" creates an even greater inner resistance against the contemplation of the conceptualization of six separate lines of development, as portrayed in Figure 7, which I am now inclined to advocate — as would be the corresponding change in a purely verbal presentation. Visual representations lend a deceptive concreteness to the psychological complexities they portray and give us a feeling of certitude which, in many instances in our field and particularly at this time and in the topic under discussion, is unwarranted. In my own former statements about this topic (see, for example, Kohut, 1971, p. 220) I was clearly of the opinion that during the earliest stage of life the child's world of experiences did not include object love — not even in a rudimentary form. If this hypothesis could be confirmed, your teacher's "Y" would be an accurate representation of the stream of development. But, as you can see from my considerations today, I have become less certain of the correctness of this view.

The question that must be answered here is whether, with regard to the child's earliest experiences, we should assume that there is no separation between parts of objects, objects, parts of selfobjects, selfobjects, parts of the self, and the whole self, and that there exists instead a unitary precursor experience which is the matrix from which these various experiences later emerge, or whether we should assume that each of these experiences, however ill-defined, exists in an archaic initial state, and is *ab initio* separated from the others. Stating our question in different terms, we will ask whether we should postulate either two separate streams of experience — from archaic part-objects via archaic whole-objects to mature love objects, on the one hand, and from archaic parts of the self (autoerotism) via the nuclear self (archaic narcissism) to the mature self (mature narcissism), on the other hand (see Figure 6, "Modern Theory B"), or whether we should postulate the existence of six separate sequences — on

Modern Theory C

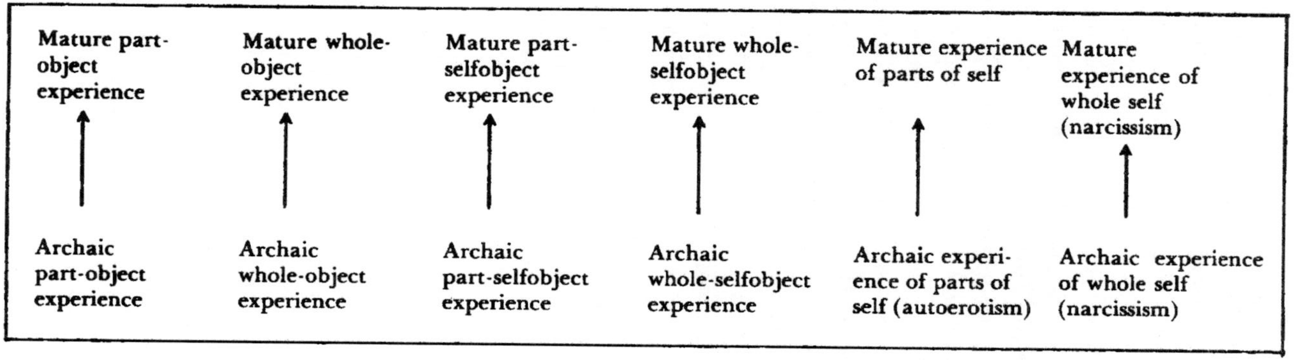

Mature part-object experience	Mature whole-object experience	Mature part-selfobject experience	Mature whole-selfobject experience	Mature experience of parts of self	Mature experience of whole self (narcissism)
↑	↑	↑	↑	↑	↑
Archaic part-object experience	Archaic whole-object experience	Archaic part-selfobject experience	Archaic whole-selfobject experience	Archaic experience of parts of self (autoerotism)	Archaic experience of whole self (narcissism)

FIGURE 7

the basis of the assumption that there exist from the beginning, side by side, archaic experiences of parts of love objects,
whole love-objects, parts of selfobjects, whole selfobjects,
parts of the self, and the whole self (see Figure 7, "Modern
Theory C") and that the development toward maturity of
each of these archaic experiences can be fruitfully investigated. If we decide to take this last position, then we will
have to undertake the separate investigation of six different
developmental lines (see Figure 7). We will, in other words,
examine how the child's archaic experience of part-objects
develops into the mature experience of parts of objects; how
the child's experience of whole objects develops from (a)
archaic beginnings via (b) the experience of whole objects as
striven-toward sources of pleasure and as avoided and fought-
against sources of pain and via (c) the objects of oedipal love
and hate to (d) the mature object that is the target of the
adult's love and aggression. And the same considerations hold
true with regard to the detailed examination of the development toward maturity of part-selfobjects, of whole selfobjects, of parts of the self, and of the whole self.

The portion of the preceding question that refers to the
appropriateness of our postulating the existence of the last-
named developmental line is, of course, the crucial one.
Should we, in other words, on the basis of our belief that
there exist archaic self-experiences, speak of a separate
stream of development of the whole self that leads from these
earliest states via definable stages to the mature self? I think
that we might find support for this postulate, indirectly, by
examining the parental attitudes toward the child. Specifically, we should determine whether, in addition to the parental
attitudes already mentioned (the parents' reactions to the
child's single parts and functions; the parents' reactions to the
whole child), there exist, *ab initio*, the germs of still another
basic parental attitude — the beginning of an attitude that involves the parents' relinquishment of the child, the precursor

of that attitude of ultimate distance which acknowledges the new separate individual, a new independent, creative self in the next generation.

I consider this question to be of great significance with regard to not only the parents' attitude but also the corresponding potentiality in the child. Are we here dealing with still another separate line of development, the development of the individual's capacity to enjoy a self-contained (creative) aloneness—one could call it a healthy estrangement from the selfobjects and from the love-objects—which is not loneliness? I am speaking here, in other words, of man's capacity to enjoy an aloneness that is not to be defined in the negative—an aloneness that is not to be seen as the result of the relinquishment of either the selfobject or the love-object, but as a positive faculty of man, i.e., as a capacity that is already present in early life, even though it is then still overshadowed by the manifestations of the child's autoerotism, narcissism, and object love.

I believe that an empathic observer, particularly an empathic parent, can discern the first beginnings of such states even in very small children and react to them with a calm amazement and the question: "Is this my child?"

One of my patients gave me a clue which helped me to comprehend one aspect of his own feeling state during the terminal phase of his analysis when he reported to me that he had watched his small son alone in the garden absorbedly moving about, kicking a stone now and then, picking up a branch and dropping it again, carelessly—self-contained, apparently listening to energized patterns within himself which strove toward expression: obviously intensely aware of himself. My patient understood that this behavior was the manifestation of a state of temporary secure independence in the child; he also understood that his own ability to recognize its meaning was due to the fact that a formerly stunted capacity from his own childhood had recently become revitalized.

Now, toward the end of his long analysis, he had become able — at least during significant moments — to experience a self-contained freedom which, up to now, had been covered over by his (mainly narcissistic) needs.

It is easy to see on the basis of the preceding reflections that, as soon as we leave diagrammatic renditions behind, the developmental lines we postulate (in order to arrange the various sequences of man's experience) become more complex and equivocal — indeed, we will admit without regret and defensiveness that we have here a number of different choices about the way in which we may wish to order our data. Does, for example, to mention still another possible theory, the developmental stream of object-love begin later than the stream of autoerotism-narcissism (as might be extrapolated from the regressive swings in the analysis of narcissistic personality disorders) — yet still springing from a separate source, i.e., without developing out of the latter? Should one speak of a prepsychological state and see both lines of development as having their separate beginnings at a later time, i.e., at a time when there is clear evidence for the existence of a rudimentary self as well as clear evidence for the manifestations of rudimentary object love? Or are there still other possibilities to be considered? At this point, I feel we should keep our options open and look at the data that analysis, child observation, and thought experimentation offer to us with all of these possibilities in mind.

And here I will end. This communication has become a good deal more extensive, and the work on it more taxing, than I had anticipated when I first sat down to express my gratitude to you. But if I have helped you and your fellow students at the Institute to see more clearly the relative positions occupied by theory and observation when we pursue our research, then I will feel fully rewarded for the hours spent on formulating my message.

46

The Self in History

[The Symposium began with a paper by Ernest Wolf, "The Self in History: Introductory Notes on the Psychology of the Self," analyzing and summarizing the key ideas of Kohut's theory of narcissism. The discussion published here begins with Kohut's extemporaneous response (as recorded at the time) to Dr. Wolf's paper.]

H.K.: I am very grateful to Dr. Wolf for this fine summary of my work of the last ten years or so. It is strange for me to hear it presented as if it were well-established shared knowledge. Until very recently it was shared only between me and myself, late at night, and hesitatingly put on paper. I am lucky to have received the kind of response to my ideas and to my work that so many of my colleagues and students have given me.

I have, since my school days, always been very interested in history. I can even say that my intellectual development was strongly influenced by a historian, a high school teacher —

A Symposium sponsored by the Group for the Use of Psychology in History and the Center for Psychosocial Studies was held in connection with the Convention of the American Historical Association, December 29, 1974. Panel: Professor John Demos of Brandeis University and Acting Director of the Center for Psychosocial Studies (Chairman); Dr. Heinz Kohut of the Chicago Institute for Psychoanalysis; Dr. Ernest Wolf of the Chicago Institute for Psychoanalysis and Associate Director of the Center for Psychosocial Studies.
A transcript of the Symposium discussion, edited by C. B. Strozier, appeared in the *Newsletter of the Group for the Use of Psychology in History* (1975), vol. 3, no. 4, pp. 3-10.

I can still see him in front of me — whose mode of thinking struck some kind of a chord in me that never stopped vibrating from the days I sat spellbound and listened to him. I remember vividly how he began to explain the absolutist regime of the late Bourbons in France by talking about the way the parks were laid out. I was impressed by his ability to demonstrate the essential unitariness of seemingly diverse phenomena of a culture, a period in history. He didn't write, he didn't grade, he was not a feared professor, and he was a very low man on the totem pole among the teachers I had. Yet, to me, he remained an unforgotten inspiration.

The first thing I ever wrote concerning the findings and theories of which Dr. Wolf spoke to you today was a short paragraph in which I said that the importance that the discovery of the remainders of the early object love and object hate had for adult psychopathology and for adult individual life would be matched by discoveries about the remainders of childhood narcissism for group behavior and for the behavior of man within groups. I was at that time president of our national association and had been puzzling about the dissensions within our group and particularly about the fact that now and then people who seemed to have been friends suddenly turned and became enemies. I learned to recognize that almost certainly, if one only looked hard, one could always find some small but nevertheless important narcissistic injury at the pivotal moment that determined the later inimical attitude of such an individual. I have since then found that the scientist's insights had been anticipated by the artists and great writers. Not long ago I was reading *Anna Karenina.* To my great delight I encountered, toward the end, a short episode describing a man who had written a scientific treatise and was now anxiously waiting for the reviews. Finally the first review came; it gave the book a tremendous panning, but cleverly and wittily, although everything was subtly distorted. The author wondered why in the world this man used his considerable intelligence and wit to distort so cleverly what he had written, in order to pan him. And then he remembered that two years ago he had met the man in a social gathering and had corrected *one* word the man had used. Now everything became clear to him. He had shamed this man in public by correcting him; and now, two years later, the opportunity for revenge arose and the man used it with glee. He knew there was nothing to be done.

In the setting of history, thwarted narcissistic aspirations, hurts to one's pride, injuries to one's prestige needs, interferences with conscious, preconscious, or unconscious fantasies concerning one's greatness, power, and specialness, or concerning the greatness, power, and specialness of the group that one identifies with are important motivations for group behavior. The refined study of these motivations will add a new dimension to the other data which historians utilize in describing historical events. I don't mean to say that hunger and the search for areas of expansion and a variety of other forces are not important. But I think that if the narcissistic dimension of these already in themselves substantial motivations is taken into account, then their explanatory power will increase greatly—they will go much further in explaining why people behave as they do, why they sometimes would rather die than live with a narcissistic injury.

The question is what do depth-psychologists and historians have in common? It strikes me that we would recognize that we have a great deal in common if we could only drop what I have recently called the tool-and-method pride or the tool-and-method snobbishness of the scientist. We all tend to see our specialness, our *raison d'être,* in the particular methodological and conceptual instruments we have learned to use, which we have made our own and with which we communicate with our friends and professional colleagues. I know that the more I ponder the relationship between depth-psychology and history, the more I realize that the important issue at the present time is to build a bridge between history and psychoanalysis on the basis of a broader awareness of the purpose of our work.

Most of us have intentionally put on blinders and narrowed our sights in consequence of our commitment to our professions. We want to understand our craft, and to work in it, as best we can, and beyond that we don't want to look. But I don't believe it is possible to maintain this attitude toward our work. Scientists subscribe to the idea that the more knowledge we acquire the better. This is our inheritance from the freeing of the individual in the Renaissance, I believe, and it reached its peak in the great scientific successes of the nineteenth and early twentieth centuries. But knowledge has a purpose. Knowledge has a purpose that we do not need to be ashamed of. Knowledge is an intermediary step toward man's over-all goal to achieve increasing mastery over his destiny. Knowledge leads in the biological and physical sciences to the curing of illness, to man's mastery of the physical surroundings; knowledge in the psychological and social sciences should lead to man's increasing mastery over his historical, political, and social fate. In this sense it seems to me that the depth-psychologist and the historian are working on the same team, that they must work together and learn from one another.

Not only our goals, our working methods, too, have much in common. In both of our fields we are looking at complicated sets of data which would remain hopelessly unintelligible were it not for the fact that the observer and what is being observed have some inner similarity. It would be impossible to understand historical events were it not for the fact that history is made by people and that we can obtain meaningful data—from which we can then secondarily derive explanatory formulations—about the behavior and the motivations of these people, even if they differ greatly from us. Similar considerations also apply with regard to depth psychology.

History and psychoanalysis should be the most important sciences of the future. They are important because humanity has reached a point in which populations will sooner or later have to become stabilized. This will have a profound influence on the psychological outlook of people in the future. It will be necessary for us to direct our resources toward the refinement of various individual activities. If humans are to survive in a way that has any similarity to what we have prized up till now as being the essence of human life, the narcissistic motivations, I believe, must come into the ascendancy. Each individual must refine and work out a new kind of psychological life, a new kind of meaningful existence, by expanding his inner skills and his inner powers. Can historians, can psychologists help man here? No historian, so far as I know, has claimed yet that his insights have influenced the course of history. Nor can we say that any particular insights of a psychological nature have made any real dent beyond their influence — I am thinking especially of the psychotherapeutic setting here — on the life of the individual. But must we resign ourselves to the conclusion that this restriction will forever prevail?

Insights gradually filtering into the population at large, and particularly into the intelligentsia and the elite groups, may indeed have some kind of influence, although it cannot be neatly discerned. I do not find it ludicrous, for example, to consider it possible that the fact that we have been living now for the better part of a century with the idea of an Oedipus complex, with an increased understanding of the child's involvement with the parental figures, has been a factor in the diminution of the generation gap that we are witnessing. The fact, for instance, that students are sitting in on faculty committees now, unheard of in previous eras, is clearly not the direct result of Freud's having described the Oedipus complex. But our increased familiarity with the child's experiences vis-à-vis his parents might very well be a factor in the general loosening of the stiffness and reserve that existed between the generations, of the diminution of the mutual suspiciousness that in turn has all kinds of political and social ramifications. In the same way, I believe it possible that the understanding of the intensity and meaning of narcissistic rage, what a narcissistic injury means for individuals and populations, as it filters through universities to science writers to newspapers and the popular media, might in the long run, and maybe not even in the all-too-long run, assert some kind of beneficial effect on our capacity to tolerate narcissistic injuries without having to fly into a killing rage, without having to be forever unable to make compromises.

Chairman: Thank you very much. Now let me just invite questions and comments in whatever order they may come up.

Q: I wonder if Dr. Kohut could explain to us why so few women have been idealized figures in society.

H.K.: I don't know the answer to this question. Classical analysis would have answered by pointing out that the absence of a visible genital in the little girl is of crucial importance in psychic development and leads to such a severe wound in self-esteem that later self-confidence remains low and idealizability therefore lessened. Now, I do not see, at least not from my own clinical experience, that the narcissistic injury that undoubtedly is connected with the absence of the visible genital in little girls is, in essence, different from the narcissistic injury to the little boy who discovers that his penis is very small as compared with the penis of a grown man.[1] I believe, however, that a child is much more signifi-

---

[1] Subsequent reactions by several colleagues to these remarks served as the stimulus for "A Note on Female Sexuality" (1975b), included in this volume.

cantly influenced by the empathic attitude of the grownups around him or her than by the givens of organic equipment. A mother's and father's admiration of a little girl as a little girl, in her sweetness, in her future bearing of children, in whatever potentials of her femininity she displays, will provide her ultimately when she becomes a woman with the same degree of security and idealizability that the man has — if *he* was accepted by his admiring and happy and glad parents when he was a little boy, even though his penis was small. The importance of the matrix of empathy in which we grow up cannot be overestimated.

It is interesting that Freud in his last technical paper, "Analysis Terminable and Interminable"—a great paper in many respects—closed with a statement of ultimate pessimism. He concluded that analysis can go up to a certain point but not beyond it. It cannot persuade a man to accept his passivity toward another man, and it cannot persuade a woman to accept the absence of the penis. Here, he says, it has reached biological bedrock. Now it would seem to me that it is up to the historian to undertake a comparative study of the attitude of adults toward children at different periods in history, in order to throw some further light on the conditions that Freud tried to explain biologically. Why, he should ask, for example, was the little girl not as welcome as the little boy? Was the little boy in early times more highly esteemed because he would later be a powerful protector and helper, as a warrior, as a tiller of the soil? I admit that I do not have answers to these questions, that I am batting the ball back to the historians. Still, I would stress that I am convinced that the research of the historian would be enriched by the insights that psychoanalysis can provide for him as he gets ready for his work, and as he carries it out.

Q: I understand that, according to psychoanalytic theory, fixations on childhood attitudes come about in consequence of excess gratification. Can you explain the frequency of such fixations in view of the fact that the *absence* of the mother and *insufficiency* of mothering are well-established historical facts, especially in nineteenth-century Europe?

H.K.: A thought-provoking question. There is in the question, however, couched a bias for which I cannot blame the questioner because it is a generally accepted bias. The bias rests in the word "mothering," and it rests in the word that is even more important behind the word mothering—namely "mother." I don't believe that these terms do justice to the complexity and the variety of relationships that can constitute a psychologically good or bad environment for the child. I have come more and more to abstain from using these terms when, in the course of my work, I discuss psychic development, and I speak instead of the "empathic responsive matrix" which the child needs for psychological survival and growth. It may not make any difference whether it is the child's biological mother who is the provider. It may not even make a crucial difference whether one or several people are involved in the mothering, as you would say, or in the empathic environment of the child, as I would say.

An interesting study, relevant to our topic, about an experiment in nature, so to speak, was written by Anna Freud and Sophie Dann about twenty years ago (1951). They reported on a group of six children who had survived the concentration camp. In the course of their three years in the camp they were taken care of by ever-changing successive sets of mothers. The children survived, but the young women who were delivered into the concentration camp were all exterminated, to be replaced by a new group of young women who, until their death, took care of the children in their turn. Now, these children were surely disturbed, no doubt—but they were not schizophrenic. These children had a reasonably cohesive self; they had had a reasonable sense of being accepted in this world. The only conclusion one can draw is that the young women, as the end of their life was approaching, fastened on the next generation with a kind of empathy, with a kind of affection, with a kind of responsiveness that gave these children a sense of the continuity and reality of their self that allowed them to become viable individuals.

I used this example to show the complexity of the psychological substance that lies behind the simple term "mother." Many times you find that the children of disturbed mothers are in comparatively good psychological health, while children of not so obviously disturbed mothers are disturbed. I have long puzzled over this matter and have come to the following conclusion: If the mothers are grossly disturbed, other adults will jump into the breach and respond to the children. But if the mothers are what we call latently schizophrenic, borderline cases, hiding their schizophrenia behind bridge cards, then such children are exposed to an emotionally empty, nonsustaining environment without being able to turn to others, without enlisting others to their cause.

I gave you a complex answer; but I think you will understand what I was aiming at. One must think not simply in terms of "mothering" and "mother," but in terms of the total complexity of an environment and whether it is positive or negative. During the era preceding our own, the overstimulating closeness with the adults to which the child was exposed led later in adult life to the hostilities and inhibitions which, as I said earlier, Freud's explanations may have ultimately helped us to overcome to a degree. Now we may see the results of a deadening distance to which children are exposed, leading in adulthood to a different kind of psychopathology, the disorders of the self, and leading also, we hope to a new set of explanations which in the long run will help us to overcome the leading psychic disturbances of our time.

Q: I have a historical question—it's a bit of turning the tables—concerning the evolution of depth-psychological thought. Please explain why the development in psychoanalysis that is represented by your ideas is taking place at this point in history when works of art and literature are being created—Pirandello, for example, on whom I am doing some research—which cannot be understood without the use of concepts like Sartre's in philosophy or like yours in psychology.

H.K.: As you can imagine, I have thought about this question before. The theory I have formed is that the greatest pioneering artists of any period are dealing with the leading psychological problems of tomorrow; that art is one day, as it were—whatever a day means in the historical sense here—ahead of science in this respect. The great artists of yesterday dealt with the experiences of people in the world of interpersonal love and hate and with the experiences of people in the sphere of the swings of narcissism to which a firmly cohesive, relatively strong self is exposed: the loves and hates, the triumphs and defeats of basically strong people were their subject matter. But now a good many artists have begun to deal with a new set of issues. This set of issues, to speak of it in the most gross terms, is the falling apart of the self and of the world and the task of reconstituting the self and the world. Among the artists who deal with this problem by verbal means is Kafka. In his stories he describes that there is nobody around to whom one can turn. One searches for a place one never gets to in *The Castle.* One searches hopelessly for a person who will at least define one's guilt, but one is killed meaninglessly in *The Trial.* One wakes up in the morning and finds with horror that one's self has become dreadfully changed and estranged in *Metamorphosis.* Perhaps the greatest expression of the central anxieties of our time was achieved by Eugene O'Neill. I don't know how many of you are familiar with *The Great God Brown*, but in this interesting play none of the personages know exactly who they are. The characters in *The Great God Brown* wonder whether they are themselves or somebody else when they put on a mask. They are always either putting on masks and becoming someone else or taking off these masks and becoming — preconsciously — themselves again. They are clearly not aware or sure of who they are. But the clearest expression of modern man's leading problem is contained in a statement by Brown who says, shortly before his death: "Man is born broken. He lives by mending. The grace of God is glue." O'Neill expressed here in Brown's words not only the sickness of modern times but also his own individual sickness. Later he told the personal story extensively in *A Long Day's Journey into Night:* about the addicted mother, the self-absorbed, vain father, and the resulting fragmentation of the selves of the sons, in particular the fragmentation-proneness of his own self. The damage suffered by his self led him, on the one hand, toward alcoholism, but also, on the other hand, through the power of his genius which enabled him to escape the addiction and to glue the fragments of his broken self, to the creation of works of art. The broken self is mended via the creation of the cohesive artistic product. These are the problems that lie in the center of the preoccupations of the artists of our time, problems that are indeed different from those with which the artists of the past had been struggling, the problems, let us say, portrayed by Ibsen's or Shakespeare's plays. But why the change?

The only answer I have is that in former times the involvement between the parents and their children was overly intense. The children were emotionally overtaxed by their proximity to adults — be they the parents or nursemaids or others. They were stimulated, touched, cajoled; and they developed all kinds of conflicts as they responded to the stimulation to which the protracted emotional interplay with the adults exposed them. In that sense we might say that the Oedipus complex, while not an artifact, was yet artificially intensified by this overcloseness between adults and children.

But now we seem to be dealing with the opposite problem. There is not enough touching, not enough genuine parental responsiveness; there exists an atmosphere of emotional flatness and sterility. Is this change to some extent due to the increasing overpopulation on earth? Is the parental self-absorption related to the need to curb the growth of the population? I don't know. But I do know that man must achieve a new psychological balance now as he learns to adapt to stable frontiers and a life without numerous children. How can he find this new balance, and what kind of inner and outer adjustment should he strive for? Here, it seems to me, lies again an area in which historians and depth-psychologists should cooperate and try, via scientifically posed questions, to provide scientifically valid solutions for these crucial problems.

47

A Note on Female Sexuality

At a recent symposium I responded with a brief discussion to a question from the audience concerning the position of women in society and, in doing so, touched on some differences between my outlook on the problems of femininity and that of classical psychoanalysis. Several colleagues who either heard my discussion or read the transcript afterwards chided me for having abandoned the psychological outlook of Freud, thus relinquishing, as they felt, some important hard-earned and valuable insights. I will go directly to the heart of the matter by questioning whether the difference between my views regarding the area of female sexuality and the views of my critics is really as great as they seem to think. I am wondering about this point on the basis of the fact that I have no quarrel with many of the classical psychoanalytic views in this area which they were upholding in the face of what they took to be my deviation from the traditionally held tenets. Specifically, I have no doubt that the sight of the male genital will inevitably make a very strong impression on the little girl, that it will become a crystallization point for her envy—the propensity for which is present in every human being, female and male—and that, among other factors, it will leave a distinctive imprint on the personality of women—just as the recognition of the possession of a penis by the little boy will

This paper (1975) was written by Kohut in reply to being criticized for some remarks he made about the psychology of women at a symposium on "The Self in History" (see pp. 776-777).

tend to reinforce (and lend a specific content to) the propensity for grandiosity which is also present in every human being, male and female, and will leave a distinctive imprint on the personality of men. At the meeting with the historians I wanted to point to areas of cooperative investigation between analysts and historians and to stress the fact that it is in the broad field of changing cultural influences where historians can assist our understanding and where, in the reverse, we can assist them by defining questions of psychological relevance.

There is a great deal more involved concerning the little girl's experience of her genitality and the influence this experience has on the formation of the woman's adult personality and the role it plays in the genesis of her psychic disturbances, than my preceding statements do justice to.[1] In pursuing the discussion of a possible divergence of my views from those considered to be classical psychoanalytic ones, I will try to avoid the traditional "nature vs. nurture" dialectics of the usual arguments among analysts concerning this matter (as Freud [1905b] attempted to do by introducing the concept of complemental series). Debates conducted along these lines have never led anywhere, and I cannot see how

----

[1] [Kohut had commented, several years earlier, on the precursors of femininity and masculinity in childhood, on the occasion of a discussion of Robert Stoller's paper, "The Male Transsexual: Mother's Feminized Phallus," presented at a Panel on "The Development of the Child's Sense of His Sexual Identity." His remarks were reported by Virginia Clower in the *Journal of the American Psychoanalytic Association* (1970), 18:165-176.

. . . Heinz Kohut agreed that the data obtained through the observation of children should be of decisive importance for analysts in formulating statements about the psychology of childhood. The interpretation of childhood behavior, however, is necessarily influenced by the knowledge of the mature psyche and of infantile residues embedded in the mature psyche which are obtained through the analysis of adults. The vital question concerns the extent to which an observer may interpret early data in the terms of later development. In this context, it seemed

they will ever be fruitful. I shall restrict my examination of this topic to evaluating the intensity of these childhood experiences concerning the nonpossession of a penis and to determining the role played by the imprints of these experiences (especially the unconscious memories concerning them) in shaping the woman's personality.

To begin with, I agree with the classical position that the experience of having suffered an injury to body narcissism is inevitable. And I do not even make a point of questioning the use of the term "innate" in this context, which one of my critics used in referring to this injury; I know he wrote his note to me quickly and did not take the time to examine the appropriateness of each word he employed. He may well not have intended a commitment to the essentially nonpsychological approach to these matters that is implied by his calling the *injury* "innate." What *is* innate are, in all likelihood, only the biological givens (the difference of the genitals) to which the little girl reacts with envy, shame, rage, and denial—even though the possibility exists that in the prehistorical past of the human race those females of the species who reacted with greater sensitivity to the experience that they had no penis had a higher survival rate—the possibility,

---

to him that, in the present papers, full gender identity was postulated in earliest life when one should instead speak, for example, of activity or passivity as precursors of masculinity or femininity.

Recalling his own work on the consolidation of the early self through the mother's "mirroring" response (repeated as "mirror transference" in the analysis of narcissistic personalities), Kohut thought that the mothers in Stoller's study might have responded to *precursors* of femininity— not to femininity in the true sense of this term—in their narcissistically passive and beautiful sons, and that these maternal responses reinforced influences toward the later establishment of true psychosocial femininity. One should, in other words, speak of femininity only when conscious or unconscious object-directed ideations (e.g., sexual fantasies about men or boys) assign a specific gender role to the child's self, i.e., when a condition has been established that clearly transcends the boy's previous narcissistic passivity.]

in other words, that this specific narcissistic vulnerability was selected into the race (and that there was a sex-linked further inheritance of this trait). But be all this as it may, I do not doubt the assertion that the injury is inevitable, that it has an incidence of one hundred percent. What I am questioning is that it is per se a significant genetic factor in the major personality deformities encountered in women, that it accounts per se for the major disturbances of self-esteem encountered in women (in particular, that it accounts for the narcissistic personality disorders of women) or, last but not least, that it is the essential motivating force that propels every girl — via reaction-formations, substitutions, displacements, and other primary processes — toward womanhood, in particular that it underlies the woman's wish for a child. That the woman's wish for children should, in the last analysis, be reducible to the wish for a penis that she experienced when she was a little girl has always struck me as one of the few badly skewed opinions held by Freud, notwithstanding the fact that fantasies about the equation of penis, feces, and baby may frequently be uncoverable in hysterical women. In contrast to this definition of the deepest psychological layers motivating a woman's wish for a child — an explanation that seems to me to have no *general* validity — I believe that the healthy woman's wish for a child is, in psychological terms, grasped much more adequately as a manifestation of her nuclear self, as a manifestation of her most central ambitions and ideals — in short, as the high point of a development that has its beginnings in the archaic self's urge toward self-expression. It is this urge which may become channelized toward motherhood at the point when physiological and emotional maturity are reached, i.e., when the convergence of biological and cultural factors may give this concretely defined content to the woman's self-expressive needs. The framework of a theory of infantile drives, in general, and the hypothesis of the propelling power of the frustration of the little girl's phallic-exhibitionistic wishes, in particular, cannot, in my opinion, serve as the basis for an adequate psychological explanation of a healthy woman's wish for a child.

I will not pursue these issues any further here; but will mention only that I have arrived at the conclusion—a hypothesis I hope to be able to present extensively in the not-too-distant future in a contribution to the theory of psychoanalysis on which I am working at the present time—that experiences of isolated drives are not primary psychological configurations but disintegration products; that they occur whenever the primary broader experiential configurations have become destroyed. The healthy self-esteem of the female baby—whose nuclear self had been mirrored empathically by an adult, experienced by the baby as a selfobject, who is proud of her—will, in other words, lead to the healthy self-esteem and to the healthy self-expression wishes of the older girl, and will, ultimately, enter into the joyful wish of the grown woman to have babies (if hormonal stimulation and the cultural milieu support this wish) or will prompt her to seek self-expression via different routes (if hormonal stimulation is lacking and the cultural milieu directs her toward the joyful pursuit of other goals). And, in the obverse, the not-empathically-responded-to, the depressed female baby, older girl, and, ultimately, woman—lacking a firmly established self which proudly wants to exhibit and express itself—will hypercathect the experience of isolated drives, and of isolated body parts and body products, in order to stimulate herself, in order to feel alive,[2] and will then, secondarily, experience the failures in the supraordinated area of the self (the depressed self, the loss of self-expressive joyfulness, the discon-

---

[2] The fact that the wish for a baby can—and often does—express a woman's striving to cure a disturbance of her self (an insufficiently cathected self; a fragmented self; the insufficient idealization of values) is of great importance not only with regard to the individual psychopathology of women, but also, and par excellence, with regard to the sociology of psy-

nectedness from sustaining idealized goals) as shortcomings of body parts and as the frustration of circumscribed drives. I am certain that the self—the basic experience of being a center of independent initiative and of being the recipient of impressions and of having cohesiveness in space and continuity in time—with its nuclear ambitions and ideals and its creativeness cannot be adequately conceptualized within a framework of drives, even though I have chosen a terminology (the grandiose-"exhibitionistic" self that needs the mirroring selfobject) and am occasionally using expressions (e.g., I may speak of the "voyeuristic" merger needs of the self that looks up to the idealized selfobject) that are meant to serve as a bridge to drive psychology.

Psychologically speaking then—and on the basis of the stance I have taken for a long time (Kohut, 1959b), namely that psychoanalysis is (and that, in its essence, it has always been) an introspective-empathic psychology of complex mental states—the need of the budding self for the joyful response of the mirroring selfobject, the need of the budding self for the omnipotent selfobject's pleased acceptance of its merger needs, are primary configurations. Just as we cannot examine physiological life even at its most primitive beginnings within the framework of inorganic chemistry, so can we not examine psychological life even at its most primitive beginnings within the framework of a theory of isolated drives. The experience of the child's need for the confirming-mirroring selfobject and of his need to merge with the omnipotent selfobject are the primary psychological configurations—despite their relative complexity. This broadly conceived "exhibitionism" and this broadly conceived "voyeurism" are not drives; they

---

chopathology. Women who have babies on the basis of the attempt to heal the pathology of their selves will not be able to respond to their babies' budding selves with appropriate mirroring acceptance and will thus, as it were, transmit their self-pathology (their own microstructural defects and deficits in the area of the self) to the next generation.

are not definable with reference to the physiological pressure of erogenic body zones; they do not relate only to the skin or to the eye, but to the total body-mind self, however rudimentary this perception of the self may be in infancy. When these primary psychological needs are not empathically responded to, then these broad configurations begin to break apart. And I am convinced of the fact that, at least in the narcissistic personality disorders (including the great majority of the perversions encountered in clinical practice), the infantile sexuality that can be detected beneath the surface of the symptoms or beneath the symptomatic behavior of these patients (and, of course, the infantile sexuality that can be detected beneath the perverse sexuality openly displayed by these patients) is not biological bedrock but psychological surface. Behind it lies the child's experience of the flawed personalities of the selfobjects who were unable to respond empathically to the needs of his self *in statu nascendi*. Having given up hope of attaining the selfobject's responses which would lead to a filling-in of the structural defects from which these patients suffer, they have turned toward the attempt to gain via the stimulation of isolated body zones, via the activity of isolated drives (sexualized voyeurism and fetishism instead of the search for the idealized selfobject; sexualized exhibitionism instead of the appeal to the mirroring selfobject), the inner cohesion and sense of being alive that only the selfobject's responses could truly provide. The addictionlike intensity of perverse activities and the addictionlike intensity of the hunger for self-esteem-enhancing nutriment in the (nonperverse) narcissistically disturbed are in the main not due to a craving activated by the drives involved, but by the intense need to fill a structural defect. Still, while the intensely exciting activities will for a moment not only give erotic pleasure but also succeed in making the self feel alive, they do not build psychological structure, and thus they lead nowhere. They are like the ravenous eating of a person with a gastric fistula; there is intense hunger, intense stimulation of an overwrought orality—the food, however, provides no nourishment.

But one doubt may yet seem to remain: could not the appearance of drives after the destruction of the broader psychological configurations be taken as proof that drives (as separate and distinct psychological entities) had been there all along, that their presence had only been covered up by the presence of the more complex configurations? The answer to this question is in the negative. Organic matter can be destroyed; it decomposes, and inorganic matter will appear. But this sequence of events does not indicate that the inorganic matter had been hidden by the presence of the organic one or that the individual organism starts out as inorganic matter. The same considerations also apply with regard to psychological life. Drive elements are from the beginning of psychological life integrated within the complex primary psychological constellations that refer to the self's needs for the responses of the selfobject.[3] The experience of a drive in isolation is not a primary configuration—it appears only as a consequence of untoward (unempathic) responses from the side of the selfobjects.

[3] The objection could here be raised that some kind of psychological life exists even before the formation of a self, and thus before a self's need for the responses of selfobjects can arise. (I am, of course, referring to the stage which Freud, in the terms of the libido theory, called autoerotism.) This objection is, however, irrelevant. Even if we should assume that at the very beginning of life no trace exists of a rudimentary self to which the zonal autoerotic experiences would be amalgamated, this assumption would have no bearing upon the topic under scrutiny. The drives with which we are concerned in the present context belong to a much later stage of libido development, the phallic stage, i.e., to a stage where there can be no doubt concerning the existence of a self and concerning the importance of the self's relation to selfobjects. I will nevertheless add here, although the statement is not needed in support of my present argument, that I have come to assume that, even at the very beginning of psychological life, the drives are already integrated into larger experiential configurations—at least as far as the all-important matrix of the selfobject's expectations is concerned (cf. Kohut, 1977).

It is not the recognition of her lack of a penis, I believe, that is the cause of serious disturbances of self-esteem in women (including serious degrees of narcissistic rage, i.e., destructive penis envy). The causal sequence proceeds rather in the opposite direction: a woman's protracted and/or recurrent (depressive) sense of being castrated, of not being up to par, and her lifelong attitudes of (paranoid) rage and vengefulness about this narcissistic injury, grow on a soil of broader and deeper narcissistic deprivations. If, in other words, the self is poorly coherent because it was deprived of the mirroring acceptance of its totality and of the opportunity to merge with an accepting idealized self-other, then the injury to phallic exhibitionism will lead to a significant (depressive) lowering of self-esteem, and, in turn, to (paranoid) chronic rage and destructiveness. And in the obverse: if there is empathic mirroring acceptance of the little girl's self, if she can merge with the idealized admired parental imago, then the recognition of the sexual difference will cause no permanent harm, will not lead to a lasting disturbance of narcissistic equilibrium.

I have, in general, obtained the impression that many of the gross events in children's lives that tend to be held responsible for the psychological disturbances occurring in adult life are only crystallization points for future pathology. To remember them does not lead to a cure — and neither does repetitive recall nor even the working-through of the resistances that surround them. The real causes must be established with the aid of the careful reconstruction — in the transference — of the more or less subtle psychopathology of the selfobjects and of their disturbed empathic responses (exemplified, for example, by their unempathic seductiveness). It is here that we can find the genetic explanation for the faultily organized or defective psychological structures of our narcissistically vulnerable patients. And the cure of their disorders, as I said, is not achieved by focusing on gross events, and on the macrostructural[4] memories of the gross traumata correlated to them, but by the careful scrutiny—in technical terms: the reconstructions which can gradually be obtained on the basis of working through the narcissistic transferences —of the disturbed psychological microstructures which, in turn, are genetically derived from the interplay with the pathogenic (parental) selfobjects.

As I come to a close, I must admit that I have not given a circumscribed answer to the question whether my statement to the historians constitutes a significant divergence from the traditional views about female sexuality. But the crucial question is not whether my views diverge from the classical ones and whether the divergence is a significant one—the crucial question is whether it is warranted, whether the view I proposed illuminates the complex conditions we observe in the psychoanalytic situation more accurately, more deeply, more relevantly than the classical view, and whether, with the aid of the reformulations suggested, our therapeutic mastery is enhanced.

---

[4] For the definition of the terms macro- and microstructures within the framework of modern physics and modern depth-psychology, see Levin (1975).

48

Creativeness, Charisma, Group Psychology

Reflections on the Self-Analysis of Freud

The Psychoanalyst and His Image of Freud

We are faced by uncertainties and difficulties when we investigate Freud's self-analysis: first, by those which in all areas of applied analysis arise because we are not participating in a living clinical situation; second, by those that arise because we might not be objective about Freud, who is for us a transference figure par excellence — we are prone to establish an idealizing transference toward him or to defend ourselves against it by reaction formation; and third, by those that arise because Freud's self-analysis is a unique event in the history of human thought.

This is not the place for an examination of the goals and methodological problems of applied analysis, but I will discuss two issues: the general difficulties we confront when we undertake the study of Freud (aspects of his personality, his biography, his significance), and the additional difficulties we face when we attempt to interpret the meaning and to evaluate the significance of Freud's self-analysis. These difficulties arise because we are here dealing with a psycho-

First published in *Freud: The Fusion of Science and Humanism* (1976), ed. J. E. Gedo and G. H. Pollock. *Psychological Issues*, Monogr. 34/35. New York: International Universities Press, pp. 379-425.

The numbered footnotes in this essay are Dr. Kohut's; the lettered ones are Gedo and Pollock's.

logical situation that — as the first scientifically orderly introspective effort to scrutinize complex psychological states — is
without recorded precedent in the history of human thought.[1]

It is always hard to achieve an objective evaluation of a
great man, whether the evaluation be by the average biographer, the historian, or the depth psychologist (R. and E. Ster-
bas' *Beethoven and His Nephew* [1954, pp. 12-17] contains
an illuminating discussion of these problems). The great man
is prone to become a transference figure for the beholder —
usually, of course, a father figure — and the childhood ambivalences of the investigator may intrude to falsify results.
Even more widespread is another pitfall: the biographer's
apparently falling in love with his subject.[a] When examined
more closely, I believe it turns out that true object love is not
involved here, but the establishment of a bond of identification. The choice of the subject is frequently determined by

[1] Here two points may need to be emphasized. I am not claiming
priority for Freud's self-analysis (and, by extension, for the science of psychoanalysis) simply because Freud used the introspective approach to the
complexities of inner life — this approach to the broad field of inner experience has been used from time immemorial by poets and mystical philosophers — but because he did so in a scientifically orderly, systematic way
and recorded and formulated the results of his observations in terms of a
more or less experience-distant theory. Nor am I claiming uniqueness for
Freud's self-analysis (and, by extension, for the science of psychoanalysis)
simply because he used the introspective approach in order to obtain scientifically valid psychological data — this claim could also be made for the
self-observations of experimental psychology — but because his subject matter was the whole of psychic life in all its breadth and depth. It is the fact
Freud used the introspective approach in a systematic, scientific way without narrowing the scope of his subject matter (and that, by extension, psychoanalysis has continued to employ the introspective-empathic approach
in the same fashion) which justifies the assertion that the introduction of
the psychoanalytic method constituted a revolutionary step in the history of
science. (For further remarks on this important topic see Kohut, 1959b,
especially pp. 205-211; 1970c, especially p. 593n; 1973, especially pp.
528-529.)

[a] For another discussion of this issue, see the remarks of B. Meyer
(Panel, 1972).

the investigator's identificatory predilections (dictated perhaps by needs emanating from structural defects or
weaknesses of the biographer who is in search of identifications) and the long preoccupation with the life of the investigated is prone to reinforce the identificatory bonds even
further.[b] Still, one might expect that the pitfalls of such a
scientific enterprise would prove to be least dangerous for the
psychoanalyst. The analyst is after all specifically trained to
observe and control his own reactions, and he should be able
either to set aside his childhood loves and hates and his narcissistic (e.g., identificatory) needs during his clinical and scientific work or at least disqualify himself when he senses his
inability to do so.

In general it would be justified to make such demands on
the analyst, and, on the whole, we may assume that there is
at least a fair chance that he may be able to live up to these
standards. As regards the figure of Freud, however, the
analyst's task is vastly increased, and objectivity is hard for
him to attain. In the following I shall discuss the two major
obstacles standing in the analyst's way when he attempts to be
objective about Freud.

The first obstacle stems from the fact that analysts usually
become acquainted with Freud during the crucial formative
years in which their professional selves as analysts take shape.
This fact alone is weighty enough. But there is, in addition, a
peculiar circumstance that must not be underestimated.
While he is a student at a psychoanalytic institute, the future
analyst does not primarily study Freud's life and his opinions,
but is forced to identify with Freud from the inside, as it
were; that is, he is asked to think himself into the most
intimate and detailed activities of Freud's mental processes.
Each student of psychoanalysis reads and rereads "The In-

[b] See the remarks of M. Zeligs (Panel, 1972) for an excellent illustration.

terpretation of Dreams" (1900a). As he undertakes the study
of this fundamental volume he undergoes over and over again
the peculiar experience of moving from the manifest content
of one of Freud's dreams toward Freud's unconscious dream
wishes, and thus he participates in the workings of the most
intimate recesses of Freud's mind: Freud's preconscious and
unconscious libidinal and aggressive strivings in the object-
instinctual and narcissistic sectors of his personality over and
over again become the student's own, and so do Freud's resistances, conflicts, and anxieties. If the student of analysis
does not want to deprive himself of the full, enriching experience of obtaining his basic knowledge from the genuine
source of the report of the discoverer, given at the time when
the discovery was still a recent, immediate, fresh experience,
he is forced to identify with the deepest layers of Freud's personality. Such empathic closeness with total sectors of another
person's mind, extending from conscious to unconscious
levels, is not available to us in our day-to-day relationships,
not even with those we are closest to—the members of our
family and our friends. True, once we are in the daily practice of clinical analysis, such contact with the inner life of
others does indeed fill our working day; but this contact is di-
luted by the simple fact that we do not experience our
empathic trial identifications with only *one* patient, but participate in the inner life of an increasing number of them.
The convergence of the facts that Freud is the great father-
figure and teacher of our science, that we are studying him
from the inside, as it were, and that this study constitutes our
first, or at least a very early and basic, experience of identification with the unconscious of someone else—combine to
produce in analysts a specific attitude toward Freud, i.e., an
attitude of firmly established identification with an idealized
figure (or, in reaction formation, of rebelliousness against this
identification). The idealization of great teacher figures is undoubtedly encountered in other branches of science, too.

However, in general, these idealizations constitute simply a new psychological content which temporarily attaches itself to the permanent unconscious idealized images of the superego; they are by no means analogous to the deeply anchored, lasting identifications that develop in the analyst with regard to Freud.[2]

Although the pull toward establishing a gross and uncontrolled identification with Freud is strong, I believe that with the aid of increasing self-understanding (e.g., as acquired during the training analysis) the student should be able to resist it. And I believe that insight would help dissolve even an already established identification with Freud — unless it is the symptomatic result of a persisting, unanalyzed, structural defect — if the causative factors that I have so far mentioned were the only ones responsible. Another factor exists, however, whose influence weighs even more heavily in the balance.

The most important obstacle the analyst faces when he tries to achieve an attitude of objectivity toward Freud is that the idealized figure of Freud plays a currently active role in the dynamics of the psychoanalytic community, i.e., that body of psychoanalytic practitioners, scholars, and researchers, which in the past was sometimes — unfortunately, and, I think, largely erroneously — referred to as "the psychoanalytic

---

[2] Some psychoanalytic educators might draw the conclusion that a simple curricular remedy is alluded to here — namely, the postponement of the study of Freud's "The Interpretation of Dreams" until later in the analyst's career and its replacement by the study of secondary writers and of more up-to-date approaches. Such a conclusion is unwarranted. The analyst must not attempt to sidestep psychological tasks by avoidance; on the contrary, the identificatory pull should be faced openly through increased awareness of its existence, of the psychological defect that tends to submit to it, and of the psychological assets that can be mobilized against it. (In this context see the discussion of the crucial difference between gross and wholesale identifications, on the one hand, and the result of the process of *transmuting internalization* on the other [Kohut, 1971, pp. 45-50, 165-167].)

movement" (see Freud, 1914a). I would like to suggest that
the idealization of Freud by the individual members of the
psychoanalytic community has played an important role —
usually a positive one, but not always — in maintaining both
the psychic equilibrium of the individual analyst and group
cohesion in the analytic community. It exerts its influence
particularly by virtue of the fact that, on the individual level,
it tends to forestall the development of certain exquisitely
painful experiences of narcissistic imbalance in the analyst
(such as the pangs of jealousy and envy) and, on the group
level, it is a counterforce to the rash and indiscriminate formation of splinter groups which tend to arise in response to
the ill-controlled narcissistic demands of certain of its creative
members (such as the tendency for new discoveries to stimulate secessionist movements instead of becoming integrated
into the previously accumulated body of knowledge). There is
no need to expand on these formulations since they are fully
in harmony with certain basic psychoanalytic tenets concerning group psychology. Ever since Freud's relevant pioneering
contribution (1921), we have taken for granted that group
cohesion is mainly established and safeguarded with the aid
of the imago of the leader who, as the ego ideal held in common by the members of the group, becomes that point to
which all individuals look up, and to whose greatness they all
submit in shared admiration and submission.

A detailed and comprehensive study of the advantages
and disadvantages for the science of psychoanalysis which are
related to the fact that psychoanalysts are held together by a
shared ego ideal, the idealized imago of Freud, should some
day be undertaken — this task, however, is beyond the scope
of the present essay. Here I would only point out one of the
advantages accruing to analysis from the fact that psychoanalysts are held together by powerful emotional bonds. The
essential continuity of a group, its essential sameness along
the time axis despite the changes brought about by growth

and development, is a precondition for the healthy productivity of the group, just as is the analogous continuity of the self-experience, despite the analogous changes within the confines of a single life span, for the healthy productivity of the individual. To state it differently: a firm group self[3] supports the productivity of the group just as a firm individual self supports the productivity of the individual. Applying this maxim to psychoanalysis and stating it in the negative, we can say: if — even on the basis of legitimate reforms in theory and practice — psychoanalysis should change so abruptly and to such an extent that the sense of the continuity of the science were lost, then the individual analyst would receive no further stimulation from his participation in the scientific community of analysts, would lose his sense of belonging to a living, developing body of scientific knowledge to whose growth he can contribute, and his productivity would cease.[4]

---

[3] The concept of a "group self" will be discussed later in the present essay.

[4] In harmony with my emphasis on the importance of a sense of historical continuity for the psychoanalyst, I continue to be an advocate of historically oriented presentations in the curricula of psychoanalytic educational institutions. Although I realize that the systematic rather than the historical presentation of psychoanalytic theory and technique would have some advantages for the learner, I still believe that there ought to be a minimum of courses that acquaint the student from the beginning of his studies with the germinal thoughts of Freud and of his early pupils. The familiarity with "The Interpretation of Dreams" and with Freud's great case histories is of particular value in this respect. The study of these works is not only a splendid and, I believe, still irreplaceable exercise in a difficult new mode of thinking (i.e., in terms of the symbolic notations of metapsychology), it also sets up a historical baseline for the future analyst from which he can trace the development that led to the modern theories and clinical methods. The advantages of retaining a minimum of historically oriented teaching are immeasurable and, to my mind, outweigh the advantages of a totally nonhistorical systematic orientation. To follow the unbroken line of development from the original discoveries in their original form through the various changes of the early formulations to their present state will allow the student to experience the development of psychoanalysis in the course of his psychoanalytic education and will provide the psycho-

Among the disadvantages arising for psychoanalysis
because analysts form strong bonds of idealization to an internalized imago of Freud, let me briefly speak of two. The
first — it seems to me to be the less deleterious one — is a tendency toward conformity. New thought, in other words, is in
danger of being viewed with suspicion because it is experienced as potentially disruptive. Many analysts may thus tend
to be overcautious with regard to new ideas, while others,
owing to the presence of a preconscious rebelliousness against
the encompassing presence of an unchanging ideal, will welcome new ideas not so much because they have convinced
themselves of their validity as because they have experienced
them as a liberation from a dimly felt internal bondage. The
second unfavorable consequence of Freud's imago having
served as a stimulus for the mobilization of idealizing cathexes
seems to me to be of even greater importance than the first.
The channeling of the flow of a large part of the individual
psychoanalyst's narcissistic energies toward the group ego
ideal creates psychological conditions unfavorable to creative
activities that emanate from the grandiose self. To describe
the situation in experiential terms: the ambitious strivings

---

analyst with that firm sense of the cohesion and continuity of analysis which
forms the secure basis of all future creative developments. Nor should the
cognitive advantages of a historical orientation be underestimated. Only by
studying the origins and the way stations can the present theories be fully
understood. And only by realizing how analysts have in the past struggled
unceasingly to formulate newly discovered data with the aid of new concepts will psychoanalysis continue to fulfill its potential for further growth.
I am convinced that the vitality of psychoanalysis as a growing science is far
from exhausted. It has so far hardly scratched the surface of the human
mind, and it will deepen its investigations for a long time to come, if — and
indeed here lies a grave danger — historical and political developments do
not stifle its activities from the outside. The recognition of this danger —
perhaps in the form of the ascendancy of an antipsychological, totalitarian,
mass society — should, in addition to the detached desire to expand the
frontiers of psychological knowledge, prompt the analyst to investigate the
field of history with the hope of increasing man's mastery over his historical
destiny.

and the cognate self-expanding urge toward new discoveries — in the physical world, to move into new territories, i.e., a derivative of archaic flying fantasies — are not sufficiently engaged and will therefore not stimulate the growth and refinement of correlated new sublimatory structures, i.e., of ego functions (talents) that would perform in accordance with the pressures emanating from the grandiose self. The potentially creative narcissistic strivings of the individual psychoanalyst may, in other words, be committed in too large a proportion to idealized goals. No doubt all creative and productive work depends on the employment of both grandiose *and* idealizing narcissistic energies, but I think that truly original thought, i.e., creativity, is energized predominantly from the grandiose self, while the work of more tradition-bound scientific and artistic activities, i.e., productivity,[5] is performed with idealizing cathexes.

But we must leave these general and speculative considerations and return to the more narrowly circumscribed area of our present concern. We are dealing with the question of how the analyst employs his nonobjective, idealizing attitude toward Freud in the service of protecting himself against a disturbance of his narcissistic equilibrium. The answer to this question will, of course, secondarily explain certain resistances against discarding the idealization of Freud, i.e., resistances that are an outgrowth of the analyst's wish that his narcissistic equilibrium remain undisturbed.

I believe the idealization of Freud protects each analyst in two ways against the experience of painful narcissistic tensions. (1) Genuine, i.e., nondefensive idealization in any form and with any content (it is most effective in the form of a strongly idealized superego, i.e., in the form of meaningful, high ideals) is always an important and valuable

---

[5] I first encountered the felicitous comparative juxtaposition of the terms "creativity" and "productivity" in a letter (February 5, 1968) to me from K. R. Eissler.

safeguard against the development of narcissistic tensions
(e.g., shame propensity) because a substantial amount of a
person's narcissistic energies will be absorbed by his ideals.
(2) The idealization of a group model protects the individual
member of the group against certain states of narcissistic
disequilibrium which are experienced as envy, jealousy, and
rage. If these narcissistic tensions remain undischarged, they
are exquisitely painful; if, however, they are discharged
(through actions, especially actions motivated by narcissistic
rage), then they are socially dangerous. If the present-day
psychoanalyst can maintain that everything of importance
in psychoanalysis has already been said by Freud, if, furthermore, the imago of Freud has been securely included in the
analyst's idealized superego and has thus become a part of
the self, then he can disregard contemporary competitors,
they are not a threat to his own narcissistic security, and he
can avoid suffering the painful narcissistic injuries that the
comparison with the actual rivals for the goals of his narcissistic strivings might inflict on him. Small wonder then that
the deidealization of the Freud imago creates strong uneasiness in the analyst and mobilizes strong resistances against
taking an objective, realistic attitude toward Freud, i.e., an
attitude in which Freud is seen as a fellow human being
with his assets and defects, his achievements and his limitations. True, as I stated before, tearing down the image of
Freud is a not infrequent occurrence in the history of
analysis. One may assume such events to be largely
defensive: in many instances, at least, they testify to a persis-
tent, unmitigated idealization of Freud in the detractor's unconscious.

Readers inimical to psychoanalysis may well gloat over
the preceding statements and may feel justified in their criticism of psychoanalysis as an unscientific, semireligious
enterprise. But I will leave aside the comparatively easy task
of formulating an anticipatory rebuttal to such potential

abuse of my considerations and instead propose that, in true psychoanalytic tradition, we should regard these insights, if indeed they are in essence valid, as a challenge to expand the domain of our awareness. Specifically, I would say they challenge us to deepen and broaden our training analyses in the narcissistic sector of our candidates' personalities. We must be particularly watchful concerning the detrimental possibility that the unconscious grandiose-exhibitionistic strivings of our candidates will escape from becoming sufficiently engaged in the psychoanalytic situation, and that, in consequence of this evasion, they will not become gradually sublimated and integrated into the reality ego of the future psychoanalyst. The incompleteness of the mobilization of the candidate's narcissism (and/or the incompleteness of the working-through process in the narcissistic sector) may be caused in a variety of ways involving the entire spectrum of resistances in the candidate and a motley array of blind spots, countertransferences, and theoretically buttressed attitudes in the training analyst. One specific mode in which the narcissistic pressures in the candidate may be shunted aside and escape analysis is via the implicit or explicit agreement between analysand and training analyst that the potentially disturbing narcissistic cathexes of the candidate are to be committed to an idealized imago of Freud. To end a training analysis on the high-minded note of a shared admiration for Freud is, because of its emphasis on fraternal and communal feelings, not only a socially acceptable step of great respectability, it can also be a moving experience for the candidate, which soothes his pain at the parting and sweetens the inevitable bitterness of having to accept the reality of his frustrations in the object-instinctual and the narcissistic realms. It cannot be denied, nevertheless, that such a termination may in some instances tend to close off certain postanalytic potentialities for the future analyst. In particular, the commitment of his still uncommitted narcissistic cathexes to the imago of Freud may deprive him of the emotional pressure to search for individually valid solutions and may increase his structural conflicts (his guilt feelings) if he, in independent assertiveness, should try to express the pattern of his own self. The clinical issues concerning this whole problem area are too complex to be dealt with in the present context, and I will add only one statement in order to give an appropriately balanced outlook: a training analysand's spontaneously arrived at, realistic, nondefensive capacity to admire Freud as one of the great minds of the Western world and as a model of scientific rigor and moral courage by no means indicates that the narcissistic sector has not been successfully dealt with in the analysis. On the contrary, it may sometimes even be considered a sign of analytic success, especially in personalities who were formerly unable to mobilize any enthusiasm for greatness, whether encountered in the form of admirable ideas or of admirable personalities.

Freud's Self-Analysis: The Transference of Creativity

After this cautionary discussion of some of the personal, social, and methodological problems posed for the psychoanalytic investigator by an examination of Freud's personal life and scientific activities, I now turn to the hub of the present inquiry: an evaluation of Freud's self-analysis during the years preceding the publication of his decisive scientific contribution and greatest work, "The Interpretation of Dreams."

The initial question to which I shall address myself is whether Freud's self-analysis should predominantly be considered analogous to all other analyses or whether its essential significance is to be sought elsewhere.

There is no doubt that the insights Freud obtained were

of benefit to his emotional health in the ordinary psychoanalytic sense of the word, i.e., his self-analysis lifted repressions, dissolved psychoneurotic symptoms and inhibitions,
and thus secondarily put instinctual forces that had formerly
been bound up in structural conflicts at the disposal of his
ego. Seen from this, the traditional viewpoint, we will say
that the success of Freud's self-analysis was the precondition
for his creativity. We may furthermore say not only that the
inner freedom obtained by his self-analysis liberated the
nameless creative forces which served as the instinctual fuel
for his achievements, but that he was in addition, on the
strength of his unique endowment, able to turn each personal insight into a suprapersonal scientifically valid psychological discovery.[6]

If we look at the relationship Freud established with
Wilhelm Fliess during the period of his self-analysis we will
quite naturally assume that, lacking an analyst (who would
become the focal point of the transference, i.e., the target

[6] Here, the objection might be raised that each analysis is simultaneously therapy and research. I would have no quarrel with such an opinion if
the term research in this context is meant to refer broadly to a specific
mental attitude (taken by analyst and analysand) of openness to the unexpected and the unknown. In this sense, analysis may indeed be looked upon
as a form of research—especially by comparison with the therapeutic
processes of medicine in which known remedies are applied to cure known
illnesses. True research, however, aims at the discovery of data and relationships that have not been seen before, while in the usual therapeutic
analysis the open-minded attitude is directed toward the recognition—the
rediscovery—of already previously discovered configurations. True research
requires, in addition, the intention—whether consciously acknowledged or
not—of formulating the newly seen configurations in more or less experience-distant terms and of communicating the findings and theories to the
broader scientific group. My claim that Freud's self-analysis was unique by
being a combination of therapy and research therefore rests on the fact
that here a therapeutic endeavor was not just combined with the rediscovery of what was already known but also with the creative discovery of
configurations that had never been recognized before, and with the
courageous intention of communicating the findings to the appropriate
representatives of society, the community of scientists and scholars.

of the object-directed and narcissistic, libidinal, and aggressive strivings from the unconscious), Freud would almost as
a matter of course search for a suitable person in his environment who could play this role for him. Indeed, we must
admire the cleverness of Freud's choice of Fliess, with whom
he was not in direct contact most of the time — the
behind-the-couch distance and invisibility of the ordinary
analyst was here replaced by the distance between Vienna
and Berlin, which likewise kept the disturbing reality input
at a minimum. It is in tune, it must be stressed, with
Freud's psychological genius that he did not — as so many of
our patients and training analysands are wont to do even
though an analyst is in fact at their disposal — live out his
transferences with his friends and family or, what must have
been most tempting, with his patients through the formation
of countertransferences. In summary, then, we will understand why Freud's analysis has been primarily taken as a specific variant of an ordinary therapeutic one and why it was
thought that no other hypothesis is needed in addition to the
assumption that Fliess was called upon to fill the void of the
empty chair behind the symbolic couch on which Freud
struggled along his way toward insight and mastery.

Freud's self-analysis was not the first analysis ever conducted. Freud and Breuer had already approached the
problems of many patients through the application of the
psychoanalytic method. Yet in certain respects — particularly
if we consider the breadth of Freud's aim and the persistence of his investigative effort as he conducted his self-
analysis — this analysis was indeed something new, even if we
disregard the absence of an analyst. It was the first
specimen of the type of analysis that the modern analyst is
in essence still practicing, i.e., it was an analysis that aimed
at the depth-psychological comprehension of the total personality and was not narrowly focused on a pathological
symptom or syndrome. It was — and indeed continued to be

almost to the very end of Freud's life—the first specimen of "analysis interminable."

Even though Freud's self-analysis was the pioneering precursor of the broadly conceived analyses of today, not all of its features are equivalent to those with which we have become familiar in our usual therapeutic work. It is the specific historical position of Freud's self-analysis, not the fact that analysand and analyst were the same person, that accounted for those elements—especially the meaning of the central transference—which set it apart. I now turn to a discussion of these distinguishing features of Freud's analysis in order to offer an alternative—or to be more exact, a complement—to the traditional hypothesis about the significance of Freud's transference to Wilhelm Fliess.

At the height of the transference neurosis of the usual therapeutic analysis, the analysand's extra-analytic activities and his capacity for full emotional responsiveness outside the analytic situation are commonly impoverished; creativeness, too, is generally curtailed and tends to appear only in the final stage of the analysis, after the insightful resolution of certain specific sectors of the transference has been achieved. During the time of his self-analysis, however, Freud was not only capable of responding to his environment with strong, deep, varied, and appropriate emotions, as can be ascertained by a perusal of his correspondence, but he was arriving at the most original insights, discoveries, and formulations of his life, as is attested by the great work which was the crowning result of the labors of this period.

If Freud's self-analysis had been primarily an act of self-healing through insight, one would have expected it to end, parallel to the termination of the analysis of the usual transference neurosis, with the discovery of the meaning of the transference and, simultaneously, its resolution. In Freud's case, however, there seems to have occurred a dissolution of the transference bondage without corresponding insight,

i.e., Freud's understanding of the full meaning of transference came only gradually, much later, and was derived from
his clinical work. Freud's transference to Fliess must therefore be viewed as a phenomenon accompanying creative
work: Freud's self-analysis was a creative spell which was
simultaneously worked through analytically.

This phenomenon is outside the realm of pathology,[7] although it is distantly related to the clinically observable fact
that a modicum of empathic contact with the analyst is
necessary for the maintenance of a newly acquired capacity
for artistic sublimation on the part of certain analytic patients.

Mr. E.,[8] for example, was suffering from a severe narcissistic personality disturbance with regressive swings that
had the appearance of fleeting psychotic episodes. As a result of the systematic working through of his analysis, he
gradually acquired the ability to channel certain formerly
pathologically employed narcissistic cathexes into emotionally absorbing and fulfilling artistic activities. Both the leading symptom of his psychopathology (a voyeuristic perversion) and his newly acquired artistic sublimation were off-
shoots of his lifelong intense concentration on the maintenance of visual contact with the world. Already in his earliest
years he seems to have shifted the focus of his contact needs
from his frustrated oral, tactile, and olfactory demands
toward his vision, as could be reconstructed on the basis of
transference fears lest his intense gaze overburden and
destroy the (mother-)analyst. (Throughout the patient's
childhood the patient's mother had been ill with malignant
hypertension—she was frequently very tired, never picked
him up when he was a baby, and was unable to give to the
child the self-confirming emotional sustenance he needed.

---

[7] Ellenberger (1970), however, uses the term "creative illness" for such
events.
[8] This patient is frequently referred to in Kohut (1971).

She died during the patient's late adolescence.) The significance of the patient's voyeuristic perversion—he was irresistibly driven by the dangerous urge to look at male
genitals—can be gleaned from the details of the situation in
which it made its first appearance. During the patient's
early adolescence the boy and his mother were at a country
fair. He had enjoyed himself alone on a high swing (undoubtedly in a preconscious elaboration of archaic flying
fantasies) and, pleased with his skill and prowess, asked his
mother to watch him perform. When the mother, who was
tired and depressed, did not respond to his wish, he suddenly felt bereft of the buoyancy he had just experienced, and
felt drained and empty. It was at that moment that he
turned away from his mother and walked to a public toilet,
driven by the irresistible wish to gaze at a powerful penis
(see Kohut, 1971, pp. 158-159).

In the present context there is no need to spell out the
metapsychological substance of the patient's perversion
beyond the minimum necessary for understanding the relation between the patient's narcissistic transference bond,
which had established itself in his analysis, and his ability to
maintain a newly cathected artistic sublimation. The essence
of the perversion could be gleaned from childhood memories
(such as the episode at the country fair) and was confirmed
over and over again as the transference was being worked
through. The patient's developing self had been badly deprived of cohesion-maintaining narcissistic cathexes because
of the dearth of appropriate responses (mirroring) to his
narcissistic (-exhibitionistic) needs. His craving to fill an
inner void, to obtain a sense of aliveness, therefore became
intense; furthermore, there is little doubt that—because of
innate endowment and accidental circumstances (e.g., the
fact that he was deprived of tactile contact)—these needs
became concentrated in the visual sphere. Deprived as it
was, and severe as his regression might be, his self would

never permanently disintegrate; he never quite gave up the hope that he would ultimately obtain the needed confirming-approving-mirroring response from the narcissistic object. As he offered himself (visually) to his mother (e.g., in the country fair), so did he within the context of the analysis in the transference.

It is instructive to compare an early, beautifully elaborated attempt by the patient to channel the analysis and its insights into the visual-artistic area with the episode late in the analysis which we are contemplating here. At that time, too, it was a separation from the analyst that was the trauma to which the patient reacted. But then, under the impact of this trauma, he erected a rudimentary structure of artistic expression which was still directly related to the self-object analyst (see Kohut, 1971, pp. 130-132). It was an emergency step into art—the artistic product was crude and ephemeral. In the present episode, by contrast, the patient responded to the same trauma not with a crude forward move but with the temporary disintegration of the advanced structures of artistic expression—the artistic product was now completely unrelated to the needed selfobject—that he had in the meantime, in the course of the analysis, acquired via innumerable microinternalizations in response to micro-traumata. And he was able now, with the aid of insight and on the basis of the different solidity of the newly acquired structures, to re-establish his interest in the artistic product, which was now elaborated and constituted an abiding discussion of his self. Still, the analytic work was not completed. Even now, the maintenance of the artistic sector of his personality depended to some extent on the presence of the analyst. Whenever the hope for an empathic mirroring response was disappointed, a regression took place, and instead of persisting in his demands and renewing his attempts to obtain narcissistic gratification on the level of "mirroring," he turned to the sexualized attempt to achieve his needed narcissistic sustenance through a visual merger with the symbol of powerful maleness with which he could thus identify.

It would be tempting to enter into a discussion of the meaning of the patient's perversion at this point, but — even in its briefest form — such an enterprise would lead us too far afield.[9] In our present context, however, we can say that in the transference the patient experienced over and over the following specific sequence of events: (1) he offered himself — or later his artistic product, i.e., the extension of his grandiose self — to the narcissistic object (the analyst in the mirror transference); (2) he was disappointed because of an empathic failure from the side of the analyst — or because of other narcissistic blows from him; (3) then followed a regression leading to the intensification of the voyeuristic perversion; (4) the analyst responded with an empathic interpretation of this reaction; (5) the perverse urge now subsided, and the patient renewed his attempt to obtain mirroring admiration. It was the working through of the repeated experience of this sequence that gradually increased the patient's mastery over the regressive trends and that buttressed his ability to persist in his creative efforts despite disappointments.

An episode that occurred after several years of analysis, when the patient had already made considerable progress, is of particular significance in illuminating the role the narcissistic object is called upon to play in support of the more

[9] Those familiar with my studies of narcissism will have no problem recognizing that here again (as I first pointed out in my discussion of Patient A. [Kohut, 1971, see especially pp. 69ff.]) we can see that the perversion is not caused by the existing pregenital sexual fixations, but that it is a manifestation of the need to fill a structural defect. The visual merger with the powerful penis (including the accompanying unconscious or preconscious fellatio fantasy) constitutes the attempt to obtain needed narcissistic sustenance (to fill a structural void) and to escape from a sense of emptiness and depression.

or less precariously maintained ability to carry on creative
activities. Mr. E.'s general condition had much improved by
that time, and his whole life was now more satisfying and on
a higher level. His homosexual voyeurism had nearly disappeared, and he was not only deriving considerable inner
satisfaction from his art, but, since luckily he did indeed
possess considerable talent, he was also receiving sufficient
external acclaim to satisfy some of his needs for approving,
accepting, and (self-)confirming responses. The patient was
now able to weather the usual week-end separations from
the analyst without feeling endangered by the pull of his
voyeurism — clearly an indication of the considerable progress he had already made. On this occasion, however, he
not only had to confront the tension created by the time gap
between the last appointment of the present and the first
appointment of the following week, he also had to confront
the feeling of an increasing separation from the analyst in
space. During this weekend it became necessary for him to
undertake a trip to a city about two hundred miles from
Chicago because of some artistic work he had been commis-
sioned to do there. As he left Chicago by train, he was not
only still in high spirits, but his mind was creatively preoccupied with the work he was going to do upon his arrival.
As mile after mile went by, however — specifically (as he reported in the Monday session), as mile after mile of distance
interposed itself between him and the analyst whom, as he
now began to realize, he had always fantasized as sitting in
his analytic chair during the weekends, waiting for him to
come back, the patient experienced again the old feeling he
had thought he had overcome: a sense of depression, a painful lowering of self-esteem, a sense of inner emptiness, and a
need to be filled up. As the train took him further and
further away from Chicago, the sense of emptiness
increased, and, simultaneously, his interest in the artistic
task, which had formerly been so stimulating to him, de-

clined. Finally, about halfway between Chicago and his destination, he suddenly felt the urge to follow a sailor into the toilet. It was at this moment that he was able to make use of the analytic insights he had acquired. He grasped the essence of what was going on in him, resisted the temptation, went through with his trip and his assignment (though not as zestfully and creatively as he had anticipated), and returned to Chicago. On the trip back he could observe in himself that his self-esteem began to rise, that the sense of inner emptiness diminished, and that his creative and artistic interests began to intensify again as the distance to the narcissistic object decreased.

I shall now return to Freud and his quasi analyst in order to examine the significance which the imago of Fliess may have had for Freud as narcissistic support with regard to the creative (nontherapeutic) aspects of his analysis. I am not overlooking the vast difference separating Freud's transference experience from that of Patient E.[10] As I said before, the phenomenon under consideration is outside the realm of psychopathology and is only distantly related to such occurrences as those illustrated by Mr. E.'s trip. Nevertheless, if we shift the focus of our attention from the specific focus of the narcissistic transference in psychopathology and examine instead the general psychological significance — whether in illness or in health — which the relationship to

[10] I am not alluding here to the fact that Patient E.'s sublimatory activities were sustained by a *mirror* transference while Freud in the lonesome uneasiness of his voyage of discovery into the depth of the mind turned toward an omnipotent idealized figure, i.e., may be said to have established a relationship which is akin to an *idealizing* transference. These are small differences, no more than variations on a basic theme, which we may disregard in the present context. People whose self is in need of sustenance, whether because of the energic drain and anxiety during a creative spell or for other reasons, will tend to establish narcissistic relationships to archaic selfobjects — whether in the form of one of the varieties of a mirror transference or through a merger with an idealized imago.

selfobjects may have for people, then the previous clinical material will serve as an acceptable background for the following constructions.

It is my main thesis that during periods of intense creativity (especially during its early stages) certain creative persons require a specific relationship with another person—a transference of creativity—which is similar to what establishes itself during the psychoanalytic treatment of one major group of narcissistic personality disorders.

In the treatment situation, the endopsychic substance of this relationship is the analysand's idealizing transference to the psychoanalyst. This transference is the manifestation of a phase of normal development, which, in consequence of the regression induced by the treatment situation, has been revived in a distorted form. During the normal phase of development that corresponds to the idealizing transference, the caretaking empathic adult is held to be omnipotent by the child, who obtains a sense of narcissistic well-being (of being whole and powerful, for example) when he is able to experience himself as part of the idealized selfobject. Under favorable conditions the adult's empathic response to the child sets up a situation in which the child's phase-appropriate need for a merger with an omnipotent object is sufficiently fulfilled to prevent traumatization. This basic fulfillment of the need, however, is the precondition for the subsequent developmental task, which involves the child's gradual recognition that the adult is not omnipotent and that he, the child, is not a part of him but a separate person. In consequence of this gradual and phase-appropriate disillusionment, the idealizing cathexes are withdrawn from the archaic object and set up within the psychic apparatus (e.g., idealizing the values of the superego). In other words, an archaic selfobject imago has been transmuted into psychological structure. If this developmental task is not completed, however, then the personality will be lacking in sufficiently idealized psychological structures. In consequence of this defect, the person is deprived of one major endopsychic method by which he could maintain his self-esteem: the self's merging into the idealized superego by living up to the values harbored by this psychic structure. Yearning to find a substitute for the missing (or insufficiently developed) psychic structure, such persons are forever seeking, with addictionlike intensity and often through sexual means (the clinical picture may be that of perversion), to establish a relationship to people who serve as stand-ins for the omnipotent idealized selfobject, i.e., to the archaic precursor of the missing inner structure. In everyday life and in the analytic transference the self-esteem of such persons is therefore upheld by their relations to archaic self-objects.

Although I believe that the transference of creativity is a phenomenon akin to the idealizing transference, I do not claim that creative people are of necessity suffering from structural defects that drive them to seek archaic merger experiences. I suspect, however, that the psychic organization of some creative people is characterized by a fluidity of the basic narcissistic configurations,[11] i.e., that periods of narcis-

[11] The metapsychological explanation of the processes of scientific and artistic creativity suggested here within the framework of the theory of narcissism (i.e., the theory of the two major narcissistic configurations and of their cathexes) should be compared with the important formulations offered by previous workers (in particular Sachs and Kris) within the frame of reference provided by the structural model of the mind.

Sachs (1942; see especially pp. 48-49) believes, in harmony with Freud (1908b), that the creative poet initially "uses his fantasy as a means of gaining narcissistic gratification for his own person." His guilt feelings, however, force him to shift his "narcissism" away from himself and onto his creation. The poet thus gives up more of his narcissism than average people, "but his work wins back immeasurably more of it than others can hope for."

Kris's relevant statements (1952b, pp. 59-62) about the sequence of "inspiration and elaboration" in the process of artistic creation are not only psychoanalytically sophisticated behavioral descriptions, they also provide us with an account of the processes of creation in metapsychological terms.

sistic equilibrium (stable self-esteem and securely idealized internal values: steady, persevering work characterized by attention to details) are followed by (precreative) periods of emptiness and restlessness (decathexis of values and low self-esteem; addictive or perverse yearnings: no work), and that these, in turn, are followed by creative periods (the unattached narcissistic cathexes which had been withdrawn from the ideals and from the self are now employed in the service of the creative activity: original thought; intense, passionate work). Translating these metapsychological formulations into behavioral terms, one might say that a phase of frantic creativity (original thought) is followed by a phase of quiet work (the original ideas of the preceding phase are checked, ordered, and put into a communicative form, e.g., written down), and that this phase of quiet work is in turn interrupted by a fallow period of precreative narcissistic tension, which ushers in a phase of renewed creativity, and so on.

I am not prepared to say whether this three-phase schema applies to the vicissitudes of Freud's work and creativity, but I can furnish some evidence in support of the idea that this is so. There is no doubt, for example, that Freud had an enormous capacity for prolonged and concentrated attention to details in the service of the completion and perfection of his work (phase two of the three-phase schema) and that he possessed high, strongly cathected, internalized values. Furthermore, one might hypothesize that his intense oral-respiratory cravings (e.g., his increasing, unbreakable

---

Kris sees the creative process, as does Sachs, within the metapsychological context of the functions of the structural model of the mind. In contrast to Sachs' emphasis, Kris does not stress the motivational importance of the superego conflict, i.e., the motivational importance of guilt feelings, but the interplay of ego and id during the collaboration of two structures in the creative activity. To put Kris's formulation in a nutshell: during the phase of inspiration, the id holds sway, while during the phase of elaboration, the ego predominates.

bondage to cigar smoking)[12] were related to a depressionlike state of precreative inner emptiness, which was the manifestation of the decathexis of the self as the narcissistic energies detached themselves and became available for the creative task.[13] Freud did indeed report that a certain disturbance of his well-being was a necessary precondition for his creativeness (Jones, 1953, pp. 345-346). Was Freud here describing the unpleasant feeling of tension that accompanies the precreative regression of narcissistic libido (i.e., an autoerotic tension state)? Did he at such times feel empty and depressed, and was there an addictionlike intensification of oral-respiratory intaking needs — all as manifestations of the decathexis of the narcissistic structures in consequence of the fact that the narcissistic energies had to remain in uncommitted suspension, waiting to be absorbed by the creative activity? I cannot do more here than to raise these questions. If these hypotheses could be confirmed, they would lend support to my interpretation of one aspect of Freud's

---

[12] Freud himself believed that there was a connection between his addiction to cigars and his capacity to work. He wrote (in a letter to Fliess of June 12, 1895): "I have again begun to smoke, because I never stopped missing it (after fourteen months of abstinence) and because I have to spoil that psychic rascal in me, or else he won't do me any work" (my translation; cf. Schur, 1972, p. 86).

[13] The feeling of estrangement the creative person often experiences vis-à-vis the product of his creativity, his work, is in many instances not the result of structural conflicts (e.g., guilt about having produced something beautiful or discovered something important) but the direct expression of the fact that at the very moment of creativity the self is depleted, because the narcissistic cathexes have been shifted from the self to the work. In the productive activities of noncreative persons and in the phase of quiet work of creative minds the narcissistic cathexes are distributed between the self and the work, with the result that the self is experienced (and later remembered) as the active initiator, the source, the shaper of the product. During the phase of frantic creativity, however, the self is depleted because the narcissistic cathexes are concentrated on the work, with the result that the self is not experienced (and is later not remembered) as the initiator, source, or shaper of the product.

relation to Fliess as a regression to the idealization of an archaic omnipotent figure.

In the foregoing, I supported the hypothesis that one aspect of Freud's relationship to Fliess should be understood as the expression of his regressively activated need for an idealized archaic omnipotent figure by demonstrating that this explanation fits meaningfully into the broader framework of a conception of creativeness in terms of the dynamics of narcissism. In the following, I will show that my interpretation is not only supported by its congruence with the aforementioned broader theory but also by empirical evidence gathered within the framework of (pre-)conscious motivations.

During creative periods, the self is at the mercy of powerful forces it cannot control; and its sense of enfeeblement is increased because it feels itself helplessly exposed to extreme mood swings which range from severe precreative depression to dangerous hypomanic overstimulation, the latter occurring at the moment when the creative mind stands at the threshold of creative activity. (For a summary of Freud's vivid description of his emotional state during creative periods, see Jones, 1953, pp. 343-345.) And when his discoveries lead the creative mind into lonely areas that had not previously been explored by others, then a situation is brought about in which the genius feels a deep sense of isolation. These are frightening experiences, which repeat those overwhelmingly anxious moments of early life when the child felt alone, abandoned, unsupported.[14][c] Freud put it

[14] See in this context Székely's perceptive contributions (1967, 1970) concerning the fear of the new and unknown in scientists. For clinical material illustrating such emotional states, see Gedo (1972).

[c] The patient described in this paper forestalled the development of feeling states of aloneness and abandonment in consequence of his highly original discoveries by arranging to publish them only with a co-author. The function of the collaborator in preparing the work was to listen to the patient's ideas and assure him of their pertinence and validity. Interestingly, in

bitterly when he said (March 16, 1896), "I . . . live in such isolation that one might suppose I had discovered the greatest truths" (1887-1902, p. 161)—a statement to which one can add only that here a sense of humor aided Freud in confronting the fact that he had indeed discovered truths that could not but cause him to stand alone in the newly opened territory, alone until a few courageous pupils began to follow him. Small wonder, then, that creative artists and scientists—the latter at times in striking contrast to their fierce rationality in the central area of their creative pursuits—often attempt to protect their creative activity by surrounding it with superstitions and rituals. But while one creative mind will have to protect himself with "a pair of tall wax candles in silver holders at the head of his manuscript" (the description of the novelist Aschenbach in Thomas Mann's *Death in Venice*) and while another (Schiller) had to work on a desk from the drawer of which the smell of rotten apples emanated (see Eckermann 1836-1848, *Conversations with Goethe*, Part 3; October 7, 1827), there are still others—among them, I believe, was Freud—who during the period of their most daring creativity will choose a person in the environment whom they can see as all-powerful, a figure with whom they can temporarily blend.

The transferences established by creative minds during periods of intense creativity are therefore much more closely related to the transferences that occur during the analysis of narcissistic personalities than to those that occur in the analysis of transference neuroses. In other words, we are dealing with either (a) the wish of a self which feels enfeebled during a period of creativity to retain its cohesion

---

the small professional community qualified to judge the work, it was invariably attributed to the patient alone. In terms of Kohut's concept of the transference of creativity, this instance illustrates a variant in which the grandiose self is expressed in the form of a *twinship*.

by expanding temporarily into the psychic structure of others, by finding itself in others, or to be confirmed by the admiration of others (resembling one of the varieties of a mirror transference) or (b) the need to obtain strength from an idealized object (resembling an idealizing transference). Thus, relationships established during creative periods do not predominantly involve the revival of a figure from the (oedipal) past, which derives its transference significance primarily from the fact that it is still the target of the love and hate of the creative person's childhood.

It would be fascinating to pursue the investigation of the varieties of the narcissistic relationships (and of the details of the narcissistic bonds by which they are maintained) that creative people establish, especially during their creative periods. In the area of the grandiose self, for example, some evidence has already been accumulated in support of the assumption that the twinship relation to an alter ego may provide the necessary confirmation of the reality of the self during creative periods. Mary Gedo's studies (1972) show convincingly that under these conditions Picasso was in need of self-cohesion-providing relationships to alter-ego figures (e.g., to the painter Georges Braque). The presence of an alter ego and the narcissistic relationship to it, one might speculate, protected the self of the artist from the danger of irreversible fragmentation to which it felt exposed while it was drained of narcissistic energies during periods when the genius-artist allowed the visual universe to break into meaningless pieces before he reassembled them and, in so doing, gave Western man a new perception of the visible world.*

* Footnote added 1978: I have recently come across one of the most striking examples of a transference of creativity of the twinship variety — the relationship between James Joyce and James Stephens. While undertaking the most daring creative step of his life, the composition of *Finnegan's Wake* involving the complete transformation of the use of language as an artistic medium, Joyce, in the words of his accomplished biographer, developed "one of the strangest ideas in literary history" (Ellman, 1959, p. 604). He

Undoubtedly, the large areas of the relation between homosexuality and creativity, first explored by Freud (1910a, p. 59), will also be illuminated when we investigate it by taking into account the vicissitudes of the narcissistic cathexes. Although I am not able to present empirical data obtained through the systematic psychoanalytic investigation of a great creative artist or scientist, I will offer a substitute: the literary testimony of a great writer. The value of this evidence is enhanced by the fact that there is good reason to assume that the relevant insights contained in the artistic document under consideration were in essence derived from the writer's own experiences, in particular with regard to the vicissitudes of his own creativity. The examination of Thomas Mann's *Death in Venice* (Kohut, 1957b) reveals that the essence of this beautiful novella is an almost scientifically exact portrayal of the disintegration of artistic sublimation. The artist Aschenbach, Mann's protagonist, had throughout his long creative life been able to channel the available free narcissistic cathexes toward his artistic productions.[15] While in his childhood he must still have been in severe jeopardy — his childhood self had been insufficiently sustained by his environment and had been in danger of fragmentation — he had later become capable of providing himself with the needed experience of psychological perfection and wholeness — i.e., the experience of basic self-esteem — through the creation of works of art. Extensions or duplications of the self were now available which he could invest with narcissistic libido: he could give them formal perfection. But, as the story begins, this ability is being lost. The artist is aging, and his power to create replicas of the perfect self is waning. On the way to

---

formed an intense attachment to Stephens, considered him to be his twin and with great intensity spun out the fantasy that he would transfer the authorship of his work to him (pp. 604-606, 630, 632).

[15] I am in these remarks expressing the conclusions reached in an early investigation (1957b) in the terms of my more recent findings.

total disintegration, however—and here lies the focus of the novella—we see the revival of the sexualized precursor of the artistic product: the beautiful boy (though frail and already marked for destruction) who is the symbolic stand-in for the core of the still unaltered childhood self which craves love and admiration. As "the cultural structure of a lifetime . . . [is] . . . destroyed," i.e., as the writer's ability to deploy the narcissistic cathexes in the performance of the creative task is lost, the narcissistic cathexes return from the work of art to the imago of the fragmenting childhood self. There they rest briefly, delaying the ultimate destruction of the personality for one more moment.

The deployment of the fluid narcissistic cathexes of creative persons toward idealized imagoes seems to be even more common than their search for replicas or expansions of the grandiose self—as exemplified by the case of Aschenbach. At any rate, man's need for the merger with a supporting idealized figure is more easily observable.

But to return to Freud's self-analysis. If we accept that in its essence Freud's self-analysis was not a self-therapeutic experience but rather the crowning achievement of his creative genius, then we will understand why he did not discover the clinical transference at that time. The end of Freud's self-analysis was not analogous to the termination of the usual therapeutic analysis, i.e., it did not occur in consequence of the fact that the analysand (Freud) had recognized the transference, i.e., the illusory aspects of his relationship with the analyst (Fliess), and that the transference had been worked through. It was rather the opposite: the transference—an idealizing transference of creativity—became superfluous and came to an end when the creative work done with the aid of the self-analysis had been consummated. In other words, for Freud during his most important creative spell, Fliess was the embodiment of idealized power; and Freud was able to dispense with the illusory sense of Fliess's greatness and thus with

the narcissistic relationship—in contradistinction to a resolution of transference by insight—after he had completed his
great creative task. [d]

Charismatic and Messianic Personalities

One subsidiary question with regard to the transference of
creativity still to be confronted concerns the problem of the
specificity of the choice of the narcissistically cathected selfobject.

In the usual clinical circumstances, given the appropriately neutral attitude of the analyst and his noninterference with
the unrolling of the endopsychic process elicited by the psychoanalytic situation, the transference will develop in accordance with preanalytically established endopsychic factors.
The transference will portray the objects of the analysand's
childhood, in particular as he loved and hated them in the
context of the crucial events which formed his personality, especially its neurotic aspects. True, some actual features of the
analyst's personality and of his actions will become
temporarily amalgamated during the analysis with imagoes
stemming from the analysand's childhood. But these details

[d] We have some evidence that a later period of Freud's creativity was
marked by a similar expansion of the grandiose self: during the creation of
his work on Leonardo da Vinci (1910b), the case histories of Little Hans
(1909a), of the Rat Man (1909b) and of D. P. Schreber (1911b), and "Totem
and Taboo" (1913b). From the Freud-Jung correspondence (McGuire, 1974)
and Jung's memoirs (1961) it should be possible to reconstruct these vicissitudes of Freud's relation to Jung. Referring to Gedo's essay on the Freud-
Jung correspondence (J. Gedo, in preparation), Kohut suggested (at a meeting of the Chicago Psychoanalytic Society, November 16, 1974) that the temporary increase of Freud's need for a powerful figure during the time of his
strongest idealization of Jung was motivated not so much by a new creative
advance as by fear vis-à-vis the consciously wished-for but unconsciously
dreaded expansion of psychoanalysis beyond the confines of Vienna—i.e.,
in the language of Freud's childhood, by fear regarding a move from a
narrow (Jewish) environment into a vast (gentile) world.

of the clinical transference, while of considerable tactical importance in clinical psychoanalysis, do not constitute its essence: their relation to the core of the transference, i.e., to the genetic center of the psychopathology, is the same as the relation between the day's residue and the unconscious dream-wish from childhood in dream psychology.

In the transference of creativity, on the other hand, the opposite may be held to be true. Here, it is a current situation that is central, a situation in which an enfeebled self, drained of its cohesion-maintaining cathexis and engaged in the daring exploration of the moon landscapes of the unknown, will seek the temporary aid that comes to it from the relation with an archaic selfobject, particularly with an idealized parent imago. True enough, the transference of creativity repeats an archaic childhood situation: it is a reversion to that phase of development in which the self in formation had not yet separated itself from the figures in its environment — had not separated itself, in other words, from the imagoes which for the social-psychological observer are the "objects" of the child. But the child still experienced these figures in the early environment as belonging to the self, they were still "selfobjects." Now, if in the analysis of a narcissistic personality disturbance the psychoanalytic situation is established appropriately, then a narcissistic transference will develop spontaneously, and it will take on the predetermined form — or the predetermined sequence or mixture of forms — that is the outgrowth of the analysand's childhood history and of the correlated fixation points in his development. These conditions, however, must not be expected to prevail in the creative personality — at least, they are not essential.[16]

[16] Creativity may be embedded in a great variety of personality make-ups, ranging from normal to psychotic. There are undoubtedly many creative persons who, if scrutinized with an eye to classifying them in terms of psychopathology, would have to be counted among the narcissistic per-

The essential ingredients of the usual clinical transference are therefore preanalytically established, and the personality of the analyst and other reality factors concerning him must in the main be taken into account only on the basis of the question whether they might *interfere* with the unfolding, the maintenance, and the working through of the transference. This maxim does not hold true with regard to the transference of creativity, however — whether a twinship is sought (in which the alter ego must fit its role, i.e., it must *in fact* resemble the needy personality of the creative person) or whether it is the archaic idealized omnipotent object that is required (which must then *in fact* have certain features that make it suitable for the role the creative person assigns to it).

And what are the characteristic features of the person who is especially suitable to become the admired omnipotent selfobject for the creative person during the period when he makes his decisive steps into new territory? Certain types of narcissistically fixated persons (even bordering on the paranoid) — they display an apparently unshakable self-confidence and voice their opinions with absolute certainty — are specifically suitable to be the objects of the idealizing needs of the creative person's temporarily enfeebled self during a creative spell. Those who fall into this psychological category are obviously not likely to offer themselves to the scrutiny of the psychoanalyst. They do not feel ill, and their self-esteem is high. What makes them specifically able to play the role of the idealized archaic object for those who are in need of it, and what makes them ready to fill it, is the fact that the mainten-

sonality disorders. While, on the one hand, the fluidity of the narcissistic cathexes in the creative mind creates vulnerabilities similar to those to which (noncreative) narcissistic personalities are exposed, and, on the other hand, the favorable outcome of the psychoanalytic treatment of narcissistic personality disorders is not infrequently due to the fact that the patient succeeds in channeling some of the formerly pathogenic narcissistic energies toward creative pursuits, spontaneous creativity is, in its essence, not related to the narcissistic personality disorders.

ance of their self-esteem depends on the incessant use of certain mental functions: they are continually judging others — usually pointing up the moral flaws in other people's personalities and behavior[17] — and, without shame or hesitation, they set themselves up as the guides and leaders and gods of those who are in need of guidance, of leadership, and of a target for their reverence. In many instances it appears that such charismatic and messianic personalities have fully identified themselves with either their grandiose self or their idealized superego. For most of us, the herd of common mortals, the ideals[18] we harbor are direction-setting symbols of perfection. They provide us with narcissistic pleasure when we come near to the target they have set for us, and they deprive us of narcissistic sustenance when we fall short of it by too wide a margin. The messianic leader figure, however, is done with the task of measuring himself against the ideals of his superego: his self and the idealized structure have become one.

Certainly, the endopsychic arrangements that support the self-esteem of the charismatic or messianic person deprive his personality of elasticity. Mobility and the reliance on several different sources of self-esteem are in the long run safer ways of psychological survival than the maintenance of a rigid narcissistic equilibrium through the employment of a single set of restricted functions. Indeed, the endopsychic equilibrium of the charismatic leader or of the messiah seems to be of the

---

[17] The role that the function of judgment plays for most people in the psychic economy of narcissism must not be underestimated. I am not speaking here primarily of the mechanism of projection, with the aim of which our faults are assigned to others, but of the innumerable nonspecific acts of judgment with regard to the behavior, the morality, the personalities of others. For example, the pleasant glow experienced by participants in judgmental bull sessions in which those not present are taken apart is, in my opinion, due not so much to the discharge of sublimated sadism but rather to the enhanced self-esteem supplied by the act of judging and the comparison with those who are being judged.

[18] I am here, for the moment, disregarding the grandiose self.

all-or-nothing type: there are no survival potentialities between the extremes of utter firmness and strength, on the one
hand, and utter destruction (psychosis; suicide) on the other.
I would nevertheless like to stress that, in reflecting about the
messianic or charismatic leader figure, the depth psychologist
should not too quickly abandon his objective stance and
espouse an attitude of moral judgment. Charismatic and messianic personalities come in all shades and degrees. Some
among them are no doubt close to psychosis. These are dogmatic persons who lack all empathy with the inner life of
others—with the notable exception of their keen grasp of
even the subtlest reactions in other people that are related to
their own narcissistic requirements. There are other messianic
persons, however, in whom the coalescence between self and
idealized superego, while chronic, is only partial, i.e., where
the nonmessianic sectors of the self, although in harmony
with the messianic substance of the personality, may at times
even retain the freedom of displaying a sense of quite nonmessianic humor. It must be stressed, in addition, that the
social effects of messianic and charismatic personalities are
not necessarily deleterious. A figure of the kind required in
times of grave crisis cannot be of the more modest, self-
relativistic personality type to which those chosen to positions
of leadership during quiescent historical periods generally belong. In a moment of crisis and profound anxiety, the nation
will turn to the messianic or charismatic personality—not primarily because it has recognized his skills and his efficiency,
but because it realizes that he will satisfy its need to identify
with his unquestioned righteousness or with his firmness and
security.

The relation between the British people and Winston
Churchill before, during, and after the greatest danger ever
faced by England (and the Western world) is a good example
in this context. Churchill (a leader, by the way, whose mystique emanated, I believe, predominantly from the grandiose

self, not from the idealized superego), who was unacceptable before the crisis, filled his role to perfection during the crisis and was the unquestioned leader of the nation. Yet he was discarded after the crisis had subsided. The British people identified themselves with him and with his unshakable belief in his and, by extension, the nation's strength so long as their selves felt weak in the face of the serious danger; as soon as victory had been attained, however, the need for a merger with an omnipotent figure subsided, and they were able to turn from him to other (noncharismatic) leaders.[19] It takes little effort to discern the parallel between the temporary needs of the enfeebled self of the creative person and the temporary needs of an endangered nation in times of crisis; in both instances, the idealization of the leader, the narcissistic transference to him, is abandoned when the need for it has come to an end.

In contrast to the endopsychic conditions prevailing in the messianic and charismatic personality, the ego of the average person, of the man who has attained that state we might refer to as average mental health, attempts to fulfill two tasks. On the one hand, it responds to the pressure of the grandiose self in the depth of the psyche; but, when it strives for the enhancement of self-esteem through activities that fulfill the

[19] Two relevant topics would be worthy of study by the psychoanalytic historian and sociologist: The first is the examination of the political genius of a people, i.e., its skills, its political savvy, as manifested in its capacity to choose the right kind of leader in various historical situations. The second concerns the specific relation between leader and followers, in particular whether (1) the leader is apt to be idealized (in this case I would designate him as a messianic personality, indicating by this term that his self has largely merged with the idealized superego); (2) the leader is apt to become the target, in the main nonidealized, for an identification with an omnipotent object (in this case I would designate him as a charismatic personality, indicating by this term that his self has largely become the carrier of the grandiose self); or (3) the leader is apt to be simply the executor of certain ego functions of those who have chosen him (in this case he is neither a messianic nor a charismatic personality).

ambitions nourished by the demands of the grandiose self, it does so in a realistic way. In particular, it takes into account the needs and feelings of others, of the fellow man with whom it is in empathic contact. On the other hand, as its second task, the normal ego attempts to exert its initiative and control in order to bring about behavior approaching that demanded by the idealized standards of the superego. In so doing, it will compare the performance of the actual self with that demanded by the idealized standards and will acknowledge the fact that perfection cannot become reality. In consequence of this recognition, however, its sense of narcissistic pleasure when the self comes close to living up to the ideals will be a limited one. And, in particular, there will again be empathic contact with others, which will prevent the development of a sense of absolute moral superiority over the fellow man. When comparing his own performance with the performance of others, the judgment of the nonmessianic person will be influenced by his empathic understanding of the fact that the others, too, experience limited failures and successes in the moral sphere, and thus no unrealistic feeling develops that the self is perfect and that the selves of other people are in essence corrupt.

But what is it that enables charismatic personalities to maintain their sense of power (as if their real self and the archaic grandiose self were one), and what bestows on messianic personalities their sense of absolute moral righteousness (as if their real self and the idealized selfobject were one) that makes them so irresistibly attractive to those who need to merge with self-assured leaders and self-righteous messiahs?

Some of these personalities appear to belong to the group to which Freud first referred, in a somewhat different context, as "the exceptions" (1916a, pp. 311-315). Freud thought that some people can allow themselves immoral actions all their lives because they feel they have suffered an unjust punishment in childhood and have therefore, ahead of time, expiated their later misdeeds, which they can now commit with inner impunity.[20]

Although, as stated earlier, messianic and charismatic persons are not likely to become willing subjects of the psychoanalyst's clinical scrutiny, I have encountered a number of patients in my psychoanalytic and psychotherapeutic practice who were close to the character type I have in mind. My clinical experience with such patients allows me to draw some tentative conclusions about the type of personality structure that may manifest charismatic and messianic features and especially about the genetic matrix that seems to favor the development of such personalities.

These persons appear to have no dynamically effective guilt feelings and never suffer any pangs of conscience about what they are doing. They are sensitive to injustices done to them, quick to accuse others — and very persuasive in the expression of their accusations — and thus are able to evoke guilt feelings in others, who tend to respond by becoming submissive to them and by allowing themselves to be treated tyrannically by them. As far as I could discern, however, these persons do not primarily maintain the conviction of having already in childhood expiated their present evilness. The dynamic essence of their current behavior appears to me to lie in a stunting of their empathic capacity: they understand neither the wishes nor the frustrations and disappointments of other people. At the same time, their sense of the legitimacy of their own wishes and their sensitivity to their own frustrations are intense. Genetically important is the fact, as formulated in gross approximation, that these persons suffered early severe narcissistic injuries mainly because of the

[20] Freud describes the psychological state of Shakespeare's King Richard III through the medium of an imaginary soliloquy about the consequences of being congenitally deformed: "I have the right to be an exception, to disregard the scruples by which others let themselves be held back. I may do wrong myself, since wrong has been done to me" (1916a, pp. 314-315).

unreliability and unpredictability of the empathic responses to them from the side of either the echoing-mirroring or idealized selfobject. To be more specific: intense feelings of self-confidence obtained through echoing-mirroring responses (e.g., the empathic mother's proud smile) and intense feelings of security obtained through the merger with the omnipotent selfobject (e.g., being held and carried empathically by the adult) seem in the childhood of these persons to have been followed by abrupt and unpredictable frustrations. As the result of this trauma, the developmental process of the gradual integration and neutralization of the archaic narcissistic structures was interrupted, and the child, perhaps with the aid of certain unusually strong congenital abilities in the realm of the maintenance of self-esteem (we might here speak with Hartmann [1939] of the primary autonomy of these functions), took over prematurely and in toto the functions that the archaic selfobjects should still have performed for him. We are thus not dealing with persons who have escaped guilt by prior expiation. These persons do not live in accordance with the standards of an inner world regulated by guilt feelings—rather, they live in an archaic world, which, as they experience it, has inflicted the ultimate narcissistic injury on them, i.e., in a world that has withdrawn its empathic content from them after having first, as if to tease them, given them a taste of its security and delights. They responded to this injury by becoming superempathic with themselves and with their own needs, and they have remained enraged about a world that has tried to take from them something they consider to be rightfully their own: the response of the selfobject, i.e., a part of the archaic self. Self-righteously, they are themselves performing functions the selfobject was supposed to perform; they assert their own perfection, and they demand full control over the other person, whom they need as regulator of their self-esteem, without regard for his rights as an independent person. In other

words, the prior injustice they suffered was the abrupt withdrawal of narcissistic sustenance, and what the world judges
to be their present misdeeds is to them the expression of justified narcissistic demands.

Since mixed cases may well be encountered most
frequently, I venture the opinion, at the risk of being over-
schematic, that those personalities who manifest charismatic
strength and self-certainty (often coupled with self-righteously
expressed self-pitying and hypochondriacal complaints) have
suffered a traumatic withdrawal of empathy from the side of
the selfobjects who were expected to respond to the child's
mirroring needs, while those with messianic features have
suffered analogous disappointments from the side of the archaic idealized object. Furthermore, if we consider the effect
of these traumata from the developmental point of view of social psychology, we can say that in both instances the withdrawal of the selfobject led to a severe reduction of the
educational power of the environment. If the needed narcissistic sustenance is self-righteously and angrily demanded,
rather than having to be earned, then the object loses his
leverage as an educational factor. It can no longer exert its
influence in leading the child toward the gradual modification of its narcissistic demands in the spheres of both the
grandiose self and the archaic precursor of the internalized
ideals.

Group Psychology and the Historical Process

The elucidation of the personality of the charismatic and
messianic person and of the psychological basis of the intense
relationship the followers of such a person establish with him
is an important task for the depth psychologist who, with the
tools of psychoanalysis, attempts to investigate group
processes and their effect on the dynamics of history.
Although, within the confines of the present essay, I do not il-

luminate the details of the interplay between the personality of a specific leader, the response of his followers, and the dynamics of the course of the correlated specific historical events, the psychoanalytic historian will have no trouble finding promising subjects for study in this area. Two brief examples here will clarify my meaning. One of them, Daniel Schreber, a historically insignificant figure, is surely better known to the psychoanalyst than to the student of general history, since he was the father of a man whom Freud described in one of his great case histories; by contrast, the other one, Adolf Hitler, needs no introduction, since he is known to everyone as one of the most fateful historical personalities of modern times.

Daniel Gottlob Moritz Schreber, the father of the *Senatspräsident* with dementia paranoides, was the leader of a very popular health cult. Like most leaders of cults and sects, he had absolute convictions within the area of his mission — in his case, convictions within the area of health morality, i.e., of the importance of physical exercise, good posture, clean living, etc. — and his teachings received an enthusiastic response not only in Germany but also in other countries, e.g., in England. So far as I know, the dynamics of his influence on the numerous devoted followers of his cult have not been investigated, but (thanks to the research done by Baumeyer, 1956; Niederland, 1951, 1959a, 1959b, 1960, 1963; and others) we have a good deal of information about his empathic and tyrannical treatment of his children, which seems to have constituted a decisive genetic factor in the development of his son's famous psychosis. And there is Hitler, still essentially enigmatic in his personality and in his seemingly irresistible effect on Germany. His convictions were absolute and, in certain areas, could not be questioned or modified. After a lonesome, hypochondriacal, self-doubting period as a young adult, he emerged with a new rigid nucleus of immovable opinions which from that time on remained untouchable whatever his changes and vacillations might be. He knew with complete certainty what was evil and had to be eradicated in this world of ours, and what good and worth preserving. His utter certainty that the Jews were an evil and destructive element which had infected the clean and healthy body of the godlike German race was from then on the center of his being and not only insured the maintenance of his own heightened self-esteem, but invited the participation of the German nation in this blissful self-image through the merger with him.

Schreber's father and Hitler — and perhaps in some more or less distantly related way personalities like Wilhelm Fliess — different as they are, what do they have in common? They seem to combine an absolute certainty concerning the power of their selves and an absolute conviction concerning the validity of their ideals with an equally absolute lack of empathic understanding for large segments of feelings, needs, and rights of other human beings and for the values cherished by them. They understand the environment in which they live only as an extension of their own narcissistic universe. They understand others only insofar — but here with the keenest empathy! — as they can serve as tools toward their own narcissistic ends or insofar as they interfere with their own purposes. It is not likely that depth psychology will find effective means to influence such persons, at least not those who present themselves in the arena of history. But the historian-analyst and the analyst-historian may well be able to make contributions that will not only increase our psychological grasp of such personalities, but will also provide answers to two interrelated questions: How do the characteristic psychological features of the messianic and charismatic person dovetail with the widespread yearning for archaic omnipotent figures? And what are the specific historical circumstances that tend to increase this yearning?

To repeat: there may well be a wide gap separating the

personality of such a nearly unique historical figure as Hitler from that of a not atypical founder of a common health cult such as Daniel G. M. Schreber. And an even wider gap may well separate personalities of the type of Schreber's father from those of the type of Wilhelm Fliess. Future investigations of the personalities of these and other notable figures who, in some historically significant setting, exerted their attraction on others—whether on whole nations, or on smaller groups, or on single susceptible individuals in times of crisis—may well be able to demonstrate what they have in common. Were there similar psychological features that made all of them so irresistible? Similar traits that were the secret of their adamant strength, their apparently all-knowing certainty? And did the effect they had on others lead to similar or analogous consequences? How did those fare—their followers, their children— who could not extricate themselves from the bonds to the charismatic or messianic figure who was their leader, their father? These and related questions will surely prove to be a worthy challenge for the psychoanalytic historian.[e]

Let us then return to one of the central themes touched upon over and over in the preceding pages: the relation of Freud to Fliess during the period when Freud's self was enfeebled while it undertook a daring exploratory venture. Is this need, which arose in Freud during his courageous voyage into the unknown, related, if ever so distantly, to the need felt by populations who follow a charismatic leader, or even to the need of a hypochondriac who swears by the teachings

---

[e] Confirmatory evidence for one of the basic assumptions of Kohut's essay, his reconstruction of Fliess's personality as (latently) psychotic, has recently become available. In his letters to Jung (McGuire, 1974), Freud was unequivocal in his assessment of Fliess as a paranoid person: indeed, he stated that he had gained his conviction of the dynamics of paranoia he elucidated by means of the example of Schreber as a result of his observations of Fliess in the course of their divergences.

of a health messiah? I think there might well be a similar set
of psychological factors active in all these relationships and
that the time will come when we will be able to turn toward
their exploration in depth, not only with regard to Freud's
relation to Fliess but perhaps also with regard to our own relation to the figure of Freud.

I am keenly aware that the preceding presentation is tentative and speculative to an unusual degree. Instead of adducing a sufficient number of specific data—data, for example, concerning Freud's experiences during his self-analysis,
or data that would illuminate the personality of Wilhelm
Fliess—I have relied largely on the internal logic and consistency of my ideas and on the indirect evidence of clinical
phenomena analogous to those for which I gave no direct
empirical support. This shortcoming is regrettable and needs
to be justified.

What was the essence of the task to which I addressed
myself? Why did it have to be approached so tentatively? And
what is the reason for the fact that it was carried out so in-
completely?

The task is to apply psychoanalytic knowledge to the investigation of group psychology with the specific aim of
making a contribution to the explanation of historical events,
of the course—or, expressed more courageously, the
process—of history. I suspect that the seemingly most
expedient application of analysis in this area, the investigation of the personalities of individuals who have exerted a decisive influence on the course of historical events, can make
only a limited contribution to a scientifically valid explanation of history within the framework of depth psychology. I
think rather that psychoanalysis must find novel approaches
if it is to provide us with more comprehensive explanations of
historical phenomena that will increase man's mastery over
his historical destiny. To be specific: in addition to the study
of historical figures, the psychoanalytic historian must also

undertake the study of historical processes, of the dynamics of historical events.

If the study of historical sequences is to be pursued successfully, however, it will have to be coordinated with a number of basic investigations of the social field. What I have in mind here is the psychoanalytic study of (more or less large) groups: their formation, cohesion, fragmentation; or, stated in more specific terms, the circumstances that favor their formation, the nature of the psychological cement that holds them together, the psychological conditions under which they begin to manifest regressive behavior and begin to crumble, etc. It will have become obvious to those who are familiar with my recent work that I am suggesting, as a potentially fruitful approach to a complex problem, that we posit the existence of a certain psychological configuration with regard to the group—let us call it the "group self"[21]—which is analo-

---

[21] I believe that here we will find a depth-psychological approach to the scientific illumination of such currently ill-defined, impressionistic concepts as national character, and the like. The notion of a nationally, ethnically, or culturally determined "identity"—a "group identity"—must also be differentiated from the concept of a "group self." The considerations which apply to the differentiation of the analogous concepts in individual psychology are also valid in the present context (see Kohut 1970a, pp. 578-580, and Kohut 1972b, pp. 623-624, the comparison between the "psychopathological events of late adolescence described by Erikson" and the vicissitudes of the self). The sense of a person's identity, whether he views himself as an individual or as belonging to a particular group, pertains to his conscious or preconscious awareness of the manifestations of a psychological surface configuration—it concerns a self-representation that relates to the conscious and preconscious goals and purposes of his ego and to the conscious and preconscious idealized values of his superego. The psychoanalytic concept of a self, however—whether it refers to the self of an individual or to the self of a person as a member of a group or, as a "group self," to the self of a stable association of people—concerns a structure that dips into the deepest reaches of the psyche. Indeed, I have become convinced that the pattern of an unconscious nuclear self (the central unconscious ambitions of the grandiose self and the central unconscious values of the internalized idealized parent imago) is of crucial importance with regard to the overriding sense of fulfillment or failure that characterizes a person's

gous to the self of the individual. We are then in a position to observe the group self as it is formed, as it is held together, as it oscillates between fragmentation and reintegration, as it shows regressive behavior when it moves toward fragmentation, etc. — all in analogy to phenomena of individual psychology to which we have comparatively easy access in the clinical (psychoanalytic) situation.

It is too early to say how successful this approach will be, but not too early to suggest that it should be tried. The difficulties are great, since the relevant depth-psychological data about the group self have to be obtained with the aid of a specific instrument of observation: introspection and empathy. It is with regard to the problem concerning the accessibility of such data that I return to the psychoanalytic group. (With renewed reluctance, I am reminded once more of the concept of a "psychoanalytic movement," but I must not shrink from it in the present nonevaluative context.) The history of the psychoanalytic movement — its formation, the crystallization and sequestration of dissident groups, its continuity despite changes — should, in a certain sense, constitute an excellent study topic for the psychoanalyst who pursues the investigation of group processes. Potentially at least — and I say this in full awareness that my suggestion will undoubtedly be greeted with humor or sarcasm — this is the group with the greatest insight about itself. It is the group, in other words, that should be expected to supply the researcher with the maximum number of useful data relevant to the study of the nature of group cohesion and of the causes of group disinte-

---

outlook on his life, to some extent independent of the presence or absence of neurotic conflict, suffering, symptom, or inhibition. And I am now suggesting that these considerations concerning the influence of the basic unconscious narcissistic configurations in individual existence are valid also with regard to the life of the group, i.e., that the basic patterns of a nuclear group-self (the group's central ambitions and ideals) not only account for the continuity and the cohesion of the group, but also determine its most important actions.

gration. Furthermore, there is no need to be defensive about the fact that the psychoanalytic community offers to the observer a rich field for the investigation of behavioral phenomena (including the whole spectrum of the manifestations of narcissistic rage—the aggressions of the members of the group against each other) that accompany group regressions.

There are, of course, many obstacles standing in the way of an objective assessment of the psychoanalytic community by psychoanalysts. Such a self-study is a difficult but by no means impossible task. I rather think it likely that despite the obvious difficulties (or, perhaps, because the difficulties are obvious) the self-investigation of the psychoanalytic community by analysts is more promising than analogous studies which could be undertaken by other groups.

When I speak here of the self-analysis of the psychoanalytic community, I am, of course, not contemplating a group enterprise. The psychological revelations that grow out of the matrix created by group meetings are obtained in consequence of the psychological regression imposed on the individual by immersion into the group. Group pressure diminishes individuality; it leads to a primitivization of the mental processes, in particular to a partial paralysis of the ego and to a lowering of resistances. The diminution of the influence of the ego is then followed by the cathartic expression of archaic (or at any rate undisguised) impulses, emotions, and ideation, i.e., by the revelation of material not accessible in normal circumstances. The insights I have in mind cannot be obtained in a regressive atmosphere. The valid self-analysis of the psychoanalytic group—or of any group—must not only rest on the clear, nonregressive perception of archaic psychological experiences that arise within the group; it also requires the intellectual and emotional mastery of this material. The validity of the insights obtained will be demonstrated by the fact that the pressure to act out (especially to act out angrily, the principal symptom of group psychopathology) will be diminished within the group. The individual who wishes to make decisive steps toward new depth-psychological insights concerning the group must therefore be able to remain deeply and directly involved in the group processes — but instead of acting them out, he must be able to tolerate the tension of seeming passivity: all his energies must be withdrawn from participating action and concentrated on participating thought. Only if he can maintain full emotional participation with the group processes of his own group, yet channel all his energies toward his cognitive functions (specifically the gathering of data through empathic observation and the subsequent explanation of the observed data) — only then will he be able to make those decisive discoveries and obtain those crucial new insights which will deepen our understanding of the behavior of the group and its members.

Group processes are largely activated by narcissistic motives. We may therefore hope that the fact that training analysts are now paying increasing attention to the narcissistic dimensions of the personality of analytic candidates will have favorable results in the area under discussion. The strengthened ego dominance over the narcissistic sector of their personalities which future generations of analysts will obtain may, in particular, be expected to facilitate the investigation of group processes within the psychoanalytic community. And we may also assume that one or another gifted psychoanalyst will be aided in his investigations concerning the influence of narcissistic motives on the behavior of the psychoanalytic community by the insights given him by his training analysis with regard to his own narcissistic strivings.

Among the various areas that will have to be studied within the context of the psychological self-scrutiny of the psychoanalytic community, the (changing) significance of the figure of Freud for the group will prove to occupy a place of paramount importance. But the time is not quite ripe for such an undertaking. Conscious hesitations dictated by considerations of tact and decorum, as well as unconscious inhibitions, still interfere too strongly with our ability to maintain the degree of objectivity required if we wish through the creative act of the group's self-analysis to make a valid contribution to psychoanalytic group psychology and to the psychology of the historical process. But I also think that, measured by the yardstick of history, the time is not far off when psychoanalysts will indeed be able to undertake such studies with the hope of reaching objectively valid conclusions.

I am therefore justifying the presentation of this speculative and tentative essay by saying that it should be regarded as a blueprint for the future. Clearly, I believe that my suggestions concerning the meaning of Freud's self-analysis and the significance Fliess had for Freud during his self-analysis will be corroborated by the detailed work of the future analytic historian, who will look upon "the origins of psychoanalysis" with a fresh eye. Although his task will remain a difficult one — i.e., he will have to reconstruct complex psychological situations across a wide gap of time on the basis of data culled from written documents[22] — his inner readiness for it will be greater than ours, and the emotional atmosphere of the social circumstances in which he will perform it will be more propitious than that in which we live. The assessment of Freud's psychological state at the peak of his creative life, the scrutiny of Fliess's personality, and, above all, the investigation of the role played by the figure of Freud in shaping the history of the psychoanalytic community (and thus in shaping the development of the science of psychoanalysis): these are

[22] The collection of historical material concerning the history of psychoanalysis undertaken by the Sigmund Freud Archives will be of inestimable value for future researchers in many of the areas referred to in this essay.

tasks that must be undertaken by future generations of analysts — perhaps even by the next one — with that favorable mixture of empathic closeness and scientific detachment not yet available to the psychoanalyst of our day.

In view of the fact that I have contemplated the possibility that the community of psychoanalytic scholars might someday, in a not-too-distant tomorrow, undertake through the work of some of its creative thinkers the task of a self-scrutiny in depth of the psychoanalytic community itself, it seems appropriate to close with a few remarks on the nature of scientific progress in psychoanalysis.

Decisive progress in man's knowledge of himself is, in my opinion, not primarily a cognitive feat, but achieved mainly as a consequence of what, expressed in everyday language, must be called an act of courage. Pioneering discoveries in depth psychology require not only a keen intellect but also characterological strength, because they are in essence based on the relinquishment of infantile wishes (see Freud, 1932) and on discarding illusions that have protected us against anxiety. I have little doubt that, even in fields outside of the investigation of complex psychological states, pioneering discoveries require an analogous measure of courage.[23] But I would assume that his cognitive detachment toward the physical universe he investigates protects a physi-

[23] These views are in harmony with Freud's opinion (1917b) that the discoveries of Copernicus and Darwin, like his own, constituted severe blows to the narcissism of man. These discoveries, I will add, rested first and foremost on the courageous overcoming of inner resistances, because the discoverers had to deprive themselves of an illusion which had protected them against coming face to face with the painful recognition of the relative smallness and insignificance of their selves. It must not be forgotten, furthermore, that attacks on grandiose fantasies elicit dangerous narcissistic rage against the offender (see Kohut, 1972b). In addition to their inner strength, therefore, the three great discoverers had to be able to muster considerable social courage when they communicated their findings to their contemporaries, whose wrath, as they undoubtedly anticipated at least preconsciously, they would now have to face.

cist, for example, or an astronomer, from the kind of fear the depth psychologist experiences when he, alone, is face to face with unpleasant psychological reality. I would at least claim that this assumption is valid in our day, when scientific findings in the physical and biological sciences are no longer effectively opposed on moral grounds.

But be that as it may in these other branches of human knowledge, I am certain that decisive progress in the area of depth psychology is tied to personal acts of courage by the investigator who not only suffers anxiety but tends to be maligned and ostracized. It is therefore not an accident that one of the greatest steps of individual psychology, a gigantic advance toward the scientific understanding of the inner life of the individual, was made as the result of the victorious outcome of the grueling process of one man's inner struggles, Freud's creative self-analysis. Could it be that the analogous step in group psychology, the decisive advance toward a valid depth-psychological understanding of the experiences and actions of the group, will be the result of a similarly courageous self-scrutiny of the psychoanalytic community by itself? I know that the future cannot be predicted with any degree of reliability by analogy with the past, that the success of Freud's genius in the field of individual psychology may not be repeatable with regard to the field of group psychology, despite the intense efforts of future analysts. But of one thing I am convinced: should any group ever be able to overcome its inner resistances and thus make a decisive step toward the understanding of the dynamics of its behavior, the nature and development of its group self, and the genetics of its conflicts and of the oscillations of its self—should a group ever be able to succeed in these tasks, it will have laid the foundations for a valid psychological understanding of history.

49

Preface to
Der falsche Weg zum Selbst,
Studien zur Drogenkarriere
by Jürgen vom Scheidt

The explanatory power of the new psychology of the self is
nowhere so evident as with regard to four types of
psychological disturbance: the narcissistic personality disorders, the perversions, the (psychogenic) delinquencies, and
the addictions. Why can these seemingly disparate conditions
be examined so fruitfully with the aid of the same conceptual
framework? Why can all these widely differing and even contrasting symptom pictures be comprehended when seen from
the viewpoint of the psychology of the self? How, in other
words, are these four conditions related to each other? What
do they have in common despite the fact that they exhibit
widely differing, and even contrasting, symptomatologies? The
answer to these questions is simple: in all these disorders the afflicted individual suffers from a central weakness, from a
weakness in the core of his personality. He suffers from the
consequences of a defect in the self. The symptoms of these
disorders, whether comparatively hazy or hidden or more distinct and conspicuous, arise secondarily as an outgrowth of a
defect in the self. The manifestations of these disorders become intelligible if we call to mind that they are all

---

Der falsche Weg zum Selbst was published (1976) by Kindler (Munich).

attempts—unsuccessful attempts, it must be stressed—to remedy the central defect in the personality.

The narcissistically disturbed individual yearns for praise
and approval or for a merger with an idealized supportive
other because he cannot sufficiently supply himself with self-
approval or with a sense of strength through his own inner
resources. The pervert is driven toward sexual enactments
with figures or symbols that give him the feeling of being
wanted, real, alive, or powerful. The delinquent repeats over
and over again certain acts through which he demonstrates to
himself that he is invulnerable and omnipotent, thus providing for himself an escape from the realization that he feels
devoid of sustaining self-confidence and of sustaining ideals.
And the addict craves the drug because the drug seems to
him to be capable of curing the central defect in his self. It
becomes for him the substitute for a selfobject that failed
him, with traumatizing intensity and suddenness, at a time
when he should still have had the feeling of omnipotently
controlling its responses in accordance with his needs as if it
were a part of himself. By ingesting the drug, he symbolically
compels the mirroring selfobject to soothe him, to accept
him. Or he symbolically compels the idealized selfobject to
submit to his merging into it and thus to his partaking in its
magical power. In either case, the ingestion of the drug provides him with the self-esteem he does not possess. Through
the incorporation of the drug, he supplies for himself the
feeling of being accepted and thus of being self-confident; or
he creates the experience of being merged with a source of
power that gives him the feeling of being strong and
worthwhile. And all these effects of the drug tend to increase
his feeling of being alive, tend to increase his certainty that
he exists in this world.

It is the tragedy of all these attempts at self-cure that the
solutions they provide are impermanent, that in essence they
cannot succeed. The praise the narcissistically disturbed in-

dividual is able to extract from others, the mergers with idealized others that he imposes on them, the sexualized reassurances the pervert procures for himself, the loudly proclaimed assertion of omnipotence forever repeated through his actions by the delinquent—they all give only fleeting relief. They are repeated again and again without producing the cure of the basic psychological malady. And the calming or the stimulating effect the addict obtains from the drug is similarly impermanent. Whatever the chemical nature of the substance employed, however frequently repeated its consumption, however cleverly rationalized or mythologized its ingestion with the support from others who are similarly afflicted—no psychic structure is built; the defect in the self remains. It is as if a person with a wide-open gastric fistula were trying to still his hunger through eating. He may obtain pleasurable taste sensations by his frantic ingestion of food, but, since the food does not enter the part of the digestive system that absorbs it into the organism, he continues to starve.

It is the great virtue of the present monograph that the author was able to seize the deepest meaning of the general formulations which were outlined in the preceding summarizing statement and could apply them, effectively, in the investigation of his subject matter. The insights contained in these formulations are therefore always present, even when they are not explicitly referred to or explicitly adduced in each explanatory context. Stated openly or implied, they participate in the richly varied descriptions and explanations offered in appropriately eclectic profusion by the author's scholarship, and they provide each of them with vitality and depth. Whether the present study deals with the pathogenic childhood situation that forms the vulnerable personality of the addict, or with the typical steps in the "career" of the addicted—his *Long Day's Journey into Night* as O'Neill called his great portrayal of the impact of a mother's addiction upon the other members of the family—or with the

pseudoremedial consequences of the social support that
addicts give to each other, or with the effective therapeutic
approaches or the effective prophylactic endeavors employed
by depth-psychologically informed therapists—in short, whatever the specific detail of the broad subject matter of
addiction with which the present work deals and whatever the
particular methodological road on which the author
proceeds, his awareness of the depth-psychological essence of
the disorder under scrutiny never fails to enrich his
descriptions and to deepen the significance of his explanations.

The enriching effect of the insights supplied by the
psychology of the self upon the data obtained within different
psychological frames of reference can be demonstrated with
special clarity with regard to the examination of the family
background, of the childhood situation, of the future
addict—a subject to which many pages of the present work
are devoted. It is evidently of great importance to determine
certain details concerning the behavior of the addict's parents
when he was a child. We might ask, for example, whether
they had been lenient or strict, or whether their identities
(e.g., as male and female; or, occupationally, the mother as a
housewife, the father as a truckdriver, etc.) were hazy or well
defined. Having obtained the answer to these and similar
questions, we will look at the significance of the sociopsychological data concerning parental behavior with different
eyes when we examine them against the background of our
knowledge concerning the factors that contribute to the
child's ability to build up a strong and cohesive self and, in
the obverse, concerning the factors standing in the way of this
crucial developmental task.

Just as we know that physiologically a child needs to be
given certain foods, that he needs to be protected against extreme temperatures, and that the atmosphere he breathes has
to contain sufficient oxygen if his body is to become strong

and resilient, so do we also know that depth-psychologically he requires an empathic environment — an environment that responds to his need to have his presence confirmed by the glow of parental pleasure and to his need to merge into the reassuring security and strength of the powerful adult — if he is to acquire a firm and resilient self. It is not enough to obtain answers to such questions as whether the mother's attitude toward toilet training is strict or lenient or whether the father's work-identity is clearly defined or not. The crucial question concerns the adequacy or inadequacy of the parents as the selfobjects of the child, i.e., the adequacy or inadequacy of the parents at a time when they are still performing for the child the psychological functions of self-esteem regulation which the child should later be able to perform on his own, the adequacy or inadequacy of the parents at a time, in other words, when the child still experiences them predominantly as extensions of himself or experiences himself still predominantly as part of their strength. The crucial question, then, is whether the parents are able to reflect with approval at least some of the child's proudly exhibited attributes and functions, whether they are able to respond with genuine enjoyment to his budding skills, whether they are able to remain in touch with him throughout his trials and errors. And furthermore, we must determine whether they are able to provide the child with a reliable embodiment of calmness and strength into which he can merge and whether they are able to serve him as the focus for his need to find a target for his admiration. Or, stated in the obverse, it will be of crucial importance to ascertain the fact that a child could find neither confirmation of his own worthwhileness nor a target for a merger with the idealized strength of the parent and that he therefore remained deprived of the opportunity for the gradual transformation of these external sources of narcissistic sustenance into endopsychic resources, i.e., into sustaining self-esteem and a sustaining relationship to internal ideals. Thus, in asking the crucial question concerning the factors in childhood that lead to the addiction-prone personality, we will say that, in the last analysis, and within certain limits, it is less important to determine what the parents *do* than what they *are*.

Let me end this prefatory note by stating explicitly what could surely already be gleaned from my preceding remarks: that I consider vom Scheidt's work to constitute a most felicitous and significant scientific step because it represents a viable and productive compounding of the insights and explanations derived from the viewpoint of the psychology of the self with the valuable insights provided by a number of other approaches and methodologies, such as those of the classical psychoanalytic psychology of the psychoneuroses, of cultural and social psychology, of the important investigations of congenital predisposition, of the statistical scrutiny of behavioral data, to mention only a few. As such, the work is a move into new territory and should become a model for future investigations, not only of the field of drug addiction, this old scourge of humanity, but also of all the many other areas in which the application of the viewpoints of the psychology of the self leads us to new and fruitful insights about man's thoughts, feelings, and actions.

Letters

December 22, 1961

I am writing you as I promised in order to clarify what I said (or intended to say?) during the afternoon sessions of the Panel on Narcissism.

I began by stating that when the term narcissism is used as part of the "lingo," some culturally determined value judgment frequently intrudes which is not made explicit, namely, that to be narcissistic (as opposed to being capable of love) is "bad" or "sick." It is comparatively easy to avoid the pitfalls of unscientific value judgments or "health morality" (Hartmann) by dealing with narcissism entirely as a theoretical concept and discussing it as a state of libido development and a type of libido distribution. It seems to me, however, that purely theoretical discussions of the concept of narcissism tend to become overcomplex, and in view of the undoubted clinical usefulness of the term we should, in the sea of theoretical uncertainty, hold on to the rock of clinical observation. Here, of course, we cannot avoid one value judgment — that of usefulness for adaptation. In this context, I stressed that we are not dealing with a simple contrast, namely, that narcissism is nonadaptive and object love is adaptive, but that there is an optimal balance, different under different circumstances, which is most desirable from the adaptive point of view. Under average circumstances, the objects or goals of our strivings are more important than the narcissistic component of the activities (such as the pleasure obtained from performance, pride in success), yet *some* admixture of narcissistic pleasure *is* a desirable component in almost all activities. It is only when the narcissistic component is not in balance, when the pride in personal achievement outweighs the pursuit of the goal and makes the goal unimportant, that we may judge narcissism as adaptationally or socially harmful; it leads to shifting goals and unreliability. There are, however, states in which a very high degree of narcissism is adaptive and socially useful. Such is probably the case during the narcissistic "regressions" during pregnancy and during certain phases of intense creative activity.

I then made a further attempt to bring theoretical concept and clinical observation closer together. I said that primary narcissism could be envisaged not only as a theoretical state of libido distribution but also as accessible to direct observation. There are differences in the degree of response of babies to the mother's offering herself as a love object; some babies respond more, some less. The relative lack of response to stimulation in some babies may be regarded as an expression of intrinsic libidinal self-investment and theoretically formulated as a high degree of primary narcissism.

I stressed the importance of "experiments in empathy" in a scrutiny of the concept of narcissism. We must attempt to approximate the significant psychological experiences empathically and must not confuse this attempt with the description of a social relation that we observe.[1] When we speak of narcissism we do not mean that there is no other person involved, but that the other person is not experienced

---

[1] Kohut first made this crucial distinction in 1959 (see pp. 217-225 above). It is easily grasped by many, but is apparently opposed to ingrained patterns of thought that are connected with the predominant role of vision (and the other senses) in our exploration of the world and the denial that the employment of empathic resonance in explaining the inner life of man is unavoidable. See also Kohut (1971, p. 219n) and the letter of February 10, 1965 in this volume (pp. 862-865).

as separate, with individual motivation and individual freedom. People who suffer the loss of an object (in the sense of social psychology) at a time when the "object" is still experienced narcissistically seem to strive all their lives for "objects" with what seems an apparently insatiable object hunger. Objects, however, do not satisfy them (nor are they important to them) since these people strive to heal a narcissistic defect, and they use objects impermanently and unsuccessfully to fill this narcissistic defect.

I ended by recommending the "borderline objects" of the depressive as a focus for the aforementioned experiments in empathy, since the empathic investigation of this area seems to me to be especially likely to deepen our understanding of the problems of narcissism. The breast, it seems, is at one moment experienced as a separate object. Yet, under the influence of frustration and rage, a regressive move to a just recently abandoned position is made, and the breast is again experienced narcissistically; thus the rage is not directed against an external object but against a self that still shows traces of the former (now abandoned) differentiation.

Perhaps this contributes to the clarification of what I said in New York; I hope I am not ending up by adding further confusion. But we are really dealing with a difficult topic, and even our errors may help by sharpening superior counter-argument. Thus proceeds, one hopes, progress in science.

November 19, 1962*

Since our Committee should be meeting tomorrow to discuss, albeit in a preliminary fashion, what we have learned about the selection of training analysts in the past two or three years, I will put down a few thoughts on paper and

* This and the following two letters were written in conjunction with a meeting of the Committee on Teacher Development of the Chicago Institute for Psychoanalysis.

attempt to bring some tentative order into my own experiences as a member of the Committee on Teacher Development. . . .

If I am not mistaken the real task (i.e., the usual "impossible" task) is the setting down of those criteria by which we have been guided in our assessment of the people that we interviewed, discussed, and, finally, evaluated. What are these criteria? Or better: what are some of the *additional* criteria (over and above those that we employ in our usual evaluations of students or of analysts in general) that we used in the assessment of candidates for potential training-analyst status?

Let me try to write down a few ideas in this area. I don't claim they are original; I don't claim they are profound; and they probably are nothing more than a statement of the obvious. Yet they may help starting us on the road.

1. *The assessment of the integration of psychoanalysis with the rest of the life of the psychoanalyst.* Although difficult to define in detail without much further thought, I put great stock by this criterion. I would be suspicious of the psychoanalytic "fanatic" who has no life, no interests other than analysis, as well as of the analyst to whom psychoanalysis has not become the major absorbing and meaningful occupation of his mature years. There are innumerable variations of "good" integrations of the devotion to the life work as a psychoanalyst and the maintenance of other absorbing interests (be they one's family; social and political interests; art, music or literature; friendships; and the like). What I pay attention to in this area is not only the coexistence of strong interests in analysis and in other areas, but how these areas relate to each other. Is one area strictly isolated from the other, or is there a smooth transition? Is there the ability to remain an analyst (without amateurish analytic parlor games, of course) even outside the walls of the office? Is there the ability to remain a human being inside the office, i.e., the

ability to be a true analyst, not an interpretation machine? The interviewing device most of us have used — to see the candidate first in a nonprofessional setting, to chat with him about nonanalytic matters, etc., and then to turn to a direct assessment of his personality without any hedging about the purpose for which this exploration is undertaken — seems to me to be particularly apt to bring out the candidate's assets and defects in this respect. You may remember that the seriousness of the personality disturbance of one candidate who otherwise managed to make a rather good impression became obvious when he was exposed to the task of making the transition from the social atmosphere of the interviewer's dining room to the professional one of the interviewer's study.

2. *The assessment of the capacity (or perhaps better: of the potential) for an attitude of "wisdom," specifically in the area of the profession though not, of course, confined to it.* Again, this is not a simple criterion. Once one orients one's evaluating and observing functions in this direction, however, it is not as vague and ill-defined as the word "wisdom" would make one suspect. I have in mind, for example, the capacity for humor without being a "wise guy," or the capacity to acknowledge the shortcomings and limitations of psychoanalysis without sarcasm or hopelessness. If I may be permitted to quote what I said during our most recent Training Analysts Seminar on October 9, 1962, about the same topic in the context of the patient's and analyst's attitude during a "good" termination, I can perhaps help to circumscribe my meaning: ". . . in the termination phase of the analysis, the analyst's knowledge of the patient, and the patient's self-understanding have taken on a coloring of wisdom, i.e., a certain detachment, which, however, is not 'isolation': an acceptance of assets and limitations, of the fact that while not all is solved, and conflicts and problems remain, they are now familiar and can be contemplated with tolerance and composure."

3. *Parental feelings toward students and younger professional colleagues.* These should be well sublimated and under the ego's control. There should be no intense need to perpetuate one's aging self through the younger colleagues, no hidden wish to form a "school" of psychoanalysis in one's own image, and the like. Yet, on the other hand, I value positively the recognition that a younger generation must take over, and even the enjoyment of the gradual lessening of the burden of responsibility toward the future of our science as a younger generation reaches professional maturity and competence.

4. *Unresolved transferences to (younger) sibling imagoes.* Finally, I pay attention to the resolution of the specific transference problems that relate to sibling rivalry, especially those that have led to attitudes of contempt or undue competition toward younger sibling imagoes. I don't look for perfection (as a matter of fact, I am rather suspicious of perfection in this area), but try to gauge the extent of the candidate's awareness about this problem area and whether he is able to avoid the repetition of *chronic* situations of competition with younger sibling figures.

I don't need to state that the foregoing doesn't aim at completeness. In practice, it may well happen that, guided by the personality of the particular candidate, we may not follow up any one of the directions described above. But there is no need for further explanations—only the hope that these thoughts may contribute to providing a starting point for our discussions and deliberations.

November 21, 1962

Let me put down a few thoughts while yesterday's fruitful meeting of our Committee is still fresh in our minds. I enjoyed the meeting, and I believe it added clarification to our tentative formulations. I am particularly glad that we did not get hung up in useless arguments whether this or that formula was too much "hot air" or too dry and sterile, but that we were all trying to move toward increasing explicitness without loss of relevance.

First, to make a general point: I believe that the term or concept of "criterion" may be more a hindrance than a help to us at this time. Judgments have to be made, and they are being made — but it seems to me better to concentrate first on defining the areas that are important for evaluation and for the time being to keep in abeyance attempts aiming at rigorously differentiating "good" from "bad" within each of the areas that we are circumscribing.

Taking the preceding reflections into account — and without reference to the minutes of our discussion, which I am sure will help us even further, we can spell out the following areas that are of importance in evaluating candidates for training analyst status: (1) professional skill and competence; and (2) the analyst's attitude toward his profession. Here belongs the integration between personal life and professional life that I discussed in my previous letter. It should be noted, however, that we pay attention to this integration as a source of *specific* information (a) about the question whether the analyst has achieved a reasonable solution of his ambivalences toward analysis and (b) what degree of autonomy from the original motivating fantasies and from other irrational motivations has been achieved. The evaluation whether the analyst has made a reliable peace with his professional choice is especially important, since the training analyst is often faced with the task of analyzing forms of psychopathology in the student analysand that are intricately interwoven with motivations for the choice of psychoanalysis as a career.

(3) Evaluation of the candidate's attitude toward the results of analysis. Is this attitude characterized by realism and wisdom — or is there sarcasm and hopelessness? The other remarks contained in point 2 of my preceding letter belong

here. In addition, however, the specific nature of the termination of training analysis should be mentioned at this point (cf. Anna Freud): i.e., that a transition from the therapeutic transference to the occupation of being an analyst involves more identificatory elements than can be optimally hoped for in therapeutic analyses. Thus, the training analyst's realism, wisdom, detachment without isolation, humor about limitations without sarcasm, etc., are specifically important areas for our investigation.

(4) Parental feelings — as described before.

(5) Sibling rivalry — as described before.

(6) The point is that all these evaluations should be made on a time axis; that a developmental assessment and a transverse-sectional assessment must go hand in hand.

I hope that the foregoing may be of some help to you as you organize your thoughts about our Committee's report to the Committee on Institutes of the Association, and to our own Education Committee.

November 27, 1962

You know, of course, that any attempt to delimit the complexities of the whole personality, even in such a comparatively circumscribed area as its professional functioning, is confronted by grave problems. How to be reductionistic without losing relevance in a field that treats the complexities of the whole man is a task that seems at times insuperable. Perfect solutions will not be found, but one can aim at reaching optimal levels of generalization. This, of course, is what I tried to do in my statements about the training analyst. He has a specific task which requires objectivity vis-à-vis his analysand's motivations and ambivalences toward his future profession. An assessment of the present integration of the potential training analyst's professional life with the rest of his interests is, to my mind, an indicator whether he can be expected to muster the necessary objectivity in the area of professional motivation.[2] It is similar with the assessment of the training analyst's attitude toward the results of his therapeutic endeavors. Has he made a true peace with his narcissistic expectations, or has he become hopeless and sarcastic? Again, we have a specific area for our assessment, since the termination of training analyses leaves the candidate with more of his analyst's attitudes toward the results of his endeavors than could be optimally expected in other analyses.

But let me stop here! This is indeed a difficult field, and first approximations will have to be pondered, elaborated, and modified through experience. At the moment I am more interested in our establishing levels of approach in these areas than in premature commitment to narrow answers.

November 17, 1964

Thank you for giving me the opportunity to read your essay "In Defence of Shakespeare's Romeo and Juliet"; I found it well written, clear, and likeable. I agree with your thesis that this is a good play and a true tragedy, even though the motive power which leads to the catastrophe is not easily discernible to the literary scholar who has no access to the insights of depth psychology. I have no doubt that an ex-

---

[2] Kohut pursued this topic further in 1968 and summarized his views in a statement to the Committee on Teacher Development at the Chicago Institute for Psychoanalysis. The following is an excerpt:

I am not primarily interested in "how the nominee's life style had developed," but in establishing that he does not experience his professional activity as an isolated part of his life. A training analyst should have achieved a level of his personal and professional development that allows him to employ his specialized technical skill and knowledge without loss of his total human responsiveness to his analysands. The "balance between personal and professional responsibilities," etc., etc., which you mention, I examine, not because of the high value that one might place on achieving it, but as an indicator of the fact that the analyst has accepted his profession fully and without undue strain.

planation of the tragedy must lead to the depth of the two personalities and that their death is the punishment they are unconsciously seeking. Freud thought that the unconscious sense of guilt was the strongest destructive force in human life, and he felt that even psychoanalysis was usually power-less against it (see, for example, the famous footnote in "The Ego and the Id" [1920, p. 50]; there are many other poignant statements by Freud to the same effect). Just as an unconscious sense of guilt will create paradoxical depressions when others would feel triumphant under the same circum-stances (see Freud, 1916a, p. 316), so there are paradoxical instances of calmness and peaceful strength when the punish-ment appears to have been achieved. This, I believe, is the explanation for Romeo's forceful clarity which you describe so well.

What is left is, of course, the question concerning the nature of the unconscious guilt. I can say nothing definite about it, but would like some time (when I have the leisure to do it) to reread *Romeo and Juliet* and give more thought to it. I have a vague impression which I will tell you, even though I cannot really substantiate it except in the most general terms. My impression is at variance with your inter-pretation that the motive power for the tragedy lies in Romeo alone; and it is also at variance with the classical interpre-tation advanced by Dr. Seitz and referred to by you. Although I agree with you that the stronger and more overt contribution to the catastrophe comes from Romeo, I believe that both Romeo and Juliet share a deep guilt and cooperate in their downfall, their guilty union in death. And what is the guilt? I had the impression that the play is (at least on a level that is reasonably accessible to perception) a portrayal of brother-sister incest. Not having studied the play in detail, I have little to say in favor of this thesis. But I am inclined to see the two (like Cocteau's *Enfants Terribles*) as removed from the old generation, love-hungry and in need of affection, and turning to each other for forbidden satisfactions for which they must then die. In contrast to one aspect of your interpretation, I am inclined to see a "twin" relationship, or at least a complementing brother-sister love in the couple. Let me assure you, however, that this interpretation (whether it is correct or not) cannot claim to be more than a hunch, based on the most general impressions.

And now let me once more thank you for allowing me to read your study and for the enjoyment that it gave me.

January, 1965*

. . . In essence, your point of view is that, even though the means are different, the verbal free association of adults and the free association play of children are alike.

I have no quarrel with this position, and I agree that it is often important to recognize the similarities of seemingly disparate phenomena. I am in agreement with your position that the analyst's attitude toward the two phenomena is identical. My question was meant to raise a problem on the basis of the dissimilarities between the child's and the adult's mode of expression in the analytic situation. And I still maintain—despite your point—that the question and the problem I raised are legitimate. I asked whether the external difference of the two modes of analytic expression was not connected with a difference in the development of the structure of the child's psyche and of the way in which the child's neurosis is structurally embedded in the psychic apparatus. Is not the balance of psychic forces different in the grown-up patient? Or phrased differently, is not the grown-up analysand capable, even with a crippling neurosis, of producing (without depleting efforts!) the split in the ego

---

* This is from a reply to two colleagues (both of them child analysts) who responded to a question Kohut raised at a presentation on child analysis at the Chicago Institute for Psychoanalysis on January 21, 1965.

that allows one part to regress and the other part to remain adult and to observe? Would not a similar task interfere with the child's psychological mobility, with the flux of libidinal and aggressive forces which are not yet securely bound to the defensive and adaptive structures in the ego, and perhaps ought not yet to be firmly bound to this position? I am convinced that these are legitimate questions which cannot be argued away on the basis of the similarity of form and meaning between the child's analytic play and the adult's free association. It was mentioned in the discussion a number of times that analysts tend to think of the child as "only a child," or as "the little child," etc. Perhaps that is so and should be corrected. Yet one may also think of the child's immature psyche as a necessarily unstable, forward-striving, creative structure which should perhaps not be prematurely rigidified in the attempt to produce the feat of a firm self-observing split (quite a task even for most adults) at a time when the psychological balance is still more on the side of the id — and perhaps should be.

Charles Kligerman, with whom I had briefly discussed the questions which you had raised, was, I believe, the first to express the view that forcing a child into a full analytic situation may impose a task on him which is out of step with his psychic development. I don't know whether I understood him correctly, but my own thought went to those cases where premature reading, writing, and mathematical training become intermingled with the libidinal and aggressive problems of toilet training and set up for a lifetime an unwholesome link between intellectual activity and anality. . . .

February 10, 1965*

I am sorry that you found yourself in such strong disagreement with the thoughts I expressed in my letter to the

* Response to a colleague who questioned Kohut's delineation of "social psychology" as expressed in the President's Newsletter to the membership of

members, and I regret even more that it made you angry. I am nevertheless glad that you did not follow the impulse to, as you say "gnash my teeth, and then go on," but that you expressed yourself and thus are offering me the opportunity to reply to your remarks.

There is, of course, no denying the fact that our theoretical positions are not the same and that therefore, in practical implementation, what appears most central to me in our science does not seem so to you. I am, however, not opposed to the application of the findings of psychoanalytic depth psychology to the social field and to social psychology. There is no question in my mind that the psychoanalytically sophis-

the American Psychoanalytic Association (Vol. V., No. 1, November, 1964, pp. 5-6). There Kohut had stated: "Let me now move on to a discussion of the work of the Committee on Social Problems. Although this committee has been in existence for only a little more than two years, it has developed in this short span of time, under the chairmanship of Dr. Joseph J. Michaels, into a cohesive team. The committee had to face the temptation of moving away from its primary tasks in either of two directions: by engaging in social action rather than remaining faithful to the aims of scientific study; and by examining the social field as social psychologists, i.e., on the (pre-)conscious levels of human motivation and from the historical point of view, rather than as analysts who, in addition, have access to the unconscious motivations and the genetic determinants of behavior. The committee is fully aware that its function is the psychoanalytic study of social phenomena; yet, either the subject matter or the specific predilection of its members has led to the tendency not only to engage in the study of social phenomena but also to participate in current social activities. Thus the Committee on Social Problems has formed a subcommittee which is gathering information about current legislation in the mental health field and would like to influence mental health laws by advice to the legislators which is based on the insights of psychoanalytic depth psychology. This laudable objective would seem to lie beyond the confines of a scientific study committee. It may be maintained, however, that, just as the scientific psychoanalyst needs the clinical field to derive empirical stimulation for new insights, so the Committee on Social Problems needs active involvement with the social problems of our time in order to be stimulated in its researches from that direction and in order to retain a grasp of the realistic circumstances and possibilities. It is obvious that the pros and cons concerning the social activities of a study committee need to be evaluated and that careful thought needs to be given to the most appropriate organizational place for such activities."

ticated observer of social phenomena will be open to the understanding of social motivations that would not even be
suspected by those who have no access to psychoanalytic data.
You are not right when you think I am against social psychology. But there is a difference between the most sophisticated
analyses of social interactions or transactions and the study of
the active influence of a split-off, asocial, narcissistic fantasy
or of deeply repressed distortions of object representations.
To weigh the fruitfulness of one approach against the other is
undoubtedly legitimate. Since, however, only the psychoanalytic method provides access to the depth of the individual's
psyche and to the irrational psychological motivations that
stem from these psychological areas, I am convinced that the
psychoanalytic approach in these central areas must be
furthered and must be considered our legitimate pursuit. I
have tried to clarify my theoretical position in a series of
papers, so allow me to enclose three reprints [1959b, 1964b;
Kohut and Seitz, 1963], with the earnest hope that you will
not brush my thoughts aside, but give them a hearing and a
chance.

    As I said, the application of psychoanalytic knowledge to
a variety of fields appears to me to be eminently proper, and
I have no quarrel whatever with the activities of a
psychoanalytically sophisticated social psychologist or social
psychiatrist. My only strong disagreement with your statement concerns your sensing "a veiled criticism and an explicit
admonition that probably psychoanalysts should not engage
in either social action or in the exploration of material which
is 'on the preconscious level of human motivation.' " To your
statement that you cannot accept this position, I can only reply that I cannot either. Please read once more the
paragraph that seemed to give you the opposite impression.
What I was discussing was not the desirability of social
action, but the importance of determining "the most appropriate organizational place for such activities." As a matter of

fact I advanced a strong argument for leaving such activities within the scope of the Committee on Social Problems by stating that "just as the scientific psychoanalyst needs the clinical field to derive empirical stimulation for new insights, so the Committee on Social Problems needs active involvement with the social problems of our time in order to be stimulated in its researches from that direction and in order to retain a grasp of the realistic circumstances and possibilities." Let me here point to one further misunderstanding. I am not arguing against "the exploration of material which is 'on the preconscious level of human motivation,'" as you believe. I think that the examination of the preconscious level of motivation is not only fascinating but indispensable. The decisive words ("in addition") are contained in the second half of the sentence you are quoting. I said: "The committee had to face the temptation of moving away from its primary tasks . . . by examining the social field as social psychologists, i.e., on the (pre-)conscious levels of human motivation and from the historical point of view, rather than as analysts who, *in addition*, have access to the unconscious motivations and the genetic determinants of behavior." The full meaning I intended to convey with these words will, I think, become clear to you if you read pages 130 to 132 of the Chapter entitled "Concepts and Theories of Psychoanalysis," which I am enclosing [see pp. 360-363]. Pages 469 to 472 of my paper on Introspection will also help you in understanding what I am driving at [see pp. 217-221].

And now let me close by expressing the hope that despite your uneasiness, you will continue to debate, to express your point of view, to disagree — and yet to remain one of us.

April 4, 1972

. . . I will stress that the differentiation [of a merger transference from a merger with the idealized parent imago in the idealizing transference] must be made during periods of tension, not during periods of equilibrium. During a satisfactory merger it is hard to know whether a humble self has made itself a part of an omnipotent archaic object or whether an omnipotent self feels it has absorbed the archaic object into itself. During periods of narcissistic disequilibrium, however, the nature of the selfobject becomes clear. Is there a yearning for an attachment to a powerful perfect object? Or are we witnessing the insistence of a grandiose self that the selfobject be totally enslaved? Would it be helpful to you to think of a married couple held together by predominantly archaic narcissistic bonds—e.g., the husband enslaving the wife who must listen to the stories of his achievements and activities, the wife looking up to him, living through him, feeling attached to his greatness? Yet neither one is able to live independently; each does not lovingly yearn for the other when they are separated, but experiences lowered self-esteem without the other.

April 11, 1972

. . . The term "nuclear self" does not occur in the index [of the *Analysis of the Self*]. The study of case J., however, (pp. 179ff.), and especially Diagram 3 on page 185, should clarify my meaning. To put it in a nutshell: the nuclear self in this case is defined by the repressed wish to be admired and accepted as an independent male child. The other "selves," [the openly exhibitionistic one and the depressive one], are peripheral. . . .

Erikson's stress on the necessity to remain tentative about "ego identity" must be considered against the background of the fact that the concept of ego identity concerns the psychological *surface*. Since people have to live in a changing society, Erikson says, they have to remain flexible in order to be able to adapt to new roles. The scrutiny of a person's ego identity, however, tells little about his nuclear self. A firm nuclear self, a deep sense of one's inner cohesiveness and continuity which rests on early experiences of acceptance and confirmation, will allow one to respond in free, autonomous choice, to the tasks of external adaptation. Since the underlying structure of the self is firm, there will be no need for *defensive* rigidity or for quick and anxious adaptation, and the commitment to the continuity of the important goals and values of the personality will not be easily given up. You ask whether one can provide adequate "confirming responses" to one's offspring — and serve as an archaic idealized object for the young, I would add — if one remains tentative in one's ego identity. I would think that the answer would have to be in the affirmative. So long as the nuclear self of the parent is firm and so long as he himself has formed a firmly internalized set of values and ideals, he will be able to be a responsive "mirror" and an unembarrassed ideal for his children — whether his external behavior and his value system are more on the side of social fluidity or of social constancy. Did I make my meaning clear?

September 12, 1972

I am writing to you with a request for help, hoping only that the task will not prove to be a great burden to you.

For many years I have tried to trace the origin of the concept "optimal frustration" in psychoanalysis which, as you know, I have used widely in my lectures and writings. Although I have elaborated the concept metapsychologically and have used it in, I believe, a novel way in the context of the explanation of structure formation, I always knew that (in its interpersonal meaning, i.e., as a quality of the education of children [and thus belonging to educational psychology]) I must have come across the concept somewhere. I have never claimed any priority with regard to the term or the concept

and have handled it carefully in a noncommittal way whenever I used it. Until recently, however, my attempts to trace it
have been fruitless, despite the help of Glenn Miller and
despite the fact that I asked a number of sophisticated people
in our field about this point. One of the people I asked to investigate the issue, Dr. Peter Kutter of Stuttgart, Germany,
seems now to have come through with the answer—or at least
with an important lead toward the answer. He discovered in
S. Bernfeld's booklet *Sisyphos oder die Grenzen der Erziehung* the phrase "optimaler Grad von Versagung."
Bernfeld's *Sisyphos oder die Grenzen der Erziehung*, according to Fenichel's bibliography, was published in 1928. I
wonder whether he had not used this concept earlier (or later)
in a more elaborate form, e.g., in his great book *Die
Psychologie des Kleinkindes* which I read many years ago and
where I might have picked up the term in question. (The
English translation of *Die Psychologie des Kleinkindes*
appeared in 1929; I am certain, however, that the original
German edition came out much earlier.) I have no library
available here in California which would have either of the
two books by Bernfeld, and I wonder whether you would be
interested in spending the time in doing the relevant research
for me on this question.

The reason for the urgency is that the manuscript of the
German translation of *The Analysis of the Self* has just gone
to the publisher. If I had the relevant information I could ask
them to insert a footnote at the first mention of "optimal
frustration" in my book—and I would feel somehow relieved
in doing so.

I am sure that you will understand the details of my
needs, even without my spelling them out, if you think
yourself into my situation. Was the phrase just mentioned by
Bernfeld in passing, as it were, or did he present the concept
as an important issue in development? Did he take it from
someone else? Is it correct when I assume that he used it in

the context of the sociopsychological, interpersonal framework of educational psychology (albeit a psychoanalytically sophisticated one), or is his contribution, like mine, essentially within the metapsychological framework of psychoanalysis (at least in the way in which I understand it, as defined in my introspection paper)? I will say no more because I am sure that you understand that the tone of the footnote I hope to be able to insert in the German translation of my book depends largely on the answers to these questions. . . .

September 23, 1972

Your letter of September 17 has reassured me, and I am at present inclined to leave well enough alone, i.e., not to insert any hurried footnotes into the German translation of *The Analysis of the Self.* The decisive step I took is after all a metapsychological one, i.e., I said that omnipotent objects become internalized every time the child discovers a flaw in them, provided that the discovery is not of traumatic degree but optimally frustrating. Structure formation is, in other words, explained not primarily within the framework of parental behavior (whether overindulgent, optimally drive-curbing, or overly prohibitive)—these aspects determine only the content of the introject—but on the basis of the psyche's need to preserve the selfobject. The situation is more complex because the *drive*-curbing behavior of the selfobject is in essence experienced by the child as a *narcissistic* injury—how can you who is part of me (or you of whom I am a part) fail me in this way?—and thus drive curbing *seems* to lead to structure formation. In reality, however, structure formation is always due to a loss of the prestructural selfobject, not of the drive-curbing true object, and it can therefore not be explained within the framework of an objectinstinctual drive psychology.

January 15, 1973

. . . Much more should be said in response to your message, in particular as regards your cogent critique concerning the use of such terms as "narcissistic libido." I tried briefly—probably all-too-briefly—to explain my point of view in my book [1971]—see the footnote on page 39. But the acceptance or rejection of my terminology hinges on the question whether my subtle but decisive shift in defining the libido theory and its subsidiary conceptualizations will attain the status of respectability I would like it to have. I am referring here to an outlook which I first advocated in my essay on introspection and empathy [1959b]. In essence, I maintain that the safest and most consistent stance the depth-psychological theorist can take is that his concepts are abstractions and generalizations that relate to an introspected and/or empathically grasped reality. The concept of narcissistic libido, then, (as an example) is an abstraction that has reference to the specific feeling tone which pervades the experience of either the self or the object. If the self is scrutinized by the ego with warm and interested objectivity, we express this state of affairs by saying that the self has been invested with object libido. The self, in other words, is experienced like an object (the term object here used in its conventional sense, i.e., within the framework of social psychology). But when the object is experienced as an extension of the self or as if our control over it corresponded to the control we expect to exert over our own body and mind, then we say that the object has been invested with narcissistic libido. . . .

March 21, 1973

. . . Yes, Kleist's final remarks fascinated me, too. As a matter of fact, when I wrote the first draft of my narcissism studies (nearly eight years ago) this hundred-page sketch, the precursor of all my later writings on the subject, began with the introduction to the narcissistic rage paper, which you just read, and ended with Kleist's final statement in the Puppet Theater. . . . I might add here . . . that I see two major sources of psychosomatic illness within the area of narcissism. The one, as you rightly state, is chronic narcissistic rage (see the footnote about Patient P.'s hypertension in the paper on rage; p. 657n). The other (perhaps sometimes combined with the first) is the decathexis of the body-self (because it had received insufficient empathic responses in childhood). Concerning the latter possibility, see *The Analysis of the Self*, pp. 63-64, especially the footnote on p. 64, and pp. 214-215.

Concerning your remark about the total surrender of Nazi Germany, I can only tell you that I have done a good deal of work on the psychology of the German resistance movement and that I have written a good deal on this topic. I distinguished between the "martyr heroes" and the "rational resisters," but devoted my attention mainly to the first group, exploring the unusual capacity of some individuals not to get swallowed up by mass movements. This work is, unfortunately, embedded in a larger investigation of history and is not yet ready for publication. . . .

Is there another kind of rage than a narcissistic one, you ask. This is a matter of definition, I think. Intense feelings of anger within the object-instinctual sphere do certainly occur and may arouse intense aggressions in support of one's object-instinctual goals. But in order to qualify as rage, I would think that, even in these cases, there ought to be a large admixture of narcissistic injury, perhaps secondary, in response to one's frustration, impotence, etc.

March 22, 1973

I read your notes on terror and terrorism. It is my impression that, on the conscious and preconscious levels, you are describing the effects of this social state very well and that the elaboration of your description should make impressive and instructive reading in your new book. I have never studied the phenomenon — I have only suffered from it and have been frightened by it. I think it occurs in many degrees. You are talking about the grossest historical examples, of course. But terror does also occur in subtler forms, and there are border-line instances. The whole McCarthy era had something of that flavor. But there are much subtler occurrences — in pro-fessional groups, in educational institutions, in industry — which could perhaps be studied with a greater hope for deep insight than the crass instances to which you address yourself. As I said in a different context: progress toward the understanding of the nature of malignancy might well come rather from the examination of the near-normal cell in the first transition toward a malignant state than from the examination of patients who are dying from widespread me-tastases.

Another point. What is the essence of the emotional state which is induced in the terrorized? What does his regression consist of? Why is there such a tendency to emotional paral-ysis? Why the absence of courage, the inability to organize resistance movements, mutual support? Would the examina-tion of great works of literature be of any aid here? I'm thinking in particular of Kafka — The Castle, The Trial—who describes impressively the state of increasing paralysis which the victim experiences vis-à-vis a world that has lost interest in him and treats him like an inanimate particle. I think, in other words, that the grasp of the nature of the psychological state which is induced by terror would shed light on the pro-cesses by which terror is brought about and would lead us toward the possible mastery of this condition.

As you can see, I have little to add to what you have said — all I could do was to ask questions.

I am sending you my good wishes for success in your research.

March 25, 1973

... My first reaction [to your letter about the patient] was that he poses a puzzling diagnostic problem. Is this a severe narcissistic personality disorder or a covered-up psychosis? The symptom picture appears often to point toward the second possibility, but the fact that he tolerated years on the couch, his relative openness, the appropriate affect, and, especially, his warm and resonant humor would argue for the first. I also had a vague feeling of the presence of some organic factor, perhaps in the nature of a mild postencephalitic disorder, which I could not substantiate. (I did not examine [the patient] neurologically, but I did notice some oiliness of his face. And there are also tics and the borderline torticollis spasms in the neck musculature.) I finally came to the conclusion that there was no point in worrying about the differential diagnosis. He himself feels that he is treatable and that he needs to be in treatment. He is, however, a bit hung up between two attitudes with respect to therapy: on the one hand, he wants to be considered as analyzable (he was resentful when he read in my book, *The Analysis of the Self*, that schizophrenics are not analyzable), yet, on the other hand, he feels that classical analysis is harmful to him. I would think that the problem lies in the verbal sphere, taking into consideration that words have probably a less symbolic and more concrete meaning for him than they have for us. He wants a form of treatment which is appropriate for him and he wants this treatment to be called (which to him means: to *be*) analysis.

All in all, I would as his therapist be inclined to worry neither about the diagnosis nor about the name of the treatment, but would try to be attentive, perceptive, and empathic in order to understand what he wants and what he needs.

I have little doubt that his mother did not provide him

with adequate mirroring responses and that his father frustrated his need for an idealized omnipotent object. But such
a statement is, of course, general and not helpful. The
essence of the treatment, regulated externally in accordance
with his specific requirements, would be for therapist and
patient to become increasingly aware of his needs in both of
these spheres: concretely as they are experienced in the present, and, as broadly and empathically reconstructed, in comparison with his present needs, as they occurred and were
frustrated in his childhood. I would not only pay close
attention to his frustrations and his angry responses to them,
but would also investigate the beneficial interactions (such as
the beneficial result of your remark about the fact that there
are better places for clams in New York than Howard John-
son's). I would respect his need for visual contact and would
nondefensively accept his resentment about any signs of the
therapist's oral needs. All in all, the therapist's stance should
be one of acceptance of his wishes and of his need to
dominate the therapeutic situation — with clear and out-
spoken limit-setting when his demands overtax the therapist
and when the patient becomes uncomfortable unless his
reactions are curtailed. In every case, however, I would in a
friendly, direct, nonmoralizing but secure and convinced way
say that this or that demand cannot be fulfilled because it
would be to the detriment of the patient to fulfill it. He seems
to need contact, stimulation to get out of his "boredom" (this
word which he used with me probably refers to feelings of un-
reality about himself). He is very grateful when the therapist
can reduce his tensions, and I see no reason why he should be
deprived in this sphere. (The idea of abstinence is a completely correct one. But in [this patient's] case the very best
that a therapist can do to respond in accordance with his intense needs will turn out to be more frustrating, more
"abstinent" than any regular analytic patient ever has to
tolerate.) But gratification is not the essence — it should be ac-

companied by insight. What are his needs, how did they
arise, in what way are they justified even though they are not
in harmony with adult life, etc.? The primitive needs, by the
way, such as oral-incorporative wishes, and the reactive biting
anger and neck-muscle tensions when he is frustrated, I
would acknowledge, but would, on the whole, see and deal
with as products of regression. They are not fixations on
primary experiences of childhood; they are psychological disintegration products following the disappointments of his
need to be accepted by the warm smile of a mother and to be
the chip off the old block of an admired father.

Enough! I hope you don't mind my having thought out
loud in this communication to you. I saw [the patient] only
once, I believe, and I cannot therefore be specific and
concrete about him, but writing this letter provided me with
the opportunity to reflect about a complex area of diagnosis
and therapy, and I hope that you don't mind my having
shared these reflections with you. . . .

April 2, 1973

Your tersely expressed, excellent question whether I consider my "departures from classical analysis as parameters (in
Eissler's sense)" would deserve the writing of an essay in reply.
Thus, although I would be tempted to undertake the task of
giving you an adequate answer, I have to restrain myself in
order to continue ongoing work to which I must give prece-
dence. The following points can be no more than hints, given
with the hope that you will treat them with charity and that
you will make the necessary effort to fill the gaps which I
myself must at this time leave unfilled.

(1) My reference on page 291 of *The Analysis of the Self*
to what I called the "reluctant compliance with the childhood
wish," should be classified as the reference to a parameter.

(2) Certain forms of behavior toward analysands, which

might by many analysts be considered as classical technique,
I consider to be based on a misunderstanding. From which
follows that I do not consider as parameters the analyst's
behaving in a different way from what is believed to be
classical. To be concrete: the patient asks a question, and the
analyst remains silent. Such behavior is not psychologically
neutral, but is in fact rude and offensive or puzzling and mysterious, etc. To consider such silence neutral rests on a confusion between a physical zero-point (no sound waves) and a
psychological zero-point. The psychological zero-point is average expected behavior, not silence. An analyst should, however, I believe, suggest to his patient after convincing himself
the repeated questions betray an underlying pressure to
find out something of which the patient himself is not aware,
that the continuation of questions and answers does not lead
anywhere, that indeed it helps to keep covered the true
meaning of the urge to ask these questions. No hard and fast
rule can here be established. It is the skill and the perceptivity of the analyst that must guide his behavior in various
situations. But there are undoubtedly many instances in
which I would be in disagreement with some of my colleagues
about my responsiveness to an analysand's demands. I would
at times consider nonresponsiveness an artifact and therefore
a parameter, while some colleagues might consider my responsiveness to be a rationalized parameter.

(3) This point concerns probably what you in essence had
in mind when you wrote your note. The expectant attitude
toward the unfolding of the narcissistic transference and the
emphasis on the legitimacy of the narcissistic demands as
understood in the reconstructed childhood situation I do not
consider parameters (except as defined in point [1]). Concerning the question of "abstinence" which might arise in this
context, I would like to refer you to pp. 196-199 of my book,
stressing again that it is the understanding of the principles of
analytic progress that counts and not the adherence to the

external features of traditional behavior in the analytic situation. Since in this context a recent letter to a colleague might be of interest to you (see in particular my remarks about "abstinence"), I am enclosing a copy of this letter for you.[3] You must, however, remember that this letter refers to a patient who, at best, is on the very lowest level of self-cohesion that might possibly still be diagnosed as narcissistic personality disorder. He might well in essence be a "borderline case," i.e., in my definition (see, e.g., the footnote on page 626 of my paper "Thoughts on Narcissism and Narcissistic Rage"), a covered-over or latent psychosis.

Does all this help you?

April 30, 1973

. . . Keep in mind the difference between empathy as a tool of observation in analysis and the patient's remobilized transference need for empathic responses from an archaic environment.

Most important: differentiate between a "corrective emotional experience" *instead* of analysis and a corrective emotional experience becoming possible as the *result* of analysis. The term "corrective emotional experience" was introduced by Alexander, French, et al. in a framework which suggested that it could replace analysis, i.e., the analyst should intentionally act in ways that differed from the behavior of the traumatic parent. This approach is erroneous because it disregards the fact that the patient's needs (e.g., for empathic understanding) are in their essential focus not available to the patient. They have to be freed through slow analytic work and then have to be maintained against continued resistances during the working-through process.

I hope all this gives you at least a glimpse of what I have

---

[3] This refers to the preceding letter, dated March 25, 1973.

in mind about the important questions to which you ask me
to respond.

May 23, 1973

Simple as your question seems, it deals with a varied and
complex set of phenomena about which, in my opinion, one
cannot make generally valid statements, but which have to be
explored in each individual instance.

In the usually encountered vertical split, for example, the
individual rarely has overt feelings of depersonalization: the
noisy, grandiose sector of the personality seems to be *the* psychic reality. It is only in the course of psychoanalysis that the
patient becomes aware of a more central, empty, depressed,
and deprived sector and begins to connect this sector with
deeply meaningful memories from his childhood. In the transition from the first to the second phase of analysis, however,
during the phase, in other words, when the patient is insecure
about the question which of the two sectors constitutes his
real person, feelings of depersonalization may occur. (I might
add that there are individuals who are able to keep contradictory sectors of the personality in awareness and, without a
permanent sense of estrangement, can accept the often
creative tensions between them.)

There are other personalities, also characterized by a vertical split, in whom the grandiose or perverse sector of the
personality is dominant only from time to time. Such
people are capable of achieving a modicum of fulfillment in
the central sector of the personality through some perfor-
mances which are the expression of the activities of their
nuclear grandiose self. When these achievements, however,
are not available to them (e.g., achievements of a creative
kind), then their conscious self becomes depleted and they
turn, in the absence of creative possibilities, to perverse activities or to regressively grandiose attitudes. A sense of deper-

sonalization (a feeling of emptiness, a painful feeling of not being alive) precedes either a renewed creative spell or a turning to the vertically split-off perverse or regressively grandiose sector.

There are other variants. But do the descriptions I supplied to you help you with the assessment of C.?

May 24, 1973

Please excuse my tardiness in acknowledging the receipt of your paper and in reacting to it. I read your description of Taijin Kyofu with great interest and became quite convinced that, despite the apparently ominous nature of the manifest symptomatology, we are here dealing with a narcissistic personality disturbance and not with a paranoid psychosis. These symptom pictures occur, of course, also in Western culture. I have seen individuals in whom the oversensitivity of being looked at and other signs of social anxiety—blushing or fear of blushing—were the cardinal symptoms. Yet, after years of careful psychoanalytic exploration, I can say with certainty that these were not psychotic individuals. Most of them, such as Mr. E., whom I described in *The Analysis of the Self* (see in particular pp. 117-118), are narcissistic personality disturbances, despite some temporary seemingly dangerous symptoms. Mr. E., for example, had a temporary delusion (after the death of his mother) that a fish he was eating was looking at him; and he had other fleeting delusions during the course of the analysis. But here is the crucial point: whenever the correct interpretation concerning the transference precipitant of the regression was made, the seemingly psychotic symptom melted away.

I hope very much that you will follow up your work with Taijin Kyofu not only through psychotherapy but through analysis. I am convinced that only the patient empathic observation of the transference situation over a long period of time will allow you to come to definitive conclusions about these disorders. Excellent as your speculations (and those of some of the other authors whom you quote) are, only the analytic situation will establish reasonable certainty about the essence of the psychopathology.

June 18, 1973

I read your "Notes on Benvenuto Cellini" with mounting absorption, feeling sorry when your essay ended, and am now eager to hear the results of your further researches about this fascinating character. One would give a great deal to see the outline of the structures that determined this man's personality: his enormous self-confidence, his sense of invulnerability, his tendency to see himself (and his childhood) in a mythological context. I would say—and I assume that you would agree—that his castration fears are of no great importance. These were present in his childhood as they are present in everybody's childhood. The unusual aspect here is the sense of invulnerability, of survival when others would die. I don't believe that this conviction is primarily defensive. Its defensive use, I would say, is again nonspecific. But the sense of specialness, of uniqueness, comes from other sources, namely—probably in the absence of other information, this is what I would assume—from the fact that he was the unexpected, miraculous child and that his parents' attitude toward him gave him indeed the primary, nondefensive feeling of being *benvenuto*—that he was adored as a young god.

Thank you so much for the intellectual pleasure your essay provided for me. I can't wait for the continuation.

P.S. Cellini could perhaps be fruitfully examined by comparing his personality and life with others who were late born and no longer expected—openers of seemingly permanently closed wombs, like St. John the Baptist. The childhood memories of episodes symbolizing survival despite a death-giving surrounding may well refer to his birth, to the mother's first successful pregnancy.

June 24, 1973

I have thought more about your speculation (on the basis of my remarks about Freud's inhibited exhibitionism, his inability to accept praise without depreciating it, his absence from public celebrations, etc.) about Freud's unresolved narcissistic fixation and your idea (on the basis of my remarks about Freud's need to distance himself from the psychotic mind) that one of the episodes of Freud's fainting occurred in reaction to the stimulation to which Jung's psychoticlike imagery exposed him on their trip to the United States. I think that Freud's petit-bourgeois belittlingly-jocular rejection of nonrealistic art can be seen in the same light and supports your hypothesis that Freud was afraid of being swept away by psychoticlike thought processes. An illustration of Freud's rejection of modern art can be found in the remarks contained in his letter to Abraham on December 26, 1922.

September 21, 1973

. . . Indeed, your communication is fascinating and thought provoking. I have little doubt that "the visual axis," as you call it, ordinarily makes a very important contribution to the formation of the self, but I do not believe that it is all-important. It rather seems to me that tactile, olfactory, gustatory experiences make their basic contributions, too, and that the visual ones furnish only the peak layer and thus perhaps are essential in the ultimate integration of the self. Judging by my analytic experiences, however, I would assume that these factors are not absolute. [In the case of Mr. E.], for example, there seems to have taken place a shift *toward* the visual axis (leading perhaps to a primitivization of vision) be-

cause the patient suffered early severe deprivations in the tactile sphere. And I would assume that profoundly musical personalities have acoustic selves rather than visual ones. Could
the specific issue with your patient have been that her parents
did not accept her blindness, that they did not adapt themselves to the required shift in their attitudes toward the patient which would have required the expression of their
responses through other sensory modalities? I don't know the
answer, but I thank you for your stimulating communication
which raises so many important issues. . . .

November 21, 1973

Thank you for letting me see your interesting clinical vignette. If the patient's pivotal childhood experience was his
being defensively put down by his mother who was disgusted
(in a reaction formation) because she had become stimulated
by the boy's penis, then we are dealing with oedipal material
and it is correct to refer to this material as either an expression of phallic narcissism or of narcissism in the phallic
phase. (Phallic narcissism *is* narcissism in the phallic phase.)
The question, however, (which I cannot answer on the basis
of the evidence contained in the material you present), is
whether the patient was indeed suffering from an oedipal
transference neurosis against which he had walled himself off
by a narcissistic defense (touchiness and active rejection in
order to ward off castration anxiety and active castration
wishes toward the father) or whether he is suffering from a
narcissistic personality disturbance. In the latter case, the
central transference experience would be the danger of the
temporary breakup of the self when he feels rejected, and the
oedipal put-down would be in the main a particularly poignant or comparatively easily remembered symbol of a much
deeper-going and long-lasting rejection. You are of the
opinion that it is the first possibility rather than the second

and, since you know your patient, you are undoubtedly right. The crucial proof is the absence of the episodes of temporary (and reversible) fragmentation swings which are pathognomonic for the narcissistic transferences. Whatever the specific form of psychopathology, however, from which your patient suffered, I have no doubt that the building into the adult personality organization of the narcissistic cathexes which fed the unmodified flying fantasies should stand the patient in good stead: from a greater elasticity of his gait and increased pride in his body posture to a greater mobility of his fantasy life and of his creative intellect.

December 7, 1973

. . . What you say about the detailed, mechanistic approach to psychological phenomena strikes a sympathetic chord in me. Again, it will not surprise you to hear that I have pursued similar thoughts. At one occasion . . . I talked about my increasing preference for the use of broad reconstructions of total feeling states in childhood rather than of narrow dynamic interpretations of drives versus defenses. And I compared the difference between these two approaches with the difference that exists between organic and inorganic chemistry. The knowledge of inorganic chemistry (the metapsychology of drives and defenses, etc.) is a necessary cognitive step in science — but the living organism and its behavior cannot be adequately explained by it. The understanding of the complexities of organic substances and of their behavior (empathically reconstructed feeling states of childhood and their corresponding feeling states in adult life) are needed in order to explain the vicissitudes of biological (and psychological) life.

I do not see what I myself can do to counteract the danger that my work will be pulled down into the theoretical world of "inorganic chemistry." This fight should not be fought by me but by those who, like yourself, have grasped my intentions. The best way of counteracting the distortions which my work appears to be suffering through the unwelcome influence of some self-appointed disciples is not only through appropriate teaching but also — and especially! — through the use of my outlook in the undertaking of new explorations. . . .

December 18, 1973

. . . As you recognized, the use of humor by the analyst is a subtle affair. If it is primarily motivated by the analyst's narcissistic needs, it often constitutes the traumatic repetition of a traumatic childhood situation when a parent used his child for his emotional needs instead of responding to the needs of the child. But humor can also be used to help the patient in his attempt to surmount his own archaic narcissistic demands. If the analyst can laugh with the patient when the patient begins to see the incongruity of his grandiose and exhibitionistic demands, when the analyst's humor is the empathic support of the patient's growing wisdom vis-à-vis the limitations of the narcissistic gratifications that can be obtained in life, then the patient is not likely to feel that the analyst is in competition with him and neither will he be enraged nor will he retreat to a self-soothing attitude. . . .

January 2, 1974

. . . I enjoyed your essay very much, and it seems to me that your investigation of Dostoyevsky's story shows that Dostoyevsky portrayed here the phenomena of narcissistic trauma and narcissistic rage. I wonder whether you could not expand this essay — either by adding other writings about the subject matter or by going into greater detail with regard to the *Notes from the Underground.* This is truly an inexhaustible topic. Recently, by chance, I came across an illustration

which parallels the underground man's reaction to Lisa,
namely, an episode in the life of Hoess, infamous commander
of the concentration camp Auschwitz. One day Hoess suddenly decreed the execution of the camp gardener, an order
which seemed incomprehensible to the subordinate officer
who was to carry it out. When the officer interrogated the
gardener, he found out that the gardener had helped Hoess
by pulling him into the shade and by sprinkling him with
cold water when Hoess had nearly fainted in the summer
heat. Then the officer understood: the gardener had to be
eliminated because he had witnessed Hoess's temporary weakness. (See Fest, C. M., *Das Gesicht des Dritten Reiches*,
Ullstein, 1969, pp. 443-444.). . .

January 2, 1974

. . . With regard to your paper, I will say that I liked your
clear differentiation of the psychopathology of structural conflict and the psychopathology of the self, in particular your
emphasis on the fact that in the first kind of disturbance the
differentiation of male and female plays an important role,
while it is of no significance in the second. The two dreams at
the end of your paper demonstrate your meaning especially
clearly. It is difficult for me to give an opinion with regard to
the terminological question you raise. I can see that for certain purposes and under certain circumstances my two concepts, the grandiose self and the idealized parent imago (a
selfobject), should be replaced by a single concept which
comprehends both of these configurations. But whether the
term "Moi-Idéal" (and in English: Ideal-Ego) would be useful
in this context, I cannot decide without some further internal
experimentation. At the moment I am inclined to see the
two developmental lines of narcissism as separate, yet I
acknowledge that they are two sides of the same coin as I said
in *The Analysis of the Self*. All these questions should be de-

cided on the basis of concrete, demonstrable usefulness, not via armchair reasoning. I suggest, therefore, that we should live with your idea for a while and not come to any decision. . . .

February 7, 1974

Thank you for your inquiry about Mr. P., who has been under my psychotherapeutic care for many years. It is difficult to define the essence of this patient's psychopathology within the established nomenclature. He is not psychotic — yet the label of psychoneurosis would not do justice to the nature of his recurrent states of emotional disequilibrium. Using a term which I have come to consider useful in describing a not infrequently encountered form of psychopathology, I would refer to him as a rather severe case of narcissistic personality disturbance, i.e., he is a person whose self-esteem is easily injured, who requires a specifically cooperative environment for his emotional well-being, and who is inclined to suffer from great irritability leading to attacks of rage and to panic states when the environment does not provide him with the understanding responses he needs.

There is not much of substance that I can contribute to the problem of his hypertension. I have always reacted to it as a physical illness to which he must adapt as best he can, and I have never suggested to him that psychological factors might play an etiological role. Yet, as a psychiatrist and depth psychologist with long years of experience and as a physician who is still reasonably well informed about the causal chains of relevant somatic factors, I must admit that, had anyone asked me years ago — before Mr. P. had shown any manifestations of hypertension — what kind of psychosomatic disease he might eventually develop if indeed he were to develop one, I would unhesitatingly have answered: hypertension. You may say that this is unscientific hindsight, and you would be right.

I can nevertheless vouch for the veracity of this report even though I cannot tell you its significance. Is it the chronic readiness toward rage, which in the long run leads to those organic changes (via endocrine stimulation), which ultimately lead to the irreversible new balance that manifests itself in hypertension? Or is the association the other way around, i.e., is there an organically definable prehypertensive constitution which also manifests itself in certain psychological propensities, such as readiness to rage? I do not know the answer, although again I would be less than truthful if I denied the fact that from what I have learned about Mr. P.'s early childhood, I am inclined to assume that environmental psychological factors must at least have interacted with constitutional givens to produce Mr. P.'s adult personality and adult psychopathology. I am thinking here in particular of Mr. P.'s mother, a very disturbed, perhaps borderline-psychotic woman, who frustrated her child's need for homeostatically attuned understanding, leading to early rages against her, and to the fact that he did not acquire the ability to regulate his self-esteem, to calm himself, to control his emotions.

So much for the background of Mr. P.'s personality. Concerning the present management, I can only repeat that he should have the benefit of all that modern medicine has to offer — from the surgical exploration of his adrenal tissue, if this seems indicated, to the management of his symptoms by antihypertensive drugs. His reactions to drug therapy are known to you. He is convinced that intensive medication accounts for the unexpected periods of intense anxiety and depersonalization from which he has occasionally suffered in recent years. I am doubtful about this connection, but am not certain concerning this view. I believe that a careful correlation of the type of drugs used, and their combination and dosage, with the occurrence of the recent anxiety spells might help — this is a task that must clearly be undertaken by the internist in charge.

I would like to close this report by telling you that I should be glad to try to answer any specific questions that you might have. I would also like very much to receive a report of your findings and conclusions.

May 16, 1974

Thank you for your note. I am glad that you enjoyed my address. As far as your challenging question about analysts is concerned, I was at first inclined to reply jokingly that it had me completely stumped — giving you thus the proof for the existence of an analyst who possesses this basic constituent of the mental equipment of the scientist: the ability not to know, to be puzzled, to tolerate the tension which ultimately should lead to new, creative insight. But the longer I thought about your question, the more I became impressed by its profundity. And I admired the simplicity and directness with which you put your finger on a serious problem.

Let me first state my conviction that analysts — some analysts, at least — *do* have the ability to be stumped. It so happens that I had felt increasingly stumped during the past fifteen years or so of my professional life by a series of cases: perhaps as many as one-third or one-half of my practice. I tried unsuccessfully to understand them on the basis of the classical assumption that they had failed to solve their emotional involvements with their parents, in particular the love and hate relationships with their parents around what is called the Oedipus complex. If I tried to explain their relationship to me, their demands on me, as revivals of their old love and hate for their parents, or for their brothers and sisters, I had more and more the feeling that my explanations became forced and that my patients' complaints that I did not understand them (see, for example, in my book *The Ana-*

lysis of the Self, p. 286) were justified. It was on the basis of feeling stumped that I began to entertain the thought that these people were not concerned with me as a separate person but that they were concerned with themselves; that they did not love or hate me, but that they needed me as a part of themselves, needed me as a set of functions which they had not acquired in early life; that what appeared to be their love and hate was in reality their need that I fulfill certain psychological functions for them and anger at me when I did not do so.

Now you might say: "Here we go again! While you admit to having been stumped for a long time, you also claim that you have found the solution." And I don't know how I could defend myself against such a response. But the question is: is there really an *essential* difference between analysis and "the kind of science" in which you are engaged, as you put it in your letter to me? Is there any intrinsic virtue in remaining stumped? Or should not the state of being stumped lead to the attempt to get at new solutions? You are, of course, saying that much yourself, yet your challenge relates to the analyst's supposed inability to admit his permanent failure by saying "I have never understood it."

But I am willing to assume that there is a difference in this respect between, let us say, the physicist, on the one hand, and the psychoanalyst, on the other hand. What does account for it? The first answer that occurs to me is that analysis is such a comparatively young science. It is not that we understand so much — it is that we understand so little. If in giving you the account of the course of an analysis I were to tell you all the things that I *don't* understand — that I *permanently* don't understand — this report would have to include the overwhelming majority of the patient's communications. My mind works all the time; all kinds of possible explanations occur to me — but convictions about explanatory insights are rare and far between. Thus, we are in-

clined to talk about the occasionally obtained secure insights we *have* acquired, report on the occasional clear-
cut connections we *have* been able to make—in particular
when we can show how such an insight can lead to increased
mastery for the patient. My story about the insight concerning the animal torturer was meant as an illustration
for a broad point I wanted to communicate. It would
have been nonsense for me, in that context, to talk about
an area in which I had remained stumped. In the case in
question, the analysis led to a certain point with moderate
but not insignificant improvement in the patient's well-being
and functioning. But there were broad areas that had us
stumped—completely and, I assume, permanently. The
patient had, for example, a peculiar, stereotyped way of examining the doctor's waiting room, of looking into corners,
behind books, of exploring the hallway. He did this over and
over again—but we never made any headway in understanding his motivations in this respect. He also had a peculiar way
of thinking. It was overly concrete—he had difficulties understanding subtle jokes—and whenever the analyst wondered
what the patient's explorations might mean, the overcon-
creteness of the patient's thinking seemed to increase. Having
come to the conclusion that the classical assumption (e.g.,
about infantile sexual curiosity) did not fit, we began to assume that his exploring was an enacted thought of some kind.
But, even if so, we could never find out what it was.

But enough! I could give you literally hundreds of
examples of feeling stumped in trying to understand psychological configurations, but will not bore you with expanding
on this issue. I might only mention that I founded a committee of the International Psychoanalytical Association
about six years ago concerning our predictions of our applicants' ability to become analysts. We are engaged in examining instances where the evaluators at psychoanalytic institutes (seasoned analysts throughout) failed dismally in

making the correct prediction (either they had thought the applicant would perform very poorly when, in fact, it turned out that he performed splendidly during training, or the other way around). I can only tell you that to our chagrin we have made very little headway so far, despite great care and effort and a thorough investigation of all the available data.

Apart from the fact that analysis is comparatively young and that it must therefore still concentrate on those instances it *does* understand, I think there is also another reason for the difference between your kind of science and mine in this respect. Analysis has not yet reached that stage where it is able to support research-scientists — a stage which, of course, has been firmly established in physics and in all the other older sciences. By far the greatest number of analysts are first and foremost practitioners. They are hard-working, devoted people; they have been trained in the skills of their craft; and they have absorbed theoretical knowledge to the extent that theory is needed in their work. Failure to understand, however, is not accepted by them as a necessary stepping stone in a research-oriented life — it is to them, quite understandably, nothing to be proud of, rather something to feel ashamed about. I will not elaborate on this simple point; but I am certain that you could find analogies in the periphery of your own field if you move from the top layer of researchers to the technologists who apply their knowledge of physics to practical goals. You would hardly expect them to be proud of having been permanently stumped in their work. . . .

May 21, 1974

. . . the only question I have is whether your distinctions between empirical or clinical theory, on the one hand, and abstract or speculative theory, on the other hand, does full justice to the contrast between empirical and speculative science. I do not know the answer but, although I realize—and have often stressed myself—that observation is "a theory-laden enterprise," there seems to me to be an important difference between (a) the (tentative and ad hoc) use of preformed, vaguely outlined configurations during the act of observation which makes possible the collection of data and (b) the development of sharply defined mental configurations, i.e., of theories (to which the researcher has a long-term conscious commitment), which is followed by a systematic series of observations designed to prove or disprove the theories. I am aware that one can here, as usual, either stress the fact that these two scientific activities form a continuum or emphasize the contrast between the two ends of the continuum (as I chose to do in the preceding).

I still maintain that there is room for evocative descriptive terms if they further communication, and I think that one should not become hypochondriacal about the use of imagery. And I know, for example, that I did not intend the coiled-spring image (for the nuclear self) versus the vending-machine image (for the area of parts) to be causal-explanatory, but evocative. (An autobiographical note: I remember a discussion with a friend when I was about nineteen. Trying to explain to him my commitment to life and my devotion to my goals, I said "Irgend etwas treibt mich vorwärts wie eine Feder!" ["There is something in me that drives me forward like a coiled spring!"].). . .

June 28, 1974

Thank you for your sensitive and cogent reaction to Mitscherlich's review of the Freud-Jung correspondence. I fully agree with your thoughts, and I share your feelings. But, to add a thought of my own: don't you think that this tragedy was a consequence of the fact that neither of the two fully grasped the enormous power of narcissistic motivations in human relationships? Thus, all their deep insights about the

revived loves and hates of the oedipal situation did not help
them.

July 14, 1974

. . . Your letter rang many bells in me, on many levels of my
responsiveness: from deep and personal to high and scientific.
Even the musical metaphor I just used is in context because
my own move toward words (writing) was by way of some unsuccessful attempts at expressing myself through music (my
father was a musician). And my interest in music has never
ceased. My first analytic paper was about music. And I am at
the present time working on a paper about the termination of
the analyses of narcissistic personality disturbances in which
(in the analysis of Mr. M.; cf. pp. 128-129 of *The Analysis of
the Self*) a decisive stretch of the movement of the exhibitionistic needs for confirming-mirroring responses was from the
way station of musical display to the final mature resting
place of written verbal performance. The thought occurs to
me (in the context of your taking up my parting remark to
you: "Keep the plane flying!") that some flying phobias, like
some acrophobias, are not the symptoms of structural-conflict
neurosis, but express a fear of the repetition of terrifyingly
violent swings in self-esteem that took place in childhood. We
might imagine that the original model of these swings in self-
esteem relate to the small child's merging into the omnipotent
idealized object while he is being carried empathically (and is
thus enabled to feel merged into the idealized adult, to feel
himself as part of him, indeed, to feel himself as being the
omnipotent figure) — but the adult's sudden lack of empathy
with the child or his sudden loss of interest in the child leads
to the sudden interruption of the merger; the child feels (or
really is) dropped. These experiences could well be prototypical for other ups and downs in the child's self-esteem vis-
à-vis the idealized object, prototypical for oscillations of ar-

chaic precursors of (what adults experience as) self-esteem,
which do not involve the child being carried and then
dropped. There is a German phrase [Goethe, *Egmont* 3],
"Himmelhoch jauchzend; zum Tode betrübt" (To heaven
exulting, cast down to death), which, on a higher level of
experience, expresses these contrasting oscillations. . . .

December 3, 1974

Thank you for your very informative letter. I am sorry
that the treatment seems to have come to an end. (As you anticipated, I had already learned about this from Mr. N.'s
mother.) What a fascinating psychological problem! And
what specific, peculiar demands such a patient makes on the
therapist! His need to be moved by a power outside himself
"like a puppet" is, I would think, the necessary consequence
of the fact that he has no self that could function as a reliable
center of initiative. His father's abrupt disappearance and his
mother's personality effectively blocked the development of
this central structure of his personality. Insight does not cure
this defect. In general, it only helps to start and to maintain
the relevant working-through processes. Thus, he could not
start treatment on his own—it had to be on the initiative of
someone else, and it had to be maintained (e.g., paid for) by
someone else. Why the couch hour marked the end of the
therapy, I do not know for certain. But I would think of this
possibility. The demand that he must for the time being perceive you as *his* personality might have been very taxing, and
thus you might have protected yourself from the feeling of
being sucked into him (by his eyes, for example) by putting
him on the couch. He, on the other hand, might now have
been deprived of the (at first grossly concrete) possibility of
building structure through identification. Visual and oral incorporation wishes for self-building psychological substance
might well have become replaced by anal incorporative urges

on the couch, as he felt deprived of contact and felt rejected by what he perceived as a break in empathy. (Thus, "homosexual" fantasies might have arisen in him as the incorporation needs became intensified and sexualized.) But all this is only speculative.

Thank you so much for tackling this enormously difficult therapeutic problem and for telling me about the events that led to the end of therapy.

February 3, 1975

. . . Concerning your inquiry, I must also be relatively brief. I do not believe that the Freudian concept of transference will be directly useful to you in the context in which you propose to use it. (Please read carefully Kohut and Seitz, 1963. I suggest that you read the whole essay, but, in particular, pp. 120ff [see pp. 246ff]). . . . As you will see, transference relates to the mature psychic apparatus, it is the influence of the repressed upon preconsciousness across a weakened repression barrier. For Freud, it concerned libidinal and aggressive strivings. I have, however, demonstrated analogous processes in the narcissistic realm. . . .

I do not believe, however, that the addictions belong to the stage of psychic maturity that is required for the process of transference. Transferences occur in a mature psychic apparatus which has been able (more or less successfully) to wall itself off from certain infantile strivings. The essence of the addictive mind, however, is not (poorly resolved) conflict between mature structures but the presence of structural defects. (For an early statement about this, see my paper on Introspection [1959b]).

To put my opinion into a nutshell. The drug experience (similar to the sexual experience of most perversions) is designed to fill a structural defect. The childhood prototype of these experiences is the following: During a developmental stage when the child needs a narcissistically experienced other person (a "selfobject") for the maintenance of his self (his self-esteem), that other person (the selfobject) fails him. (The failure can be the selfobject's absence or, most often, the selfobject's inability to provide empathic responses to the child.) The child is thus confronted with the loss of psychological structure (the selfobject is at that time the child's psychological structure). In order to replace the selfobject (the selfobject's empathy, the selfobject's soothing, the selfobject's responsiveness), the child turns to self-stimulation. For this purpose he uses oral, anal, and phallic masturbation; he uses self-inflicted pain (which is better than feeling nothing); and he uses imagery. With all these activities he attempts to replace the absent selfobject and the lack of psychic structure. (Psychic structure was not formed because the means by which structure is built is the gradual loss of the selfobject. Since the child lost the selfobject traumatically, no structure was formed.) I believe that the drug experience repeats the childhood attempt to replace the selfobject (the psychic structure) and to counteract the feeling of deadness — which comes about in consequence of the absence of the empathic milieu that should be provided by the selfobject. Self-generated fantasies (later: fantasies generated by hallucinogenic drugs) are the means by which in these instances the selfobject is replaced and the sense of deadness is fought.

Are these tersely expressed formulations helpful to you? I hope so.

February 19, 1975

I think that you are making a very valuable contribution in your paper on the self and the Oedipus complex. I also believe, however, that your important insights deserve to be communicated in a clearer and more sharply outlined form than your presentation provides for the reader. Even though I could at this point devote only limited time to the study of your paper, I believe I understood your aims. But, in view of my familiarity with the subject matter, I am not a representative sample of the average psychoanalytic audience. Here is my suggestion. I think you should provide, before you give your own new interpretation of the data, the two different ways of looking at the material that are already more or less established in psychoanalysis; and I think that you should give them both in the most cohesive and persuasive way you can find. It is only after you have given these alternatives that you should undertake the task of presenting the new theory, demonstrating its advantages, its greater explanatory power, its greater internal consistency, etc. The two other theories against the background of which you should outline your own proposition are these.

(a) The theory that we are in essence dealing with an Oedipus complex, and that the narcissistic manifestations which emerge in the transference and/or which are remembered by the patient from her childhood (or can be reconstructed) are only the secondary accompaniments of the central drive-determined conflicts. (The girl wants a baby from her father, for example; she realizes that she cannot compete with her mother who in fact gets the real baby; she is crestfallen, her self-esteem is low.)

(b) The theory that you are dealing with a mixture of self pathology and oedipal-conflict pathology. To be exact: the girl's self had been insufficiently responded to early in life, and it is therefore poorly consolidated when she enters the oedipal phase. Responding to the organizing and synthesizing push of the oedipal aspirations, the self consolidates sufficiently to experience the conflicts of the oedipal rivalry, but, from time to time, it breaks down and the child re-experiences the earlier disintegrations of her body-mind-self. There exist indeed patients who alternate between the pathological results of true oedipal conflicts and the pathological results of self-pathology. The movement in the transference in such individuals is usually (but by no means always) in the direction toward the ever more clearly experienced oedipal-conflict situation as the self consolidates.

It is against the background of these two alternative possibilities that you should outline your own contribution as a third formulation: a child whose self is well consolidated in its basic configuration, as a unit in time and space, as a center of initiative, and as a recipient of impressions; and a child, furthermore, who does not suffer (at least not to a disabling degree) from the narcissistic blows which are always dealt out in the oedipal situation. What you are presenting is a child whose ambitions and ideals are damaged by the pathogenic responses either of the mirroring or of the idealized selfobject (or by both) at that phase in which the self-experience as a male or as a female needs confirming support or needs to be goal-settingly idealized. It is the damage coming from this specific late failure of the selfobjects (who up to now have reacted with comparative acceptance toward the child and its preoedipal development) that you want to outline by contrasting it as sharply as you can with the two other syndromes I mentioned before.

After you have gone through with the task that I described in the foregoing, you may then — indeed you should — tackle certain refinements, such as the fact that there are surely no pure forms of isolated oedipal malfunctioning of the selfobjects, that evidence of earlier disturbances in the narcissistic realm are undoubtedly discernible. At any rate, I would imagine that among those who seek analysis for their self-disturbance on this level, more broadly based weaknesses of the self will also be found. (Are there, however, perhaps comparatively healthy inverts in whom an earlier self-damage is minimal?)

Thank you for giving me the opportunity to study your

essay. And my sincere wishes for continuing, satisfying productivity.

March 7, 1975

Your interest in my paper on narcissistic rage gives me great satisfaction, and I am glad to send you a reprint. As you know, it is one of the essential aspects of my conception of psychological development that I do not see narcissism developing into object love and that I do not see narcissistic rage developing into object-related rage. Object love develops from primitive to mature stages; object-related aggression (assertiveness) develops from primitive to mature stages; narcissistic love develops from primitive to mature stages; and narcissistic rage, too, develops from primitive to mature forms. Anger with regard to infringements on one's self is, in other words, no more in and of itself pathological than are self-esteem, ambitions, ideals, creativeness, humor, and wisdom (i.e., the mature forms of narcissism). I am at the present time working on a long contribution [*The Restoration of the Self*] in which I am again discussing all these problems in detail, and from a somewhat different point of view. . . .

April 10, 1975

. . . It is, as you know, my view that the normal, neutral, atmosphere — from the beginning of life — is empathic acceptance. That silence, nonresponsiveness, is a crass deviation from the basic axis of psychological neutrality. . . . I would stress, in other words, that the spontaneous warm reactions of the analyst are the "neutral" environment for an analysis — that everything else is a strained artifact. . . .

There are probably a number of causes for the fact that Freud and the other early analysts set this artificial pattern (which was then rationalized in complex ways by the theorists). Some of the present-day staunch defenders of an emotionally depriving atmosphere do so, I believe, because to them (either because of the traumata of their training analyses or because of their own basic personality structure) warm emotional responses seem in fact artificial. If they behaved in a warmly responsive way, it would not be neutral for them. And they thus generalize and proclaim their attitude to be the only appropriate one. Paradoxically, on first sight—but really quite understandably—many patients of such analysts will adapt without undue harm to being "treated" in this fashion. They grasp after a while that this is indeed the analyst's personality, and/or the analyst's conviction, and that he means well. They supply to the image of their analyst, probably in an unspoken way, a fantasy of a warm heart beneath a cold surface which sustains them during the analytic work. And I believe that the analysts are pleased with these responses (they preconsciously grasp what their patients are doing) and that they let these fantasies go by without interference or interpretation. . . .

April 15, 1975

I was finally able to read your essay on Kleist's "Puppet Theater" during the last weekend. It is a skillfully written, carefully thought out, and well-balanced presentation which gave me a great deal of enjoyment. I liked especially your elaborations on the theme represented by the relation between the puppeteer and the puppet. It is beautiful to see how Kleist alludes simultaneously to three psychological issues and synthesizes them. (1) The dim memories which all human beings harbor deep in their personality of a phase of normal development in which the baby still felt himself to be a part of an idealized omnipotent self-object. (2) The danger of the pathological revival of this phase in a schizophrenic regression in which the self as a center of independent initiative is put out of action — here I would refer you especially to a particular symptom of a certain type of schizophrenia that is called "automatic obedience." And (3) the leading psychological problem of an era (specifically the dangers posed by mass society: the anonymity of the individual) for which the description of the individual psychopathology of the artist is only a vehicle.

Once more my thanks for giving me the copy of your paper, and good wishes for your professional and personal future.

May 30, 1975

. . . As far as your essay is concerned, I believe that I am a very poor judge of the accuracy and relevance of your comparison. Although you are to my knowledge the first person to point out similarities between my work and Adler's, you are not the first person to compare my work with the work of others.

While I can recognize that a number of associative bridges can be built between my work and the work of these others, no bell rang in me, and I did not get a sense of the existence of any real similarity between my work and the work of those whom I supposedly have followed. And the same held true when I read what you had to say about Adler's and my work in this context.

I have no doubt that Adler's interest concerned the area of narcissistic injury and of the psychological reactions to it. It is therefore not surprising that through selective quoting one can demonstrate similarities. But even disregarding the fact that I undertook a broad, empirically based investigation of the transferences that develop in a certain group of individuals with defects in the structure of their self and demonstrated how specific working-through processes become activated which revive the developmental task that could not be completed in childhood, while Adler, to my understanding, did nothing of the kind—even if we disregard this fact, I have the impression that Adler's central outlook (as I gleaned it from your quotes) is in a basic way the very opposite of mine. I emphasize the original, basic positive narcissistic experience of the child, which I take to be the primary given; and I see the interferences with this experience as being of two kinds: optimal ones (i.e., phase-appropriate and limited ones) which lead to structure formation in the area of the regulation of self-esteem; and traumatic ones (i.e., phase-inappropriate and extensive ones) which lead to structural defects in this area. As a matter of fact, I believe that the traditional psychoanalysts could, in your sense, be called more Adlerian than I, because in general they have assumed that grandiosity is an overcompensation. (See, for example, the relevant statement on p. 83 of *The Analysis of the Self*, about Anna Freud's and Dorothy Burlingham's remarks concerning the grandiose "fantasy father.")

As you can see, it is not easy for me to recognize the similarities you are pointing out. I also know, of course, that it would be very difficult for me to be objective. My ideas grew from the soil of my clinical experience and were organized on the basis of a theoretical stance I delineated long ago in my essay "Introspection, Empathy, and Psychoanalysis" [1959b]. Work that has been done by others on the basis of a differently ordered set of experiences will therefore strike me as dissimilar to mine, even though the sector of psychological reality it investigates might be the same as the one I tried to illuminate.

I will close my response to you by these final remarks. Even though I cannot find myself in agreement with your thesis, I enjoyed your work. The attempt to fit the ideas of a science into a historical context is very worthwhile, and I am grateful to you for having undertaken the task of fitting my contributions into a historical context. Whether others will agree with your conclusions is hard for me to predict. But whatever the response, I think it will be a stimulus to the further re-examination of psychoanalytic contributions of the past, an enterprise which, in turn, will lead to a clearer understanding of the contributions made in the present time. . . .

June 18, 1975

. . . Your review is a delight — clear, humorous, level-headed; it could hardly be better. I have only one (perhaps idiosyncratic) objection: I did not like your making fun of the fact that the therapist was so tardy in confronting the patient with her having left the session early, i.e., only after the event had been repeated for a third time. Much could indeed be said in favor of the analyst's "bringing it up" immediately. And I have no doubt that most analysts would bring such a parapraxis to a patient's attention without delay. But there is also something to be said on the side of waiting — and I myself might at times, quite unselfconsciously and relaxedly, refrain from confronting a patient with his or her unconscious act. Although confrontations are consciously intended by the analyst as incentives to analyze motivations, they are frequently, I believe, rationalized expressions of the analyst's impatience, reactions of his frustrated need to know, i.e., reactions to a narcissistic injury. I do not doubt that being overly patient can also be a manifestation of unresolved narcissistic needs in the analyst, e.g., the enactment of that godlike benevolence about which you rightly joke when you say that it makes you doubt your "libidinal cathexis." But waiting, even protracted waiting, may also be rational — and natural — as long as it forms part of a total attitude of commitment to empathic cognition. It may well be claimed, on the one hand, that the habitual use of confrontations tends to create an atmosphere in which the intrusions from the unconscious begin to be experienced as if they were misdemeanors about which the patient feels guilty, while on the other hand, that the analyst's habitual waiting (until the spontaneously emerging material enables him to speak out not only about the symptomatic act but also simultaneously about its position in the current dynamic equilibrium) can set up an atmosphere in which the patient might, nondefensively, discover the self-assertive, positive meaning of an act that he was formerly able to undertake only outside of his awareness. Be all this as it may, I neither insist that an attitude of nonconfronting expectancy is the only appropriate one nor would I myself always assume it.

. . . I agree with you . . . that Freud took a psychobiological stance when he formulated his observations in terms of drives and psychic energy. Still, I believe that the basic meaning of Freud's theoretical system has gradually changed, that (see my paper on Introspection and Empathy) the terms Freud originally meant to fit into a biological frame of reference have now indeed become metaphors that refer to psychological data and psychological relationships. I am convinced, for example, that our references to the degrees and the distribution of energic cathexes should now be understood as the metaphorical vocabulary of a system of symbolic logic that is attuned to the task of formulating the content of complex psychological experiences and events. The relationship between structure formation and optimal frustration (structural defect and traumatic frustration) could serve as one illustration of the use of the metaphors of analytic metapsychology. Or, as another illustration, think of my recent metapsychological formulation of the affect of shame and rage (see pp. 654-657 of my paper on narcissistic rage [1972b]). I do not consider this metapsychological exercise to be a major contribution; still, in support of my present argument, I will here advance the claim that I have succeeded in clarifying a variety of complex relationships by speaking — metaphorically—of drives, drive discharge, inhibited drive discharge, and the response of the selfobject. I am not asserting that these metaphors are optimal, that they will not be gradually superseded, that these experiences could not have been expressed by using other terms. And, in particular, I would grant you the full right to express your findings without the use of the traditional psychoanalytic symbols—in fact, I am increasingly doing so myself. Still, I do think you should treat the traditional system with greater respect, demonstrate that you understand how well it has served us, and how well it may indeed still serve us if it is buttressed by appropriate definitions. I have never felt the need to change established modes of expression on purely theoretical grounds—I change them only (e.g., in my introducing the concept of selfobject transferences, etc.) when clinical insights force me to do so.

July 17, 1975

I read your letter attentively and enjoyed it very much. Mrs. M. is certainly a fascinating case—truly "borderline," i.e., in danger of permanent or protracted fragmentation. Yet her very rages, though delusional, seem to me to have also a cohesion-producing capacity, a fact which may explain why certain paranoiacs, despite their psychotically skewed personalities, appear to have a firmly delimited, strong self. I might add that anger, particularly anger that is responded to sensibly (even with pride) by the selfobject, undoubtedly contributes to the consolidation of the self in childhood.

March 19, 1976

I read your letters (February 4 and February 22) several times, and I thank you for them. Although they are thought-provoking in many respects, I will address myself today only to your most challenging suggestion: that we should posit, not two as I do, but four lines of psychic development: (1) one for our experience of the self and of the selfobject, (2) one for our experience of the other person insofar as he is not a self-object (i.e., of the other person experienced as a center of independent initiative), (3) one for our experience of the group, and (4) one for our experience of "transcendental meanings" (my translation of your term *die spirituelle Ebene*).

Let me begin by saying that I am not against your theory, i.e., that I am not rejecting it in the sense in which Freud, for example, rejected the opinion that religious experience — the psychological content of your fourth line of development — was a basic or primary human response, and that it concerned a genuine aspect of reality [cf. Freud, "The Future of an Illusion," 1927a; "A Religious Experience," 1928; his letter to Binswanger of October 8, 1936]. But while I am not rejecting your theory — I am here dealing only with your claims concerning group experiences and religious experiences, i.e., with your third and fourth lines of development — which indeed seems important and challenging to me, neither can I accept it.

Why can't I accept it? My answer is simple. I can't accept it because it seems to me to be purely speculative. It lacks those — however tentatively outlined — reconstructions of early experience that are formulated in such a way as to allow empirical evidence for and against them to be marshaled by you and other investigators. Only if this condition begins to be fulfilled can your ideas claim the serious attention of the scientific depth psychologist.

It is not enough to demonstrate that grownups feel attached to groups or that belonging to a group will provide an increment of security for them. What you have to show is that the group has an important meaning for the small child.

Does the small child experience an emotional echo to the fact that he is surrounded by a multiplicity of voices or that he perceives in some way the odor of many human beings who surround him without touching him? Does he experience in some specific archaic way a sense of belonging to a tribe, and is he beset by some specific archaic fear of being abandoned by the tribe? Are the child's reactions to groups as groups different from his reactions to the empathic or nonempathic responses of this or that or of several individual others who hold him, respond to him, care for him?

Similar questions also arise, of course, with regard to the spiritual line of development you are positing. Freud, as you undoubtedly know, took up the challenge posed by the claim that the "oceanic feeling" was the *fons et origo* of the need for religion. But he rejected this theory on the grounds that the experience in question could be convincingly explained in a different way and that to connect it with the later religious experience of grownups was only a rationalization. (See his letter to Romain Rolland of July 14, 1929 [in E. Freud, 1960] and "Civilization and Its Discontents," Chapter 1 [1930].) Now, you might be able to adduce arguments that invalidate Freud's explanation of the oceanic feeling; or you might be able to adduce archaic precursors of religious feelings in the child other than the oceanic feeling (see in this context my positing precursors of the experience of "grace" and of "original sin" in my interview with Dr. Moss [1976]). I am not denying these possibilities. I am saying that when or until you proceed in this fashion your theories will be a kind of poetry — pleasing and beautiful, and perhaps evocative; as I said before, however, they will not engage the serious attention of the scientific depth psychologist which they would otherwise deserve.

Thank you once more for having shared your ideas with me. . . .

December 1, 1976*

It will not surprise you to hear that many of my colleagues did not respond favorably to your recent lecture, "Psychoanalysis and the Misinterpretation of Literature." Some, it is true, were fascinated by what you had to say and, despite strong misgivings, felt positively in the balance. Others, including me, not only admired the formal brilliance of your presentation but were grateful to you because you had chosen a most significant topic and had confronted us with a number of crucial questions. But even this group of admirers, of which I am here making myself the spokesman, had some reservations and, above all, felt certain deep regrets.

Let me say at the outset that I do not insist on an even-handed approach. Like the good old-fashioned hellfire-and-brimstone preacher, you delivered a sermon meant to stir up guilt and contrition in the congregation; and, while my own tastes don't run in this direction, I have no wish to impose my predilections on you and recognize your right to make your points in the form of your choosing. And I was gratified to note that your scorn was mitigated by an occasional dram of wise, above-the-mêlée objectivity and by an ounce of welcome humor that took you mercifully out of the pulpit and put you behind the lectern of a scholar talking to other scholars — thus, for precious moments, transforming the attack into a tolerant sharing of that knowledge perhaps most prized in the community of the truly learned: the knowledge how little one knows for certain, how little one can ever hope to know.

But, to get into *medias res*, what was the most substantial question that you raised in your address to us? Put in my own

<hr />

*This and the following letter were prompted by a lecture entitled "Psychology and the Misinterpretation of Literature," given by Erich Heller under the auspices of the Chicago Institute for Psychoanalysis in November, 1976. The lecture, as well as the letters—in a slightly different form — were originally published in *Critical Inquiry* (1978), 4:433-450. Chicago: University of Chicago Press.

words, it was this: What is the purpose of the psychoanalyst's efforts outside the clinical setting, in particular when his contributions take the form of a pathography? That is, to what end do analysts study the psychopathology of the creators of great works? I, too, have asked myself this question, and, since you read my old essay "Beyond the Bounds of the Basic Rule," you know some of my answers. But important basic questions are hardly ever answered once and for all; and I will therefore under the impact of your lecture, respond as if I had heard the question for the first time.

My immediate reply is simple. The inquiring human mind, I say, will not be stifled by prohibitions. We don't know what the purpose of such examinations is, we don't know whether anything of value can be obtained by them. But here is the mystery of creativity—so we dig and look, and we try to apply the insights obtained in the laboratory of our clinical experience with ordinary patients, and with our ordinary selves, to the psychology of the genius. We don't know what will ultimately come of it, but we do it anyway. This is what man has done since his mind first began to be active. There is a bit of childhood playfulness in scientific inquiry that no parental disapproval—and that includes your sermon to the analyst-child—can suppress.

Is that all I can say in response to this crucial question? you might ask. All right then, go and play, but leave the rest of us alone with the results of your playfulness—at least until such time as you come up with results that have reached the level of sophistication that the results of *our* games have already reached. And I would here have to agree with you: my argument that the analyst be given license to engage in playful, seemingly purposeless inquiry goes only part of the way in meeting your objections to our work. What I must show is that there is indeed meaning in our meaning, that there is a significance—on a higher level, outside the enjoyment of our own play—to our findings.

Let us, for the sake of argument, assume that the hypothesis that you rejected was correct. Let us assume, in other words, that Kleist had suffered from sexual impotence, and that this experience had profoundly shaken him, had come to be a permanent, deeply felt wound in his self-confidence, and that this deeply felt hurt cried out for expression. *"Und wenn der Mensch in seiner Qual verstummt, gab mir ein Gott, zu sagen wie ich leide."* ("And as my tortured human self was silenced, a god gave me the voice to tell my pain.") Tasso's immortal words acknowledge, I believe, this source of artistic creativity. If an experience of impotence had indeed been the center of a deep wound in Kleist's self-esteem, would it be a negligible task for a psychoanalyst to show how an individual tragedy, a deeply felt personal hurt, became in a genius the motivating force for the creation of something beautiful and broadly meaningful — vastly transcending the original disturbance, yet still in unbroken psychological contact with it? You may say that if this were the case, it does not interest you. That the context of ideas is enough for you, that you do not feel enriched by the knowledge of how some personal suffering is interwoven with an aesthetic, spiritual, intellectual performance on the most sublime level of human achievement. If you said this, I would have to grant you the right to your prejudice — but I would consider *you* the narrow-minded one here. As I said to you immediately after your lecture, it seems to me a worthy enterprise to show how a great artist can raise his lonely suffering to a supraindividual level and can thus become the spokesman for the suffering of his age.

But now to the next issue — your censure of analysis for disregarding the influence of the historical moment on the experiences of man — which you raised in connection with your critique of Freud's demoniacal-neurosis paper. You criticized Freud's attempt to take the measure of a seventeenth-century phenomenon — Christoph Haizmann's belief that he was possessed by the devil — with the aid of a twentieth-century yardstick. Seventeenth-century man, you said, is not modern man — modern thought in general and modern depth psychology in particular do not apply to him. The interpretation of his experience in terms of being possessed by the devil is as valid within the framework of seventeenth-century man's outlook on the world and his position in it as is the interpretation of certain hallucinatory experiences occurring in a contemporary of Freud within the framework of nineteenth-century science, that is, as a symptom of psychopathology.

Clearly, there is much room for argument here. No one would deny the vast differences that separate the world view that prevailed hundreds of years ago from the one prevalent today. But while I agree with you that meanings must be evaluated within the total framework of the world view of a historical period, there are also abiding hierarchies of meaning. The relativistic position of modern science, for example, which you take in your argument, occupies to my mind a higher position as a guide in man's attempt to understand himself and the world in which he lives than does the absolutistic outlook of mythology — however valuable the religious stance might be in supporting man or in providing him with a medium to express the otherwise inexpressible. The question, in other words, is not whether Haizmann as a seventeenth-century man could have grasped Freud's hypothesis concerning his experiences but whether we expect either the devil theory or a psychological theory — be it Freud's theory of the Oedipus complex or some other theory, perhaps one that has not yet been formulated — ultimately to explain these experiences most encompassingly, flawlessly, and completely. Devil theories had existed before Haizmann's time, and they continue to exist today. But the scientist's capacity *not* to know, to search in puzzlement, playfully, as I like to say, to apply first one theory and then

another, has also always existed—during Haizmann's time
and long before, side by side with the mythological stance,
just as is true today.

I think, therefore, that it is not inappropriate to examine
the past with the best conceptual tools at the disposal of the
modern investigator, notwithstanding the fact that the
present tools will undoubtedly be superseded by other, hopefully improved ones, tomorrow. Still, your critique is cogent,
I believe—though not in the form in which, if I grasped your
meaning correctly, you expressed it in your address to us.
What you should have said—or was that indeed your
message?—is this: You analysts, or at least some among you,
make it much too easy for yourselves when you jump with
both feet into the past. You of all people should know how
long it takes to grasp the essence of the world in which
another individual lives—the specific meaning that his communications have, etc.—even if this other individual shares
your own cultural background. You of all people should
know how long it takes to familiarize oneself with another
person's outlook, how long it takes to understand his
language. And yet, all too often, you disregard this
knowledge when it comes to the interpretation of biographical data of individuals who lived long ago in different surroundings, or when it concerns the investigation of the
meaning of the work of artists and writers of the past.

I, for one, would welcome such an admonishment to analysts, especially when it comes from an accomplished master
in a neighboring field such as yourself. But I would not draw
from it the conclusion that a bridge of understanding to the
past cannot ever be built by psychoanalysts or that the psychoanalyst should be prohibited from attempting to build it.
While we should acknowledge that the difficulties are great,
while we should realize that perfection cannot be attained,
the modern depth psychologist should continue to make the
attempt to understand not only people from different cultures

but also the man of the past. However difficult the task, we
should not cease the attempt to extend our empathic understanding toward those whose experiences are separated from
ours by a vast distance of space and time. And if our conclusions are sometimes in error, don't forget — or should I say,
begin to realize — when evaluating their significance, how
young modern depth psychology still is. Hardly a hundred
years old — a very short span of time when you consider the
radical newness of the enterprise.

But now I have done with preliminaries and am ready
to state my essential message. I hope that through this letter I
can persuade you to address the analyst as an equal among
scholars. Analysts are not likely to listen when they are
scolded — even when the scolding comes from as fine a mind
as yours and is given in as beautiful a lecture as the one you
presented to us. But it is in your power to employ your essay
in the future in a more constructive way. Instead of aiming
your paper at an audience that is ready to laugh about the
foibles and narrow-mindedness of the analytic profession, I
hope that you might consider the attempt of establishing a
true communication between yourself and analysts.

I trust that you will consider my request in the positive
spirit in which it is made. Far from trying to persuade you to
alter the important critique of applied analysis that your essay contains, I want your valuable points to be stated in such
a way that they will be heard and understood by those who
are most in need of hearing and understanding them. This
letter, then, is an attempt to further the development of a
fruitful dialogue between disciplines — a dialogue that
analysts need, a dialogue that, I am convinced, would also
not be useless for broad-minded scholars of other disciplines.
It would not take much to transform your beautiful paper
from a rejecting critique into the beginning of a potentially
fruitful and mutually enriching conversation between representatives of two disciplines that are engaged in the unend-

ing, fascinating study of man and of his creations.

I send you my warm personal regards.

July 31, 1977

Thank you for the letter and for the typescript of your essay "Psychology and the Misinterpretation of Literature." I shall not take issue with your conclusion, based on recent readings, that instances of reductionism are met with frequently in psychoanalytical interpretations of literature. Nor shall I address myself further to the question whether you had presented your critique of applied psychoanalysis in a way that encouraged constructive debate. In view of the fact that you went to considerable pains to soften the tone of your disapproval in this, as I assume, final version of your paper and in view, furthermore, of the fact that you allude to your intention of writing another essay on applied psychoanalysis, the issue of style and tone has become of only peripheral concern.

What has become of central importance to me is that I can see more clearly now why you cannot easily shift from the stance of a critic of psychoanalysis to that of a collaborator with it. I have come to realize not only that your disapproval of applied psychoanalysis is of long standing but also, most significantly, that it is but one of the several manifestations of your broadly based distrust of modern science and its pre-eminent position in our time in general and of modern depth psychology and its impact on the "climate of opinion" of our century, in particular.

So here we are at an impasse beyond which it seems very hard to move. But, as you must have recognized by now, I do not like to throw in the sponge, hoping against hope that a searching mind like yours will respond to a reasonably stated appeal to question even its long-established attitudes and opinions.

Let me immediately go to the heart of the matter. My paramount concern about your essay — and the same holds true for a number of others you have written in the course of your productive life — is with your enmity toward science, or, to put it more accurately, I am concerned about the manner in which you depict man's choice as either his espousal of science or of the humanities; of his either leading a life devoid of values but filled with facts or of his retaining or regaining a life filled with valued beauty and meaning.

I am a committed scientist. I am a committed psycho-analyst. And yet it seems to me that in certain respects I treasure art more highly than even you. You argue that depth psychology, by doing away with the irrational in man, is harmful because it interferes with art, yet laudable because, via the same mechanism, it opposes the horrors of de-humanized political totalitarianism. It is in the context of this comparative exposition that you pose the following significant rhetorical question: "Who would not gladly forego the blessings of art," you ask, "if the sacrifice had spared the world such curses as Hitler?" The answer you imply is clearly that, when faced with the choice, we would — or at any rate should — want an all-rational world; that we should choose total rationality, even at the sacrifice of art, if by making this choice we would be spared a Hitler. The more I try, however, to think myself into the horrible dilemma evoked by this question, the more I come to feel that I do not agree with the answer you suggest. To this scientist at least, to this psycho-analyst at least — and I am sure that there are others like me — a world permanently devoid of art is no less horrible to imagine than a world debased by the occasional appearance of a Hitler.

I am convinced, however, that the sense of an opposition between the two realms which your essay on applied psycho-analysis — and the same holds true for a good many passages in your other writings — tends to create in the reader is wrong.

We are not facing the choice between a scienceless, art-full, Hitler-breeding world, on the one hand, and a world dominated by scientific rationalism that has killed art and Hitler alike, on the other. Science *and* art, together, will save us, if indeed we can be saved. The challenge which the human race is facing is not that of having to decide between an artless world dominated by the scientific mind, on the one hand, or a world without the benefits of science but maintaining the values of beauty and meaning, on the other — our challenge is to find ways and means to further the cooperation between art and science, between meaningful beauty and fact.

Why am I making the effort to write you this second long letter? I am writing because I feel that, in a limited and modest way, I can show that our two disciplines have something to offer to each other. I want these letters to acknowledge that the depth psychologist not only can learn something from the humanist but has something to offer in return.

Let me now, therefore, speak again on behalf of the potential value of the contributions of the depth psychologist with regard to the artist and his productions by addressing myself to three specific topics that relate to issues that you raised in your "Misinterpretation" essay: (1) your claim that the differences between the various history-bound "souls" of man are so great that the psychoanalyst — *even* the psychoanalyst, I would say, because I am convinced that he is the person most fully trained to perceive the complexities of man's inner life via the scientifically disciplined use of the introspective-empathic approach — has no chance of bridging them and that he will, therefore, arrive at ludicrously misleading results; (2) your view that scientific psychology must of necessity destroy artistic creativity by making man rational; and, finally (3) my assertion that the latest developmental phase of depth psychology, the psychology of the self, comes indeed close to fulfilling the demands made by the humanist that a psychology applied to the field of artistic creation must not destroy the meaning of art and beauty through the doctrinal application of an irreversibly reductionistic approach. And I will add that depth psychology is able to do this without the loss of its essence: it remains committed to the task of giving explanations in the form of empirically testable hypotheses — it does not become art or philosophy disguised in scientific garb.

I have already, in my earlier letter, addressed myself to your contention that, as I paraphrased you before, the differences between the various history-bound "souls" of man are so great that the professional depth psychologist can never bridge the gap and that he should therefore not undertake the attempt to do so. Instead of continuing my argument in the abstract, let me give you a concrete example — a very simple and personal one. One day when, after a few weeks in Italy, I drove from the Chicago Southside toward the Loop, I was suddenly struck by the similarity between the pattern of the skyscrapers against the sky and the pattern of the *"torre de nobilità"* as one approaches San Gimignano from Siena, and I realized that this formal similarity expressed a similarity of meaning and significance: that there was a significant identity in psychological attitude and motivation between the builders of the Chicago skyscrapers, the men who control the powerful industries in the United States, and the men who had controlled the powerful aristocratic families of northwest Tuscany hundreds of years ago. Clearly, however economically advantageous it might be to build tall buildings on high-priced building lots in downtown Chicago, there can be no doubt that propaganda and pride are the true motivating force for the undertaking. Hundreds of millions of dollars, in other words, are spent on tall buildings by the giants of modern industry so that people will know the Sears Tower, the John Hancock, and the Standard Oil building, and be impressed by the power they express through their height. And, however militarily advantageous it might have been to fight one's neighbor from the taller tower or, again, however economically advantageous to build tall buildings on high-priced city ground, the *torre* of San Gimignano and of other Italian cities served the same purpose (cf. Waley, 1969, pp. 176-177). The taller the tower that the family built, the more impressively was the power of the family clan held up, in exhibitionistic assertion, to the eyes of the beholder.

There are certain human propensities that remain unchanged across the centuries. My illustration concerns one of them: examples of man's inclination toward conspicuous consumption, prideful display, the assertion of power via the erection of structures pointing toward the sky can be found throughout his history, perhaps ever since his race lifted itself up to a biped stance — an experience, I might add, that is repeated by each generation of toddlers.

Have I defeated your assertion that it is "unimaginable that the totems of savages, the pyramids of Egypt, the temples of the Acropolis, the cathedral of Chartres, the Sears Tower and that of Babel are all the creations of identical souls?" Of course not. But I have gone some way, I believe, in demonstrating that there is no single, simple answer to the question whether the trained empathy of the historian, the literary historian, or the depth psychologist is able to bridge the gap to the soul of the man of the past as it is accessible to us via the scrutiny of his recorded deeds and of the works of art that he has left behind. Clearly, there are great differences between the man of our time and the man of the more or less distant past. But clearly also, there are similarities. Some basic human experiences remain the same over long stretches of human history, perhaps across the whole of known human history, while other experiential contents and styles will change. To acknowledge these complexities, however, does not, to my mind, mean that we must abandon the attempt to extend our empathy toward those different from us, but rather that we must strain it to the utmost to come to valid results.

I now turn to your view that science in general and depth psychology in particular are inimical to art, that, to express your fear most specifically, the psychoanalytic treatment of an artist would destroy his creativeness by depriving him of the wellspring of his need to create and of the deepest source material for the content of his creation by transforming the seething cauldron of feelings that strive for artistic expression into a coolly rational but sterile mode of mentation.

This letter is not the proper medium for a discussion of the problems that arise in the psychoanalytic treatment of unusually gifted and creative people. A great deal has been said and written, by Freud and others, about this subject matter, and the various relevant views and findings that one could cull from the psychoanalytic literature would fill a monograph. It is, however, not only the extent of the labor that would be required that makes me unwilling to undertake the task of giving a summary of these older views, but my conviction that, while we have in fact been helpful rather than harmful to many creative people in the past, the theoretical model with which we were working has not appropriately served us to understand and formulate the dynamics of our failures and successes. The cognitive model of the mode of action of psychoanalytic therapy ("to make the unconscious conscious"), even in its more relevant ego-psychological extension ("where id was, there ego shall be"), does not do justice to the most important problems faced by the creative personality. Not even simple inhibitions (such as the hysterical paralysis of the hand of a writer or the arm of a virtuoso) are always fully encompassed by the classical model. Still, many circumscribed conflicts of the artist can be adequately explained and neurotic inhibitions that interfere with the mechanics of artistic productivity can be adequately treated via an approach that is based on the conceptual

framework of classical psychoanalytic psychology. But as concerns the essence of creativity itself, this central activity of
mankind as it is carried out in proxy by its artists, these conflicts and inhibitions occupy only a peripheral position. In
order to deal with creativeness itself, and with its essential,
central disturbances, I must now move to my next—and
final—topic, namely, to my assertion that the latest development in scientific depth psychology, the psychology of the
self, has indeed increased the capacity of our theoretical formulations to encompass creative man and to deal therapeutically with him, and, furthermore, that it has enabled us to
make significant explanatory statements about the products
of his creativity.

I shall begin this last section of my letter by addressing
myself to a specific passage (on pp. 423-425) in your essay,
namely your opposition of, on the one hand, Yeats's celebration of the "unity of Being and Doing" in the last stanza of
his poem "Among School Children" and, on the other hand,
the interpretation, which you believe to be representative of
the psychoanalyst's contribution to the explanation of art and
artists, of an episode in Kleist's essay on the marionette
theater as an expression of the writer's preoccupation with
sexual impotence, feminine sexual identification, and anal-
penetration fantasies. Let me first acknowledge that the question "How can we know the dancer from the dance?" with
which Yeats defines "the unity of Being and Doing" is
beautiful—hauntingly beautiful and evocative—while an
analyst's analogous comments about the integration of the
self and its actions—even meaningful and important
comments, not drive-psychological reductionism—are not.
But I admit this without shame. It is the very function of
art—the essence of its "being," as you might say—to be beautiful and evocative; it is the very function of science—its essential objective, as I would say—to be explanatory and clear,
to concentrate on the content of its communications and to

put formal considerations second to the unambiguous pre-
ciseness of its statements.

But now it is my job to find and to present to you explanatory psychoanalytic comments on the vicissitudes of the relationship between "being and doing" which do not destroy
the significance of a profound human problem by reducing it
to a conflict in the realm of sexuality, but, while remaining
scientifically exact and unambiguous, maintain contact with
the essential meaning of the total phenomenon to be investigated. I would point to a passage in my own writings that
shows you that psychoanalysts know that the unity or the lack
of unity between the self and its actions may be a decisive
indicator with regard to whether we are dealing with psychological disturbance or psychological health, and that they
know, furthermore, that a feebly constituted self will be
threatened by its own actions, while a firmly constituted
self—or a self that has been restored through psychoanalysis
—will feel itself enhanced, not threatened, by its activity.

I wrote in *The Analysis of the Self* (1971, p. 128) that

many patients with narcissistic personality disturbances
complain of a feeling of fragmentation, consisting specifically of a sense of separation of their self-experience from
their various physical and mental functions. [Such] fragmentation . . . is rather frequently encountered temporarily in the later phases of successful analyses of narcissistic personality disturbances. The greater cohesiveness of
the self which has been achieved in the analysis brings
about . . . the channeling of interests toward vocational
and interpersonal aims. Fascinated by the novel experience, the patient may have lost himself in a particular
pursuit when he suddenly becomes aware of anxious hypochondriacal preoccupations concerning his physical and
especially his mental functions. These tensions, however,
tend to disappear quickly when—at first with the aid of

the analyst's interpretations, and later spontaneously—the patient comprehends that the condition is due to the fact that his self . . . had been uncontrolledly siphoned into his actions.

Or take note of another passage in my work (1977, pp. 120-121) that relates more directly to the substance of the experiences of Kleist's young man who becomes self-conscious and clumsy when asked to assume a specific attractive pose that, a few seconds earlier, he had achieved with effortless grace. The passage describes the conditions that bring about a disturbance in a balanced, rounded, secure self-experience:

> While a relationship to an empathically approving and accepting parent is one of the preconditions for the original establishment of a firm . . . self, and while in analysis disturbances in this realm are once more open to correction, the opposite sequence of events (the movement from a cohesive self to its fragmentation) can often be observed . . . in a child's interplay with his pathogenic parents. . . .
>
> Patient B., for example, remembered from his childhood the following destructive reaction of his mother. When he would tell her exuberantly about some achievement or experience, she seemed not only to be cold and inattentive, but, instead of responding to him and the event that he was describing, would suddenly remark critically about a detail of his appearance or current behavior ("Don't move your hands while you're talking!" etc.). This reaction must have been experienced by him . . . as an active destruction of the cohesiveness of his self-experience (by shifting attention to a *part* of his body) just at the most vulnerable moment when he was offering his total self for approval.

It is easily seen that the preceding statements apply to the paralyzing self-consciousness that overcomes Kleist's young man when his companion asks him to reinstate his former graceful position. Just as Mr. B.'s mother by her critical remark about a detail of his behavior at a moment when he offered her his total self for approval destroyed the cohesiveness of his self-experience, so was, in Kleist's story, the young man's cohesive self—the integrated unity of "action" and "being"—destroyed by his companion's malicious request that he repeat a spontaneous action, because the request brought about a split between volition (the self as initiator of the act) and performance (the self within the act).

But even if you agree with my explanations so far, I believe that you will still say that, while they may elucidate some circumscribed problems of individual psychology, they are unrelated to the broad and general meaning of Kleist's story. You will continue to insist, in other words, that Kleist did not deal with the individual's experiences—that, in particular, he did not aim at charming the reader by presenting a fetching psychological vignette—but, on the contrary, used the psychological moment as carrier for the allegorical rendition of a timeless meaning; that he wanted to have the reader think about mankind's fall from innocence and grace, about self-consciousness, not in the narrow sense of the psychological experiences of the individual, but as a problem of the race.

It is in response to this last objection which I am ascribing to you that I would like to make my boldest assertion. It is the assertion that, with the advent of the psychology of the self, depth psychology can for the first time begin, however haltingly and cautiously, to deal with the problems and activities of the whole man. That it can now attempt to make contributions—*scientific* contributions—to the understanding of some of the most important activities of man, such as his religions or his art, that do not dissolve these activities into their elemental constituents and, by doing so, become blind to their essential significance or, at any rate, disregard it. While remaining science, in other words, and not becoming art, philosophy, or religion, depth psychology can now examine these complex activities of mankind against the background of psychological considerations that take into account their meaning as an expression of man's self, that take into account their significance as safeguards and supports of this core of man's personality.

No doubt, when approached from the point of view of the drives, or wish fulfillment and the pleasure principle, religion is seen as an unacceptable illusion for those who cannot bear the stark realities of existence. And art becomes an acceptable one for those who want temporarily to turn away from the burdens of life to a voluntarily undertaken and knowingly self-deceptive consolation. But these formulations, however irrefutable they may be within the normative framework of the truth- and reality-values of the scientific world view, do not do justice to the meaning that religious and artistic activities have when evaluated within the supraordinated normative framework that is correlated to the needs of man's developing and expression-seeking self. The truth-values of classical science have, of course, not been abandoned by the psychology of the self, but they are broadened to encompass the search for truths concerning the significance of truth-seeking itself. To see reality undistortedly remains an important achievement, requires courage; and man in general, and scientific man in particular, have the right to take pride in it. The recognition, however, that the crumbling self of man is as great a danger to his psychological survival in our time as was the stifling and infantilizing intellectual obscurantism that man fought in the Renaissance and in the era of Enlightenment, gives us the right to evaluate truth-seeking as being now first and foremost an important tool in the service of man's efforts to strengthen and to maintain his self.

Perhaps you will tell me now that you do not need the formulations of scientific depth psychology in support of views to which you are already subscribing, of convictions which you already hold. But should you indeed feel prompted at this point to decline the aid of science, allow me to give expression to the suspicion that you are whistling in the dark. You, too, like all of us, have lost your innocence, have fallen from grace. You, too, like all of us, must have your moments of doubt whether our values, our meanings as portrayed by our art, philosophy, and religion, are not, in truth, illusions. And you, too, like all of us, cannot always call up the sense of inner security, wholeness, and joyful certainty that is given to us at times—cannot always call up that affirmative attitude toward our existence which, notwithstanding the acknowledgment of the ultimate extinction not only of our individual lives but also of the physical and biological universe, is the precariously held precious possession of those whose self has been established in a matrix of empathic responsiveness. You, too, like the rest of us, must therefore realize, as Kleist concludes at the end of his essay, that there is no return passage to paradise—only a forward move. That we must strive toward what Kleist called "infinite consciousness," that the fruit from the tree of knowledge is our only available sustenance, is our only, quite unreligious, salvation.

I am convinced, in other words, that modern man, having suffered a more complete loss of his innocence, having fallen from grace more definitively than previous generations, is therefore in even greater need than the man of earlier centuries of the buttressing of an affirmative attitude toward life in the form of scientific explanations concerning the significance which the values and meanings that are continuously created by art, religion, philosophy, and by science itself have for him. These scientific explanations are no more than tiny steps on mankind's path toward increasing consciousness—tiny steps in the direction of that state of "infinite consciousness" which according to Kleist is the only substitute for the lost, never to be recovered original state of innocence, the unrecoverable state before the Fall.

Does our acceptance of Kleist's theory of the development of the human spirit mean that we ought to bemoan the fact that the expansion of consciousness proceeds slowly, and that we must admit that total knowledge — Kleist's *infinite* consciousness — will be forever beyond our grasp? And must we, in particular, therefore abandon our commitment to science, cease to consider it as our most trustworthy friend? I do not think so. The aim that Kleist defined for us is not concrete; it is an ideal goal, an indicator of the direction of our cognitive strivings. Indeed, I believe that we can even be grateful for the fact that the disturbed wholeness of our self will never be fully and permanently restored — neither by religion and philosophy nor by science and art — because it is the very incompleteness of man's self, O'Neill's "Man is born broken," that spurs him to his greatest achievements, that keeps alive in him, to the end of time, the attempt to recapture the lost wholeness of his self. The myth formations and communal experiences of man's religions, the meaningful beauty of the integrated symbols of his self in his works of art, the formulations of his various scientific world views, the definitions of the meaning of experience and existence contained in his systems of philosophy, they are all, in the last analysis, motivated by man's "fall from grace," are all, to state the issue again in the language of modern depth psychology, motivated by the loss of the secure cohesion, continuity, and harmony of his self. Despite the full acknowledgment, therefore, of the tentativeness of the formulations supplied by the psychology of the self, despite the smallness of the progress on the road toward "infinite consciousness" that they constitute, I believe that our generation of depth psychologists can be proud of the new conceptualizations. Whatever their limitations and shortcomings, I know, not only that the psychology of the self explains more meaningfully certain areas of man's psychological experiences in mental illness and health than previous scientific approaches, but also that its formulations can be more relevantly applied outside the field of normal and abnormal psychology. The new psychology of the self has moved us one inch forward on our unending road.

August 13, 1977

I am very grateful to you for sending me the typescripts of your papers "Certains Aspects du Narcissisme" and "Réflexions sur le Rêve d'Être Nu," not only because I enjoyed them and profited by them, but also because they gave me some understanding for the reason why my recent work has found so little echo in France up to now.

Although I can read French fairly well (and can even speak it a little), the language barrier is an obstacle for my full appreciation of your essays. But I believe I grasped your meaning well enough to say that you understand the essence of my ideas well and that you are applying them appropriately in the clinical situation. Two passages, occurring toward the very end of your "Certains Aspects" paper, I found especially significant: The brief paragraph in which you say that my theories are based on a metapsychology that is not accepted in France, and the paragraph in which you raise the rhetorical question whether, even if the criticism of Hartmann's theories is justified, all work that accepts the notion of a self must, therefore, *eo ipso* be rejected. These two passages — and there were other similar ones, though none as directly expressed — gave me the sense that you are truly in touch with my basic outlook. The theoretical framework that I used at the time of *The Analysis of the Self* and of "Thoughts on Narcissism and Narcissistic Rage" was that of classical libido theory. But your remarks demonstrate to me that you realize that the framework I then used was not the essence of my work — that I used it because I needed to present my new findings in a language that was known among those with whom I am in the closest scientific contact, namely, in the main, my colleagues in the United States. As you will see when you read *The Restoration of the Self,* I had to undertake further steps in order to adapt my concepts and theories to my new findings.

It is my impression that theory has achieved a position of somewhat exaggerated significance in modern psychoanalysis. I love theory, and I am unable to conceive of our science without the serious-minded pursuit of framing relevant general statements. But theory must not become our master; it must be our servant.

I hope that you will continue to follow my line of thought, including my attitude toward theory, by lending your attention to my most recent work, especially *The Restoration of the Self.* I will be happy to hear from you so that I can learn from you how you react to my new formulations. In the meantime, I want to express to you only that I am very happy to see that a fine mind like yours has found that my ideas are helpful.

March 11, 1978

Your question whether I advocate providing the patient with "the approximately correct measure of love" is not easy to answer because of the ambiguity of the term "love" and of the specific connotation of the term "provided"—but, on the whole, I am inclined to say "no." It is not in order to avoid being "misunderstood as advocating a nonscientific form of psychotherapy" that I take this position, but because I feel that it would be erroneous to do otherwise. The essential curative process in cases of self pathology is structure-building via transmuting internalizations. This process can only take place in a therapeutic milieu that is psychologically neutral,

i.e., in an atmosphere free from gross psychological overstim-
ulations and rejections. The analyst tries to be in empathic
touch with the patient's inner life at all times, with the result
that his failures are sufficiently small and of sufficiently short
duration to allow the patient to respond to them via structure-building — just as should have happened in childhood.
Friendliness is not curative in this sense — persistently pursued
and, on the whole, successful empathic responses, however,
are. Empathic resonance is a transformation of narcissism —
it is not love. I reject love, as I understand this term, not only
because it is not essential, but because it is to my understanding a faulty, unempathic response. It is true, as I said on
page 122 of *The Restoration of the Self,* that all mature love
relationships are also simultaneously self-selfobject relationships. But the reverse is not always true, especially not in the
treatment of patients with defects in the structure of their
self. These patients don't require love — they require a milieu
in which they can activate their old need for the specific
responses of selfobjects. The analyst's help does not consist in
fulfilling the patient's needs, but in telling him what he feels
and how he reacts and showing him that these feelings and
reactions make sense dynamic-structurally (they are due to
certain real shortcomings in his psychological equipment) and
genetically (they are due to the faultiness of the selfobject
environment of childhood). I see no advantage and many
disadvantages in calling love the analyst's ability to be in
touch with the patient's needs and to tell him about them in a
noncensorious, accepting way.

Conclusion

The Search for the Analyst's Self

I am impressed by Paul Ornstein's analysis of my work, in particular by his having been able to demonstrate that the unfolding of my contributions during my scientific life occurred in accordance with a predetermined, consistent, logical plan. It all sounds very convincing to me when I look at it from the outside. But I must admit that I knew nothing about any program laid down within me. All I knew when I wrote a paper during my earlier years was that I was writing this or that particular paper. In no case did I know that any specific work belonged in any larger pattern or program, that it was logically connected with other works. Only about ten years ago did I begin to have a sense of where I might be going. But, as I said, that was not the case in my earlier life. Some of my writings, for example, were purely accidental. I was asked to undertake a particular job, and I agreed to do it. Still, I can recognize in retrospect that, even when I was merely responding to external promptings, such as, for example, the preparation of the discussion of somebody's paper at the request of a program committee, I often managed to insert something into these productions that I wanted to express but that I was not yet ready to put forward in the form of a clear-cut, definitive, separate contribution.

I have been asked what the external factors had been that

Remarks in response to a presentation by Paul H. Ornstein of parts of his introduction to this volume of essays at a meeting of the Chicago Workshop on the Psychology of the Self, June 25, 1977.

931

had most strongly and decisively influenced the direction my
work has taken. No doubt the knowledge acquired through
reading in the course of my life exerted its influence on my
thinking. But ideas alone don't fire me up. Something must
happen between me and my observations before I will write.
In order to move forward in my theoretical formulations I
must first have gained some new understanding about something that I am observing — either in myself, or in others;
either within the clinical situation, or, outside of it, in the
field of applied analysis.

At first, not having enough clinical data at my disposal,
yet feeling I had a good grasp of the material supplied to me
by art, I worked a good deal in applied analysis. That is why
many of my early writings focused on the field that I eventually came to define as lying "beyond the bounds of the basic
rule." But even then I was already especially interested in
nonverbal experiences, was fascinated by the problem of
understanding contentless traumatic states. It was this specific interest that led me to the attempt to come to a psychological understanding of music, to formulate a psychological
theory of music.

Paul Ornstein has set himself the task of tracing the intellectual history of the development of my ideas. To do that
with anybody's life work who writes sufficiently frequently is
an interesting undertaking — independent of the value of the
work under scrutiny. I myself can make only small and
peripheral contributions here. I can now clearly see, on the
basis of Ornstein's scrutiny of my writings, that all my later
insights were alluded to from the beginning. And the question is: why was I so slow in expressing them clearly and
firmly? The obstacles that stood in my way lay partly in the
emotional and partly in the cognitive realm.

Foremost among the forces that restrained me was my intellectual and emotional commitment to classical analysis. I
had studied classical theory and knew it well. I knew it well

enough to be able to separate the wheat from the chaff. That allowed me, in the metapsychology courses that I taught for many years at the Chicago Institute, to de-emphasize those parts of traditional theory that did not seem to me to be relevant and explanatory and to emphasize those that did. For a long time I was able by these means, without introducing major modifications, to adjust the classical tenets to the data that I accumulated as I added year after year of clinical experience. But as time went on, I began to realize increasingly that I had to strain more and more, that I was building more and more elaborately constructed logical bridges, had to give more and more complex explanations, in order to make the classical theory relevant with regard to certain data of observation, particularly in the clinical field. And I felt increasingly uncomfortable in doing so.

My account of the earlier period of my professional life would be incomplete if I omitted a fact that was of great significance to me, namely, that during those years I became acquainted with some of the leading personalities of contemporary psychoanalysis and established friendly ties with them. That was, of course, a very valuable experience for me. Yet these relationships with revered leaders in our field who upheld the classical tradition and expected me to do likewise also increased my inner conflicts because I was becoming increasingly doubtful whether analysis could continue its development along the lines they thought were the correct ones.

This conflict reached its climax at about the time my administrative duties with the American Psychoanalytic Association had come to an end. I had given many years to administrative work and had reached a position of some influence. I made use of it by encouraging analysts to remain analysts, by trying to inspire the younger generation and to impress them with the importance of our field. The response of the older generation was one of gratitude and pleasure, and I know that I felt greatly sustained by their response. But, as I said before, this support was not an unmixed blessing because I felt more and more guilty about my "new" thoughts. You will appreciate the extent of my misgivings when you gauge the extent of the intellectual change that ultimately took place by comparing my summarizing statement of the classical position, the 1963 paper with Seitz, with the first "new" paper, the 1966 paper on narcissism.

True, so far as I could see, the 1966 paper was fully accepted by the older generation. Nor were there open objections to the much more daring paper of 1968. Still, some time after 1966, the emotional support that sustained me in my scientific endeavors began to come to me from a new direction. When formerly, as I said, this support had come from a group of colleagues who were older than I, it now came from a group of younger people. These younger people—several of them are sitting here in this room, and are not quite so young anymore—began to tell me that my work had struck important chords in them and that they were grateful to me for what I had done. All these responses provided me with the invaluable reassurance and support that comes from feeling understood and appreciated. I have no doubt that my work and productivity were greatly enhanced by the reverberations I received from this younger group, and I, in turn, am deeply grateful to them for their generosity toward me. These younger colleagues not only told me that they could use my work clinically, and to great advantage, but also that it was of great personal significance for them.

But soon the enthusiasm of this younger group confronted me with a new dilemma. Some at least of these younger people wanted me to go faster now than I felt I should go, urged me to discard the traditional framework and undertake the construction of a new one.

I well remember the conflict I felt. On the one hand, I was willing to acknowledge that our theories would ultimately have to assign a position to the self that would be in harmony with the importance that, as we could recognize with increasing clarity, the self had in our clinical work. On the other hand, I felt that we must proceed slowly, that we must not make changes on the basis of armchair speculations, but introduce new theories only insofar as they were needed in order to accommodate the new observations. I was convinced, in other words, that any newly constructed experience-distant theory of the self at this point in the development of psychoanalysis would have to be firmly based on the experience-near theories which could already be derived from clinical data. Thus, when my colleagues urged me to formulate a new metapsychology of the self, I replied: not yet, we must not precipitously discard the valuable modes of thought that have sustained us up to now. But I also knew that if we should come to see that a significant number of observations, especially in the clinical field, could no longer be explained within the framework of classical metapsychology, but required an independent psychology of the self, then we should not hesitate to formulate such a psychology.

I finally realized that an independent psychology of the self was needed not primarily in order to explain this or that clinical observation but because it encompassed a different dimension of the experiences of man, a whole dimension of man that had not been addressed by psychoanalysis up to now. At bottom, then, my hesitation in taking the step toward an independent self psychology was grounded in my preconscious recognition of the magnitude of the move that was involved here.

As you surely recognize, I am speaking here of the fact that the essentially new assertion at which I arrived — formulated first in 1974 in the essay "Remarks About the Formation of the Self" — is that the scientific observer of the inner life of man will only achieve a partial view of the field that he examines so long as he restricts himself to the use of the conceptual tools of conflict psychology. Conflict psychology, in other words, sees only Guilty Man—the psychology of the self is needed in order to observe, understand, and explain the experiences of Tragic Man. An essential aspect of human life, which was heretofore the exclusive domain of philosophy, theology, and art, can now, through the application of the psychology of the self, become the target of empirical observation and scientific scrutiny. And I came to see furthermore that, by thus widening the scope of scientific examination, the psychology of the self allows us to focus our attention on a dimension of human life, in health and disease, that, while it has of course always been ubiquitous as part of man's experience, is of especial relevance in our time.

Conflict psychology and the theory of the drives had, on the whole, successfully explained the important but narrow field of the classical neuroses. It had been much less successful vis-à-vis the psychopathology of the self (from the narcissistic personality disorders to the psychoses) and vis-à-vis the vicissitudes of man's behavior in the arena of history. Freud's daring theory, in particular, that man's failure in history is due to the fact that his aggressions are the manifestations of a death instinct, is neither a satisfactory scientific explanation—it involves too great a leap from behavioral data to experience-distant abstraction—nor does it increase our ability to master our destiny through insight. Our acceptance, however, of the psychological primacy of the self and of its aspirations and our examination of the causes and consequences of its defects allow us to see man's pathological drives in a meaningful psychological context and lead us, in particular, to the recognition that even the most severe and long-lasting instances of human destructiveness are to be understood as reactions of his injured self.

No wonder then, in view of the fact that a whole new concept of man was here involved, that I had hesitated for some time before I could attempt to draw the outlines of a psychology of the self. But once I had recognized that this step was indeed necessary, that it involved neither an abandonment of the viewpoints of science, in general, nor of those of scientific depth psychology, in particular, I could proceed to confront the essentials of the intellectual task. Specifically, I felt that in order to create a satisfactory new framework, I had to outline a theoretical structure that would be adequate to fulfilling three demands, which I will now set down in the order of their increasing importance: (1) the new psychology of the self must remain in an unbroken continuum with traditional psychoanalytic theory to preserve the sense of the historical continuity of the group self in the psychoanalytic community; (2) the new theoretical system must, at this point in the development of psychoanalysis, not disregard the fact that the classical theories, especially as expanded in the form of modern ego psychology, though applicable only in a restricted area, are neither in error nor irrelevant; (3) the new theory, while clear, must not be dogmatic and definitive, but open to change and capable of further development.

You know the solution at which I ultimately arrived. I formulated a set of two complementary theories: a theory of a psychology of the self in the narrow sense — in which the self is a content of a mental apparatus — and a theory of psychology of the self in a broad sense — in which the self lies in the center of the theoretical structure. The solution I found was in harmony with my three demands. It preserved the continuity with the past, it acknowledged the adequacy of classical tenets within a limited field, and, by stressing the relativity of all theorizing, did not impose undue restrictions on future creative developments.

And where do we go from here? What will the future bring? What will be the creative developments that the looseness and tentativeness of our present formulations are meant to enhance? It is obvious that I do not know the answer to these questions. If I did, the future would have become the present — and the same questions would again have to be asked. All I know is that we will see further developments, that the growth of psychoanalysis will continue. There will be small steps forward within the new psychoanalytic psychology of the self — refinements in our classification of the various narcissistic transferences, for example — and larger steps leading us to a more profound understanding of the formation of the self in childhood and of its vicissitudes throughout the life of the individual. The question whether I myself will make further contributions to the psychology of the self does not concern me very much. What matters to me now and gives me great satisfaction at this point of my life is the realization that a door toward a new area of psychological reality has been opened sufficiently widely and that a first path into this area has been made passable far enough to anticipate with confidence that others will further extend the explorations and that they will lead us toward new doors which, in turn, will not remain closed. If you who are contributing to the growth of the psychoanalytic psychology of the self obtain through your work the sense of being participants in the ongoing struggle of enhancing the worthwhileness of life through the expanding insights of scientific depth psychology, then you will be rewarded by one of the most satisfying experiences available to man: the satisfaction that comes from the realization that our individual productivity and the productivity of the generations that will follow us are one. As for myself, I have no doubt that the sense of participation in the ongoing development of science has been the greatest satisfaction that my efforts have given to me.

References

Abraham, H. C. & Freud, E. L., eds. (1965), *A Psychoanalytic Dialogue: The Letters of Sigmund Freud and Karl Abraham.* New York: Basic Books.

Abraham, K. (1919), A particular form of neurotic resistance against the psycho-analytic method. In: *Selected Papers.* New York: Basic Books, 1953, pp. 303-311.

Adler, A. (1907), *Study of Organ Inferiority and Its Physical Compensation.* New York: Nervous & Mental Disease Publishing Co., 1917.

Aichhorn, A. (1936), The narcissistic transference of the "juvenile imposter." In: *Delinquency and Child Guidance,* ed. O. Fleischmann, P. Kramer, & H. Ross. New York: International Universities Press, 1964, pp. 174-191.

Alexander, F. (1938), Remarks about the relation of inferiority feelings to guilt feelings. *Internat. J. Psycho-Anal.,* 19:41-49.

—————— (1943), Fundamental concepts of psychosomatic research. *Psychosom. Med.,* 5:205-210.

—————— French, T. M., et al. (1946), *Psychoanalytic Therapy: Principles and Application.* New York: Ronald Press.

Antrim, D. K. (1943), Music in industry. *Musical Quart.,* 24:275-290.

Aristotle. *Politica.* Bk. 8. New York: Oxford University Press, 1957.

Auden, W. H. (1945), *The Collected Poetry of W. H. Auden.* New York: Random House.

Bach, K. P. E. (1856), *Versuch über die wahre Art das Clavier zu spielen.* Fifth Edition. Berlin: F. Stage.

Baer, L. (1932), *The Concept and Function of Death in the Works of Thomas Mann.* Philadelphia: Privately printed.

Baumayer, F. (1956), The Schreber case. *Internat. J. Psycho-Anal.,* 37:61-74.

Benedict, R. (1946), *The Chrysanthemum and the Sword.* Boston: Houghton Mifflin.

Bennis, W. (1974), Discussion remarks at Round-Table Conference: "Empathy and the Scientific Method," University of Cincinnati, April 20, 1974.

Bing, J. F., McLaughlin, F., & Marburg, R. (1959), The metapsychology of narcissism. *The Psychoanalytic Study of the Child*, 14:9-28. New York: International Universities Press.

Binswanger, L. (1936), Freud's concept of man in the light of anthropology. In: *Being in This World*. New York: Basic Books, 1963, pp. 149-181.

_____ (1957), *Sigmund Freud: Reminiscences of a Friendship*. New York/ London: Grune & Stratton.

Bonnard, A. (1963), Impediments of speech: A special psychosomatic instance. *Internat. J. Psycho-Anal.*, 44:151-162.

Bracher, K. D. (1969), *The German Dictatorship: The Origins, Structure, and Effects of National Socialism*. New York & Washington: Praeger, 1970.

Breuer, J. & Freud, S. (1895), Studies on hysteria. *Standard Edition*, 2:1-305. London: Hogarth Press, 1955.

Chijs, A. V. D. (1923), An attempt to apply objective psychoanalysis to musical composition. Abstracted in: *Internat. J. Psycho-Anal.*, 4: 379-380.

Churchill, W. (1942), *My Early Life*. New York: Macmillan.

Coeuroy, A. (1951), Schumann et Bach. *Contrepoints*, 7:27-33.

Coriat, I. H. (1945), Some aspects of a psychoanalytic interpretation of music. *Psychoanal. Rev.*, 32:408-418.

Croce, B. (1902), *Estetica come scienza dell' espressione e linguistica generale*. Milan: R. Sandron.

Darwin, C. R. (1872), *The Descent of Man and Selection in Relation to Sex*. New York: Appleton.

Eckermann, P. (1836-1848), *Conversations with Goethe*. London: Dent, 1930.

Eggar, K. (1920), The subconscious mind and the musical faculty. *Proceedings of the (Royal) Musical Association*, 47:23-38.

Eidelberg, L. (1954), *An Outline of a Comparative Pathology of the Neuroses*. New York: International Universities Press.

_____ (1959), A second contribution to the study of the narcissistic mortification. *Psychiat. Quart.*, 33:634-646.

Eissler, K. R. (1953), Notes upon the emotionality of a schizophrenic patient and its relation to problems of technique. *The Psychoanalytic Study of the Child*, 23:199-251. New York: International Universities Press.

_____ (1962), *Goethe: A Psychoanalytic Study*. Detroit: Wayne State University Press.

_____ (1963), Die Ermordung von wievielen seiner Kinder muss ein Mensch symptomfrei ertragen können, um eine normale Konstitution zu haben? *Psyche*, 17:241-291.

_____ (1971), *Talent and Genius*. New York: Quadrangle Books.

Ellenberger, H. (1970), *The Discovery of the Unconscious*. New York: Basic Books.

Ellman, R. (1959), *James Joyce*. New York: Oxford University Press.

Eloesser, A. (1925), *Thomas Mann, sein Leben und sein Werk*. Berlin: S. Fischer.

Epstein, L., ed. (1962), *Hebrew and English Edition of the Babylonian Talmud*. London: Soncino Press.

Erikson, E. H. (1956), The problem of ego identity. *J. Amer. Psychoanal. Assn.*, 4:56-121.

Federn, P. (1936), On the distinction between healthy and pathological narcissism. In: *Ego Psychology and the Psychoses*, ed. E. Weiss. New York: Basic Books, 1952, pp. 323-364.

Fenichel, O. (1939), The counterphobic attitude. In: *Collected Papers*, 2nd Series. New York: Norton, 1953, pp. 163-173.

_____ (1941), *Problems of Psychoanalytic Technique*. New York: Psychoanalytic Quarterly, Inc.

_____ (1945), *The Psychoanalytic Theory of Neurosis*. New York: Norton, pp. 236-267.

Ferenczi, S. (1909), On the interpretation of tunes that come into one's head. In: *Final Contributions to Psychoanalysis*. New York: Basic Books, 1955, pp. 175-176.

_____ (1911), On obscene words. In: *Contributions to Psychoanalysis*. New York: Basic Books/R. Brunner, 1950, pp. 132-153.

_____ (1913), Stages in the development of the sense of reality. In: *Contributions to Psychoanalysis*. New York: Basic Books/R. Brunner, 1950, pp. 213-239.

_____ (1914), On the nosology of male homosexuality (homo-erotism). In: *Contributions to Psychoanalysis*. New York: Basic Books/R. Brunner, 1950, pp. 296-318.

_____ (1921), The further development of an active therapy in psychoanalysis. In: *Further Contributions to Psychoanalysis*. New York: Basic Books, 1952, pp. 198-217.

_____ (1924), *Thalassa: A Theory of Genitality*. New York: Norton, 1968.

Fergusson, F. (1949), *The Idea of a Theater*. Princeton: Princeton University Press, pp. 111-112.

Fermi, L. (1954), *Atoms in the Family*. Chicago: University of Chicago Press.

Fisher, C. (1954), Dreams and perception: The role of preconscious and primary modes of perception in dream formation. *J. Amer. Psychoanal. Assn.*, 2:389-445.

_____ (1965), Psychoanalytic implications of recent research on sleep and dreaming. *J. Amer. Psychoanal. Assn.*, 13:197-303.

Fleming, J. & Benedek, T. (1964), Supervision: a method of teaching psychoanalysis. *Psychoanal. Quart.*, 33:71-96.

Freud, A. (1936), *The Ego and the Mechanisms of Defense. Writings*, 2. New York: International Universities Press, 1966.

_____ (1951), Obituary: August Aichhorn. *Writings,* 4:625-638. New York: International Universities Press, 1968.

_____ (1962), Assessment of pathology in childhood. *Writings,* 5:26-59. New York: International Universities Press, 1969.

_____ (1966), The ideal psychoanalytic institute: A utopia. *Writings,* 7:73-93. New York: International Universities Press, 1971.

_____ & Dunn, S. (1951), An experiment in group upbringing. *Writings,* 4:163-229. New York: International Universities Press, 1968.

_____ Nagera, H., & Freud, W. E. (1965), Metapsychological assessment of the adult personality: The adult profile. *Writings,* 5:60-75. New York: International Universities Press, 1969.

Freud, E. L., ed. (1960), *Letters of Sigmund Freud.* New York: Basic Books.

Freud, S. (1887-1902), *The Origins of Psychoanalysis.* New York: Basic Books, 1954.

_____ (1896), Further remarks on the neuro-psychoses of defence. *Standard Edition,* 3:159-185. London: Hogarth Press, 1962.

_____ (1898), Sexuality in the aetiology of the neuroses. *Standard Edition,* 3:263-285. London: Hogarth Press, 1962.

_____ (1900a), The interpretation of dreams. *Standard Edition,* 4 & 5. London: Hogarth Press, 1953.

_____ (1900b), Die Traumdeutung. *Gesammelte Werke,* 2 & 3. London: Imago Publishing Co., 1942.

_____ (1901), The psychopathology of everyday life. *Standard Edition,* 6. London: Hogarth Press, 1960.

_____ (1904), Freud's psycho-analytic procedure. *Standard Edition,* 7: 247-254. London: Hogarth Press, 1953.

_____ (1905a), Jokes and their relation to the unconscious. *Standard Edition,* 8. London: Hogarth Press, 1960.

_____ (1905b), Three essays on the theory of sexuality. *Standard Edition,* 7:125-245. London: Hogarth Press, 1953.

_____ (1905c), Fragment of an analysis of a case of hysteria. *Standard Edition,* 7:7-122. London: Hogarth Press, 1953.

_____ (1907), Delusions and dreams in Jensen's *Gradiva. Standard Edition,* 9:7-95. London: Hogarth Press, 1959.

_____ (1908a), Character and anal-erotism. *Standard Edition,* 9:168-175. London: Hogarth Press, 1959.

_____ (1908b), Creative writers and day-dreaming. *Standard Edition,* 9:141-153. London: Hogarth Press, 1959.

_____ (1908c), Some general remarks on hysterical attacks. *Standard Edition,* 9:229-234. London: Hogarth Press, 1959.

_____ (1909a), Analysis of a phobia in a five-year-old boy. *Standard Edition,* 10:3-149. London: Hogarth Press, 1955.

_____ (1909b), Notes upon a case of obsessional neurosis. *Standard Edition,* 10:153-249. London: Hogarth Press, 1955.

———— (1910a), Leonardo da Vinci and a memory of his childhood. *Standard Edition*, 11:59-137. London: Hogarth Press, 1957.

———— (1910b), The psychoanalytic view of psychogenic disturbance of vision. *Standard Edition*, 11:209-218. London: Hogarth Press, 1957.

———— (1911a), Formulations on the two principles of mental functioning. *Standard Edition*, 12:215-226. London: Hogarth Press, 1958.

———— (1911b), Psychoanalytic notes on an autobiographical account of a case of paranoia (dementia paranoides). *Standard Edition*, 12:3-82. London: Hogarth Press, 1958.

———— (1912a), The dynamics of transference. *Standard Edition*, 12: 99-108. London: Hogarth Press, 1958.

———— (1912b), Recommendations to physicians practicing psycho-analysis. *Standard Edition*, 12:111-120. London: Hogarth Press, 1958.

———— (1913a), The predisposition to obsessional neurosis. *Standard Edition*, 12:313-326. London: Hogarth Press, 1958.

———— (1913b), Totem and taboo. *Standard Edition*, 13:1-164. London: Hogarth Press, 1955.

———— (1914a), On the history of the psycho-analytic movement. *Standard Edition*, 14:7-66. London: Hogarth Press, 1957.

———— (1914b), On narcissism: An introduction. *Standard Edition*, 14: 69-102. London: Hogarth Press, 1957.

———— (1914c), Remembering, repeating and working-through. *Standard Edition*, 12:145-157. London: Hogarth Press, 1958.

———— (1915a), Instincts and their vicissitudes. *Standard Edition*, 14: 117-140. London: Hogarth Press, 1957.

———— (1915b), Repression. *Standard Edition*, 14:146-158. London: Hogarth Press, 1957.

———— (1915c), The unconscious. *Standard Edition*, 14:166-204. London: Hogarth Press, 1957.

———— (1916a), Some character types met with in psychoanalytic work. *Standard Edition*, 14:310-355. London: Hogarth Press, 1957.

———— (1916b), On transience. *Standard Edition*, 14:305-307. London: Hogarth Press, 1957.

———— (1916-1917), Introductory lectures on psycho-analysis. *Standard Edition*, 15, 16. London: Hogarth Press, 1963.

———— (1917a), A childhood recollection from "Dichtung und Wahrheit." *Standard Edition*, 17:145-156. London: Hogarth Press, 1955.

———— (1917b), A difficulty in the path of psycho-analysis. *Standard Edition*, 17:137-144. London: Hogarth Press, 1963.

———— (1917c), Mourning and melancholia. *Standard Edition*, 14:239-258. London: Hogarth Press, 1957.

———— (1920), Beyond the pleasure principle. *Standard Edition*, 18:7-64. London: Hogarth Press, 1955.

———— (1921), Group psychology and the analysis of the ego. *Standard Edition*, 18:67-143. London: Hogarth Press, 1955.

———— (1922), Dreams and telepathy. *Standard Edition,* 18:196-220. London: Hogarth Press, 1955.

———— (1923), The ego and the id. *Standard Edition,* 19:23-66. London: Hogarth Press, 1961.

———— (1924a), The loss of reality in neurosis and psychosis. *Standard Edition,* 19:183-190. London: Hogarth Press, 1961.

———— (1924b), Neurosis and psychosis. *Standard Edition,* 19:149-154. London: Hogarth Press, 1961.

———— (1925a), An autobiographical study. *Standard Edition,* 20:3-74. London: Hogarth Press, 1959.

———— (1925b), On negation. *Standard Edition,* 19:233-239. London: Hogarth Press, 1961.

———— (1926), Inhibitions, symptoms and anxiety. *Standard Edition,* 20:87-174. London: Hogarth Press, 1959.

———— (1927a), The future of an illusion. *Standard Edition,* 21:3-56. London: Hogarth Press, 1961.

———— (1927b), Humour. *Standard Edition,* 21:161-166. London: Hogarth Press, 1961.

———— (1928), A religious experience. *Standard Edition,* 21:167-172. London: Hogarth Press, 1961.

———— (1930), Civilization and its discontents. *Standard Edition,* 21:59-145. London: Hogarth Press, 1961.

———— (1932), The acquisition and control of fire. *Standard Edition,* 22:185-193. London: Hogarth Press, 1964.

———— (1933), New introductory lectures on psycho-analysis. *Standard Edition,* 22:3-182. London: Hogarth Press, 1964.

———— (1935), Letter to Thomas Mann. *Standard Edition,* 22:255. London: Hogarth Press, 1964.

———— (1937), Analysis terminable and interminable. *Standard Edition,* 23:211-253. London: Hogarth Press, 1964.

———— (1941), Psychoanalysis and telepathy. *Standard Edition,* 18:177-193. London: Hogarth Press, 1955.

Gebsattel, V. E. (1947), *Not und Hilfe.* Freiburg i. Br.: Caritas Verlag.

Gedo, J. (1969), Discussion of S. Pulver (1970). Unpublished.

———— (1972), On the psychology of genius. *Internat. J. Psycho-Anal.,* 53:199-203.

———— (1975), To Heinz Kohut: On his 60th birthday. *The Annual of Psychoanalysis,* 3:313-322. New York: International Universities Press.

———— (in prep.), Magna est vis veritatis, tuae, et praevalebit! *The Annual of Psychoanalysis,* 7.

———— & Goldberg, A. (1973), *Models of the Mind.* Chicago: University of Chicago Press.

———— & Pollock, G. (1976), *Freud: The Fusion of Science and Humanism: The Intellectual History of Psychoanalysis. Psychological Issues,* Monogr. 34/35. New York: International Universities Press.

Gedo, M. (1972), Picasso's self image. Unpublished manuscript.

Gitelson, M. (1954), Therapeutic problems in the analysis of "normal" candidates. In: *Psychoanalysis: Science and Profession.* New York: International Universities Press, 1973, pp. 211-238.

Glover, E. (1932a), On the etiology of drug-addiction. *Internat. J. Psycho-Anal.,* 13:298-328.

———— (1932b), A psycho-analytic approach to the classification of mental disorders. In: *On the Early Development of Mind.* New York: International Universities Press, 1956, pp. 161-186.

———— (1939), *Psychoanalysis.* London: Staples Press. Second edition.

———— (1947), Basic mental concepts. *Psychoanal. Quart.,* 16:482-506.

———— (1950), Functional aspects of the mental apparatus. In: *On the Early Development of Mind.* New York: International Universities Press, 1956, pp. 364-378.

———— (1955), *The Technique of Psychoanalysis.* New York: International Universities Press.

Goethe, J. W. (1828), Selige Sehnsucht. In: *Goethe's Werke: Vollständige Ausgabe letzter Hand,* Vol. 5. Stuttgart: Cotta.

Goldstein, K. (1948), *Language and Language Disturbances.* New York: Grune & Stratton.

Greenacre, P. (1955), *Swift and Carroll.* New York: International Universities Press.

———— (1957), The childhood of the artist. In: *Emotional Growth.* New York: International Universities Press, 1971, pp. 479-504.

———— (1964), A study of the nature of inspiration. In: *Emotional Growth.* New York: International Universities Press, 1971, pp. 225-248.

Hanslick, E. (1896), *Vom Musikalisch-Schönen.* Ninth Edition. Leipzig: J. A. Barth.

Hartmann, H. (1927), Understanding and explanation. In: Hartmann, 1964, pp. 369-403.

———— (1939), *Ego Psychology and the Problem of Adaptation.* New York: International Universities Press, 1958.

———— (1950), Comments on the psychoanalytic theory of the ego. In: Hartmann, 1964, pp. 113-141.

———— (1953), Contributions to the metapsychology of schizophrenia. In: Hartmann, 1964, pp. 182-206.

———— (1956), The development of the ego concept in Freud's work. In: Hartmann, 1964, pp. 268-296.

———— (1964), *Essays on Ego Psychology.* New York: International Universities Press.

———— & Kris, E. (1945), The genetic approach in psychoanalysis. In: Hartmann, Kris, & Loewenstein, 1964, pp. 7-26.

———— ———— & Loewenstein, R. M. (1946), Comments on the formation of psychic structure. In: Hartmann, Kris, & Loewenstein, 1964, pp. 27-55.

—————— ———— ———— (1949), Notes on the theory of aggression. In: Hart-
mann, Kris, & Loewenstein, 1964, pp. 56-85.
—————— ———— ———— (1964), *Papers on Psychoanalytic Psychology. Psy-
chological Issues,* Monogr. 14. New York: International Universities
Press.
—————— & Loewenstein, R. M. (1962), Notes on the superego. In: Hart-
mann, Kris, & Loewenstein, 1964, pp. 144-181.
Havenstein, M. (1927), *Thomas Mann, der Dichter und Schriftsteller.*
Berlin: Wiegand & Grieben.
Heisenberg, W. (1952), *Philosophical Problems of Nuclear Science.* New
York: Pantheon.
Helmholtz, H. (1865), *Die Lehre von den Tonempfindungen.* Second
Edition. Brunswick: F. Vieweg & Son.
Hentoff, N. (1964), The crackin', shakin', breakin' sounds. *The New
Yorker,* 40:64-90, October 4, 1964.
Hesse, H. (1930), Notizen zum Thema Dichtung und Kritik. *Die Neue
Rundschau,* 41:761-773.
Hitschmann, E. (1956), *Great Men: Psychoanalytic Studies.* New York:
International Universities Press.
Holt, L. E. & Howland, J. (1940), *Holt's Diseases of Infancy and Child-
hood.* Revised by L. E. Holt Jr. & R. McIntosh. Eleventh Edition.
New York: Appleton.
Isakower, O. (1939), On the exceptional position of the auditory sphere.
Internat. J. Psycho-Anal., 20:340-348.
Jacobson, E. (1954), The self and the object world. *The Psychoanalytic
Study of the Child,* 9:75-127. New York: International Universities
Press.
—————— (1964), *The Self and the Object World.* New York: International
Universities Press.
Jones, E. (1913), The God complex. In: *Essays in Applied Psycho-Analysis,*
2:244-265. London: Hogarth Press, 1951.
—————— (1953, 1955, 1957), *The Life and Work of Sigmund Freud,* 3 Vols.
New York: Basic Books.
Jung, C. J. (1961), *Memories, Dreams, Reflections.* New York: Pantheon.
Kant, I. (1790), *Kritik der Urteilskraft.* Berlin: Lagarde & Friederich.
Kasdorff, H. (1932), *Der Todesgedanke im Werke Thomas Manns.*
Leipzig: H. Eichblatt.
Kavka, J. (1962), Meetings of the Chicago Psychoanalytic Society: A
Report. *Bull. Phila. Assn. Psychoanal.,* 12:174-176.
Kerr, W. A. (1945), *Experiments on the Effects of Music on Factory
Production.* (Applied Psychology Monogr. 5, American Association
for Applied Psychology.) Stanford University Press.
Kierkegaard, S. A. (1843), De unmiddelbare erotiske stadier; eller, Det
Musikalisk Erotiske. From *Enten-eller.* Copenhagen: C. A. Reitzel.
Klein, H. R. (1965), *Psychoanalysts in Training: Selection and Evaluation.*

New York: Psychoanalytic Clinic for Training and Research, Columbia University.

Kleist, H. von (1808), *Michael Kohlhaas*. Clarendon German Series, ed. J. Gearey. New York: Oxford University Press, 1967.

―――― (1811), On the marionette theater. Translated by T. G. Neumiller. *Drama Rev.*, 16:22-226, 1972.

Knight, R. P. (1946), Determinism, "freedom," and psychotherapy. *Psychiat.*, 9:251-262.

Kohut, H. (1951a), Discussion of Samuel D. Lipton's paper: "The function of the analyst in the therapeutic process." *The Search for the Self*, Chap. 4.

―――― (1951b), The psychological significance of musical activity. *Music Therapy*, 1:151-158.

―――― (1952), Book review: *Psychanalyse de la Musique* by André Michel. *The Search for the Self*, Chap. 5.

―――― (1953), Discussion of Henry von Witzleben's paper: "Natural science and humanism as fundamental elements in the education of physicians and especially psychiatrists." *The Search for the Self*, Chap. 6.

―――― (1954), Discussion of Iago Galdston's paper: " 'Eros and Thanatos': A critique and elaboration of Freud's death wish." *The Search for the Self*, Chap. 7.

―――― (1955a), Book review: *The Haunting Melody* by Theodor Reik. *The Search for the Self*, Chap. 8.

―――― (1955b), Book review: *Beethoven and His Nephew: A Psychoanalytic Study of Their Relationship* by Editha and Richard Sterba. *The Search for the Self*, Chap. 9.

―――― (1956a), Discussion of Annette Garrett's paper: "Modern casework: the contribution of ego psychology." *The Search for the Self*, Chap. 10.

―――― (1956b), Discussion of Thomas S. Szasz's paper: "The role of the counterphobic mechanism in addiction." *The Search for the Self*, Chap. 11.

―――― (1957a), Book review: *The Arrow and the Lyre: A Study of the Role of Love in the Works of Thomas Mann* by Frank Donald Hirschbach. *The Search for the Self*, Chap. 14.

―――― (1957b), *Death in Venice* by Thomas Mann: A story about the disintegration of artistic sublimation. *The Search for the Self*, Chap. 1.

―――― (1957c), Discussion of Louis Linn's brief communication: "Some comments on the origin of the influencing machine." *The Search for the Self*, Chap. 15.

―――― (1957d), Discussion of William G. Niederland's brief communication: "A note on beating fantasies." *The Search for the Self*, Chap. 16.

―――― (1957e), Observations on the psychological functions of music. *The Search for the Self*, Chap. 13.

_____ (1959a), Childhood experience and creative imagination: Contribution to a panel on the Psychology of Imagination. *The Search for the Self,* Chap. 18.

_____ (1959b), Introspection, empathy, and psychoanalysis: An examination of the relationship between mode of observation and theory. *The Search for the Self,* Chap. 12.

_____ (1960a), Beyond the bounds of the basic rule: Some recent contributions to applied psychoanalysis. *The Search for the Self,* Chap. 19.

_____ (1960b), Discussion of William G. Niederland's paper: "Further data and documents in the Schreber case." *The Search for the Self,* Chap. 20.

_____ (1961), Discussion of David Beres's paper: "The unconscious fantasy." *The Search for the Self,* Chap. 21.

_____ (1962), The psychoanalytic curriculum. *The Search for the Self,* Chap. 22.

_____ (1964a), The position of fantasy in psychoanalytic psychology. Chairman's introductory remarks to the symposium on fantasy. *The Search for the Self,* Chap. 24.

_____ (1964b), Some problems of a metapsychological formulation of fantasy. Chairman's concluding remarks to the symposium on fantasy. *The Search for the Self,* Chap. 25.

_____ (1964c), Values and objectives. *The Search for the Self,* Chap. 27.

_____ (1966a), Discussion of Max Schur's paper: "Some additional 'day residues' of 'the specimen dream of psychoanalysis.'" *The Search for the Self,* Chap. 31.

_____ (1966b), Forms and transformations of narcissism. *The Search for the Self,* Chap. 32.

_____ (1968), The psychoanalytic treatment of narcissistic personality disorders: Outline of a systematic approach. *The Search for the Self,* Chap. 34.

_____ (1970a), Discussion of D. C. Levin's paper: "The self: A contribution to its place in theory and technique." *The Search for the Self,* Chap. 38.

_____ (1970b), Narcissism as a resistance and as a driving force in psychoanalysis. *The Search for the Self,* Chap. 36.

_____ (1970c), Scientific activities of the American Psychoanalytic Association: An inquiry. *The Search for the Self,* Chap. 39.

_____ (1971), *The Analysis of the Self.* New York: International Universities Press.

_____ (1972a), Discussion of Ernest S. Wolf, John E. Gedo, & David M. Terman's paper: "On the adolescent process as a transformation of the self." *The Search for the Self,* Chap. 41.

_____ (1972b), Thoughts on narcissism and narcissistic rage. *The Search for the Self,* Chap. 40.

_____ (1973), Psychoanalysis in a troubled world. *The Search for the Self,* Chap. 35.

_____ (1974), The self in history. *The Search for the Self,* Chap. 46.

_____ (1975a), The future of psychoanalysis. *The Search for the Self,* Chap. 42.

_____ (1975b), A note on female sexuality. *The Search for the Self,* Chap. 47.

_____ (1975c), The psychoanalyst in the community of scholars. *The Search for the Self,* Chap. 43.

_____ (1975d), Remarks about the formation of the self. *The Search for the Self,* Chap. 45.

_____ (1976), Creativeness, charisma, group psychology: Reflections on the self-analysis of Freud. *The Search for the Self,* Chap. 48.

_____ (1977), *The Restoration of the Self.* New York: International Universities Press.

_____ & Levarie, S. (1950), On the enjoyment of listening to music. *The Search for the Self,* Chap. 3.

_____ & Seitz, P. F. D. (1963), Concepts and theories of psychoanalysis. *The Search for the Self,* Chap. 23.

Kramer, M. (1959), On the continuation of the analytic process after psychoanalysis. *Internat. J. Psycho-Anal.,* 40:17-25.

Kramer, P. (1955), On discovering one's identity. *The Psychoanalytic Study of the Child,* 10:47-74. New York: International Universities Press.

Kris, E. (1933), A psychotic sculptor of the eighteenth century. In: Kris, 1952b, pp. 12-150.

_____ (1936), The psychology of caricature. In: Kris, 1952b, pp. 173-188.

_____ (1952a), Book review: *Freudianism and the Literary Mind* by F. J. Hoffman. In: Kris, 1952b, pp. 265-272.

_____ (1952b), *Psychoanalytic Explorations in Art.* New York: International Universities Press.

_____ (1955), Neutralization and sublimation. In: Kris, 1975, pp. 151-171.

_____ (1956), The recovery of childhood memories in psychoanalysis. In: Kris, 1975, pp. 301-340.

_____ (1975), *The Selected Papers of Ernst Kris.* New Haven: Yale University Press.

Kuhn, T. (1962), *The Structure of Scientific Revolutions.* Chicago: University of Chicago Press, Second Edition, 1970.

Laufer, M. (1965), Assessment of adolescent disturbances. The application of Anna Freud's diagnostic profile. *The Psychoanalytic Study of the Child,* 20:99-123. New York: International Universities Press.

Levin, D. C. (1969), The self: A contribution to its place in theory and technique. *Internat. J. Psycho-Anal.,* 50:41-51.

_____ (1975), Physics and psychoanalysis: An epistemological study. Unpublished manuscript.

Lewin, B. D. (1946), Countertransference in technique of medical practice. In: Lewin, 1973, pp. 449-458.

_____ (1953), The forgetting of dreams. In: Lewin, 1973, pp. 213-226.

_____ (1954), Sleep, narcissistic neurosis, and the analytic situation. In: Lewin, 1973, pp. 227-247.

_____ (1973), *The Selected Writings of Bertram D. Lewin*. New York: Psychoanalytic Quarterly, Inc.

_____ & Ross, H. (1960), *Psychoanalytic Education in the United States*. New York: Norton.

Lewisohn, L. (1934), *The Permanent Horizon*. New York & London: Harper.

Lipton, S. D. (1955), A note on the compatibility of psychic determinism and freedom of will. *Internat. J. Psycho-Anal.*, 36:355-356.

Loewenberg, P. (1971), The unsuccessful adolescence of Heinrich Himmler. *Amer. Hist. Rev.*, 76:612-641.

Lorenz, K. (1952), *New Light on Animal Ways*. New York: Crowell.

Ludwig, E. (1926), *Kaiser Wilhelm II*, tr. M. Colburn, London & New York: Putnam.

_____ (1947), *Dr. Freud: An Analysis and a Warning*. New York: Helman, Williams, 1948.

Macalpine, I. & Hunter, R. A., eds. (1955), *Daniel Paul Schreber, Memoirs of My Illness*. Cambridge, Mass.: Robert Bentley.

McGuire, W. ed. (1974), *The Freud/Jung Letters*. Princeton: Princeton University Press.

Mahler, M. S. (1952), On child psychosis and schizophrenia: Autistic and infantile psychoses. *The Psychoanalytic Study of the Child*, 7:286-305. New York: International Universities Press.

Mann, T. (1918), *Betrachtungen eines Unpolitischen*. Berlin: S. Fischer.

_____ (1921), *Wälsungenblut*. Munich: Phantasus-Verlag. (Privately printed.)

_____ (1930), Lebensabriss. In: *Die neue Rundschau*. Berlin: S. Fischer, June, p. 732.

_____ (1945), Dostoevsky—in Moderation. In: *The Short Novels of Dostoevsky*. New York: Dial Press, pp. vii-xx.

Michel, A. (1951), *Psychanalyse de la musique*. Paris: Presses Universitaires de France.

Mitscherlich, A. (1946), *Freiheit und Unfreiheit in der Krankheit*. Hamburg: Classen & Goverts.

_____ (1957), Meditationen zu einer Lebenslehre der modernen Massen. *Merkur*, 11:201-213, 335-350.

_____ (1963), *Society Without the Father*. (Translated by Eric Mosbacher.) New York: Harcourt Brace & World, 1969.

_____ (1965), *Die Unwirtlichkeit unserer Städte*. Frankfurt a. M.: Suhrkamp.

_____ (1966), *Krankheit als Konflikt*, Vol. 1. Frankfurt a. M.: Suhrkamp.

_____ (1967a), *Krankheit als Konflikt*, Vol. 2. Frankfurt a. M.: Suhrkamp.

_____ (1967b), Menschenversuche im Dritten Reich. In: *Wissenschaft und Ethos*, ed. P. Scheider & O. Saame. Mainz: Universität.

_____ (1969), Könige sind archetypische Gross-Väter. *Der Spiegel*, 23: 100-110.

_____ & Mitscherlich, M. (1967), *Die Unfähigkeit zu trauern*. Munich: Piper.

Mosonyi, D. (1935), Die irrationalen Grundlagen der Musik. *Imago*, 21:207-226.

Moss, D. M. (1976), Narcissism, empathy and the fragmentation of self: An interview with Heinz Kohut. *Pilgrimage*, 4, No. 1, Summer, 1976.

Mozart, W. A. (1938), *The Letters of Mozart and His Family*, ed. E. Anderson. London: Macmillan, Vol. II, p. 826.

Nagera, H. (1964), Autoerotism, autoerotic activities, and ego development. *The Psychoanalytic Study of the Child*, 19:240-255. New York: International Universities Press.

Niederland, W. G. (1951), Three notes on the Schreber case. In: Niederland, 1974, pp. 39-48.

_____ (1959a), The "miracled-up" world of Schreber's childhood. In: Niederland, 1974, pp. 69-84.

_____ (1959b), Schreber: Father and son. In: Niederland, 1974, pp. 49-62.

_____ (1960), Schreber's father. In: Niederland, 1974, pp. 63-67.

_____ (1963), On the "historical truth" in Schreber's delusions. In: Niederland, 1974, pp. 93-100.

_____ (1974), *The Schreber Case: Psychoanalytic Profile of a Paranoid Personality*. New York: Quadrangle/New York Times Book Company.

Ornstein, P. H. (1974), On narcissism: Beyond the introduction, highlights of Heinz Kohut's contributions to the psychoanalytic treatment of narcissistic personality disorders. *The Annual of Psychoanalysis*, 2:127-149. New York: International Universities Press.

Palombo, J. (1972), Psychic trauma: The adventitious organizer. Paper presented to the Panel on Trauma, Amer. Assn. of Psychiatric Services for Children, Washington, D.C., November, 1972.

Panel (1961), The Selection of Candidates for Psychoanalytic Training, R. R. Greenson, reporter. *J. Amer. Psychoanal. Assn.*, 9:135-145.

_____ (1972), The Methodology of Psychoanalytic Biography, J. E. Gedo, reporter. *J. Amer. Psychoanal. Assn.*, 20:638-649.

Piaget, J. (1937), *The Construction of Reality in the Child*. New York: Basic Books, 1954.

Piers, G. & Singer, M. (1953), *Shame and Guilt*. Springfield, Illinois: Charles C Thomas.

Plato, *De republica*. Bk. 3.

Poetzl, O. (1917), Experimentell erregte Traumbilder in ihren Beziehungen zum indirekten Sehen. *Ztschr. f. Neurol. u. Psychiat.*, 37:278-349.

Pulver, S. (1970), Narcissism: The term and the concept. *J. Amer. Psychoanal. Assn.*, 18:319-341.

Rangell, L. (1954), The psychology of poise. *Internat. J. Psycho-Anal.*, 35:313-332.

Rank, O. (1911), Ein Beitrag zum Narzissmus. *Jb. Psychoanal. Psychopath. Forschungen*, 3:401-426.

Rauschning, H. (1938), *Die Revolution des Nihilismus.* New edition with introduction by G. Mann. Zurich: Europa Verlag, 1964.

Reich, A. (1960), Pathologic forms of self-esteem regulation. In: *Psychoanalytic Contributions.* New York: International Universities Press, 1973, pp. 288-311.

Reich, W. (1933-1934), *Character-Analysis.* New York: Touchstone Books, 1974.

Reichenbach, H. (1951), *The Rise of Scientific Philosophy.* Berkeley and Los Angeles: University of California Press.

Reik, T. (1953), *The Haunting Melody.* New York: Farrar, Straus, & Young.

Riemann, H. (1900), *Die Elemente der Musikalischen Aesthetik.* Berlin & Stuttgart: W. Spemann.

Rosenbaum, M. (1954), Psychoanalysis at the Hebrew University: The Freud-Eitingon-Magnes correspondence. *J. Amer. Psychoanal. Assn.*, 2:311-317.

Rousseau, J. J. (1781), *Traités sur la Musique.* Geneva.

Sachs, C. (1929), *Geist und Werden der Musikinstrumente.* Berlin: D. Reimer.

Sachs, H. (1942), *The Creative Unconscious.* Cambridge, Mass.: Sci-Art.

_____ (1944), *Freud, Master and Friend.* Massachusetts: Harvard University Press.

Sadger, J. (1909), Heinrich von Kleist: Eine pathographisch-psychologische Studie. *Grenzfragen des Nerven- und Seelenlebens*, 70. Wiesbaden: Bergmann, 1910.

Sandler, J., Holder, A., & Meers, D. (1963), The ego ideal and the ideal self. *The Psychoanalytic Study of the Child*, 18:139-158. New York: International Universities Press.

Saul, L. (1947), *Emotional Maturity.* Philadelphia: Lippincott.

Schafer, R. (1973), Action: Its place in psychoanalytic interpretation and theory. *The Annual of Psychoanalysis*, 1:159-196. New York: Quadrangle Books.

Schilder, P. (1938), Psychoanalytic remarks on *Alice in Wonderland* and Lewis Carroll. *J. Nerv. & Mental Disease*, 87:159-168.

Schopenhauer, A. (1877), Die Welt als Wille und Vorstellung. In: *Sämmtliche Werke.* Second Edition. Leipzig: F. A. Brockhaus.

Schur, M. (1966), *The Id and the Regulatory Principles of Mental Functioning.* New York: International Universities Press.

_____ (1972), *Freud: Living and Dying.* New York: International Universities Press.

Sechehaye, M. A. (1950), *Journal d'une Schizophrène.* Paris: Presses Universitaires de France.

Silberer, H. (1909), Report on a method of eliciting and observing certain symbolic hallucination-phenomena. In: *Organization and Pathology of Thought,* ed. D. Rapaport. New York: Columbia University Press, 1951, pp. 195-207.

Speer, A. (1969), *Inside the Third Reich: Memoirs of Albert Speer.* New York: Macmillan, 1970.

Spencer, H. (1902), The origin and function of music. In: *Facts and Comments.* New York: Appleton.

Spitz, R. A. (1946), The smiling response: A contribution to the ontogenesis of social relations. *Genet. Psychol.* Monogr., 34:57-125.

Stekel, W. (1909), Beiträge zur Traumdeutung. *Jb. Psychoanal. & Psychopath. Forschungen,* 1:458-512. Abstracted in: *Psychoanal. Rev.,* 3:111-113, 1916.

Sterba, R. (1934), The fate of the ego in analytic therapy. *Internat. J. Psycho-Anal.,* 15:117-126.

_____ (1946), Toward the problem of the musical process. *Psychoanal. Rev.,* 33:37-43.

_____ & Sterba, E. (1954), *Beethoven and His Nephew.* New York: Pantheon.

Strachey, J. (1934), The nature of therapeutic action in psycho-analysis. *Internat. J. Psycho-Anal.,* 15:127-159.

Stumpf, K. (1883-1890), *Tonpsychologie.* Leipzig: S. Hirzel.

Sullivan, H. S. (1940), *Conceptions of Modern Psychiatry.* Washington: William Alanson White Psychiatric Foundation, 1947.

Székely, L. (1966), Letter to the Pre-Congress Organizing Committee (C.O.P.T.).

_____ (1967), The creative pause. *Internat. J. Psycho-Anal.,* 48:353-367.

_____ (1970), Über den Beginn des Maschinenzeitalters: Psychoanalytische Bemerkungen über das Erfinden. *Schweiz. Z. Psychol.,* 29: 273-282.

Tausk, V. (1913), Compensation as a means of discounting the motive of repression. *Internat. J. Psycho-Anal.,* 5:130-140, 1924.

_____ (1919), On the origin of the "influencing machine" in schizophrenia. *Psychoanal. Quart.,* 2:519-556, 1933.

Terman, D. (1972), Summary of the Candidates' Pre-Congress Conference, Vienna, 1971. *Internat. J. Psycho-Anal.,* 53:47-48.

Tolstoy, L. N. (1866), *War and Peace.* New York: Simon & Schuster, 1942.

Trilling, L. (1947), *Review of Emil Ludwig's Dr. Freud.* New York Times, December 14.

Trollope, A. (1857), Baby worship. In: *Barchester Towers.* New York: Doubleday, Chapter 16, pp. 133-144, 1945.

van Ophuijsen, J. H. W. (1920), On the origins of the feeling of perse-
cution. *Internat. J. Psycho-Anal.*, 1:235-239.
Varendonck, J. (1921), The psychology of day-dreams. In: *Organization
and Pathology of Thought*, ed. D. Rapaport. New York: Columbia
University Press, 1951, pp. 451-473.
Waelder, R. (1951), The structure of paranoid ideas. In: *Psychoanalysis:
Observation, Theory, Application.* New York: International Univer-
sities Press, 1976, pp. 207-228.
_____ (1961), *Basic Theory of Psychoanalysis.* New York: International
Universities Press.
Waley, D. (1969), *The Italian City-Republics.* New York: McGraw-Hill.
Whitehead, A. (1927), *Symbolism: Its Meaning and Effect.* New York:
Macmillan.
Wolf, E. (1974), The self in history. Unpublished.
Wundt, W. (1911), *Einführung in die Psychologie.* Leipzig: R. Voigt-
länder.

Name Index

Abraham, H. C., 687
Abraham, K., 188, 552, 881
Adler, A., 628-629, 901-902
Aichhorn, A., 131-133, 495, 496
Alexander, F., 215, 387-388, 442, 507, 629, 637, 752n, 877
Alvarez de Toledo, L. G. de, 409-411, 414-415, 417
Antrim, D. K., 148
Archimedes, 345
Aristotle, 135, 136
Auden, W. H., 514-516

Bach, J. S., 13, 168, 169, 238-239
Bach, K. P. E., 136-137
Baer, L., 122
Baumayer, F., 833
Beethoven, L. van, 155, 157, 158, 191-193, 275-277, 290-293, 299, 302, 303
Beigler, J. S., 341
Bénassy, M., 381-383, 385
Benedek, T., 418
Benedict, R., 442, 638
Bennis, W., 706
Beres, D., 271, 309, 312, 313, 318
Bernfeld, S., 868-869
Bernstein, H., 443n
Bing, J. F., 430n
Binswanger, L., 436-437, 469n, 500, 906
Bird, B., 461-463, 470
Bonnard, A., 650-651
Bornstein, B., 405
Bracher, K. D., 635

Brahms, J., 148
Braque, G., 820
Breuer, J., 29, 211, 301-302, 337, 527, 578, 583, 584, 688, 697, 806
Brill, A. A., 615
Brody, M. W., 267-269
Burlingham, D., 902

Calder, K., 461-462
Calixtus, G., 328
Camus, A., 751
Carroll, L., 278, 290, 293-294, 296-300, 302, 303
Cellini, B., 880-881
Chijs, A. V. D., 138
Churchill, W., 88, 443-445, 827-828
Clower, V., 784-785
Cocteau, J., 860
Coeuroy, A., 239
Copernicus, 344, 515, 548, 689, 842n
Coriat, I. H., 142
Croce, B., 137

Dann, S., 778-779
Darwin, C., 136, 344, 515, 518, 544, 548, 634, 689, 714, 722, 842n
da Vinci, L., 279, 283, 823
Debussy, C. A., 168
Demos, J., 771
Deutsch, H., 326
Dewald, P., 416

Subject Index

as driving force in psychoanalysis, 554-561
ego dominance in, 620-621
empathy and, 450-453, 742-745
fear of death and, 183-184
forms of, 430-444
infantile, 47-48, 556-557, 617-618, 742-745, 899
and object love, 65-67, 556, 618
organ inferiority and, 628-632
primary vs. secondary, 180, 430-431
psychology of self and, 92-100
rage and, see Narcissistic rage
as resistance, 547-554
in schizophrenia, 260-261
self-mutilation and, 632-634
shame and, 69-72
transformations of, 440-460, 899
Narcissistic personality disorder, 556-557, 742-745
clinical examples of, 873-875, 879-880, 882-883, 886-888
concept of, 739-740, 845-846, 921-922
and structural neurosis, 554-555
and transference neurosis, 627-628
treatment of, 477-509, 652-653; see also Psychoanalytic technique
Narcissistic rage, 69, 615-658
chronic, 656-657
clinical example of, 638-639, 649-652
concept of, 71-72, 104, 636-640, 654-656, 756, 870-871, 899
ego dominance over, 646-649
experiential content of, 643-645
related phenomena, 640-643
transformation into mature aggression, 649-654
see also Aggression
Narcissistic self
concept of, 434-438
ego and, 440-443, 456-457

exhibitionism and, 438-439
grandiose fantasy and, 439-440
and idealized parent imago, 430-434
see also Grandiose self
Negative therapeutic reaction, 20
Neurosis, 17, 161, 354, 405-407
organ, 18-19, 215, 245, 249-250
pseudotransference, 624-628
and psychosis, 21
see also Transference neurosis
Nuclear self, 184n, 443n, 741, 747-749, 757n, 866-867

Object relations
narcissism and, 60-62, 65-67, 621-628, 764-766, 899
selfobject vs. true object, 18, 60-62, 67-68
in transference, 60-62
see also Selfobject, Transference
Observation (psychoanalysis), 205-212, 217, 749-750; see also Psychoanalysis
Oceanic feeling, 456, 907
Oedipus complex
beating fantasy and, 263-264
development of self and, 622-627, 882-883, 896-898
fantasy and, 312, 375
in Hamlet, 281-282
psychoanalysis of, 78-80
see also Child, "Guilty Man," Sexuality
Organ inferiority, 628-632

Parapraxes, 550-551, 580
and development of compulsive personality, 124-125
and development of intellect, 406-407
and development of self, 617-618
and development of superego, 241
see also Child, Idealized parent imago, Mother